Praise for the 4th Edition
Eating Expectantly

"Newly revised and busting with practical information for moms-to-be, this comprehensive guide offers easy tips for maximizing nutrition, and sound advice on common pregnancy challenges, like combating morning sickness, fighting fatigue, and shedding baby weight. Kudos to Bridget!"

- Joy Bauer, MS, RD, New York Times Bestselling author and Nutrition Expert for NBC's TODAY Show

"Eating Expectantly is designed to provide relevant, practical, useful information for the expectant mom- but, in fact, much of the information, including that in the panels and the tables is useful to any reader. The QR codes are an innovative and great way to provide the reader additional and updated information."

- Chairperson, Dept. of Nutrition and Dietetics University of North Florida and Past President of the Academy of Nutrition and Dietetics, 2010-2011

"This is the ultimate guide for nutrition and pregnancy. It answers every question you might have on how to eat in order to have a healthy baby, starting before you even get pregnant right on through to after pregnancy. It should be every woman's pregnancy bible!"

- Sharon Palmer, RD, Editor, *Environmental Nutrition Newsletter* and author of *The Plant-Powered Diet*

"I truly wish this wonderful book was available when I had my 3 children. Bridget's up-to-date sound advice and practical tips is a must-have for anyone planning on starting a family."

- Toby Amidor, MS, RD, CDN, Nutrition expert and columnist, *Today's Dietitian Magazine*

*"No matter how your diet is now, the easy-to-follow tips in **Eating Expectantly** can guide you towards a healthier diet and baby. I love the interactive feature of the book: links to more information are just a click away with QR codes and your smart phone."*

- Dawn Jackson Blatner RD, Huffington Post Food and Nutrition Blogger and Author of *The Flexitarian Diet*

"She's done it again! Bridget Swinney has compiled THE go-to nutrition book for moms-to-be and those who love them. Her first edition was my favorite baby shower gift and I plan to keep a few of this new one on hand. Well-researched and up-to-the minute advice is all there!"

- Christine M. Palumbo, MBA, RD, Columnist, *Chicago Parent*

Praise for Previous Editions of
Eating Expectantly

"Eating Expectantly is the complete guide to good nutrition for pregnant women."

- Self Magazine

"Her illustrations, charts, liberal use of bullets and a warm colloquial style of writing make this guide very easy to use. For everyday food questions and current practical information, Swinney's book is a recommended purchase…"

- Library Journal

"Once again, Bridget Swinney has found a way to make important nutritional concepts practical and easy to understand. This latest edition of Eating Expectantly belongs in the library of every expectant mother."

- Bryan S. Vartabedian M.D., F.A.A.P., Texas Children's Hospital

"I commend Bridget Swinney for her timely and informative guide. You should get your copy now and not wait until you are pregnant."

- Michael Hambidge MD, ScD, Former Director, Center for Human Nutrition, University of Colorado Health Sciences Center and former member Food and Nutrition Board.

"Eating Expectantly offers a wealth of practical information as well as recipes that will appeal to everyone—pregnant or not."

- The Gazette, Colorado Springs

"Eating Expectantly…stands out as the kind of comprehensive guide you'll find yourself turning to for years to come."

- San Diego Union Tribune

Eating Expectantly
Practical Advice for Healthy Eating Before, During and After Pregnancy

4th Revised Edition

Bridget Swinney MS, RD

healthy food zone

El Paso, Texas

Eating Expectantly: Practical Advice for Healthy Eating Before During and After Pregnancy

Publisher's Cataloging-In-Publication Data
(Prepared by The Donohue Group, Inc.)
Swinney, Bridget, 1960-
   Eating expectantly : practical advice for healthy eating before, during and after pregnancy / Bridget Swinney. -- 4th rev. ed.
    p. ; cm.
   Previous editions published by various publishers.
   "... significantly re-written and re-designed."--Supplied by publisher.
   Includes bibliographical references and index.
   ISBN: 978-0-9632917-0-7
   1. Pregnancy--Nutritional aspects. 2. Mothers--Nutrition. 3. Prenatal care. I. Title.
RG559 .S949 2013
618.2/42

Copyright © 2013 by Bridget Swinney

Healthy Food Zone Media
8001 North Mesa-E #142
El Paso, TX 79932

Disclaimer: The information in this book is true and complete to the best of our knowledge. It is intended to provide nutrition information and not to replace medical advice. We recommend that when in doubt about anything pregnancy or health-related, you consult with your personal physician. The author and publisher disclaim all liability in connection with the use of this book.

Trademark designations: Many of the designations used by manufacturers, sellers and brands to distinguish their products are claimed as trademarks. Where those designations appear, and Healthy Food Zone Media was aware of the trademark claim, the designations have been printed with initial capital letters.

Cover Illustration: Pat Steinholz
Cover and Interior Design: Frank Blando
Editing: Judith Swinney JD, Angela Wiechmann; AMW Editing
Proofreaders: Ricardo Barrera JD, James Rolph, Madiha Ahmad MS
Contributions by Connie Evers MS, RD, Dave Grotto RD, Sharon Palmer RD, Judy Simon MS, RD, CD, Tamara Duker Freuman MS, RD, Angela Grassi MS, RD, Tammy Lakatos Shames RD, LD, CDN, CFT, Marissa Van Dommelen MS, IBCLC, Diane Welland MS, RD, Jo Lichten PhD, RD.
Publicity: Kate Bandos KSB Promotions
Marketing: Sharon Castlen, Integrated Book Marketing

Available at special discounts for bulk purchasing. Contact Healthy Food Zone at 1-800-284-6667. More information see www.HealthyFoodZone.com.

About The Author

Bridget Swinney MS, RD is a health communicator, award-winning author and well-regarded nutrition expert in the field of prenatal nutrition, child nutrition, and family eating matters. A frequent speaker and media guest, she is a Registered Dietitian with a Master's Degree in Nutrition.

Her other books include *Baby Bites: Everything You Need to Know about Feeding Babies and Toddlers in One Handy Book* and *Healthy Food for Healthy Kids: The Practical and Tasty Guide to Child Nutrition*. She is co-author of the *Healthy Heart Formula*.

The first edition of *Eating Expectantly* (1994) won the Child Magazine's Top Ten Parenting Books of the Year, and *Baby Bites* (2007) was awarded an iparenting.com Media Award. *Eating Expectantly*, in its three previous editions, has more than 100,000 copies in print. The book has been used in university dietetic and nurse midwife programs. Bridget's books have been translated and published internationally.

Bridget's writing has also appeared in *Parents, Healthy Kids, Parenting and American Baby Magazine*. She has been quoted in *Good Housekeeping, Child, Parents, Parenting*, and online in GoRedForWomen.org, mom.me, education.com, BabyCenter.com and BabyZone.com. She has appeared on "Good Morning America", "The Food Network", Fox, "Later Today", WGN, the Canadian Broadcasting Corporation and local stations in Atlanta, San Francisco, San Diego, Chicago, Houston, El Paso, Dallas, Seattle, Portland and Vancouver BC.

As a nutrition consultant, Bridget has done a variety of work, both as a nutrition therapist in clinical and public health settings and as a speaker to consumers and health professionals. She has helped hundreds of thousands of pregnant women through one-on-one counseling and through her books and media interviews. Bridget continues to consult with moms and is an advisor to BabyCenter.com. She has served as a Media Representative for the Texas Academy of Nutrition and Dietetics and the Colorado Academy of Nutrition and Dietetics and been active in the Women's Health Dietary Practice Group of the Academy of Nutrition and Dietetics. Her most important job of all, however, has been, and still is, being a mom to Nicolas and Robert. She enjoys traveling, hiking and cooking with her husband Frank. She is happiest when inspiring others.

Follow me on twitter! 🐦 @EatRightMama

 Join the conversation on Facebook!
www.facebook.com/pages/Eating-Expectantly/278800748805263

We'd love to hear your comments about *Eating Expectantly*!
Send to EatingExpectantly@gmail.com

Acknowledgements

They say it takes a village to raise a child. In some ways writing a book, especially one of this magnitude, is like bringing up a baby. Lots of late nights, weekends, early mornings and a few headaches and heartaches. But luckily, family, friends and colleagues were there with encouragement, assistance and some delicious meals.

I have to start by thanking my husband Frank, who has supported me in my writing career through six other books, which meant sharing diaper, soccer, carpooling and cub scout duties through the years, and doing everything around the house for the past the two years, while I toiled at this edition of *Eating Expectantly*. (I promise you will have your wife back soon!) To my sons Nicolas and Robert—for your support and hugs. To my sisters (and friends) Judy and Colleen, who I can always count on to be my best cheerleaders.

To my friends John and Alicia, who have been there cheering me on through two editions of *Eating Expectantly* and to Jim and Elvira, friends and walking buddies, who sometimes were the only contact I had with the outside world during long weekends when knee-deep in the book. Thanks for the encouragement and feedback! To my facebook friends—too many to mention—who helped me "crowdsource" the subtitle, and various other questions I posed. Thanks to my editors and proofreaders, Ricardo Barrera, Judith Swinney, Jim Rolph and Angie Wiechmann. for their witty and insightful editing. Thanks to Shannon Bodie with Lightbourne for helping with the interior design and George Foster for his cover design advice. Thanks to my publicist Kate Bandos and book marketer Sharon Castlen for their expertise and patience. Gratitude also goes to my previous publisher Bruce Lansky and Meadowbrook Press.

Thanks to other colleagues for their contributions to the book; I appreciate you sharing your expertise! Connie Evers MS, RD, Dave Grotto RD, Sharon Palmer RD, Judy Simon MS, RD, CD, Tamara Duker Freuman MS, RD, Angela Grassi MS, RD, Tammy Lakatos Shames RD, LD, CDN, CFT, Carrie Zisman RD, Elizabeth Ward MS, RD, Ann Dunaway Teh MS, RD, Kelli Mangold LMSW, Marissa Van Dommelen MS, IBCLC, Diane Welland MS, RD, Christin Chan MBA, Jo Lichten PhD, RD and Miriam Erick MS, RD. Thanks to registered dietitians and other colleagues who assisted with reviewing the book: Connie Evers MS, RD, Jacquie Craig RD, CDE, Melissa Joy Dobbins MS, RD, CDE, Maria Duarte PhD, RD, Rosa Macintyre Valenzuela RN, Celina Ramsdale MSW, Kathy Vega, Judy Barron, Esther Rodarte and Caroline Peaslee MS, RD. Thanks also to Marcia Hays MS for her research assistance. Thanks to the "Fab Five" peer group for their ongoing support: Karen Collins, MS, RD, Jennifer Neilly MS, RD, Sharon Palmer RD and Jill Weisenberger MS, RD, CDE.

I was lucky to have a whole team of dietetic students, some who are RDs now, assisting from around the country. I joked that I had interns in every time zone, and even one in Australia! Thanks for stepping up and I hope the experience you had will help you in future endeavors: Julie Usdavin, JoAnne Usdavin, Krystle Klosterman, Sara Cook, Katie Small, Caitlin Fields, Amber Smith, Kathryn Cook, Rachel Dayan, Danielle Letzler, Michelle Manz, Amber Bozarth, Christin Chan and Julia Moszkowicz. I couldn't have completed the book or cookbook without the ongoing help of Madiha Ahmad MS, who was both research assistant and recipe analyst.

Thanks! Gracias! Merci!

To Moms-To-Be Around the World

Healthy eating isn't always easy, but it's worth it!
My hope is that **Eating Expectantly** will inspire you to give your baby
the gift of good nutrition.

TABLE OF CONTENTS

Introduction 13

1 - Contemplating Pregnancy 15
Why Planning Your Pregnancy Is Best 16
The Pre-Pregnancy Quiz—Are You Ready? 18
The Importance of Good Nutrition Before and During Pregnancy 19
How Pre-Conception Nutrition & Lifestyle Affects Pregnancy 23
Planning a Healthy Pregnancy - A Step-by-Step Guide 26
Eating Expectantly Diet: Before Baby 31
Questions You May Have 34

2 - Fueling Your Fertility 37
Weight Matters 38
Polycystic Ovary Syndrome (PCOS) 40
Other Fertility Factors You Can Control 43
Dad's Diet and Lifestyle: YES—They DO Play a Role in Fertility 50
Seven Tips to Fuel Your Fertility 52

3 - The Knowledgeable Pregnancy 55
Changing Your Mindset for Pregnancy 56
Twelve Steps to a Healthier Diet (and Life) 57
Carbs 101: What You Need to Know 62
What About Sugar & Other Sweeteners? 70
Going Gluten-Free 75
Fat: The Good, the Bad, and the Ugly 78
Allergy Prevention During Pregnancy 83

4 - Eating Expectantly Diet   85

The Eating Expectantly Diet   86
What's a Serving?   87
Vitamins and Supplements: What You Need to Know   94

5 - Weight Gain: What You Need To Know   103

Where the Weight Goes   104
How Much Should You Gain?   105
What's Your Goal?   105
Having Trouble Meeting Your Goal?   107

6 - Keeping Your Baby's Environment Safe   111

Bad Habits   112
Environmental Chemicals   119
Bad Bugs and Food Poisoning   129
Water   132
Food Safety   134
Around the House   146
Beauty Care   149
In a Nutshell: Greener Living   153

7 - First Trimester   155

How Baby Is Growing   156
Fueling Your Little Bump: Weight Gain and Calorie Needs   157
Protein Power   160
First Trimester Power Nutrients   164
First Trimester Diet Challenges   168

8 - Second Trimester   179

How Baby Is Growing   180
Feeding Your Bump: Weight Gain and Calorie Needs   181
Second Trimester Power Nutrients   187
Focus on Fruits and Vegetables   195
Choosy Mothers Snack Smart!   199
Healthier Travel   201
Second Trimester Diet Challenges   201

9 - Third Trimester   205

How Baby Is Growing   206
What Could Happen This Trimester   207
Feeding Your Big Bump: Weight Gain and Calorie Needs   210
Third Trimester Power Nutrients   214
Third Trimester Diet Challenges   222
How's Your Diet?   226

10 - Vegetarian Eating   227

Vegetarians: The Healthy Minority   228
The Pregnant Vegetarian   230
Vegetarian Meal Planning Tips   230
Questions You May Have   244

11 - High-Risk Pregnancy   245

Expect the Unexpected   246
Problems with Blood Sugar: Diabetes   247
Keys to Controlling Gestational Diabetes   250
High Blood Pressure   256
When You're Expecting Twins or More   261
Coping with Bed Rest   267
Older Moms   271
Pregnancy After Gastric Bypass Surgery   273

12 - Considering Breastfeeding   275

Breastfeeding: 100% Natural   276
Why Choose Breastfeeding?   277
Possible Obstacles   279
Going Back to Work   285
Nutrition during Breastfeeding   289
Drugs and Breastfeeding   297
Breastfeeding for Special Groups   297
Questions You May Have   300

13 - First Weeks With Baby   303

What to Expect after Delivery   304
The Baby Blues   306
Losing That Baby Fat   306

Eating Expectantly Diet: Lose That Baby Fat   316
Your Next Pregnancy—WHAT?   321

14 - Fitting Fitness In   323
Why Exercise?   324
Two All Star Pregnancy Exercises   326
Ten Tips for Smarter Exercise   328
Fitting Fitness into Your Busy Lifestyle   333
Exercise After Pregnancy   339
Questions You May Have   341

15 - Stocking The Pregnant Kitchen   343
Your Kitchen: Time to Take Inventory   344
A Peek in My Kitchen   344
Using Food Labels to Your Advantage   346
Eating on a Budget   355
Stocking the Kitchen Toolbox   359
Keeping the Vitamins in Your Veggies   360
Boost Your Veggies: Twelve Ways   362
Cooking Meats, Poultry and Fish   363
Eating Cleaner And Greener   365

16 - Eating Out And Eating In   375
Kitchens are Gathering Cobwebs   376
Pitfalls of Eating Out   376
At Your Favorite Type of Restaurant   383
Get a Healthier Meal, Just by Asking   390
Choosing Nutritious Fast Foods   392
Last Minute Meals from What's in the Pantry   394
Choosing Frozen Meal Options   397

References   399

Index   447

Recommended Resources   457

A Note From Bridget: Why I Wrote This Book

Shortly after my first son, Nicolas, was born, I had the opportunity with two other authors, to contribute to a book in the making about pregnancy nutrition. While that book never came to fruition, I decided to forge ahead on my own, writing the first edition of *Eating Expectantly*. The eating challenges of pregnancy were fresh on my mind; I knew that it wasn't always easy to eat well during pregnancy. Coupled with my experience as a public health nutritionist and a hospital clinical dietitian, I knew that the millions of women who give birth in the US each year needed practical eating advice. I felt passionate about spreading the "good word" about how nutrition can make a big difference—both to how you feel when you're pregnant, and how healthy your baby is at birth—and beyond.

Fast-forward 20 years. My first-born is now in his 20's and my second son Robert just started college. There are two updated editions of *Eating Expectantly*—and I've written two follow-up books about feeding infants and children. After working with pregnant women, children and adults of all ages during my career, I approach the newest edition of *Eating Expectantly* with an even stronger passion. I know that this book can make a profound difference in the health of your baby—not just at birth or the first few years of life—but also in his/her risk of chronic diseases as an adult.

I became a registered dietitian with a simple goal; to help others enjoy longer, healthier lives with a better quality of life through good nutrition. I quickly learned that counseling one person at a time was not going to make a lasting impression on the world. With media—books, TV, radio, and now through the web, I've been able to impact hundreds of thousands of people with practical advice about eating better.

With the current technology, you could be reading this book in a library in College Station, on your Droid in Portland, your iPad in London, your Kindle in Killarney, your Nexus in Sydney or your Kobo in Victoria. Wherever you are, and however you are reading this book, I hope it makes a positive difference in your life as well as your children's lives.

Remember to check out the *Eating Expectantly Cookbook,* featuring more than 150 recipes and menus for every trimester and "eating mood" of pregnancy.

Happy reading...

Bridget

How To Use This Book

The book is written in chronological order, starting with pre-conception and then moving on to general information that everyone needs to know, including how to keep baby's environment safe, followed by specific nutrition advice for each trimester. Then there are tips for vegetarian eating, as well as some specifics for high-risk pregnancy. Then it's info for post-baby—breastfeeding, surviving the first weeks with baby and that all-important postscript—losing weight. It closes with advice about keeping fit, stocking the kitchen, eating out, and choosing healthier convenience foods.

Eating Expectantly can be started at any point in the book—with it's easy-to-read lists and quizzes, it's perfectly doable to read the book in small chunks. Of course if you aren't pregnant yet, you'll definitely want to start with the first two chapters. Everyone should read chapters three thru six. After that, you can skip around to the chapters that most appeal or apply to you.

The Metric Measurements

The world is getting smaller! So with this edition, we decided to add metric measurements, so that it would be useful to people more familiar with that system. For the metric conversion we rounded to the nearest multiple of "5". Sometimes the conversions have been adjusted to represent the most commonly used measurements rather than the exact calculation.

QR Codes: Making This Book Interactive!

Have you ever read an article with a recommended website and wish you could check it out without having to type in a long web address? Well, me too! Enter QR codes—those funny looking squares that are sprinkled throughout this book. They can be read with your smart phone using a free QR code reader, which you can download from your phone's "app" store. I use the ATT Scanner, which can scan bar codes and QR codes. Each QR code redirects through EatingExpectantly.com.

Typically, when you scan a QR code, it can link to a website, video, product information or even a phone number or address. In *Eating Expectantly*, when the QR code is at the beginning of the chapter, it links to chapter updates, friendly notes and even an occasional video message from me. When the QR code is in the margin of the chapter, it links to the website that's listed nearby on the page, to more information or charts that are too long for the book. Recommended websites are monitored to make sure they are active and up-to-date. I hope you enjoy this cutting edge feature of the book—**a first for a pregnancy book!**

Scan this QR code for a video message from Bridget! (For best result hold phone about 3-5 inches / 7-13 cm away)

1

CONTEMPLATING PREGNANCY

What You'll Find:

- Why Planning Your Pregnancy Is Best
- The Importance of Good Nutrition Before and During Pregnancy
- How Pre-Conception Nutrition & Lifestyle Affects Pregnancy
- Planning a Healthy Pregnancy—A Step-by-Step Guide
- Eating Expectantly Diet: Before Baby
- Questions You May Have

Frequently Asked Questions:

- Is my body ready for a baby?
- What's the most important thing to discuss with my health care provider?
- What if I'm underweight or overweight?
- Can stress affect my fertility?
- Which foods may help my fertility?
- Does Dad's diet make a difference to fertility?

SCAN HERE FOR CHAPTER UPDATES

Why Planning Your Pregnancy Is Best

Thinking about having a baby? It's a smart move to plan ahead. In addition to learning about pregnancy on your own, you'll want to visit with your health care provider. Depending on your health, you'll want to make this visit at least 3 months prior to conception. The Centers for Disease Control and Prevention (CDC) recommends that pre-conception health promotion be available to all women of childbearing age.[1] Why? Here's what you'll gain from a pre-pregnancy visit with your health care provider:

1. Information you need to change lifestyle habits that may affect your pregnancy, especially smoking, drinking, caffeine intake, and eating habits.
2. An opportunity to better control chronic medical conditions, such as high blood pressure, diabetes, kidney disease, hypothyroidism, or eating disorders before you get pregnant. For example, women with poorly managed asthma have a 25% greater chance of having a preterm birth and a 50% increased risk of developing preeclampsia.[2] Being in optimal health will help you have the healthiest baby possible!
3. Time to start eating a well-balanced diet, build up nutrient stores, start exercising regularly and lose or gain weight, if needed.
4. A chance to learn about fetal development so you understand the importance of changing your habits before pregnancy. Critical development takes place during the first weeks after conception. This is when poor diet or lifestyle habits can damage the fetus the most—and can prevent you from getting pregnant. Most of a fetus's brain cell division, for example, occurs before most women know they're pregnant.

What's That? Preeclampsia

Preeclampsia is a potentially dangerous late-pregnancy complication in which a woman develops high blood pressure and has protein in her urine. It can cause harm to both mom and baby and the only "cure" is early delivery. Nutrition in the first trimester can affect the risk of preeclampsia.

The CDC recommends you follow these tips before you get pregnant:[3]

1. Take 400 micrograms of folic acid a day for at least 3 months before becoming pregnant to reduce the risk of birth defects.
2. Stop smoking and don't drink alcohol.
3. If you currently have a medical condition such as asthma, diabetes, high blood pressure or epilepsy, be sure these conditions are under control.
4. Reach and maintain a healthy weight.
5. Get mentally healthy.

6. Get help for violence.
7. Be sure your vaccinations are up-to-date.
8. Talk to your health care provider and pharmacist about any over-the-counter and prescription medicines you are taking, including dietary and herbal supplements.
9. Avoid exposures to toxic substances or potentially infectious materials at work and home, such as chemicals, or cat and rodent feces.

Make Your Pre-Pregnancy Visit Count!

Health care provider visits are often brief: be prepared to get the most out it by being prepared—and being honest. This is not the time to hold back information! Bring a list of questions and concerns to your appointment. Mention that you are planning a pregnancy and then, make sure this happens:[4]

♦ Discuss your health history including previous pregnancies, fertility, and birth control, eating and weight history, as well as health issues like high blood pressure, diabetes and thyroid disease.

♦ Talk about current lifestyle factors that could affect your ability to become pregnant or the health of a fetus. This includes alcohol use, drugs, mental health issues and domestic violence concerns as well as workplace hazards (for both you and your partner) that could be harmful.

♦ Review medications and supplements: Make sure your health care provider is aware and approves of any medications and nutrition supplements that you plan to continue during pregnancy. This includes prescription as well as occasional over-the-counter medications.

♦ Bring your immunization record to make sure you are current with vaccinations, including the flu shot, which is recommended during pregnancy.

♦ Have screening tests like blood tests, urinalysis, Pap smear and blood pressure.

What Is Genetic Counseling?

Genetic counseling is the process of evaluating family history, ordering genetic tests and helping parents interpret the results. Anyone with unanswered questions about diseases or traits in the family or who is concerned about being at increased risk for having a child with a birth defect or inherited disorder might want to consider genetic counseling.

For more information on genetic counseling consult the March of Dimes www.marchofdimes.com/pregnancy/trying_geneticcounseling.html

To find a genetic counselor, contact The National Society of Genetic Counselors www.nsgc.org

The Pre-Pregnancy Quiz—Are You Ready?

The following quiz will help you and your partner determine whether your diet and lifestyle are ready for pregnancy. Circle "Yes" or "No" after each statement; then follow the scoring directions at the end.

	Health Habit	Answer	
1.	I eat at least 2 cups (500 ml) of fruit and 2½ cups (625 ml) of vegetables on most days.	Yes	No
2.	I eat a vitamin-C-rich food daily. (Examples include citrus fruit or juice, berries, papaya, mango, pineapple, melon, broccoli, cauliflower, tomato, and vegetable juice.)	Yes	No
3.	I eat a wide variety of foods, including many types of protein foods.	Yes	No
4.	I do some type of aerobic exercise at least twice each week.	Yes	No
5.	I don't smoke and I avoid secondhand smoke.	Yes	No
6.	I drink no more than one caffeinated beverage each day.	Yes	No
7.	I avoid taking drugs of any kind: prescription drugs, over-the-counter drugs, herbal preparations, or "street drugs."	Yes	No
8.	I am at or close to my ideal body weight.	Yes	No
9.	I avoid exposure to radiation, pesticides, herbicides, solvents, PCBs, and other chemicals.	Yes	No
10.	I avoid eating shark, swordfish, king mackerel and tilefish.	Yes	No
11.	I usually eat three balanced meals a day and watch my trans fat and saturated fat intake.	Yes	No
12.	I eat three servings of calcium-rich foods daily. (Examples include milk, yogurt, cheese, high-calcium vegetables, calcium-enriched soymilk or tofu, and juice fortified with calcium.)	Yes	No
13.	I take a multivitamin/mineral supplement containing 400 micrograms of folic acid daily.	Yes	No
14.	I have a regular source of Docosahexaenoic Acid (DHA) and other omega-3 fats in my diet.	Yes	No
15.	I avoid drinking alcohol.	Yes	No
16.	I avoid eating raw milk, eggs, shellfish, or foods that are made with these. (Examples include homemade Caesar salad dressing, mousse with uncooked egg, and sushi.) I also stay away from uncooked sprouts.	Yes	No
17.	I eat three servings of whole-grain breads, cereals, or other whole-grain products on most days.	Yes	No

Health Habit	Answer	
18.	I live a moderately paced lifestyle, get eight hours of sleep most nights and generally feel happy.	**Yes**	**No**
19.	I have not followed any drastic diets or had an eating disorder in the last three months.	**Yes**	**No**
20.	I am a vegetarian who eats no animal products, though I do take vitamin B12 and calcium supplements.	**Yes**	**No**
21.	I have visited my health care provider and discussed a future pregnancy.	**Yes**	**No**

How Did You Do?

Count your "Yes" answers and see how you scored below.

17–21: Congratulations! Your body is ready for pregnancy!

13–16: You're doing pretty well; you have just a few things to work on for the healthiest pregnancy possible.

9–12: You may need a few months to change your habits for the healthiest possible pregnancy.

0-8: Oops! Your lifestyle may need an overhaul! Talk to your health care provider before trying to conceive, and read **all** of this book!

The Importance of Good Nutrition Before and During Pregnancy

To get started, let's explore the benefits of eating well for your baby—not only now, but in the future.

What Is Prenatal Programming?

Imagine if you could "program" your baby for future good health. You'd buy that "app", no matter what the cost, because a lifetime of good health is invaluable. You have the power to do that right now with your food and lifestyle choices.

Developmental Programming (also called prenatal programming) is any negative condition that occurs during a sensitive or critical period of development, which has lasting or lifelong impact on health or function.[5,6] To put this into simple terms, this means the foundation for your baby's health is like modeling clay and you (and your habits) are the sculptors.

Research now confirms that a baby's long-term health is sensitive to the fetal environment during pregnancy—especially the nutrition environment.[7,8,9] The fetal environment includes everything a baby is exposed to—including what a mom breathes, the stress she experiences as well as temperatures she is exposed to and medications, drugs or herbs she might take. The "nutrition environment" includes your pre-pregnancy weight, weight gain, everything you eat and drink and blood sugar levels, which may affect your baby's risk of future disease including heart disease, stroke, high blood pressure and type 2 diabetes. Both an excessive and an inadequate nutrition environment could "program" a baby for some major health problems later in life.[10]

Excessive Nutrition Environment

Being overweight, gaining too much weight, and having gestational diabetes or high blood sugar or eating an "excessive" diet, can increase your risk of pregnancy complications and of having a baby that is large for gestational age.

Excessive Diet

You may eat an "excessive diet" if you often feel that you eat too much, you regularly drink sugar-sweetened drinks and other high-sugar foods, regularly eat fried and snack foods, and say things like "I know I should eat better." An excessive diet can lead to nutrient deficiencies and weight gain. This can affect your ability to get pregnant, as well as you and your baby's health, now and later.

Overweight

Research shows that women who are overweight are three to seven times more likely to have gestational diabetes, two to four times more likely to have preeclampsia and are also more likely to have an infant with a lower Apgar score (a score of your baby's physical condition at birth). The risk increases with degree of overweight.[11] Women who are overweight also are at greater risk of having a baby born before 34 weeks, and are more likely to have a C-section.[12,13,14] There is also evidence that being overweight can change the action of certain genes, which may increase the risk of heart birth defects.[15] Being overweight is also one cause of infertility.

Being overweight during pregnancy increases the risk that your baby will be overweight[16,17] or have metabolic syndrome later in life.[18] Metabolic syndrome is a combination of risk factors: high blood sugar, abnormal cholesterol levels, high blood pressure and a large waist size, which can lead to heart disease and diabetes.

What You Can Do Now:

✔ If you are overweight, and especially if you are 20 percent or more over your ideal weight, lose weight before you conceive. A small loss can make a difference!

✔ Take a pledge to start eating healthier now. Consider the other benefits of changing your diet now—you'll look better, feel better and possibly get pregnant sooner.

✔ If you don't already exercise, start moving! Begin with a daily 10 to 15 minute walk and every week increase the amount of time. Or join the gym or jump on an exercise bike—just start somewhere! Consider getting at least 30 minutes of moderately vigorous exercise 5 days a week, as recommended by the Physical Activity Guidelines for Americans.[19]

✔ Spend less time being inactive. This may be just as important as trying to exercise more. Sitting at a desk for hours at a time? Take a five-minute break every hour to walk and stretch a bit. Hours in front of the TV can be turned into walking time—even marching your legs while sitting can help improve circulation, improve muscle tone and burn calories.

✔ Seek the help of a registered dietitian—to find one, go to www.eatright.org. Also, see advice found in the "Lose that Baby Fat" section.

Inadequate Nutrition Environment

Not getting all the nutrients your body needs over time, starting your pregnancy underweight and not gaining enough weight during pregnancy are all considered an "inadequate" nutrition environment. This type of environment can lead to infertility issues, pregnancy problems and health issues later in life for your baby.

Undernourished: Overweight or Underweight

No matter what your weight is, you may be undernourished. This may describe you if you eat lots of processed foods with few fruits, vegetables, whole grains or other whole foods. Your diet may contain plenty of calories—just not enough nutrients. You may also be undernourished if you have inadequate amounts of specific nutrients due to a chronic medical condition, or if you regularly take certain medications.

Underweight/Inadequate Weight Gain

Being underweight or not gaining enough weight increases your chances of having a baby that is too small. Interestingly enough, having a baby that is small for gestational age (SGA) can have some of the same health issues as infants who are too big at birth. It is thought that the fetus makes physical, hormonal and developmental adjustments to a limited supply of nutrients, which can increase the risk of being overweight, having metabolic syndrome[20], kidney disease[21], heart disease and diabetes.[22] Rapid catch-up growth during the first few years of life is thought to add to the risk of being overweight.[23]

What You Can Do Now:

✔ Begin by improving your diet, one food group at a time. Focus on eating foods closest to their natural state—fresh fruits and veggies, whole grains, lean protein foods and low-fat dairy products. Cut back on sugar and "extras."

✔ If you are underweight, try to gain weight to get closer to your ideal weight before trying to conceive. As easy is this sounds for the "rest" of us—people who are underweight often find it more difficult to gain weight than others do to lose it. See page 109—Not Gaining Enough, for tips on how to tip the energy balance toward weight gain.

✔ If you currently have an eating disorder or a history of one, try to resolve any issues about weight and body image before pregnancy.

✔ While exercise is recommended and good for health, if you are burning more calories in exercise than you can eat, consider reducing exercise time.

✔ Focus on foods that are both nutrient rich and higher in calories.

How's Your Weight?

In this chapter, there's a lot of talk about weight. You probably have an idea of where your weight falls in the weight categories of normal, overweight or underweight. But just in case you don't, here's a great way to find out: figure out your BMI or Body Mass Index. BMI is a number calculated from a person's weight and height. BMI is a pretty good indicator of body fatness for most people and is used to screen for weight categories that may lead to health problems. BMI can overestimate body fat when a person is more muscular than average.

◆ The easy way to find your BMI is to find an online BMI calculator or smart phone "app". www.cdc.gov/healthyweight/assessing/bmi/adult_bmi/english_bmi_calculator/bmi_calculator.html

◆ Or see the chart here: www.nhlbi.nih.gov/guidelines/obesity/bmi_tbl.htm

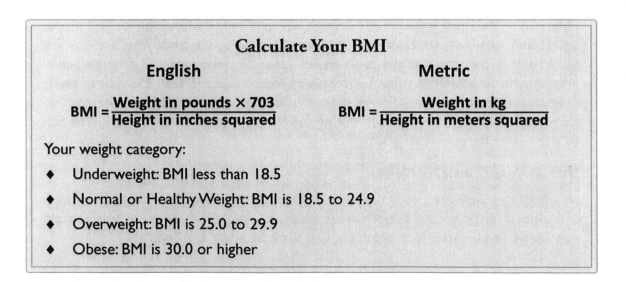

Calculate Your BMI

English	Metric
$BMI = \dfrac{\text{Weight in pounds} \times 703}{\text{Height in inches squared}}$	$BMI = \dfrac{\text{Weight in kg}}{\text{Height in meters squared}}$

Your weight category:

◆ Underweight: BMI less than 18.5

◆ Normal or Healthy Weight: BMI is 18.5 to 24.9

◆ Overweight: BMI is 25.0 to 29.9

◆ Obese: BMI is 30.0 or higher

How Pre-Conception Nutrition & Lifestyle Affects Pregnancy

Diet

The Standard American Diet—"SAD" for short, includes excess consumption of calories, refined carbohydrates, fatty meat, added fats and sugars; and lacks fruits, vegetables and whole grains. The SAD diet has been blamed for obesity and diet related diseases like diabetes, hypertension and heart disease—that are rampant not only in the US, but in many other countries.[24]

Many women start their pregnancies with eating habits that need improvement. In a survey, only 28% of women ate 5 fruits and vegetables per day.[25] Women in general don't eat enough fruits, vegetables or milk[26] and during pregnancy are not meeting the Dietary Reference Intakes (DRI) for iron, zinc, calcium, magnesium, vitamin D, vitamin E and omega-3 fatty acids.[27]

For the general population, a SAD diet increases the risk of dying from heart disease, stroke or cancer. For women who are pregnant or about to be, the stakes are much higher—the SAD diet is associated with a higher risk of having a baby that is small for age.[28] A healthier diet may increase longevity and quality of life—for you AND your baby.

Birth Defects

Much of the crucial organ development—including the brain, spinal cord and the heart as well as birth defects of those organs—occur in the first months of pregnancy. The brain and spinal cord is also referred to as the "neural tube." Because this development sometimes happens before a woman knows she is pregnant, it's important to eat a nutrient-rich diet before pregnancy. Some nutrients are stored for later use and this can come in handy if you experience nausea in early pregnancy. Not having enough nutrients such as folate, choline and vitamin B12 has been linked to an increased risk of birth defects. Women with low intakes of dietary choline have four times the risk of having a baby with neural tube defects as women with the highest intakes.[29] See page 33 for food sources. See page 220 for food sources.

Folate is so important to the prevention of neural tube defects, that mandatory fortification of wheat flour with folate is in place in 53 countries around the world, including the US, Canada and Chile. In the US, it is estimated that the added folate in enriched cereal grains adds 100-200 micrograms of folate to the diet of women of childbearing age and that it has decreased neural tube defects by 19-32%.[30]

Focus on Folate: Do You Get It?

Folate, also called folic acid or folacin, is a B vitamin that is very important before and during pregnancy; it plays a critical role in making new cells and in making hemoglobin in red blood cells. It's the role folic acid plays in cell division that increases risk of birth defects if you don't have enough. This is why it's recommended that ALL women of childbearing age get enough folic acid—400 micrograms from a synthetic source such as a multivitamin or cereal that has that amount.

Women in the US in general don't get enough folic acid—one estimate is that only 24% of women of childbearing age do have enough. Of the women taking vitamin supplements however, 72% met recommended intake amounts.[31] Food sources of folic acid include black-eyed peas, spinach, great northern beans, asparagus, green peas and broccoli. Folic acid can be destroyed by cooking, so prepare vegetables in as little water as possible for as short a time as possible. Certain medications, including some anti-convulsants and birth control pills increase folic acid needs even more. If you have had a baby with a neural tube defect, a prescription level of folic acid is usually recommended; discuss with your health care provider.

Tea Drinkers Beware

A substance found in green and oolong tea—ECGC, affects the metabolism of folic acid, important before and in early pregnancy to prevent neural tube defects. While more studies are needed, for now, it's best to switch to black tea (which has very little ECGC) or an herbal tea that's safe during pregnancy, like mint.[32]

Nutrient Deficiencies

Small nutrient deficits of vitamins and minerals including iron, zinc, vitamin C and E, omega-3 fatty acids, and B vitamins including B12 and folic acid can affect the fertility of both men and women. Find more detail below and in the next chapter. Lower intakes of some nutrients during pregnancy can also affect a child's lifelong health: For example, reduced intake of some nutrients—including vitamin D, Vitamin E, selenium and zinc—may have an impact on the risk of asthma in children.[33]

Iron deficiency before 26 weeks of gestation is associated with various problems later in pregnancy such as having a baby that is low birthweight, born prematurely or delayed in neurological development.[34,35] Have your iron stores checked before pregnancy to determine if you should take an iron supplement. You can beef up your current iron status by choosing more lean beef, dried beans (especially lentils), and iron-fortified cereals.

Depression

Depression during pregnancy can not only have an impact on the health of your pregnancy but also on your ability to take care of your baby and nurture his development once he's born. Many nutrients play a role in mental health including vitamin B1, vitamin B6, vitamin B12, folic acid, vitamin D, iodine, selenium, zinc and omega-3 fatty acids.[36] The risk for depression during pregnancy is very real because of the increased nutrient needs during pregnancy, which sometimes go unmet. While postpartum depression gets a lot of media attention, depression during pregnancy may be even more prevalent—occurring in as many as one in five women.

Depression left untreated during pregnancy has been shown to increase the rate of miscarriage, low birthweight, and babies that are small for gestational age.[37] Good nutrition before and during pregnancy as well as treatment for depression are vital for the healthiest baby and mom.

Diabetes

For women with pre-existing diabetes, blood sugar control is very important because high sugar levels in early pregnancy increases the risk of birth defects. It's a good idea to discuss your current diabetes management, as well as how your medication regimen might change during pregnancy, with your health care provider before trying to conceive.[38]

Bariatric Surgery

Women who have had bariatric surgery are at risk for multiple nutrient deficiencies including iron, vitamin B12, calcium, vitamins A, D, E, K, folate, thiamin, as well as protein.[39] Because these nutrient deficiencies could seriously affect the health of your baby, it is best to consult with your health care provider before pregnancy about correcting any possible nutrient deficits. Also check in with a registered dietitian who can develop a specialized meal plan for your specific needs.

Lack of Sleep

The quality of sleep a woman gets in the first and third trimester appears to be related to preterm birth.[40] Sleep quality is a subjective assessment that measures how long you sleep, interruptions in your sleep, the use of medications needed to sleep and not being able to function well due to lack of sleep. If you are a problem sleeper, try to get this fixed before you get pregnant.

Alcohol

Girls' night out, after-work happy hour: fun times for sure—BUT—there's a time and a place for drinking—and pregnancy isn't one of them! There's no safe level of alcohol intake during pregnancy. What does this mean? Any amount of alcohol could harm a fetus—including causing birth defects, mental retardation, hyperactivity, stillbirth and low birthweight.[41] If you're a regular drinker, start now in cutting down, so that by the time you are ready to conceive, you can stop altogether and become the designated driver. Your friends will love you for it!

Drugs

All drugs, whether over-the-counter, prescription, or illegal have the potential to harm a fetus. Check out these facts sheets (from the Organization of Teratology Information Specialists) to find out how drugs can affect fetal development: www.otispregnancy.org/otis-fact-sheets-s13037#5

Tobacco Smoke

Exposure to tobacco smoke during pregnancy—whether it's you or someone else smoking—has very negative effects on a baby: increased risk of low birthweight, and overweight[42], birth defects, smaller head circumference and an increase in cancer risk.[43] Smoking also increases your risk of having an ectopic pregnancy or stillbirth. The chemicals in cigarette smoke also increase the need for some nutrients—like vitamin C. Third-hand smoke—considered the toxic particles like lead and arsenic left behind from smoke on clothes, furniture, rugs, etc. can also be hazardous to you and your baby's health. See page 112 for more information about smoking hazards.[44]

Planning a Healthy Pregnancy
A Step-by-Step Guide

Several months before you become pregnant, both you and your partner should follow the advice below. Men are often left out in the cold when it comes to pregnancy planning—but now we know their health and well-being can be just as important! This step-by-step guide brings together many of the tips and concepts discussed throughout the chapter.

Make a Pre-Pregnancy Visit to Your Health Care Provider

During this visit you can discuss your current health as well as your immunity to diseases such as chickenpox and rubella. These diseases are fairly harmless most of the time, but if you get infected during pregnancy, they could cause serious problems to the fetus. You may want to get immunized.

Carefully Consider Medications

Visit with your health care provider about medications you currently take, if they are OK or if there are better alternatives. Why? A few medications, like Accutaine and other brands of isotretinoin used for acne therapy, cause major birth defects and miscarriages. However don't stop prescription medications unless you discuss with your health care provider; sometimes it's riskier to stop a medication than to keep taking it. It's especially important to discuss medication for depression or anxiety; pregnancy is a risky time for depression relapse—and anxiety during vulnerable development could increase your child's risk for attention deficit, hyperactivity and anxiety problems.[45] Also ask your health care provider about the safety of over-the-counter medications you sometimes take—such as pain, cold and allergy medications.

Ditch Drugs and Alcohol

Don't drink alcohol, smoke or take street drugs. They both affect your ability to get pregnant and can also affect your child's long-term health. If you can't quit smoking, try to cut down as much as possible. Remember that quit smoking aids like nicotine patches and gum still give nicotine to your baby, so discuss these with your health care provider before using. See page 114 for more information and resources.

Take Care of Teeth and Gums

Having gum disease (periodontal disease) can increase the time it takes to conceive.[46] That's because the bacteria can cause inflammation throughout the body. Gingivitis and an increase in periodontal (gum) disease are more common during pregnancy due to hormones. Gingivitis causes red, puffy gums that bleed more easily. There is some evidence that gum disease during pregnancy is related to increased risk of preterm birth, low birthweight and preeclampsia, so don't ignore it![47]

However, there are many misconceptions about dental care before and during pregnancy—even among health care providers. Most women don't seek dental care during pregnancy, even though about half of all pregnant women have dental problems. So, see your dentist now for preventive treatment including a cleaning.

Your dentist can check for the eruption of wisdom teeth, which can be another source of inflammation and bacteria in the mouth. And don't be afraid to visit your dentist while you are pregnant if any issues pop up. For more information about dental health see page 176.

Follow the Eating Expectantly Before Baby Diet

Diet affects fertility for both men and women; so both moms-to-be and dads-to-be should follow the Before Baby Diet (page 31) for at least 3 months before you plan to conceive. It takes about 9 weeks for a cycle of sperm production, so an improvement in diet for a few months could improve not only the health of both partners, but it also may result in a faster conception and healthier pregnancy. See page 50 about Dad's Diet and Lifestyle.

Keep Your Environment Safe

For both partners, this means avoiding exposure to pesticides, herbicides, radiation (x-rays), certain plastics and fumes from paint, chemicals, and glue. Avoid exposure to lead, which can cause premature birth, brain damage, learning disabilities, and kidney and liver damage. Lead is stored in the body and can be passed to the baby, especially when calcium intake is too low. (See Chapter 6 for a complete discussion.)

Cap the Caffeine

A little caffeine (up to 100 mg) seems to be OK before and during the first trimester. See page 115 for the details.

Don't Forget the Folate!

In the US and many countries around the world, women who could become pregnant are advised to take 400 micrograms of folic acid from either vitamin supplements or fortified foods such as breakfast cereal and other fortified grain products. Why? To prevent neural tube defects like spina bifida.

Remember Your Multivitamin!

Why? Many women start their pregnancies with low vitamin stores. It's an easy way to get your folic acid, and taking a multivitamin may improve your odds of getting pregnant.[48] It may also help prevent other birth defects, such as heart and limb defects and oral cleft problems. Some single supplements, like calcium, vitamin D, and iron, if needed, may improve your pregnancy. But be suspicious of some single supplements, which can contain excessive amounts. For example, too much vitamin A from a supplement may cause birth defects. However, don't worry about beta-carotene, the plant-derived source of vitamin A—your body only makes the amount of vitamin A it needs from it. (Avoid liver before pregnancy and during the first trimester because it contains large amounts of vitamin A.)

Say Hello—and Goodbye—To Stress

If you are pregnant or trying to get pregnant you have one more reason to feel stressed! (As if you needed another reason!) To better deal with stress, first you have to recognize it. Take a look at your life and identify situations which are stressful and try to modify them or how you deal with them. Why? Extreme stress is thought to affect fertility and according to the March of Dimes, very high levels may contribute to preterm birth or low birthweight. Ways to cope with stress include: talking about it, writing about it in a journal, practicing meditation or yoga, relaxing with music, and exercise.

Chill!

Increased temperatures in the scrotum area can decrease sperm count. Things that can increase scrotal temperature include driving for long periods of time (especially on a heated seat)[49] sitting in a hot tub, sitting with a laptop on the lap or even wearing tight briefs or jeans. Increasing the amount of time spent at sedentary activity, such as sitting at a desk, increases testicular temperature, and the temperature also increases at night.[50]

Women exposed to hot temperatures during the first trimester (such as from experiencing a high fever, or being in a sauna or hot tub or using an electric blanket) are at higher risk of having a baby with a neural tube defect.[51,52] The bottom line—if you are trying to conceive, men and women should "keep cool!"

Ready For Take-Off? Read the Label Before You Take Airborne

Herbal supplements are becoming so mainstream, you may not think twice about taking an over-the-counter alternative therapy for the cold or the flu. Please use extreme caution. Airborne, an effervescent herbal supplement, can contain A LOT of vitamin A; the highest level is 5,000 IU per tablet. Three tablets would exceed the recommended upper limit for vitamin A recommended during pregnancy. Some Airborne doesn't contain any vitamin A; so read the label carefully. Vitamin A has been shown to cause birth defects when taken in large amounts.

Take herbal supplements with caution—they can have drug-like effects. Many are not tested for their safety during pregnancy.

React to Workplace Reproductive Hazards

Anything that can affect the reproductive health of women or men or the ability for couples to have healthy children is called a "reproductive hazard". Radiation, chemicals, drugs, temperature, cigarettes and alcohol are examples. The health of your baby or your ability to become pregnant could be affected by what you and your partner are exposed to at work (and in other places, too). Some examples:

♦ Certain chemicals found at work and in the environment are thought to reduce sperm counts.

♦ People who work in health care or who work with infants and children may be exposed to viruses like Cytomegalovirus (CMV) or Rubella or Chicken Pox, which can cause birth defects and low birthweight. Avoid sharing food, drinks and utensils with young children as well as other exposure to saliva such as toothbrush or pacifier, to cut the risk of exposure to CMV.

♦ Those whose work includes making batteries, welding, painting, or home remodeling may be exposed to lead, which can lead to infertility, miscarriage and developmental disorders.

♦ Some hobbies like making stained glass and those that involve using special glues can expose you to harmful chemicals, too.

You can be exposed to chemicals by breathing them, from skin contact and from swallowing them. The chemicals can be passed on to others in the family on clothes, shoes, tools, hair or skin—so do your best to limit that by removing clothes and shoes outside or shortly after entering your home.

Employers are required to provide a Material Safety Data Sheet (MSDS) for any hazardous material used in the workplace. Read the MSDS to make sure you are not exposed to any materials that would pose reproductive hazards. Also talk to your supervisor about protective gear and other precautions. For more information, contact the National Institute for Occupational Safety and Health (NIOSH) at 800-CDC-INFO. You can also request a Health Hazard Evaluation for your workplace. Find resources on workplace reproductive hazards including podcasts at www.cdc.gov/niosh/topics/repro. A detailed Art and Craft Safety Guide can be found at www.cpsc.gov/cpscpub/pubs/5015.pdf

For more info about keeping your baby's environment safe see Chapter 6.

Be Safe at the Plate

Unfortunately, you're more at risk for a foodborne illness during pregnancy, so food safety is essential for the health of your baby. For example, a foodborne illness caused by *Listeria monocytogenes* can cause miscarriage or stillbirth. Listeriosis has been associated with eating soft white cheeses, deli meats, hot dogs, and unpasteurized milk. Toxoplasmosis is a parasitic infection that can cause mental retardation and blindness. It has been found in uncooked and undercooked meat, unwashed fruits and vegetables, and cat feces. For more information on food safety, see page 134.

Improve Your Posture

Weight gain and a major change in your center of gravity can cause back and pelvic pain during pregnancy—especially if your posture is less than perfect to start with. Take inventory of your posture. Are your ears centered over your shoulders? Are your shoulders rolled forward? Do you experience neck or back pain? If you answered yes to any of these questions, you could have "dysfunctional posture" which can be improved with exercise. According to Juli Hunt, PT, DPT, CSCS owner of Leonardo Physical Therapy in Wilmington, MA, "there is no one best exercise to do—but instead the focus should be on maintaining good posture—so for some that may mean more hip strengthening (gluts) and others it may be more middle/upper back strengthening (traps / lats).

Eating Expectantly Diet: Before Baby

It's easy to have a high quality diet as you ready your body for pregnancy—just follow the Before Baby Diet, including eating as many "Before Baby Superfoods" (page 33) as possible. As soon as you find out you're pregnant, you can switch over to the Eating Expectantly Diet on page 86. The two diets are not very different, so your transition will be easy. If you're wondering how to begin eating a healthy diet, see Chapter 15: Stocking the Pregnant Kitchen.

See more details of all the eating plans in Chapter 4.

What's That? Inositol

Inositol is a B vitamin linked to improved insulin levels, decreased testosterone and triglyceride levels—which may lead to normal menstrual cycles in women with Polycystic Ovary Syndrome (PCOS.) D-Chiro Inositol (DCI), the form of inositol most often linked to improving fertility, is found in buckwheat.[53,54] Buckwheat is also rich in iron, zinc, magnesium and potassium—and that makes this gluten-free, starchy seed a fertility superfood. A type of buckwheat flour reported to be an especially good source of DCI is "Farinetta" available only from its grower: www.minndak.com. See the *Eating Expectantly Cookbook* for a buckwheat recipe.

Eating Expectantly Diet: Before Baby

6	Carb servings. Best choices: whole grains like whole-wheat breads, pasta and cereals, barley, oatmeal, quinoa, and starchy vegetables: winter squash, potatoes, dried beans, peas and corn, plantain, yuca / cassava and taro.
	Ounces (190 g) of Protein Foods: choose fish twice a week and some plant protein daily. Fish and shellfish (up to 12 oz. / 375 g per week), dried beans and legumes, nuts, tofu, cottage cheese, lean beef, lamb, poultry and pork. Be sure to eat a variety!
5	Teaspoons Fats/Oils. Best Choices: avocado, nuts and seeds, olive oil, canola oil, nut oils, olives, soft spread margarine and mayonnaise. Limit saturated fats like butter, cream and coconut oil.
3	Servings of Dairy Foods: 1 serving is 1 cup (250 ml) of milk, yogurt or calcium-fortified soymilk; 1.5 ounces (45 g) natural cheese or 2 ounces (60 g) processed cheese. Choose nonfat or low-fat.
2½	Cups (625 ml) Vegetables: choose a dark leafy green or red/orange vegetable daily. Best Choices: Broccoli, cauliflower, carrots, spinach, cabbage, leaf and romaine lettuce, greens, sweet peppers, mushrooms, bok choy, artichokes and tomatoes.
2	Cups (500 ml) Fruit: choose a vitamin C-rich fruit daily. Best choices: papaya, mango, melon, berries, watermelon, apricots, peaches, grapefruit, orange, grapes and kiwi.
Splurge	200 Calories (Including up to 6 teaspoons added sugar—including what's added to food like yogurt.)

Before Baby Superfoods

In addition to the Before Baby Diet, start eating better now by eating more pre-pregnancy Superfoods.

Food	Rich in These Fertility Boosting Nutrients
Buckwheat	D-Chiro Inositol, magnesium, iron, zinc, potassium
Crab and shrimp	Zinc, selenium, iodine
Blueberries, artichokes, Plum Smart juice, pomegranate juice, red / purple grape juice, dark chocolate, natural cocoa	Polyphenolic antioxidants
Eggs, cod, lean beef, Brussels sprouts, broccoli, cauliflower	Choline
Guava, watermelon, grapefruit, kiwifruit, papaya, cantaloupe, apricots, orange, strawberries, blueberries, raspberries, lemons	Vitamin C and other antioxidants
Quinoa, chick peas, lentils and other legumes	Iron, zinc, B vitamins including folate
Milk and yogurt	Calcium, vitamin D, iodine, zinc
Potato (white and sweet)	Iodine, vitamin C, potassium, beta carotene
Spinach, asparagus, kale, arugula (rocket), avocado, broccoli	Folate, beta carotene and other antioxidants
Almonds, pecans, pistachios and walnuts	Omega-3 fat (alpha linoleic acid), antioxidants, zinc, fiber, vitamin E, magnesium, manganese, copper
Sunflower seeds and pumpkin seeds	Vitamin E, thiamin, manganese, copper, magnesium, selenium, vitamin B6 and folate
Super Spices: Black Pepper, Chili Powder, Cinnamon, Cloves, Cumin, Garlic Powder, Ginger, Oregano, Red Pepper, Rosemary, Thyme, Turmeric	Antioxidants
Wheat germ and oatmeal	Zinc, iron, vitamin E, fiber, magnesium, folate

Questions You May Have

Q: I've been taking birth control pills for five years. Is there anything special I should do before I become pregnant?

A: The effects of birth control pills are quickly reversible, so you could potentially ovulate within a few weeks of being off the pill. Waiting to have at least one period off the pill before you get pregnant helps to establish a due date in case you become pregnant immediately. Check in with your health care provider to see when you should start trying to conceive.

Nutritionally, you should make sure your diet is better than average, since any medication taken over a long period of time can affect your nutritional status. There is evidence that some nutrients are affected by oral contraceptives, including vitamin B6, folic acid, riboflavin, vitamin C and vitamin A, iron, zinc and copper. The Institute of Medicine's iron recommendation for women taking birth control pills is 10.9 mg vs. 18 mg for those not taking them. This is due to the assumption that women on the pill lose less blood during their period. Because having more iron than you need is not a good idea either, take notice of the amount of iron in dietary supplements that you are taking.[55]

Q: I have diabetes and am wondering what I should do to get ready for pregnancy?

A: Kudos to you for thinking ahead! It is essential to have good blood sugar control BEFORE you get pregnant, and in the first trimester. Doing so will decrease your risk of having a miscarriage and having a baby with a birth defect.

- It's best if you start your pregnancy as close to your ideal body weight as possible. Extra body fat and body weight increases insulin needs, thus making blood sugar harder to control.

- Visit your diabetes specialist and obstetrician while you're in the planning stages for[56]:

    » Medication review, especially those for blood pressure and diabetes.

    » Blood sugar control. The American Diabetes Association and other international guidelines generally recommend a pre-conception A1C of less than 7. However the National Institute for Health and Clinical Evidence (United Kingdom) recommends an A1C of <6.1%. These are strict guidelines and you may not be there yet, but with some work, you can be!

    » A comprehensive eye exam, cardiovascular assessment and kidney function test is also recommended prior to pregnancy, as is treatment for gum disease. (See page 247 for more advice for diabetic moms-to-be.)

    » Assessment for family history, lifestyle and need for extra folic acid.

Q: I'm forty-two and I'm finally ready for a baby. What can I do before pregnancy to ensure the health of my baby?

A: Visit your health care provider to get a checkup and a clean bill of health. Older women who are in good health and who receive early and regular prenatal care can have perfectly healthy babies—but it may take you longer to get pregnant! Preparing for your pregnancy and establishing good lifestyle habits can start your baby out right. However, older moms do face increased risks during pregnancy. This is mostly because as women get older, conditions such as diabetes and high blood pressure are more common. (See page 271 for more information.)

Fueling Your Fertility

What You'll Find:

♦ Weight Matters

♦ Polycystic Ovary Syndrome (PCOS)

♦ Other Fertility Factors You Can Control

♦ Dad's Diet and Lifestyle: YES—They DO Play a Role in Fertility

♦ Seven Tips to Fuel Your Fertility

Frequently Asked Questions:

♦ How can diet help with PCOS?

♦ Does my partner need to watch his diet too?

♦ Can an antioxidant-rich diet help me conceive?

♦ What kinds of carbs are the healthiest to eat?

♦ Is there such a thing as "fertility foods"?

SCAN HERE FOR CHAPTER UPDATES

While Chapter 1 looked at pre-conception planning in general, this chapter discusses in more detail how nutrition can improve your fertility. For conception to occur, the reproductive organs and hormones must be in perfect sync—in both partners. A weak link in the chain of events can prevent pregnancy and even cause a miscarriage. This chapter reviews factors that can affect women and/or men.

Infertility, defined as not conceiving after one year of unprotected intercourse, affects about 10-15% of couples. Infertility testing and treatment is a costly and emotional "adventure" you may be able to avoid by taking a proactive approach when planning for pregnancy. Take a look at lifestyle issues you can change. Many factors can affect fertility:

- Age

- Body weight

- Diet

- Tobacco smoke

- Stress

- Alcohol

- Exercise

- Chemicals in the environment

- Medications

- Street Drugs

There's a good chance that improving your diet, becoming more active, dealing with stress better or just taking a vacation will help your odds of getting pregnant. Perhaps one of the most important factors that affect fertility is weight. Let's explore the issues.

Weight Matters

The female body is very protective of an unborn baby. Conceiving is more difficult if you are underweight or overweight; in fact, 12% of infertility is thought to be due to weight issues. Body fat seems to be the synchronizing factor (or the conductor) for the harmonious hormonal symphony that must take place in order for pregnancy to occur and be carried to term. Because fat cells make estrogen, having too many or too few fat cells affects the amount of estrogen in the body, which therefore affects fertility.[1] It's best to get closer to your ideal weight before you seek help with fertility treatments since this simple change can often result in normal ovulation and pregnancy. It can also reduce your risk of pregnancy complications and of having a too large or too small baby.

Underweight

A certain amount of body fat is needed for the regular ovulation and menstrual cycles because some estrogen is produced in our body fat. In fact, body weight changes of just 10-15% below normal can disrupt menstrual cycles.

If you're seeking help for infertility, please make sure you're not underweight. Research shows that being underweight increases your chances of having a low birthweight infant or a baby that is born preterm.[2] Some fertility treatments greatly increase your chances for having twins or more, and this further increases the odds for having low birthweight infants.[3]

A maternal body weight closer to your ideal weight is best for conceiving and for carrying a healthy baby to a healthy weight at term. See page 109 for how to tip the energy balance toward weight gain.

Overweight

For women, excess body fat can affect the amount and types of circulating hormones, which influence fertility. It's estimated that 25% of ovulatory infertility can be attributed to being overweight.[4] Overweight is linked to Polycystic Ovary Syndrome (PCOS), a cause of infertility. Insulin resistance, which can result from having PCOS or being overweight, is also related to infertility.[5] Both PCOS and insulin resistance are discussed in more detail later.

But there's good news: studies show that overweight women have great success in conceiving once they are closer to their ideal body weight. In fact, just losing 5-10% of total body weight can dramatically improve ovulation and pregnancy rates. In one small study, just losing 14 pounds (6 kg) drastically improved ovulation and pregnancy rates.[6]

An expanding waistline can also affect a man's fertility. In fact, it's double trouble if both partners are overweight; it increases the likelihood that it will take more than a year to get pregnant.[7] Overweight men tend to have lower testosterone and increased estrogen levels and decreased ejaculate volume. Men with a BMI > 35 are more likely to have a lower sperm count and higher numbers of sperm with DNA damage, compared to normal weight men.[8] Sleep apnea, which is more common in obese men, can also cause a decrease in testosterone levels. Excess fat in the inner thighs and pubic region may also cause warmer temperatures in the pubic area, which is enough to change sperm production.[9]

Polycystic Ovary Syndrome (PCOS)

PCOS affects as many as 10% of women. Seventy-five percent of women diagnosed with PCOS are thought to have problems with infertility.[10] PCOS tends to run in families; pay attention if women in your family have problems with irregular periods, acne past adolescence, excessive facial hair or diabetes.

PCOS is caused by an imbalance of hormones—especially insulin—which leads to an overproduction of male sex hormones (or androgens) which can lead to small benign cysts on the ovaries, irregular, heavy or no periods, acne and excessive hair growth on the face and body (hirsutism). While being overweight is often common in women with PCOS, you can be of normal weight and still have it.

Issues about body image and self-esteem as well as problems with depression, anxiety, eating disorders and bipolar disorder are also more common in women with PCOS. If left untreated, PCOS can lead to diabetes and heart disease.

Other symptoms of PCOS may include[11]:

♦ Unexplained fatigue

♦ Low blood sugar (hypoglycemia) after meals. Symptoms include light-headedness, sweating, sudden fatigue or urge to eat

♦ Mood swings

♦ Hot flashes

♦ Recurrent spontaneous miscarriages

♦ Rough or velvety dark skin in skin folds, such as the neck, armpits, thighs (also called Acanthosis Nigrigans or AN)

♦ Sleep disorders including sleep apnea

Something Else To Consider: Sleep Apnea

Do you wake up tired or do you find yourself falling asleep at your desk—or worse, while driving? Have you been told you snore? You could have obstructive sleep apnea. A recent research report indicated that women with PCOS may be up to 30 times more likely to have obstructive sleep apnea, which can be a significant factor in the development of metabolic problems such as weight gain and impaired glucose tolerance. Continuous Positive Airway Pressure (CPAP) has been shown to reverse those problems as well as improve blood pressure.[12] Sleeping with a mask may not be the sexiest thing—but if it can improve your health and your fertility, it's all worth it! Discuss this with your health care provider.

Treatment for PCOS includes weight loss, physical activity, a low glycemic index diet and treatment with a medication to improve insulin sensitivity (such as metformin). Because depression and low self-esteem can go hand-in-hand with PCOS, spending time with a therapist is often helpful. If you suspect you have PCOS, speak with your health care provider about it and seek help from a registered dietitian familiar with PCOS, who can individualize a diet that will help with weight loss and help normalize insulin levels. According to Angela Grassi MS, RD, author of *The PCOS Workbook: Your Guide to Complete Physical & Emotional Health,* a healthy eating plan for PCOS often includes:

♦ A diet with a lower intake of carbohydrates (but not a "low-carb" diet)

♦ Eating more lean protein and monounsaturated fats

♦ Eating mostly whole grains

♦ A minimum of 25 grams of fiber per day

♦ Avoiding of sweet beverages including juice, juice drinks and soda

♦ Daily physical activity

♦ Vitamin D supplementation

If you suspect you have PCOS, consult with your health care provider or gynecologist, who may refer you to an endocrine specialist. Also try these tips:

1. Manage Your Weight—managing insulin resistance with medication is also a common approach.
2. Eat a "Smart Carb" Diet with high fiber and low glycemic index foods at every meal. Check out a full discussion of the glycemic index on page 63.
3. Move More—try two 15 minutes walking breaks at work. Build up to an hour or more of moderate to vigorous exercise every day.
4. Lower Your Stress—too much can affect hormone and blood sugar levels and can also lead to unhealthy binges of food or alcohol.

While it's easy to get discouraged, know that many women with PCOS do become pregnant, sometimes with medical intervention. For more information:

♦ www.PCOSnutrition.com

♦ Polycystic Ovary Syndrome Association: www.PCOSupport.org

♦ The PCOS Network: www.pcosnetwork.com/

♦ PCOS at Northwestern University: www.pcos.northwestern.edu/

♦ Project PCOS: www.projectPCOS.org

- The PCOS Challenge: www.pcoschallenge.com

- www.soulcysters.com

Insulin Resistance, PCOS, and Fertility

Insulin Resistance is when your body resists the normal action of insulin—the hormone that lets glucose into your cells. Because insulin doesn't work as efficiently as it should, the amount of glucose in your blood increases and your body secretes even more insulin. Abnormally high levels of insulin (hyperinsulinemia) cause inflammation and can lead to weight gain, high blood pressure, diabetes, heart disease and sometimes PCOS. Insulin resistance is more common in people of Asian descent, in Native Americans, Australian Aboriginals and Pacific Islanders. Not enough physical activity and a diet with too many processed carbs play a role in insulin resistance; weight gain can also trigger it. During pregnancy, some insulin resistance is normal due to hormones secreted by the placenta. However, when it becomes severe enough, it can result in gestational diabetes.

Insulin resistance is common in women with PCOS. Excessive insulin can cause growth of cells in the ovary, which can cause the ovaries to grow small cysts. Ovarian cells are in "hyper" mode, and produce excess amounts of both testosterone and estrogen. The extra testosterone causes male characteristics like excessive hair growth and acne.[13] Insulin and hormones also affect the hypothalamus, which secretes more luteinizing hormone in the brain, which in turn, stimulates even more hormones to be made by the ovaries. And thus begins the vicious cycle of PCOS. Your health care provider may check for high levels of hormones including testosterone and luteinizing hormone to help with the diagnosis of PCOS.

Being overweight increases insulin resistance. That's why weight loss, a Smart Carb diet as well as exercise, are all keys to breaking the cycle of PCOS—and increasing your chances of becoming pregnant.

The Road to Pregnancy with PCOS by Angela Grassi, MS, RD

Having PCOS can pose some unique challenges to conceive, but more is known now than ever about the relationship between PCOS and fertility. There is no question that diet and physical activity have a major impact on ovulation. Establishing healthy eating habits and a regular exercise routine now will not only increase your chances of getting pregnant, but will set the stage for a healthy pregnancy.

Although I'm a registered dietitian who specializes in PCOS, I have PCOS myself. Faced with the fear of having to undergo fertility treatments or far worse, not being able to get pregnant at all, I decided to devote a year to focus on getting my body as healthy and fertile as possible before attempting to conceive.

My yearlong pre-conception period started with a visit to my health care provider who checked my weight and blood pressure and ordered blood tests. The lab results from my blood work revealed that I had a trait of a Mediterranean type of anemia, low vitamin D and elevated insulin levels. My health care provider prescribed me a prenatal vitamin and a mega-dose of vitamin D. Because I was overweight and insulin resistant, my health care provider encouraged me to lose some weight and explained that even losing 15 or 20 pounds (7-9 kg) would significantly improve my fertility. She also prescribed metformin, an insulin-sensitizing medication, to help decrease my insulin levels and improve my ovulation.

Exercise has been shown to help improve not only insulin but ovulation. I had been maintaining a routine exercise program that consisted of mostly cardio but also added two days a week of strength training. As for my diet, I made sure to eat plenty of whole grains plus organic and local produce each day. I included some full-fat dairy, ate less meat and more fish and cut way back on sweets and sugar and avoided artificial sweeteners. My biggest challenge was limiting coffee to no more than 2 cups daily. I cut back on both my total calories and carbohydrate content to achieve weight loss. In addition to the prenatal vitamin, I also took extra fish oil each day.

I was reexamined a year later by my health care provider. My vitamin D levels were in normal range and my insulin improved along with the anemia. I had lost 18 pounds (8 kg) and my menstrual cycles were shorter and occurring monthly. My body was ready to try for a baby. Within a few months, to my great surprise, I was pregnant.

I maintained the changes I made in my diet and exercise throughout my pregnancy and continued taking metformin. I had no complications and had a healthy baby boy. Although the road was not always easy, in the end I became pregnant without fertility treatments. My advice to you is be patient and don't give up!

Angela is the author of *The Dietitian's Guide to Polycystic Ovary Syndrome* and *The PCOS Workbook*. Find out more at www.pcosnutrition.com.

Other Fertility Factors You Can Control

In addition to addressing your weight, there's a good chance that working on other things that are within your control, like your diet, fitness routine and stress, will help your odds of getting pregnant.

Taking a more holistic path to improving fertility is also catching on in the medical community—Duke University and Mt. Sinai Medical University have both opened Holistic Fertility Centers. This more natural approach to fertility includes a wide range of services, from yoga and stress management to relaxation classes, acupuncture, and massage therapy. So let's get started!

Caffeine

Does caffeine affect fertility? Possibly. Some research does show an effect (mostly in large amounts) but in the large Nurses' Health Study, researchers found no association between caffeine intake and reduced ovulatory fertility.[14] Bottom line? Moderation: keep your caffeine to no more than 200 mg a day. And if you have to choose between coffee and soda for your caffeine, go with the coffee. Sodas, with and without caffeine, appear to have a negative effect on fertility. See page 115 to find a full discussion of caffeine.

Exercise

Women involved in competitive sports (and those who just exercise a lot) sometimes reduce their body fat so much that they stop menstruating. Strenuous exercise, low body weight and body fat are related to reproductive problems, including infertility. Regular exercise is important for good health, and can improve or control many conditions that lead to infertility, including overweight, emotional stress, and PCOS. However, if you take exercise to the extreme and are having trouble conceiving, you may need to slow down.

If your guy is an "armchair athlete" encourage him to get off the couch and be more active. A recent study showed that men who watched 20 hours of TV a week had 50% less sperm, while those who worked out frequently had up to 73% more sperm than those who didn't. If your man is a dedicated athlete, encourage him to tone down his routine a bit or mix it up to keep the family jewels cool as a cucumber and unencumbered. If he's a biker, ask him to switch to swimming or running for a while (or if he insists, buy him a bike saddle with fertility-boosting engineering.) If he likes to pound the pavement in the heat of summer, encourage him to run when it's cool instead, or to switch to the treadmill or elliptical at the gym. And remember, tight briefs and shorts may look good, but they're not good for his fertility!

The Vicious Cycle for Athlete Dads-To-Be

In movies, the "jock" always gets the girl. But ironically, nature is unforgiving of male athletes when it comes to fertility. Endurance athletes have been reported to have lower sperm count, decreased sperm motility and more sperm with abnormal shape or size. Cycling is one of the major risk factors for erectile dysfunction due to pressure on perineal arteries, which decreases blood flow to the penis. In addition, up to 30% of all types of athletes (compared to 10% for all men) have varicocele (enlargement of veins in the scrotum—similar to varicose veins) with up to 60-80% of body builders having the problem. A common cause of male infertility, it results in increased scrotal temperature and sperm damage. Male endurance athletes appear to have reduced levels of testosterone, which could also affect fertility.[15]

Cigarette Smoke: Yours and Theirs

For women, the hazardous chemicals in cigarettes are poisonous to ovaries, by decreasing blood flow, interfering with estrogen production and causing genetic abnormalities in the eggs. Women who smoke take twice as long to conceive and are more likely to have a miscarriage. The effects of smoking are dose-responsive. While some of the damage that smoking does to ovaries is irreversible, stopping smoking can improve fertility rates.

In men, smoking causes lower sperm count and motility, abnormalities in sperm shape and function and can cause oxidative damage to sperm, which could be responsible for birth defects and other diseases.[16]

That said, tobacco is extremely addictive and quitting is not easy. Because the effects on fertility depend on how much you smoke, start now by cutting down with the goal of quitting for good—for you and your partner. For stop smoking resources, see page 112.

Smoking and Assisted Reproductive Therapy

According to the American Society for Reproductive Medicine, Women smokers receiving IVF treatments need nearly twice as many IVF attempts as non-smokers to become pregnant. Women who smoke also need higher levels of gonadotropic drugs to stimulate their ovaries, and have lower peak estradiol levels and lower implantation rates.[17]

Second Hand Smoke also Snuffs Your Fertility

There's almost no getting away from tobacco smoke—especially if your town doesn't have any legal bans on smoking. Even if it does, when entering or leaving a building, you've got to hold your breath long enough to get by all the smokers huddled at the front door's ashtrays. If you work in the hospitality industry, even in the non-smoking section, the smoke lingers in the air where it can enter your lungs or collect on your clothes and hair. Let's face it; we all breathe the same air!

Sidestream (second hand) tobacco smoke contains more than 7,000 chemicals including at least 69 known to cause cancer. It's estimated that 40% of nonsmokers are exposed to tobacco smoke. Sidestream smoke is just as bad as or even worse than the smoke inhaled by a smoker, because it isn't filtered. Recent research suggests that sidestream smoke, like mainstream tobacco smoke, may also cause mutations in the DNA of sperm.[18]

You may not want to share your plans for conceiving with co-workers, family or the stranger on the elevator… and even if you did, they might not think their smoking is a problem to you. Try this tip from the authors of "Before Your Pregnancy": Tell them you have (or recently developed, if they know you) a sensitivity or allergy to cigarette smoke. Embellish if you must, (throw a few sneezes or coughs in for good measure) and claim that it can bring on an asthma attack, depending on the brand. Who would argue with that? OK, pesky Uncle Gene might, but try to avoid him (and other uncooperative friends and relatives) while you are trying to conceive.

Alcohol

While many a babe has been conceived after a New Year's eve party or other celebration, this is not a tradition you want to follow. Alcohol intake by men and women in the week of conception is associated with a higher risk of miscarriage. Alcohol can be found in semen shortly after drinking, thus it can interfere directly with conception, implantation, and it may impact early miscarriage. Even small amounts of alcohol increase the formation of free radicals and the amount of antioxidants you need; so if you were a regular drinker before, you may need to boost your antioxidant intake.[19] For all these reasons, when you're serious about trying to conceive, both men and women should avoid alcohol. If you choose to have that rare drink while trying to conceive, it's safer for women to indulge during their period—the time that ovulation and conception are unlikely. For men, sex and alcohol don't mix—at least when you're trying to make a baby!

Celiac Disease

While you can't control whether or not you have celiac disease, you can control the disease through diet. Celiac disease, (CD) also called celiac (coeliac) sprue, or gluten enteropathy, is an autoimmune disease that leads to an inability to digest gluten, a protein found in wheat, rye, and barley. Research suggests a higher rate of undiagnosed celiac disease in women having trouble conceiving. Untreated celiac disease also may be associated with recurrent miscarriage and other pregnancy problems such as low birthweight.

Celiac disease, once thought to be a rare disorder, now is estimated to affect as many as 1 in 133 people (both in the US and Europe) but that less than 1% have been diagnosed.[20] Symptoms of CD can occur at any time in life, and because the symptoms are sometimes vague and may have no gastrointestinal symptoms at all, it's often mis- or undiagnosed. One study showed the average time between first symptoms and diagnosis was 11 years[21]! CD is most common in first and second-degree relatives with the disease.

Common symptoms include abdominal pain, diarrhea, unexplained anemia, and unexplained weight loss with large appetite, or weight gain. Some people with CD have a chronic skin condition called dermatitis herpetiformis, a burning, itchy rash, and no other symptoms. Some have more inconspicuous signs like bone or joint pain, mouth ulcers, migraine headaches and tingling or numbness in the hands or feet. Infertility and recurrent miscarriage can also be a symptom of celiac disease. The incidence of CD is more common in people with other autoimmune disorders like type I diabetes, lupus, rheumatoid arthritis and autoimmune thyroid disease like Hashimoto's and Graves' disease.[22]

If you suspect you have CD, visit your health care provider; a simple blood test that looks for the presence of certain antibodies is one common test. A biopsy of the small intestine, done during an endoscopy, can confirm the diagnosis. For more info on eating for a gluten-free pregnancy see page 75.

Gluten Sensitivity

People whose tests for celiac disease are negative may still have some form of gluten sensitivity—also called gluten intolerance. The only way to know for sure is to try a gluten-free diet. For more information about gluten-free eating.

Thyroid Disorders

The thyroid gland is responsible for controlling your metabolism and makes a hormone that affects every cell, tissue and organ in the body. So understandably, either an underactive thyroid (hypothyroidism) or an overactive thyroid (hyperthyroidism) can affect your fertility. One in eight women will develop a thyroid disorder in her lifetime.

Hypothyroidism can be a cause of infertility and in pregnancy can increase the risk of miscarriage, preterm delivery and developmental problems in children. Hyperthyroidism can cause problems with sperm motility in men. Checking your thyroid hormone levels requires a blood test; the American Thyroid Association recommends that everyone over 35 be screened for thyroid disease.[23]

Eating Disorders

Amenorrhea (lack of menstrual periods) and oligomenorrhea (infrequent periods) often occur in women with anorexia nervosa and bulimia. Reproductive hormones are also reduced in women who maintain a lower-than-normal body weight. An increase in body weight and a balanced food intake will help restore normal reproductive functions.

If you have an eating disorder, you should try to resolve the underlying causes of the disorder for a permanent recovery. The eating habits and health problems associated with eating disorders vary from one disorder to the other; they can put your baby at risk for birth defects, low birthweight, or prematurity as well as being born large. So, it's best to get eating habits on track and make sure you're not below your ideal body weight prior to pregnancy. Comprehensive programs involving a psychologist, physician, and dietitian are most helpful.

Resources:

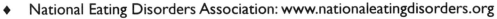

♦   National Eating Disorders Association: www.nationaleatingdisorders.org

♦   Anorexia Nervosa and Related Eating Disorders: www.anred.com

Emotional Stress

You can't control all the stress in your life, but you may have more control than you think. Always saying yes to volunteer projects and in general over-scheduling yourself can increase stress. Take an inventory of your stress and see how you can decrease it, or deal with it in a healthy way. Make your health and stress level a priority.

Oxidative Stress and Antioxidants

You've heard a lot about antioxidants and their overall health benefits. In fact, they also play an important role in your fertility.

Oxidative stress occurs when there's a shortage of antioxidants in the body to neutralize "free radicals" or reactive oxygen species (ROS)—formed during normal biochemical processes in the body (such as more oxygen use during exercise) and as a result of ionizing radiation (x-rays, sunshine) and chemicals in the environment. Free-radicals are also formed when one smokes or drinks alcohol. Pregnancy itself is a cause of increased oxidative stress—simply because your body is more metabolically active—growing new tissues uses more oxygen. The reaction of free radicals in the body can cause inflammation and damage to DNA, the main underlying cause for many age-related diseases including heart disease, cancer, diabetes, macular degeneration, memory loss and cataracts.

Free-radicals can also damage the reproductive system—and have been correlated with problems of sperm motility, sperm number, and DNA damage in sperm. Free-radicals can affect virtually every step in the reproductive process from egg maturation to pregnancy in women. In fact, researchers have now been able to determine the amount of ROS that makes it unlikely for a pregnancy to occur in women receiving assistive reproductive technology.[24] There is increasing evidence that free radicals may have an effect on endometriosis, miscarriage, preeclampsia, and preterm labor.[25] Increasing age, being overweight and of course, lower nutrient intake are associated with lower antioxidant levels in the body.[26]

That's why an antioxidant-rich diet, like the Eating Expectantly Diet, for both mom and dads-to-be, could improve your fertility. Examples of antioxidants include vitamin C, vitamin E, folate and carotenoids like beta carotene and lutein, as well as minerals like selenium, zinc and copper. Folate and zinc have antioxidant properties which affect both male and female fertility.[27] A diet containing fruits, vegetables, lean protein and whole grains could insure your entry into "Club Mom."

What About Fertility Supplements?

Research shows that some antioxidant supplements may improve sperm quality in men.[28] The latest research In this area shows promise for older men. Men over 44 years with the highest dietary and supplement Intake of vitamin C, E, folate and zinc had significantly less sperm DNA damage than younger men.[29] (Sperm damage is associated with both male infertility and genetic defects in children.) For women, it's a little trickier. Some supplements may improve ovulation and fertility, while others are dangerous to take once you're pregnant. Certain lifestyle habits like smoking increase the need for antioxidant vitamins—but excessive doses of some antioxidant supplements have been linked to *increased* cancer risk. A safe approach: take a multivitamin with antioxidants that contain only the current Dietary Reference Intake for each nutrient, plus eat an antioxidant-rich diet.

Check out www.consumerlab.com for unbiased research on the safety and quality of vitamins and herbs.

There are several ways that scientists use to measure the antioxidant activity of foods. The antioxidant measurement of a food doesn't necessarily translate into antioxidant action in the body: however, these rankings can still be useful in guiding food choices. The following foods are considered some of the richest in antioxidant capacity and should be included in your "Before Baby" diet and beyond:[30,31]

♦ Blackberries, red currants, raspberries, strawberries, blueberries

♦ Oranges

♦ Pineapple

♦ Plums

♦ Pomegranate

♦ Spinach

♦ Chile peppers

♦ Olives

♦ Mushrooms

♦ Asparagus

♦ Arugula

Cherries: A Sweet Way to Fight Inflammation

Add some fresh cherries to your diet in the summer, or some frozen cherries or cherry juice in the winter, to help boost your level of the antioxidants called anthocyanins, which research shows may reduce inflammation. Cherries also score low on the glycemic index.[32]

- ◆ Radicchio
- ◆ Beets
- ◆ Broccoli
- ◆ Artichoke
- ◆ Red peppers
- ◆ Walnuts, pecans, sunflower seeds, chestnuts, peanuts, pistachios
- ◆ Buckwheat, millet, barley

All culinary herbs and spices have antioxidants too, but these have the most: Clove, allspice, mint, sage, thyme, nutmeg, rosemary, saffron, tarragon, oregano, ginger, cinnamon, and natural cocoa.

Pesticides and Other Chemicals

It's not news that we live in a world of toxins. However, we are learning what a profound effect those chemicals we meet in our daily lives can have on our health and fertility, and the health of our children. Some chemicals in the environment, called endocrine disrupting compounds (EDC), are similar in structure to hormones and thus can mimic as well as block their action. These chemicals have been known to decrease sperm count, cause miscarriages, menstrual cycle irregularities and infertility[33]:

- ◆ Polychlorinated biphenyls (PCBs)
- ◆ Dioxins
- ◆ Polycyclic aromatic hydrocarbons
- ◆ Phthalates
- ◆ Bisphenol A (BPA)
- ◆ Pesticides
- ◆ Alkylphenols
- ◆ Heavy metals (arsenic, cadmium, lead, mercury)

Not to worry—Chapter 6 has a full discussion of environmental chemicals.

Dad's Diet and Lifestyle: YES—They DO Play a Role in Fertility

We used to think that Dad's role in pregnancy was simple—his contribution of the X chromosome—and that his diet and lifestyle habits had little or nothing to do with the time it took to get pregnant, or in having a healthy baby. Research now shows us that nothing could be further from the truth! While dads can follow all the tips in this chapter to take more control of their fertility, this section is written just for guys. We begin with a special note from author Dave Grotto.

A Note to Dads-To-Be from Dave Grotto RD, LDN

Not only does it take "two to tango" but it most certainly takes two to make a baby. And not in the obvious ways that may first come to mind, but rather in the equal responsibility that guys have in the whole baby-making process—namely, keeping themselves healthy and supporting their loved one.

My favorite saying is "if it's good for the heart, it's good for every other part." Though the #1 killer of both women and men is heart disease, many of those same lifestyle choices that lead to heart disease can gum up the plumbing in the rest of the body. For women we know that heart disease, infertility and PCOS are strongly associated with increased collection of belly fat. Same holds true with metabolic syndrome and diabetes and also erectile disorder in men. Sperm quality, quantity and prostate health are also impacted by poor diet and lifestyle factors that lead to increased belly fat.

Guys always want more sex but tend to do dumb things like smoking cigarettes, which cause vasoconstriction in the arteries. Translated? It's like taking a four-lane highway and closing down three of the lanes but you still have the same amount of traffic going through. Not only is that a problem for the heart but also when you are expected to "rise" to the occasion…Wink, Wink… Same holds true with alcoholic beverages. A drink or two every now and then to set the mood and help you relax is fine but excessive drinking most certainly can impact performance anywhere from erectile disorder, premature ejaculation and worse yet, passing out at the moment of truth! Excess alcohol negatively affects the quality and quantity of sperm produced. I also always share with guys: if they want to "get more" they better "weigh less" (if overweight). Besides, who wants a big belly to stand between a man and his woman… of course, unless it's a woman's pregnant belly!

Dave is a registered dietitian, dad and author of The Best Things You Can Eat and 101 Optimal Life Foods. www.davidgrotto.wordpress.com/

Fertility Tips for Dads-To-Be

While much of this chapter mentions how Moms and Dads-to-be can improve their diet and lifestyle, these tips are directed to the guys.

Eschew the Chew

Research shows that chewing tobacco can affect fertility similarly to that of cigarette smoke—and the effect is dose dependent. In fact, men who chewed more than 6 times a day were 14 times more likely to have some semen samples containing no sperm compared to those who chewed less than three times a day.[34]

Watch What's In Your Pocket

While the evidence is far from conclusive, a few studies show that Radio Frequency Electromagnetic Waves (RF-EMWs) emitted from cell phones may have a negative effect on sperm; potentially causing negative effects on sperm count, motility, viability, shape and size.[35,36] An increase in oxidative stress is also thought to be caused by RF-EMWs, and the damage to sperm appears to increase with increasing cell phone use. There may be other long-term effects of cell-phone use—the World Health Organization recommends using a hands-free device and using a cell phone in an area of good reception to reduce power usage.[37] While trying to conceive, it's best for dads to avoid carrying a phone in the pants-pocket.

Take Control of Diabetes

Men with type 2 diabetes have been shown to have a lower level of testosterone and a higher level of DNA fragmentation in their sperm, which can affect fertility. Insulin resistance is also known to reduce testosterone levels.[38]

Steer Clear of the Chemicals

As jobs are divided around the house, men usually grab the chores that involve chemicals: pesticides insecticides, gasoline, adhesives and solvents. They may affect fertility and, due to potential DNA damage to sperm, can affect your child (or maybe even your grandchild's) risk of having a birth defect.[39] While your partner is trying to conceive, it's best to stay away from chemicals as much as possible. If you can't avoid them completely, use gloves and masks to keep them out of your body.

Seven Tips to Fuel Your Fertility

If you're ready to fuel your fertility, start by following these easy tips.

1. Lose (or Gain) a Few Pounds

Whether you need to lose or gain, getting closer to your ideal body weight can increase the odds of pregnancy.[40] But don't just focus on calories; also eat a healthier diet, because that can also improve your fertility.

2. Get enough antioxidants

Vitamin C, Vitamin E, selenium, lycopene, beta carotene and zinc intake are all positively associated with sperm quality (number, concentration, and motility).[41] Lycopene is a carotenoid pigment found in cooked tomato products like tomato soup, tomato sauce, and ketchup, and in watermelon, fresh tomato and grapefruit. Interestingly, lycopene is absorbed up to 2.5 times better in cooked as opposed to fresh tomato products.

3. Eat the Right Kind of Fat

For women, increased amounts of trans fat in the diet nearly double the risk of infertility.[42] For men, dietary fat plays a direct role in the structure, concentration and activity of sperm. The bottom line: if you want to decrease your risk of ovulatory infertility, have more sperm and better swimmers with good shapes, limit trans and saturated fat and make sure to have omega-3 fats like DHA in your diet.[43,44,45] See page 79 and page 101 for a full discussion about fat as well as sources of DHA.

4. Be Carb-Smart

Whether it's eating whole grains, limiting portions or cutting out simple sugars, being "carb smart" can improve blood sugar, help you eat less, lose weight and thus help you get pregnant. In fact, in the Women's Health Study, women who drank 2 sodas a day were 50% more likely to experience ovulatory infertility than those who drank soda less than once a week. (The caffeine in the soda was not the culprit.) The Harvard researchers concluded that the amount and quality of carbohydrates in the diet may be important determinants of ovulation and fertility.[46]

In particular, try to make at least half your grain servings "whole." A recent study shows that eating more whole grains makes a reduced-calorie diet more satisfying, can improve insulin sensitivity, and decrease "belly" fat, which can help lower the risk of metabolic syndrome and heart disease.[47] It can also lower oxidative stress, which is increasingly associated with male infertility problems. Emerging research shows that resistant starch, a type of carbohydrate that can't be digested by the body, improves insulin sensitivity, which can also enhance fertility.

5. Consider Cleaner Eating

What's that? It's simply eating foods as close to their natural state as possible. For example, choosing fresh or flash frozen instead of canned vegetables and fruits, and choosing whole-grain foods over processed ones. It also means limiting additives in foods, such as pesticides and artificial preservatives. It's nearly impossible to eat a perfectly clean diet—unless you have unlimited money and time—which few of us do! But there are simple ways to eat cleaner, which you'll find throughout this book!

6. Eat More Chocolate

Move over acai; dark chocolate has more antioxidant power than blueberry, cranberry, and acai, according to recent research. Cocoa powder and dark chocolate are very rich in polyphenols, which are strong antioxidants. Keep in mind however that when cocoa is alkalyzed or "dutched" it loses much of its antioxidant power, so to get the benefits; you'll need to use natural cocoa powder or dark (at least 60% cacao) chocolate.[48] Having 1-2 tablespoons of natural cocoa a day could be good for blood pressure. Contrary to popular belief, the darker the color of cocoa, the lower the flavonol content.

You may be one who swears by chocolate's emotional benefits, but now there is some research to back up the notion that dark chocolate decreases levels of stress hormones.[49] Nonetheless, chocolate is still an "extra" food that can be high in calories, so limit yourself to an average of a half-ounce serving a day.

7. Eat these Top Fertility Foods

As you think about eating and cooking while trying to conceive, make sure to include these fertility foods!

- Walnuts
- Pecans
- Legumes, especially black eyed peas and great northern beans
- Asparagus
- Artichokes
- Whole grains-especially those with whole pieces of grains in them
- Lean beef
- Eggs
- Berries-all kinds
- Guava
- Natural cocoa and dark chocolate
- Pomegranate
- Spinach
- Kale
- Sunflower seeds
- Sweet potatoes
- Cherries

Walnuts, a nut known for its omega-3 content, may be just what the doctor ordered for men who want to improve their fertility. Eating just 2.5 oz. (75 g) of walnuts a day for 12 weeks helped men improve their sperms' quality, motility and morphology. The sperm also had fewer chromosome abnormalities.[50] See the *Eating Expectantly Cookbook* for a walnut recipe.

3

The Knowledgeable Pregnancy

What You'll Find:

- Changing Your Mindset for Pregnancy

- Twelve Steps to a Healthier Diet (and Life)

- Carbs 101: What You Need to Know

- What About Sugar & Other Sweeteners?

- Going Gluten-Free

- Fat: The Good, the Bad, and the Ugly

- Allergy Prevention During Pregnancy

Frequently Asked Questions:

- Do I need more vitamin D?

- What is the Glycemic Index and how can it help me?

- What is resistant starch?

- How can I cut the sugar in my diet?

- Should I eat gluten-free?

- How much fat should I eat and which fats are healthiest?

SCAN HERE FOR CHAPTER UPDATES

So you're pregnant. Congratulations! You're about to begin the most exhilarating, exhausting, challenging, and special time of your life. No doubt you will find yourself daydreaming in the months to come: "What will my baby look like? How will I be as a first-time (or second- or third-time) mom? What will my baby grow up to do—discover the cure for cancer or become President?" And your thoughts will inevitably drift back to one important question: "Will my baby be healthy?"

Fortunately, the answer to that question depends a lot on you. Although genetics and pure chance can affect your baby's health, taking good care of yourself gives your baby the best possible odds of good health—both now and in the future. The good habits you start now can be with you and your family for life!

Changing Your Mindset for Pregnancy

Up to now you've been the perfect model of health (—or not). Before, you never let trans fat pass your lips, you hit the gym five times a week, and you haven't eaten anything fried in years. Now you're craving onion rings, don't feel like exercising (or doing much of anything, for that matter), and a biscuit with gravy sounds real good. Or maybe you *weren't* the poster child for healthy behaviors before pregnancy. Perhaps you never set foot in a gym, your refrigerator produce drawer was usually empty and you *certainly* never went out of your way to get salad instead of fries. But now that there's a new life growing inside you, you want to clean up your habits.

You're in the right place, no matter what scenario fits you. While pregnancy is a perfect time to change your habits, it's not the time to beat yourself up if you're not perfect. There's no such thing as a perfect parent either, so you'd better get used to it now!

This chapter offers basic info as well as some myth busting about healthy eating during pregnancy. It's also the foundation for much of the rest of the book, so you'll want to read it first and refer to it again later. Before we begin, let's take a step back to get a little perspective on eating during pregnancy…

Habits are Hard to Change

While you may *want* to eat perfectly for the next months, know that it may not be easy. That's because you've probably eaten a certain way for 10 or 20 years. Take it one step at a time—any healthy food you eat is a step in the right direction. Congratulate yourself for the good choices you make.

Most Foods Fit

And some foods, which maybe you've thought weren't that good, have a health halo after all. A few examples: While the average American diet contains too much saturated fat, eating lean red meat in moderation is fine. You just need to choose lean cuts like top round, eye of round, and flank steak. Red meat is rich in iron, and small amounts of red meat can help your body absorb iron from non-meat sources. It is also a good source of zinc, an important nutrient during pregnancy. Even though some types of fish contain mercury, it's no reason to avoid all fish! I believe a variety of protein sources are best, including a good proportion of plant proteins. Eggs are also high on my list of foods to eat. They're considered the perfect protein—and are one of the best sources of choline, a B vitamin needed for your baby's developing brain. And in case you haven't noticed yet, this book is *chocolate friendly!*

Expect Change

Your body is going through a tremendous amount of change (no kidding!), and feeling sluggish may be your "new normal." You may also feel uncomfortable about the size or look of your "body with baby." Try to get used to it—your size is going to get a lot bigger, so you might as well go with it. Your expanding body is not the only thing changing—your moods will have their ups and downs too.

You're in Control

While it may seem like aliens have taken over your body, brain and moods, in the end it's still your daily choices about everything you do, eat and drink that will make the difference in your baby's health. In fact, with smart choices, you can actually "program" your baby for good health. Unfortunately, the opposite is also true. Read a full discussion of this on page 19.

Twelve Steps to a Healthier Diet (& Life)

Because there is so much conflicting advice about nutrition and health today, I've put together twelve easy tips to follow, now and after your pregnancy.

1. Focus on Whole Foods

Try to eat as many whole foods as possible—meaning as close to their natural state as possible. In general, look for a short ingredient list to find the least processed food—if the list is more than a few lines long, skip it!

Instead of This:	Eat That:
White rice	Quinoa, bulgur wheat, corn
Saltines	Tortilla chips, crackers with whole grain as first ingredient, and with as few ingredients as possible
Applesauce	Whole apples
French fries	Baked white or sweet potato

2. Eat (and Live) Cleaner and Greener

Minimize foods containing artificial colors and preservatives. Choose organic when possible, especially of foods that contain the most pesticides. (See page 364 for more info.) Eat locally as much as possible.

3. Savor the Flavor of Food

Too often, we eat too quickly or don't take the time to cook food that tastes good—which can lead to overeating. Food is more satisfying when it tastes good and when we take the time to enjoy it. By learning to choose and prepare foods that are tasty AND nutritious—and to savor them—you will have a healthier relationship with food. The eating and cooking advice in *Eating Expectantly* is meant to guide you on the road to eating well forever.

4. Make Moderation & Variety Your Mantra

They are the keys to a healthy pregnancy. As long as you eat a variety of nutrient-rich foods you can fit small amounts of "splurge" foods into your diet. Variety helps insure that over time you get the right mix of nutrients. Knowing that it's OK to have an occasional treat may help you avoid going overboard.

5. Eat At Least Three Times a Day

Eating small meals with snacks in between is a simple way to avoid some of the problems of pregnancy like heartburn and nausea. It's also linked to a smaller risk of having your baby prematurely.[1] Breakfast, long touted as the most important meal of the day, may help prevent cravings for sweets and sweet drinks later in the day.[2] Use the Eating Expectantly Diet, which is based on MyPlate, as a guide to eating well during pregnancy. If your grocery cart doesn't reflect MyPlate, you need to re-write your shopping list!

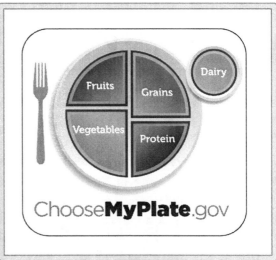

    For a personalized meal plan based on your height, weight and due date, go to www.choosemyplate.gov/supertracker-tools/daily-food-plans/moms.html

6. Bone Up on Calcium—and Vitamin D

Calcium and vitamin D (as well as magnesium, vitamin K and others) are vital for your baby's bone development. In fact, vitamin D supplementation and UV sun exposure during pregnancy predicts childhood bone mass.[3] If possible, it's best to get your calcium along with vitamin D—either in milk or a fortified food or beverage. Many studies have proven the power of calcium to prevent preeclampsia—a hypertensive disorder of pregnancy—especially among women at high risk.[4,5]

Of course, calcium is well known for helping to build bones to their maximum strength and keep them that way, which helps prevent osteoporosis. You start losing bone mass in your thirties, so be sure to consume adequate calcium and vitamin D, either from your diet or supplements from now on. Weight bearing exercise is also vital for good bone mass—walking, dancing and weight resistance exercises are perfect examples.

Next, let's discuss vitamin D in more detail.

D Does Double Duty

Just a decade ago, Vitamin D barely had a mention—now it appears to be the nutrient superstar—being studied for everything from bone mass, to cancer and gestational diabetes to autism. Vitamin D insufficiency can have profound effects on your pregnancy and on the health of your child later in life as demonstrated by these studies: Low vitamin D levels early in pregnancy are related to a five-fold increased risk of preeclampsia[6] and nearly double the risk of type 1 diabetes in children of moms with a lower level of vitamin D.[7] A new study shows that women with Vitamin D insufficiency in the second trimester are twice as likely to have children with language difficulties.[8] Adequate vitamin D at birth also seems to protect against Respiratory Syncytial Virus (RSV) the first year.[9]

The bad news is that many of us aren't getting enough of the sunshine vitamin. A study of pregnant women in Pittsburgh found that 83% of blacks and 47% of whites were either vitamin D deficient or insufficient.[10] In a study of Caucasian women in Southampton, UK, 31% were vitamin D insufficient and 18% were considered deficient. For Asian women living in the North of England, 95% were considered vitamin D insufficient and 26% had outright deficiencies.[11]

You are considered vitamin D "Insufficient" if your Serum 25(OH)D (serum 25-hydroxyvitamin D) is between 52.5-72.5 nmol/liter (<21-29 ng/ml). This level is considered to be inadequate for bone and overall health. You are considered deficient if your level is <50 nmol/liter (<20 ng/ml); this level can lead to rickets in children and osteoporosis in adults. The Endocrine Society suggests that it might require at least 1,500-2,000 IU of supplemental vitamin D to maintain normal serum levels during pregnancy.[12]

Vitamin D Recommendations Differ Around the World

The U.S. and Canada both follow the Institute of Medicine Guidelines for vitamin D during pregnancy of 600 IU or 15 micrograms.[13,14] The Tolerable Upper Level of intake for pregnancy is 4,000 IU. However, a position statement for vitamin D supplementation for Canadian mothers and infants from the Canadian Paediatric Society with the First Nations, Inuit and Métis Health Committee, recommends: Consider giving 2,000 IU, especially in the winter months to maintain vitamin D levels.[15] In France, women without an underlying vitamin D deficiency are suggested to take one dose of 80,000 to 100,000 IU (prescription level) at the beginning of the 7th month of pregnancy.[16]

Research shows that women taking prenatal vitamins containing vitamin D still have low serum levels[17], pointing to the fact that current recommendations may not be high enough. The best way to find out how much vitamin D you need is to have your serum levels tested. That way your health care provider can recommend a supplement specific to your needs.

We produce vitamin D in the skin from exposure to sunshine—however, many factors decrease the actual vitamin D that gets made—sunscreen, dark skin, windows, air pollution, being overweight, living in a not so sunny climate or living at a higher latitude. Even if you were to expose some skin in the winter, the angle of the sun prohibits vitamin D production. And of course, if you spend little time outside or your skin is covered with sunscreen or clothes when you do, it's virtually impossible to make the vitamin D you need.

It's unclear exactly how much sun exposure you need at the minimum to make enough D. For example a fair-skinned person at noon in the summer in Miami would need only 6 minutes in the sun to produce 1,000 IU of vitamin D; a brown skinned person would need 16 minutes. The same people in Boston would need 1 hour and 2 hours respectively.[18] While it was once thought that incidental exposure on the arms and face is enough, now some research indicates that little vitamin D is made in the skin of hands and face, while some is made in the skin of arms and legs. The skin of the torso makes the most vitamin D.[19]

Vitamin D is found naturally in fatty fish like salmon, mackerel, sardines, and in cod liver oil. The only natural vegetarian source is mushrooms—a few are naturally high in vitamin D. But just like with people, when exposed to ultraviolet light, the vitamin D content of mushrooms increases. Three ounces of UV exposed mushrooms has about 400 IU—the amount found in 4 cups (1 liter) of milk. Milk and milk alternatives (soymilk, rice milk) are fortified with vitamin D, as are some yogurts and cheeses. Read the label to make sure.

If your health care provider doesn't mention vitamin D, it doesn't necessarily mean that it's not important. A recent survey in London, a location that has many cloudy days, showed that only 10% of General Practitioners and 29% of Midwives recommended vitamin D supplementation during pregnancy and only 11% of General Practitioners knew more than one risk factor for Vitamin D supplementation.[20] It's important to be an advocate about your own vitamin D level.

7. Don't Skimp on Iron

It is estimated that 10% of women of childbearing age are iron deficient and half don't have the iron stores necessary for pregnancy. Iron-deficiency anemia in the first (especially) or second trimester can double or even triple the risk of premature birth and low birthweight: the earlier in the pregnancy and the more severe the anemia, the greater the risk. (However, iron deficiency in the third trimester is not associated with premature birth.)[21] Iron deficiency anemia is also associated with a larger risk of your child having wheezes the first year of life and asthma at 6 years. To find out how to make sure you have enough iron in your diet, see page 187.

8. Go for Whole Grains

Few foods have the many benefits of whole grains! Recent research links eating whole grains with reduced risk of heart disease, diabetes, digestive system problems and some cancers. Whole grains help with weight management and insulin sensitivity.[22] Whole grains also contain trace minerals that are important for your pregnancy but might otherwise be in short supply in your diet: chromium, selenium, zinc, copper, manganese, and magnesium. Leave "low carb" behind and embrace "slow carbs"—a diet based on whole grains, fruits and vegetables. Eating whole grains is easier than ever—quick cooking brown rice and bulgur, whole grain cereals, and whole-grain pastas are widely available. Experiment with some different whole grains—quinoa, amaranth, kamut, millet and spelt, available at natural food stores. For more info, visit www.wholegrainscouncil.org.

9. Get Moving!

Benefits of moving more (otherwise known as exercise) are many: stress reduction, improved endurance, lowered resting heart rate and blood pressure, improved cardiovascular efficiency, improved self-esteem and body image, better sleep habits, and reduced risk of heart attack, stroke, diabetes, and even some types of cancer. During pregnancy, exercising regularly can help you manage your weight (and thus that of your baby) and prevent gestational diabetes. Even if you don't officially "exercise," spending less time being inactive also helps. Staying limber can ease aches and pains, help reduce fatigue, and get you ready for the "mother's marathon"—labor and delivery. For tips on exercise, see Chapter 14: Fitting Fitness In.

10. Get your Fill of Fluids

You need to drink more fluid during pregnancy because of increases in blood volume, new tissues and your baby's cushiony new home surrounded by amniotic fluid. Fluid needs can vary depending on the temperature and humidity, your weight, calorie and fiber intake—even your use of a heater. About ten glasses per day are recommended during pregnancy. You can get your fluid in the form of milk, 100% juice and decaffeinated tea but try to drink most of it as clean, filtered water.

Thirst is the first sign of dehydration, but it lags behind actual need. By the time you feel thirsty, you are already behind in your fluid intake. You'll want to avoid becoming dehydrated—it can make you feel tired and sluggish, and in extreme cases, can bring on premature labor.

11. Focus on Fiber

Try to get about 30 grams of fiber each day from whole foods such as fruits, vegetables, legumes and whole grains. Fiber combats constipation and hemorrhoids—and may even reduce the risk of preeclampsia. Many foods have added fiber and resistant starch and provide an easy way to get your fiber.[23]

12. Take it Easy on the Extras

The Eating Expectantly Diet contains 200 splurge calories—which can be used for extra fat and sugar in foods. With all the extra nutrients you need during pregnancy, you can't afford to eat many empty-calorie foods.

Carbs 101: What You Need to Know

Carbs are still a hot topic—and there's just as much confusion regarding the glycemic index, the gluten-free diet and even the health benefits of potatoes. This section will detail some of the main issues. One thing that's known for sure: the quality of the carbs you eat during pregnancy can make a difference to you and your baby's health.

What are Smart Carbs?

"Smart Carbs" are mentioned often in this book! It's a term I use to describe carbohydrate foods that are digested more slowly. Because they are whole foods or only lightly processed, they also have more nutrients and fiber. The benefits of eating smart carbs include having stable blood sugar and insulin levels, and helping you feel full so you are less likely to overeat. Examples of Smart Carbs (also called "Slow Carbs" or "Quality Carbs") include:

◆   Whole grain breads, cereals and pastas: quinoa, wild rice, bulgur wheat, popcorn

- Whole fruits (including dried fruits) and vegetables

- Legumes and starchy vegetables: beans, peas, corn, pumpkin, butternut squash

- Foods containing resistant starch: beans, oatmeal, cooked and cooled pasta

What is the Glycemic Index?

If you've looked at diet books in the last few years, there's no doubt you've seen a few bestsellers boasting the merits of the Glycemic Index or GI. The GI is a ranking of carbohydrate foods from 0 to 100, based on how much the food raises blood sugar, compared to eating the same amount of pure glucose. Ranking for Glycemic Index: Low: 55 and under; Medium: 56 to 69; High: 70 and up. So, the higher a food's GI, the faster it's digested and the more it raises blood sugar. A diet that has many high GI foods has been linked to increased risk for diabetes, high cholesterol, heart disease and overweight.[24] On the other hand, a diet rich in low GI foods appear to help control diabetes, blood sugar and helps with weight loss. Another thing to consider about using the glycemic index—most of the time we eat a mix of foods that have a range of GIs.

Many factors affect a food's Glycemic Index, which explains why similar foods can have such different GIs[25]:

- Type of starch—some varieties of grain are digested and absorbed into the bloodstream more quickly. For example, arborio rice has a higher GI than converted (parboiled) white rice.

- Fiber content and solubility—the more fiber a food has, the less digestible carbohydrate it has. Soluble fiber, found in oats, beans and apples, for example, slows down digestion of starch. (For more info on fiber, see page 191)

- Ripeness—the more ripe the fruit, the more sugar it contains—and the higher it's GI. For example a very ripe banana has a higher GI than a slightly green one.

- The fat, protein and acidity of a food slows down the digestion of starch. Chocolate has a lower GI than jelly beans.

- Food processing: the more a food is processed, the higher it's GI. Think instant oatmeal compared to old fashioned oats; fruit juice vs. whole fruit.

- Cooking: causes starch to absorb water, so it is easier to digest. Soft, well cooked pasta has a higher GI than pasta cooked "al dente".

- Refrigerating: when pasta, potatoes and rice are cooked and cooled they have more resistant starch and a lower glycemic index.

What about Glycemic Load?

Glycemic load is also a ranking system of carb-rich foods; it takes into account both a food's carbohydrate content (which depends on serving size) and its glycemic index. Glycemic Load (GL) is really a better indicator of how a food will affect blood sugar. Foods with a GL less than 10 are considered Low; between 10 and 20—Moderate (Medium); above 20—High. Foods low in carb, like non-starchy vegetables, have a very low GI and GL. For a good explanation of Glycemic Load, and a way to find the estimated Glycemic Load for your favorite foods see nutritiondata.self.com/help/estimated-glycemic-load.

How to Lower the Glycemic Load of Your Diet

◆   Eat more beans, legumes and nuts.

◆   Eat high fiber cereals and bars for snacks. Look for ones that contain whole grains like oats, wheat, barley, bran, dried fruit and nuts.

◆   Choose dense, whole grain breads and crackers or those with pieces of grains and seeds in them.

◆   Eat five cups of fruits and vegetables daily, with an emphasis on low GI: fresh whole fruits and vegetables.

◆   Limit carb-containing beverages to half-cup portions of fruit or vegetable juice.

Don't get caught up in the numbers; just make sure to include a low GI food in most of your meals.

Food/Serving Size	Glycemic Load	Glycemic Index
Beverages		
Tomato Juice, ½ cup (125 ml)	2 (Low)	38 (Low)
Soymilk, original, low-fat, 1 cup (250 ml)	3 (Low)	36 (Low)
Milk, skim, low-fat and whole, 1 cup (250 ml)	4 (Low)	32-34 (Low)
Apple juice, ½ cup (125 ml)	6 (Low)	40 (Low)
Prune juice, ½ cup (125 ml)	9 (Low)	43 (Low)
Rice milk, unsweetened, 1 cup (250 ml)	9 (Low)	79 (High)
POM Wonderful, ½ cup (125 ml)	11 (Med)	67 (Med)
Orange juice, ½ cup (125 ml)	12 (Med)	50 (Low)
Gatorade, 12 oz. (375 ml)	19 (Med)	89 (High)
Cola drink, 12 oz. (375 ml)	22 (High)	63 (Med)
Fruit-flavored soda, 12 oz. (375 ml)	28 (High)	68 (Med)

Food/Serving Size	Glycemic Load	Glycemic Index
Breads & Cereals		
All Bran Kellogg's, ½ cup (125 ml)	5 (Low)	34 (Low)
Tortilla, corn, 1	5 (Low)	52 (Low)
Rye bread, light, 1 slice	7 (Low)	68 (Med)
Whole grain bread, 1 slice	9 (Low)	62 (Med)
White bread enriched, 1 slice	9 (Low)	71 (High)
Puffed rice or wheat, 1 cup (250 ml)	10 (Med)	80 (High)
Oatmeal, old fashioned, plain with water ¾ cup (190 ml)	10 (Med)	55 (Med)
Muesli, 1 oz. (30 g)	16 (Med)	66 (Med)
Bran flakes, 1 cup (250 ml)	17 (Med)	74 (High)
Pancake, one 6 inch (15 cm)	18 (Med)	67 (Med)
White dinner roll or Kaiser roll, 1	22 (High)	73 (High)
Oatmeal, Instant Maple, 1 packet with water	23 (High)	83 (High)
Corn flakes, 1 cup (250 ml)	23 (High)	93 (High)
Shredded wheat, 1 cup (250 ml)	24 (High)	75 (High)
Raisin bran, 1 cup (250 ml)	27 (High)	73 (High)
Grains & Pasta		
Couscous, ¾ cup (190 ml)	9 (Low)	65 (Med)
Spaghetti, whole wheat, ¾ cup (190 ml)	10 (Med)	42 (Low)
Bulgur, cracked wheat, ¾ cup (190 ml)	12 (Med)	48 (Low)
Quinoa, ¾ cup (190 ml)	13 (Med)	53 (Low)
Uncle Ben's Converted white rice, ¾ cup (190 ml)	14 (Med)	38 (Low)
Spaghetti white, ¾ cup (190 ml)	14 (Med)	46 (Low)
Brown rice, ¾ cup (190 ml)	16 (Med)	50 (Low)
Millet, ¾ cup (190 ml)	21 (High)	71 (Med)
White rice, ¾ cup (195 ml)	43 (High)	89 (High)
Fruits		
Peach, 1 small	4 (Low)	42 (low)
Strawberries, raw, 1 cup (250 ml)	4 (Low)	40 (Low)
Prunes, 3	5 (Low)	30 (Low)
Apple, Orange, Pear, fresh, 1 small	6 (Low)	40 (Low)
Mango, fresh, ¾ cup (190 ml)	8 (Low)	51 (Low)
Cherries, sweet, 15	9 (Low)	63 (Med)

Food/Serving Size	Glycemic Load	Glycemic Index
Raisins, 2 Tablespoons	9 (Low)	63 (Med)
Banana, ripe, 1 medium	16 (Med)	62 (Med)
Starchy Vegetables / Legumes		
Chick peas, ½ cup (125 ml)	2 (Low)	10 (Low)
Other beans (lentils, black, pinto, split peas etc.), ½ cup (125 ml)	4-6 (Low)	30 (Low)
Butternut squash, mashed, ½ cup (125 ml)	6 (Low)	51 (Low)
Corn, canned, ½ cup (125 ml)	12 (Med)	48 (Low)
New potato, boiled, with peel, 5 oz. (155 g)	16 (Med)	78 (High)
Sweet potato, boiled, 5 oz. (155 g)	18 (Med)	70 (High)
Instant mashed potatoes, prep with water ¾ cup (190 ml)	18 (Med)	92 (High)
Russet potato, baked 45-60 min	23 (High)	78 (High)
Potato, Microwaved, 5 oz. (155 g)	27 (High)	82 (High)
Dairy		
Ice cream, ½ cup (125 ml)	9 (Low)	57 (Med)
Yogurt, low-fat, with fruit, 6 oz. (190 g)	10 (Med)	33 (Low)
Snack Foods		
Dark chocolate, 1 oz. (30 g)	5 (Low)	41 (Low)
Popcorn, 3 cups (750 ml)	6 (Low)	72 (High)
Corn chips, 1 oz. (30 g)	7 (Low)	42 (Low)
Potato chips, average, 1 oz. (30 g)	7 (Low)	51 (Low)
Ryvita Original Dark Rye Crispbread, 2	8 (Low)	65 (Med)
Breton wheat crackers, 5	9 (Low)	67 (Med)
Oatmeal cookie, 1 (17 g)	9 (Low)	54 (Low)
Melba toast, 4	10 (Med)	70 (High)
Saltines or soda crackers, 7	11 (Med)	74 (Med)
Graham crackers, 3 squares	12 (Med)	77 (High)
Fruit roll ups, 1	12 (Med)	99 (High)
Pretzels, sticks, 53 pretzels (1 oz.)	18 (Med)	83 (High)

Note: Glycemic Index and Glycemic Load vary by brand, variety, cooking method and serving size. Source: www.glycemicindex.com, www.health.harvard.edu/newsweek/Glycemic_index_and_glycemic_load_for_100_foods.htm Find the Glycemic Index Foundation blog at: ginews.blogspot.com

Prebiotics

A prebiotic is a non-digestible food ingredient that promotes the growth or activity of beneficial probiotic bacteria in the large intestine. (A probiotic is a bacteria that provides digestive and immune system benefits, and is found in fermented foods like yogurt, kefir, miso, Yakult, kimchi, and sauerkraut.) Think of prebiotics as the fuel for probiotics. Prebiotics can improve bowel function, may decrease the risk of colon cancer; may increase the absorption of calcium and magnesium and improve cholesterol levels. (Some of breast milk's health benefits are the result of prebiotics.)

Inulin is the name of a prebiotic naturally found in the foods listed below; it's also extracted from chicory root and added to many processed foods like cereals, breads, yogurt, high fiber bars and infant formula. The terms to look for on the label for added prebiotics are: inulin, chicory root, oligofructose, oligofructose-enriched inulin, fructooligosaccharides (FOS), and galactooligosaccharides (GOS). Another term you might see on the label—"bifidogenic"—meaning the prebiotic stimulates the growth of a specific probiotic—bifidobacteria. A word of caution—because prebiotics are fermented instead of being digested, they can cause gas. So if they are not already a part of your diet, increase them gradually.

Foods that naturally contain inulin—listed in order of content[26]:

- Chicory root
- Jerusalem artichoke
- Dandelion greens
- Garlic
- Salsify
- Leeks
- Yacón
- Artichokes
- Jicama
- Onion
- Burdock root
- Wheat
- Asparagus
- Rye
- Banana
- Barley

> ### What's That? FODMAP
>
> A small number of people, especially those with Irritable Bowel Syndrome, can't tolerate inulin and other fermentable carbohydrates and follow the FODMAP diet. The diet limits Fermentable Oligo-, Di- and Mono-saccharides And Polyols. For more information: www.todaysdietitian.com/newarchives/072710p30.shtml and www.webmd.com/ibs/features/finding-right-diet-ibs?page=2

Resistant Starch: Passing Fad or Here to Stay?

Resistant starch (RS) is the new buzzword to add to your Glycemic Index glossary. That's because the more resistant starch a food contains, the lower its glycemic index. Resistant starch is a type of fiber and also a prebiotic. It's "resistant"

Carb Smart Pasta

Dreamfields pasta with added inulin, has only 5 grams of digestible carbs in a 1 cup (250 ml) serving and it includes 5 grams of fiber. Now that's a pasta to wrap your fork around! www.dreamfieldsfoods.com

---

to digestion, which give it numerous health benefits—including possibly cutting the risk of colon cancer. Besides the other prebiotic health benefits listed above, foods with RS are more filling—even though they contain fewer calories. RS doesn't affect the texture or taste like other fibers do, so it can be added to many foods and be "invisible."[27]

While there is no recommendation in the US or Canada about intakes of resistant starch, in Australia, 20 grams a day is recommended.[28] So—how do you get more resistant starch? You can get more resistant starch by eating more beans, oatmeal, breads containing pieces of whole grains, and slightly unripe bananas. RS is also formed when starchy foods like rice, potatoes and pasta are cooked and then cooled, as potato or pasta salad. Yes—potatoes can be a smart carb! High-amylose corn is also very rich in resistant starch and is found in King Arthur Hi-Maize High Fiber Flour and Hi-Maize Fiber. You can replace ¼ cup (65 ml) of flour in recipes with the flour—which has 20 grams of fiber per cup (250 ml). See www.kingarthurflour. com. Look for the Hi-Maize symbol on food labels of breads and snack bars.

For more information about resistant starch:
www.resistantstarch.com/ResistantStarch/About+RS/

 A wonderful resource about improving your digestive health with food:
Gut Insight: Probiotics and Prebiotics for Digestive Health and Well-being by Jo Ann Hattner MPH, RD with Susan Anderes MLIS www.gutinsight.com

Snack Bars: Best Choices

Speaking of Carbs and Resistant Starch, one place you'll find both of those things is in snack bars. Here's a list (not all inclusive) of snack bars I recommend during pregnancy. While snack bars are processed, these are made with more whole ingredients. All of these bars contain zero trans fat and no artificial flavors, colors or preservatives. There are many more varieties available from the brands listed.

Snack Bar Brand Name	Contains Organic Ingredients?	Gluten-Free?	Calories	Total Carb (g)	Sugars (g)	Protein (g)	Total Fat (g)	Saturated Fat (g)	Dietary Fiber (g)	Sodium (mg)
Zing Bars (www.zingbars.com)										
Peanut Butter Chocolate Chip	✓	✓	200	21	15	13	10	3.5	4	160
Almond Blueberry	✓	✓	210	23	12	11	9	1	5	130
Oatmeal Chocolate Chip	✓	✓	210	25	12	10	9	2	4	95
Kind (www.kindsnacks.com)										
Fruit and Nut Delight		✓	180	20	11	5	11	1.5	4	15
Blueberry Pecan + Fiber		✓	180	23	12	3	10	1	5	25
Cashew & Ginger Spice		✓	200	16	4	6	14	2	5	15
Soyjoy										
Apple Walnut		✓	140	16	12	4	6	2.5	3	50
Berry		✓	130	17	12	4	4.5	2	3	50
Banana		✓	130	16	11	4	6	3	2	30
Larabar										
Lemon		✓	220	28	22	6	11	1.5	3	5
Peanut Butter and Jelly		✓	210	27	19	6	10	1.5	4	50
Chocolate Chip Cherry Torte			190	28	22	3	8	2.5	3	40
Luna										
Blueberry Bliss	✓		180	27	13	8	5	2	3	115
Nuts over Chocolate	✓		180	25	10	9	6	2	4	190
Lemon Zest	✓		180	27	13	9	5	2.5	3	210

Snack Bar Brand Name	Contains Organic Ingredients?	Gluten-Free?	Calories	Total Carb (g)	Sugars (g)	Protein (g)	Total Fat (g)	Saturated Fat (g)	Dietary Fiber (g)	Sodium (mg)
Kashi										
Soft-Baked Chocolate Square	✓		160	24	9	2	6	1.5	4	140
Layered Peanutty Dark Chocolate			130	20	7	4	4.5	1	4	80
TLC Pumpkin Spice Flax			130	20	5	5	5	0.5	4	65
Clif Kit's Organic										
Berry Almond	✓	✓	180	27	16	4	9	0.5	5	65
Peanut Butter	✓	✓	200	25	15	6	11	2	4	95
Cashew	✓	✓	170	27	15	3	8	1.5	3	85
Gnu Bars (www.gnufoods.com)										
Blueberry Cobbler	✓		130	30	9	4	4	1	12	30
Carrot Cake	✓		140	30	8	3	5	0	12	85
Chocolate Brownie	✓		140	30	9	4	4	1	12	30
Taste of Nature (www.tasteofnature.ca)										
California Almond Valley	✓	✓	180	18	10	5	11	1.5	3	10
Go Ontario	✓		130	26	14	3	1	0.3	2	1
Caribbean Ginger Island	✓		180	21	13	4	9	1	2	10

Note that sugar listed on the label includes natural sugar from fruit. Source: Manufacturer's websites. Because ingredients often change, check ingredient label to confirm. *Thanks to Katie Small for her assistance with this chart.*

What About Sugar & Other Sweeteners?

Sugar is a term collectively used for caloric sweeteners—sugar, honey, corn syrup, molasses, etc. In recent years, other types of caloric sweeteners have popped up on the labels of "natural" and "health" foods—agave, evaporated cane juice, invert sugar, brown rice syrup and fruit juice concentrate. Regardless of the name, all are considered sweeteners and act similarly in the body. Sweeteners can be quite controversial. It's been suggested that pregnant women avoid agave nectar due its content of saponins, but—no scientific studies can be found to back this up.

We eat a lot of "sugar"—about 95 pounds (43 kg) per year per person in the US. That adds up to about 450 calories or 28 teaspoons a day.[29] Some nutrition experts believe that the global rise in obesity is related to our love for simple sugars—especially high fructose corn syrup (HFCS). However, America has decreased its sugar consumption (including HFCS) by 24 pounds (11 kg) since 2000 and the obesity epidemic rages on.

Here are some facts about sugar:

♦ Sugar contains 16 calories per teaspoon, but the calories can add up in large amounts. A 12 oz. (33 cl) soda, for example, has almost 10 teaspoons of sugar and about 150 calories—all from sugar. But, who drinks 12 oz. (33 cl) sodas anymore? The new standard serving size in the US is more like 20 oz. and 500 ml in "metric" countries—piling on up to 16 teaspoons of sugar and 240 (very empty) calories.

♦ Sugar doesn't cause diabetes, though it does cause the body to produce more insulin in order to use the sugar. During pregnancy, placental hormones interfere with the activity of insulin—making you more susceptible to having increased blood sugar levels and gestational diabetes. Watching simple sugar and carb intake—especially in the morning, can make a difference in blood sugar. Choosing smart carbs also keeps blood sugar at a healthy level. Bottom line: make sure the serving of food you eat doesn't contain more than a few teaspoons of added sugar—practice portion control!

♦ Sugar causes tooth decay, as do many other carbohydrate foods.

♦ Lactose, or milk sugar, is a natural sugar found in milk, yogurt, and to a smaller extent, cheese. It is listed on the Nutrition Facts label as a sugar, which is somewhat misleading. When you look at the label of a 6 oz. (170 g) container of Chobani fat-free Lemon yogurt, it shows 18 grams of sugar—however 7 of those grams come from the natural sugar in milk. Only 11 grams are added sugar.

♦ Fructose is found naturally in fruits and vegetables and is listed on the ingredient label as a sugar.

Organic Brown Rice Syrup: Not So Healthy After All?

Much to the shock of many who have diligently chosen foods containing brown rice syrup instead of sugar, a new study shows that many of those products contain concerning levels of arsenic.[30] Arsenic is not regulated in food, though there are limits for bottled water. Rice absorbs arsenic from the soil and it varies by location. Until standards are set for arsenic in food, it's best to avoid (or at least limit) foods that list organic brown rice syrup as the first ingredient.

- While calorie-free sweeteners (non-nutritive or artificial) are one way to cut the sugar in your diet, those are also best used in moderation too. See page 368 for full discussion.

- Many of my clients say they don't eat any added sugar—but they drink a lot of it! From the green tea in the bottle that you've painstakingly chosen over a juice drink or soda, to the decaf coffee whipped drink that's your morning ritual, you may also be drinking most of your sugar. The label on most drinks shows nutrient info for an eight-ounce serving, which is very misleading—unless when you buy a 20 oz. or a 500 ml bottle of something, you intend to share it with a friend or two! To cut the sugar you slurp, consider choosing one with a non-nutritive sweetener (see page 368 for full discussion), or make your own tea and juice drinks at home. They will have much less sugar—and be more nutritious too! See recipes for agua fresca in the *Eating Expectantly Cookbook*.

Sugar Alcohols

Remember learning in high-school chemistry that any chemical ending in "ol" is an alcohol? Well, what's it doing on the label of that sugar-free ice cream? Sugar alcohols, made by adding hydrogen atoms to sugar, aren't considered sugar and won't make you tipsy. However they can have calories; the amount varies depending on how much your digestive system absorbs. Maltilol has 12 calories per teaspoon vs. 16 in sugar—not a huge calorie saver. But erythritol is not absorbed, so it has zero calories—a safe alternative if you're looking for a low-calorie sweetener. In fact, I consider it the best choice if you're looking to avoid sugar. Check out Nectresse, a new erythritol-based sweetener made from monk fruit—it's very tasty.

Sugar... By Any Other Name

Look on the ingredient label for these sugar "aliases"—and this list doesn't include sugar alcohols, which can also have calories!

- Agave nectar
- Barley malt syrup
- Brown rice syrup
- Brown sugar
- Cane crystals
- Cane sugar
- Corn sweetener
- Corn syrup
- Crystalline fructose
- Dextrose
- Evaporated cane juice
- Evaporated cane juice syrup
- Fructose
- Fruit juice concentrates
- Glucose
- High-fructose corn syrup
- Honey
- Invert sugar
- Lactose
- Maltose
- Malt syrup
- Maple syrup
- Molasses
- Raw sugar
- Sucrose
- Sugar
- Syrup

Sugar alcohols have a smaller effect on blood sugar levels than regular sugar, which is why they're found in many foods marketed to people with diabetes. However, there is one caveat. When eaten in excess (20 grams of mannitol; 50 grams of sorbitol, per day) some sugar alcohols can cause a "laxative effect." The other good thing about erythritol is it doesn't have the same gastrointestinal side effects.

Sugar Alcohols:

- Erythritol
- Lactitol
- Mannitol
- Xylitol
- Isomalt
- Maltitol
- Sorbitol

How Much Sugar Should You Eat?

The American Heart Association has made an official recommendation on the amount of sugar we should eat—no more than half of the "empty calories" suggested by the MyPlate/MyPyramid eating patterns.[31] The 2010 US Dietary Guidelines also give a nod to decreasing sugar, suggesting no more than 5 to 15% of calories come from SoFAS—Solid Fats and Added Sugars. The Eating Expectantly Diets are based on MyPlate with 200 calories of "splurge" calories for the second and third trimesters. That translates to 100 calories from sugar, which adds up to 6½ teaspoons for your "sugar budget". Here's how sugar adds up in some common foods.

Food/Serving Size	Teaspoons Added Sugar
Beverages	
Cola or Citrus Soda, 20 oz. (620 ml)	16.5
Snapple Kiwi Strawberry, 20 oz. (620 ml)	14
Snapple Raspberry Tea, 20 oz. (620 ml)	11
Lipton Green Tea with Citrus, 20 oz. (620 ml)	11
Cola, 12 oz. (375 ml)	10
Starbucks Mocha Frappuccino, 13.7 oz. (405 ml) bottle	9
Gatorade or Vitamin Water, 20 oz. (620 ml)	8
Silk Chocolate Soy Beverage, 1 cup (250 ml)	5
Silk Very Vanilla or Chocolate Soy Beverage, 1 cup (250 ml)	4
Almond milk, chocolate, 1 cup (250 ml)	4
Almond milk, vanilla, 1 cup (250 ml)	3
Chocolate milk, 1 cup (250 ml)	3*
Sunny Delight Tangy Original, 1 cup (250 ml)	3
Plain soymilk, 1 cup (250 ml)	1.5

Food/Serving Size	Teaspoons Added Sugar
Desserts	
McFlurry with M & Ms, 12 oz. (375 ml)	18*
Burger King Small Chocolate Shake	14*
Burger King Peach & Granola Sundae	9*
McDonald's Vanilla Reduced Fat Ice Cream Cone	3*
Oreo cookies, 2	3
Pepperidge Farm Bordeaux cookies, 4	3
Lu Le Petit Beurre cookies, 2	1
Maria cookies, 2	½
Candy	
Skittles, 2.2 oz. (60 g) bag	12
Jelly beans, 14	7
Milk chocolate, 1.6 oz. (50 g)	6
Dark chocolate, 1.6 oz. (50 g)	3.4
Milky way, fun bar (17 g)	2.5
Chocolate kisses, 3	2
Breakfast	
Grands Cinnabon roll with cream cheese icing	6
Fruit yogurt, low-fat 6 oz. (190g)	3-4*
Glazed donut	3.5
Frosted flakes, ¾ cup (190 ml)	3
Cinnamon Toast Crunch, 1 cup (250 ml)	3
Pancake syrup, 2 tablespoons	3
Fruit Loops, 1 cup (250 ml)	3
Oatmeal, Maple & Brown Sugar, 1 packet	3
Kashi GoLean Crunch! Honey Almond Flax, 1 cup (250 ml)	3
Total Whole Grain Cereal, 1 cup (250 ml)	1.5
Kashi Go Lean Original, 1 cup (250 ml)	1.5
Cheerios Multi-Grain, 1 cup (250 ml)	1.5
Bear Naked Fit Vanilla Yogurt, ¼ cup (65 ml)	1
Reduced calorie pancake syrup, 2 tablespoons	1
Cheerios, Original, 1 cup (250 ml)	¼
Uncle Sam's Cereal, 1 cup (250 ml)	< ¼

Food/Serving Size	Teaspoons Added Sugar
Snacks	
Clif Kit's Organic Peanut Butter	4
Luna Chocolate Peanut Butter Protein Bar	3
Taco Bell Cinnamon Twists, 1 serving	2.5

Sources: USDA National Nutrient Database for Standard Reference, Release 24, September 2011, www.calorieking.com and manufacturer's websites.
*Approximate added sugar, not including lactose

Going Gluten-Free

Gluten-free diets are becoming so popular that gluten-free foods line the grocery store shelves and some restaurants promote their gluten-free menu items. In fact, the worldwide sale of gluten-free foods is approaching 2.5 billion dollars. Wow!

Eating gluten-free appears to be the sexy new diet of the day. Do you need to be gluten-free? No, not unless you have signs of celiac disease or gluten sensitivity, described below. Check with your health care provider for advice.

Celiac (coeliac) disease, also called gluten enteropathy, is an autoimmune disease in which gluten, the protein found in wheat, barley and rye, sets off an immune reaction which damages the intestinal wall. The damage can prevent the absorption of vitamins and minerals and cause a long list of possible symptoms. While gastrointestinal distress like diarrhea or gas is common, some people don't have any stomach issues—but may complain of fatigue, headaches, "foggy brain" or numbness in the legs, arms or fingers. Celiac Disease has been associated with recurrent miscarriage, growth restriction, preterm delivery and low birthweight. Some people who don't have actual intestinal damage (a gold standard for diagnosis of celiac disease) may still react to gluten; this is called gluten sensitivity.

A gluten-free diet contains no wheat (including spelt, kamut, einkorn, graham flour), barley, rye, or triticale (a cross between barley and rye). Many processed foods may have gluten, such as: bouillon cubes, brown rice syrup, potato chips; lunch meats and hot dogs; French fries, gravy, imitation fish, rice mixes, soups and sauces; soy sauce and seasoned tortilla chips, to name a few. (FYI, some beers, including non-alcoholic ones may contain gluten, depending on the grain they're made with.) Gluten-free grains (and grain-like foods) include corn, rice, quinoa, amaranth, arrowroot, buckwheat, millet, teff and wild rice. Look for oats labeled gluten-free; they naturally contain no gluten but may be contaminated by other grains.

As you can guess, a gluten-free diet can be hard to navigate alone; consult with a registered dietitian familiar with a gluten-free diet. Some great books on gluten-free eating include:

♦ Gluten-Free, Hassle Free: A Simple, Sane, Dietitian-Approved Program for Eating Your Way Back To Health by Marlisa Brown RD, CDE

♦ Gluten-Free Diet: A Comprehensive Resource Guide- Expanded and Revised Edition by Shelley Case RD, Iona Glabus and Brian Danchuk

♦ Gluten-Free Quick & Easy: From Prep to Plate Without the Fuss - 200+ Recipes for People with Food Sensitivities by Carol Fenster PhD

For more information:

♦ National Digestive Diseases Information Clearing House: www.digestive.niddk.nih.gov/ddiseases/pubs/celiac

♦ www.CeliacCentral.org

♦ University of Chicago Celiac Disease Center: www.CureCeliacDisease.org

♦ www.MayoClinic.org/celiac-disease

My Big, Fat, Gluten-free Twin Pregnancy

Tamara Duker Freuman, MS, RD, CDN

As a dietitian and expectant twin mother with Celiac Disease, I knew that a successful pregnancy outcome depended on me picking up the slack in my gluten-free diet, and taking extra precautions to prevent accidental gluten ingestion.

No more picking French fries off my husband's plate at restaurants under the assumption that they were "probably OK," or scraping the frosting off a piece of birthday cake to eat, since it only had "a few tiny crumbs" stuck to it. It was time to get back to the gluten-free basics: reading food labels, grilling restaurant waiters about ingredients, and not taking chances when I couldn't verify if something was safe.

The first trimester was tough, since all I craved were carbs, and my aversions to so many other foods—especially meat and fish—were strong. I must have dreamt about salt bagels with cream cheese for a month straight! Since they were off limits, obviously, I had to find some satisfying gluten-free substitutes. And they had to be effortless to make, since I was way too nauseous and tired to spend time preparing meals. Some of my staples included: baked potatoes with broccoli and cheese; egg & cheese sandwiches on a gluten-free hamburger roll; gluten-free brown rice pasta with pesto; and toasted gluten-free bread with cottage cheese or peanut butter. I also kept a box of Barbara's Bakery Multigrain Puffins cereal (one of the two gluten-free Puffins varieties) by my bedside to help quell the early morning queasiness.

As pregnancy progressed and the carb monster was tamed, my focus switched to protein: since I was carrying twins, my goal was to take in an extra 50 g of protein per day! Plain or vanilla Greek yogurt, eggs, cottage cheese and peanut butter were daily staples, all naturally gluten-free. (Greek yogurt is very low in lactose, and lactose-free cottage cheese is available, if lactose intolerance is an issue!) I kept a box of Sunshine Burgers—a sunflower-seed based, gluten-free veggie burger—in the freezer for when my husband had to work late and I was on my own for dinner. When my spicy cravings kicked in, soft tacos from a Mexican restaurant (corn tortillas are gluten-free), Sweet Potato and Black Bean enchiladas from my favorite gluten-free recipe blog (glutenfreegoddess.blogspot.com), or an Indian curry dish with basmati rice always scratched the itch.

Eating nutrient-dense, wholesome foods during my gluten-free pregnancy was a great warm-up for the yearlong calorie-fest that followed: I needed 1,000-1,200 extra calories per day to breastfeed my twins!

Tamara is a New York City-based registered dietitian and mom of boy/girl twins. You can read her gluten-friendly blog at www.tamaraduker.com. She also blogs for the *US News and World Report*.

Tamara's Favorite Gluten-free Products

These are some of my favorite gluten-free packaged foods. They're all higher in fiber than their standard gluten-free competitors, which is important to help keep things running smoothly during pregnancy!

- Bob's Red Mill Mighty Tasty Gluten-free Hot Cereal

- Bob's Red Mill Gluten-free Steel Cut Oats

- Canyon Bakehouse San Juan 7-Grain bread

- Udi's Gluten-free Whole Grain Hamburger Buns

- Barbara's Bakery Multigrain Puffins cereal

- Nature's Path Mesa Sunrise cereal

- Crunchmaster Multi-seed crackers

- Sunshine Burgers

- Beanitos Bean Chips

Fat: The Good, the Bad, and the Ugly

Watching the types and amounts of fat you eat is important—for you and your baby's short and long term health:

♦ Fat has many functions in the body; it's needed for nutrient absorption, nerve transmission, and in maintaining cell membranes. During pregnancy, it's vital for your baby's nervous system and eye development. Fat and cholesterol are the main components of brain tissue!

♦ Fat plays an important role in many functions in the body because some fat is converted to prostaglandins—hormone-like substances that affect body functions such as blood pressure, blood clotting, and immune response, so the right balance could make a profound difference in overall health.

♦ Ounce per ounce, fat has more than twice as many calories as carbohydrate or protein. Because fat doesn't take up a lot of volume, it can easily sneak into your diet when you're not looking.

♦ Too much saturated and trans fat contributes to heart disease and certain types of cancer, especially breast, prostate, and colon cancer. During pregnancy it is thought to contribute to the risk of gestational diabetes.

♦ A high-fat diet—especially containing fried foods—can aggravate the nausea of early pregnancy and heartburn later in pregnancy.

♦ The fat you eat and store up now becomes a source of fat for your baby when you breastfeed. Choose your fats wisely.

Here's a short chemistry lesson about fat. Don't worry—there will be no chemical formulas, structures to memorize or quizzes! But it is helpful to understand the basics about fat, especially since the kind of fat you eat has such an impact on your health. Confused about fat? Check out Know Your Fat by Mary Enig PhD. Dr. Enig is a nutritional biochemist who spent many years studying fats at the University of Maryland.

All fats contain a blend of fatty acids. Fats are categorized as saturated, polyunsaturated and monounsaturated depending on which type of fatty acid predominates. (Saturation refers to number of double bonds—a saturated fatty acid contains no double bonds, monounsaturated fat contains one and polyunsaturated fat has two or more.) Some fats are considered short and others are long. Short chain fatty acids combine to form long chain fatty acids. A chart that shows the fatty acid content of various fats as well as their smoke points can be found at canola. ab.ca/canola_oil.aspx

The Good: EFAs & Omega-3s

While we're programmed to consider all fats as unhealthy, there are some "good fats" that can be part of a healthy diet, when eaten in proper amounts. Essential Fatty Acids (EFAs) are fats that can't be produced in the body, so they must be eaten in the diet. There are two:

♦ Linoleic Acid (LA) is an omega-6 fatty acid that is converted by the body into Arachidonic Acid (AA), which is a component of your baby's brain tissue. All vegetable oils contain some omega-6 fat—but safflower oil is richest, followed by corn and cottonseed oil. In general, the "Western" diet contains excessive amounts of omega-6 fats—which is not a good thing, because omega-6 fats tend to be "pro-inflammatory" meaning they can cause more inflammation in the body. Too much omega-6 fat can prevent the body from making enough DHA—also not good because DHA is also critical for your baby's brain and eye development. The Dietary Reference Intake (DRI) for LA is 13 g per day for pregnancy and while breastfeeding—the amount in about a little over a tablespoon of oil. Although you may not think you eat a tablespoon of oil a day, much of the oil in most people's diet is found in processed foods.

♦ Alpha-linolenic Acid (ALA) is an omega-3 fat the body converts to Eicosapentaenoic Acid (EPA) and finally to DHA—however the conversion process isn't very efficient. The DRI for ALA is 1.4 g per day—which adds up to just less than half a teaspoon. DHA is needed for your baby's brain and visual development—60% of the fat in the brain is DHA. Unfortunately several things—too much omega-6, too much saturated fat and too much trans fat—decreases the conversion of ALA to DHA, prompting several health organizations to recommend a regular dietary source of DHA or a DHA supplement. Ground flaxseed, chia seeds, hemp seeds and walnut oil are richest in ALA, followed by canola oil and walnuts. Soybean oil and soy products are also considered good sources of omega-3 but also contain omega-6. Keep nuts and seeds and oils made from them in the refrigerator to keep them from oxidizing.

♦ DHA: You hear a lot about this superstar of fats. Why? It's the fat that appears to be in short supply in the diet of most North Americans, and it is critical for brain and visual development that happens during pregnancy and the first year of life. A recent study also found that women who had more DHA and its chemical cousin EPA in their diet had children who had a lower risk of obesity at age 3. The European Commission recommends women have an average dietary intake of at least 200 mg of DHA per day.[32] Health experts in the US have similar recommendations. Many prenatal supplements have a DHA supplement included. If yours doesn't, it's easy to find a DHA supplement with 200-300 mg of DHA. See page 101 for amounts found in food.

Which Oils to Use?

So what oils do I recommend for cooking? I actually keep a variety of oils in the house: olive oil for most cooking and salad dressings; canola oil for baking; and sesame oil and peanut oil for stir-frying. I also have flaxseed oil in the refrigerator and I add a squirt to my salad when I think of it. I like olive oil because it's a clean food and rich in antioxidants. I like canola oil because of its low saturated fat content and rich omega-3 content.

The Bad: Saturated Fat

Saturated fat (also called solid fat) is found mostly in animal fat. It's solid at room temperature; picture a stick of butter, the skin of a chicken or fat you trim off your steak. It's also found in fried and bakery foods made with hydrogenated shortening. It's the kind of fat that increases cholesterol levels and leads to clogged arteries.

Three saturated fats come from plants—palm and palm kernel oil and coconut oil. Twenty years ago, palm oil and coconut oil were avoided like other saturated fats, but have recently seen a resurgence as companies replace shortening with palm oil so that they can take the trans fat off the food label. In the research and policy making world, the tide is slowly turning toward looking beyond a fat's saturated fat content to what effect the specific fatty acids have on health. Stay tuned.

Coconut Oil

Coconut oil has made a grand re-entrance into the diets of many people. Is this the result of great marketing or does coconut oil have nutritional merits? It turns out that coconut oil contains a large percentage of lauric acid, a saturated fatty acid that has antimicrobial properties. In fact, breast milk owes some of its illness fighting properties to lauric acid. Although health authorities like the USDA, American Heart Association, British National Health Service, Academy of Nutrition and Dietetics and Dietitians of Canada all recommend limiting significant amounts of coconut oil due to its high saturated fat content, emerging research shows that coconut oil may have important health benefits.[33,34,35] But for now, use coconut oil as you would any other saturated fat to insure your total saturated fat intake isn't excessive.

The Ugly: Trans Fats

Types of fat called trans-fatty acids (also called trans fat) are made when liquid oils are hydrogenated for storage or cooking—for example, when oil is made into shortening or stick margarine. What's so ugly about them? Plenty—they raise LDL cholesterol, triglycerides and insulin levels while reducing HDL (the good cholesterol). They promote cancer, immune dysfunction and obesity. According to new research, trans fat increases the risk of ovulatory infertility and it can affect fetal growth. Trans fat is mostly found in margarine, shortening, and products made from these, such as bakery goods, commercially fried foods, and snack foods. Trans fat is listed on the food label—but beware—if a food contains up to 0.4 g of trans fat, "0" is listed on the label. So even if a food has very little trans fat, it can easily add up to an amount that can have negative effects on your health!

The American Heart Association recommends we limit our trans fat to 1% or less—that translates to only 2-3 grams per day during pregnancy. But the less you eat, the better! Here are a few ways to stay away from trans fats:

♦ Avoid stick margarine or use as little as possible. Choose a soft margarine spread that has liquid oil or water as the first ingredient.

♦ Keep high-fat processed foods to a minimum.

♦ Remember that high trans fat foods typically include donuts, French fries, onion rings, pie crust and other bakery goods. Although some chain fast food restaurants have switched to no trans fat oil, it's best to check their websites.

Just the Fat Facts: What's the Goal?

Now that you know more about the types of fats found in foods, the next step is to know how much to include in your own diet. The American Heart Association recommends these fat guidelines for everyone over age two:[36]

Type of Fat: Recommended Amount	How Does That Translate To Calories?		
	2,000 Calories	2,200 Calories	2,400 Calories
Fat: 25-35%	500-700 calories 56 - 77 g fat	550-770 calories 61-85 g fat	600-840 calories 66 - 93 g fat
Saturated Fat: less than 7%	<15 grams	<17 grams	<19 grams
Trans fat: Less than 1% of calories	<2.2 grams	<2.4 grams	<2.6 grams

In general, it's recommended that 20 to 35% of total calories be from fat. The average pregnant woman needs 2,200 to 2,400 calories, and 30 percent of those calories would be about 70 to 80 grams of fat. This may sound like a lot. In *Eating Expectantly*, you'll notice there is emphasis not so much on the amount of fat but the type of fat you eat. Low-fat and nonfat dairy products, lean protein, and plant sources of protein are recommended. Processed foods are shunned. That's because processed fats are not as healthy as natural fats found in avocado, nuts, seeds and olive oil. There's even some evidence that natural saturated fats that we have eaten for centuries (butter, coconut oil, lard) but now avoid, may not be so bad after all.

The bottom line: avoid trans fats and choose a variety of fats which are close to how nature intended: olive oil, canola oil, nuts and seeds, avocado, flaxseed oil, and even a bit of coconut oil or butter.

Are you savvy about fat? Look at the menu below and guess how much fat: it contains:

Breakfast

- Cereal with 1 cup (250 ml) 2% milk
- 2 slices toast with 2 teaspoons margarine
- Fresh fruit

Snack

- 1 ounce (30 g) cheese
- 10 wheat crackers

Lunch

- Deluxe cheeseburger
- Fries
- Side salad with 2 tablespoons dressing

Snack

- 2 tablespoons peanut butter on Melba toast
- 1½ cups (375 ml) 2% milk

Dinner

- 6 ounces (190 g) fish sautéed in safflower oil
- Baked potato with 2 tablespoons sour cream and 2 teaspoons margarine
- Fresh, steamed spinach
- Tomatoes and cucumbers with 2 tablespoons vinaigrette dressing

Snack

- Ice cream
- Chocolate-chip cookie

Believe it or not, the above menu has 160 grams of fat, or double the amount recommended. Let's change a few things and see how the fat adds up:

Breakfast

- Cereal with 1 cup (250 ml) low-fat milk
- 2 slices toast with 1 teaspoon margarine and 2 teaspoons fruit spread
- Banana

Snack

- 1 ounce (30 g) low-fat cheese
- 8 wheat crackers

Lunch

- Grilled chicken sandwich
- Side salad with light vinaigrette dressing
- Peaches and pineapple
- 1 cup (250 ml) low-fat milk

Snack

- 2 tablespoons peanut butter
- 3 Rye-crisp crackers
- Vegetable juice

Dinner

- 6 ounces (190 g) fish baked with a topping of bread crumbs, Parmesan cheese and 1 teaspoon butter
- Steamed new potatoes
- Steamed fresh spinach drizzled with 2 teaspoons olive oil vinaigrette
- Melon balls
- 1 cup (250 ml) Low-fat milk

Snack

- Frozen low-fat yogurt
- 2 Graham crackers

We've cut the fat in half with just a few changes! The menu now has about 80 grams of fat, a much better number. You can check the vitamin and mineral aspects of your diet by taking the nutrition quiz on page 226.

Want to know more about vitamins and minerals? Check out this chart online, which has all the details.

Allergy Prevention During Pregnancy

Allergies are on the rise all over the world. Researchers have been vigorously looking for the reason behind the exploding increase in allergies, as well as how to prevent them. Because diet during pregnancy sets the stage for immune health, its effect on allergies has been an enthusiastic area of research in recent years.[37]

Avoiding allergenic foods during pregnancy is controversial. There is evidence that dietary proteins can be found in amniotic fluid, which can potentially sensitize a fetus to allergens. However, in placebo controlled, double-blind studies avoiding allergenic foods during pregnancy did not decrease the risk of allergy.[38] There is currently not enough evidence to recommend a restrictive diet during pregnancy: following one that omits nuts and seeds for example, would decrease vitamin E intake, which has been shown to increase the risk of childhood asthma and allergy.[39]

Currently, neither the American Academy of Pediatrics, The American Academy of Allergy, Asthma and Immunology, the Australasian Society of Clinical Immunology and Allergy, nor the European Academy of Allergy and Clinical Immunology, recommend dietary restriction during pregnancy to decrease allergy risk.[40,41,42,43]

Dietary Factors Related to Allergies

Peanuts

Analysis of more than 60,000 infants in the Danish National Birth Cohort showed that children of moms who ate peanuts and tree nuts regularly while pregnant actually had a lower risk of asthma.[44] A smaller study found that eating nuts *daily* increased the risk of childhood wheeze.[45] This suggests the importance of moderation.

Probiotics

Using probiotics during pregnancy, either as a supplement or in food has shown promise in decreasing the risk of eczema and atopic dermatitis in children at 2 years.[46,47] The research points to several different strains of probiotics, confirming the importance of choosing probiotic foods with a variety of "good bugs".

The Mediterranean Diet

The Mediterranean Diet is known to be good for the heart; it recommends plenty of fruits, vegetables, along with fish, nuts, seeds, olive oil and cheese. The Mediterranean Diet, as well as frequent fruit consumption has been shown to decrease the risk wheezing, asthma and allergy.[48]

Low intake of leafy vegetables, apples, pears, quince, loquat and chocolate during pregnancy is related to an increased risk of wheeze in children at 5 years, but there appears to be no food link between those foods and asthma. This study underscores the importance of fruits and vegetables and perhaps chocolate?[49]

Dietary Fat

Low intake of alpha-linolenic acid (an omega-3 fat) and total intake of omega-3 fats, as well as a diet containing more saturated fat and palmitic acid appear to be linked to a higher risk of asthma. However fish oils and fish intake and their effect on allergies is controversial.[50,51] Using olive oil during pregnancy also may reduce the risk of wheeze during the first year of life.[52]

The Bottom Line: Eating a wide variety of foods with a healthy balance of fats, limiting saturated fat, and eating plenty of fruits and vegetables, but not avoiding allergenic foods are the best ways to decrease the risk of allergies for your baby. These strategies can be achieved by following the Eating Expectantly Diet. Remember that avoiding cigarette smoke while pregnant is a primary way to prevent allergies.

EATING EXPECTANTLY DIET

What You'll Find:

♦ The Eating Expectantly Diet

♦ What's a Serving?

♦ Vitamins and Supplements: What You Need to Know

Frequently Asked Questions:

♦ How many servings of carbs should I eat?

♦ What does 3 ounces (95 g) of fish look like?

♦ What are splurge calories?

♦ What should I look for in a prenatal vitamin?

♦ Should I take extra calcium?

♦ What's a probiotic?

SCAN HERE FOR   CHAPTER UPDATES

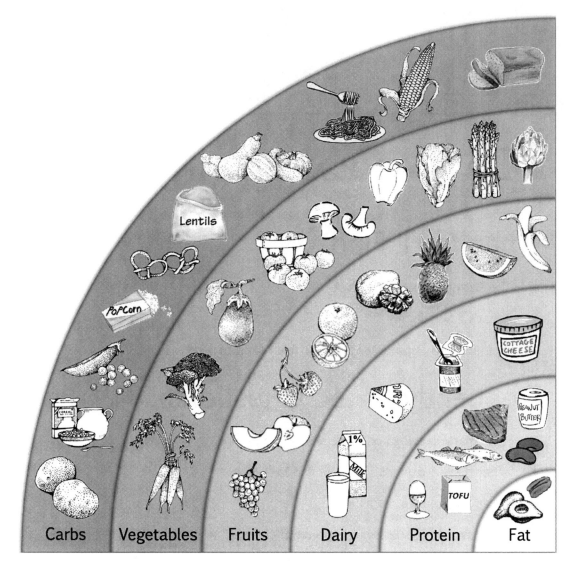

Carbs | Vegetables | Fruits | Dairy | Protein | Fat

The Eating Expectantly Diet

The Eating Expectantly Diet is a system to help guide you towards all the right foods for your baby. It's a hybrid of sorts—based on MyPlate—the USDA eating tool, plus some principles from carbohydrate counting—used in diabetic diets. The end result is a balanced diet that won't leave you hungry—but will help you gain the right amount of weight for a healthy baby.

If you're familiar with MyPlate, (and the tool's predecessor MyPyramid) you know that they're both based on food groups and suggested servings from each group.

The chart below shows the calories needed for an average sized woman pregnant with a single baby for pre-pregnancy and each trimester. (Postpartum plans are found on page 316.) Calorie needs vary a lot—depending on your size, how active you are and if you're expecting more than one baby. It's important to eat to your appetite while aiming for the weight gain goal your health care provider has recommended specifically for you. If you need more food, just eat a little more in all food groups, rather than just upping the "splurge calories."

You can get your own personalized plan from www.choosemyplate.gov/ supertracker-tools/daily-food-plans/moms.html. There's also an interactive food tracker and exercise tracker available.

	Before Baby & First Trimester	Second Trimester	Third Trimester
Carbs	6 Servings	9 Servings	9 Servings
Vegetables	2.5 cups / 625 ml	3 cups / 750 ml	3 cups / 750 ml
Fruits	2 cups / 500 ml	2 cups / 500 ml	2 cups / 500 ml
Protein	6 oz. / 190 g	7 oz. / 220 g	7 oz. / 220 g
Dairy	3 cups / 750 ml	3 cups / 750 ml	3-4 cups 750-1,000 ml
Fats & oils	5 teaspoons	7 teaspoons	7 teaspoons
Splurge calories	200 calories	200 calories	200 calories
Total calories	2,000	2,340	2,450

What's a Serving?

The Eating Expectantly Diet is based on a specific number of portions from each food group. Does that mean you must measure everything you eat? Absolutely not! But if you're not familiar with typical portion sizes, it helps to take a close look at them—even measuring some typical foods you eat to see how they count. To help you gauge servings and sizes; let's take a look at each food group.

What Counts as a Carbohydrate Serving?

This group includes grains as well as starchy vegetables and this is where this plan differs from MyPlate. The Eating Expectantly Diet suggests you think of potatoes, corn and other starchy vegetables as the carbohydrate foods that they are. (You can also count them towards your vegetable servings.) One carb serving has 15-20 g of carbohydrate and is generally a one-ounce (30 g) serving of bread, cereal or dry pasta. This is useful when reading the nutrition facts label. For many grain foods (like pasta or bulgur) and starchy vegetables (like corn or potatoes), ½ cup (125 ml) is a typical serving size. When choosing grains select mostly whole grains.

Breads	Serving Size
◆ Bagel, large (4 oz. / 120 g)	¼
◆ Bagel, mini	1
◆ Bread, any type	1 slice (1 oz. / 30 g)
◆ Bun, hamburger or hot dog	½
◆ English muffin	½
◆ Pancake, 4.5 inches (12 cm)	1
◆ Pita bread	½
◆ Tortilla, corn or flour, 6 inches (15 cm)	1

Grains and Cereals	Serving Size
◆ Barley, cooked	⅓ cup (85 ml)
◆ Bulgur wheat, cooked	½ cup (125 ml)
◆ Cereal, ready-to-eat unsweetened flakes	¾ cup (190 ml)
◆ Cereal, bran, shredded wheat or frosted	½ cup (125 ml)
◆ Cereal: granola, muesli or bran buds	¼ cup (65 ml)
◆ Cereal, puffed unsweetened	1 ½ cup (375 ml)
◆ Cereal, Weetabix	1 biscuit
◆ Cornmeal	3 tablespoons
◆ Flour, any type	3 tablespoons
◆ Millet, cooked	⅓ cup (85 ml)
◆ Pasta, cooked	½ cup (125 ml)
◆ Quinoa, cooked	½ cup (125 ml)
◆ Rice, cooked, brown or white	⅓ cup (85 ml)
◆ Wheat germ	¼ cup (65 ml)
◆ Wild rice, cooked	½ cup (125 ml)

Starchy Vegetables	Serving Size
◆ Corn	½ cup (125 ml)
◆ Corn on the cob	1 small or ½ large
◆ Green peas	1 cup (250 ml)
◆ Potatoes, white or sweet	½ cup (125 ml)
◆ Pumpkin, unsweetened	1 cup (250 ml)
◆ Squash, acorn or butternut	1 cup (250 ml)

Snack Foods	Serving Size
◆ Crackers, any type	1 oz. (30 g)
◆ Crackers, saltines	6
◆ Graham crackers	3 squares
◆ Popcorn	3 cups (750 ml)
◆ Pretzels	40 sticks or ¾ oz. (22 g)
◆ Rye Crispbread	2

What Counts as a Cup of Vegetables?

Veggies are easy—no matter how you like them—sliced, diced, or juiced—a cup is a cup, with one exception. When you eat raw leafy greens, 2 cups (500 ml) counts as a 1 cup (250 ml) serving. (Remember this group includes the *non-starchy* vegetables.)

Here's how "awkward to measure" vegetables add up to 1 cup (250 ml):

Vegetable	Serving Size
◆ Baby carrots	12
◆ Bell pepper	1 large: 3 x 3.5 inches (7 x 9 cm)
◆ Broccoli	3 spears, 3 inches (7.5 cm) long
◆ Celery	2 large stalks, 11 inches (28 cm) long
◆ Tomato-fresh	1 large, 3 inches (7.5 cm) in diameter

Counting Your Fruits and Veggies

While you're definitely not expected to go around measuring your fruits and veggies, it is interesting to see just how many strawberries or grapes constitute one cup (250 ml). Quench your curiosity and measure a few things, then you can eyeball it! And it's always OK to eat more than the recommended five cups, as long as you fit in all the other foods too! Another way to make sure you get enough: simply make sure half your plate is full of fruits and veggies.

What Counts as a Serving of Fruit?

Two cups of fruit a day is recommended; a small fresh fruit generally counts as a half cup (125 ml) portion, while a large one counts as a cup (250 ml). And for other fruits, the actual measurement works. But this list is a bit different; the serving sizes of fruits listed below all contain about 15 g of carbohydrate. Again, don't get caught up in the numbers—just know that some fruits have more natural sugar than others, which is important if you are watching your carbohydrate intake due to high blood sugar.

Fruits	Serving Size
◆ Apple	1 small, 2 inches (5 cm) diameter ½ large, 3.5 inches (8 cm) diameter
◆ Cantaloupe or honeydew	¼ of a medium or 1 cup (250 ml) cubed
◆ Cherries	12
◆ Dates	3
◆ Dried cranberries or raisins	2 tablespoons
◆ Grapes	17
◆ Grapefruit	½ large
◆ Kiwi	1 (3.5 oz. / 110 g)
◆ Mango	½ cup (125 ml) cubed
◆ Nectarine	1 small (4 oz. / 120 g)
◆ Orange	1 small (6½ oz. / 200 g)
◆ Papaya	1 cup (250 ml) cubed
◆ Peach	1 medium, 2¾ inches (7 cm) 2 canned halves
◆ Pear	1 small (3.5 oz. / 110 g) ½ large (7.5 oz. / 230 g)
◆ Plums	2 small, 2 inches (5 cm) diameter (60 g)
◆ Raspberries	1 cup (250 ml)
◆ Strawberries	1¼ cup (315 ml)
◆ Tangerines	2 small
◆ Watermelon	1¼ cup (315 ml)

What Counts as an Ounce of Protein?

Proteins from different sources contain different nutrients, so choose a variety! Choose lean beef and pork, low-fat cheeses and skip the skin on poultry.

Each serving provides about 7 g of protein:

Protein	Serving Size
◆ Egg	1 whole or 2 egg whites
◆ Egg substitute	¼ cup (65 ml)
◆ Fish, shellfish, beef, chicken, turkey or pork	1 oz. (30 g)
◆ Nut or seed butter	2 tablespoons
◆ Nuts or seeds	¼ cup (1.5 oz. / 45 g)
◆ Tempeh	¼ cup (65 ml / 45 g)
◆ Tofu	⅓ cup (85 ml / 90 g)
These are also listed under the dairy group:	
◆ Cheese	1 oz. (30 g)
◆ Cottage cheese	¼ cup (65 ml)
◆ Fromage Blanc / Fromage Frais	3 oz. (95 g)
These plant-based foods also contain carbohydrate, so they are also listed under the carb group:	
◆ Beans, peas or lentils, cooked	½ cup (125 ml)
◆ Edamame	½ cup (125 ml)
◆ Hummus	½ cup (125 ml)
◆ Meat substitutes: soy-based foods like "burger" or "chicken" patty	1 oz. (30 g)

What Counts as a Cup in the Dairy Group?

The dairy group includes fluid milk and foods made from milk that are calcium-rich, as well as soymilk that is calcium-fortified. Choose skim or low-fat. These foods all provide about 300 mg of calcium per listed serving. Other "milks" may have calcium added but they have less protein and other nutrients.

Dairy	Serving Size
◆ Milk, yogurt or calcium-fortified soymilk	1 cup (250 ml)
Cheese provides protein too so it's also listed under the protein group:	
◆ Natural cheese like Cheddar, mozzarella, Parmesan, Swiss	1.5 oz. (45 g)
◆ Processed cheese (like American)	2 oz. (60 g)
◆ Ricotta cheese	½ cup (125 ml)
◆ Cottage cheese	2 cups (500 ml)

What Counts as a Teaspoon of Oil?

All of these portions contain about 5 g of fat per serving. You'll notice that some foods from other food groups are listed here too, such as avocado, seeds, and nuts.

Food	Serving Size
◆ Avocado	¼ (also counts as a vegetable)
◆ Flaxseed	2 tablespoons
◆ Oil, any type	1 teaspoon
◆ Margarine, soft made with liquid oil	2 teaspoons
◆ Mayonnaise	1 teaspoon
◆ Mayonnaise-style salad dressing	2 teaspoons
◆ Mayonnaise, reduced fat	1 tablespoon
◆ Salad dressing, Ranch or Blue Cheese	2 teaspoons
◆ Salad dressing, Vinaigrette style	1 tablespoon
◆ Salad dressing, reduced fat	2 tablespoons
◆ Seeds: pumpkin, sesame, hemp, chia or sunflower	1 tablespoon
◆ Tahini (sesame seed butter)	2 teaspoons
◆ Nuts	1-2 tablespoons
◆ Peanut or Sunflower seed butter	½ tablespoon
◆ Olives, large	8
These fats contain a lot of saturated fat and should be limited:	
◆ Clotted cream	1 teaspoon
◆ Coconut oil or butter	1 teaspoon
◆ Cream cheese, light	2 tablespoons
◆ Cream cheese, regular	1 tablespoon
◆ Crème fraiche	1 tablespoon
◆ Half and Half (aka light cream)	3 tablespoons
◆ Half and Half, low-fat	6 tablespoons
◆ Heavy cream, whipped	2 tablespoons
◆ Heavy cream	1 tablespoon
◆ Sour cream	2 tablespoons
◆ Whipped topping (Cool Whip)	6 tablespoons

How Do You Count Splurge Calories?

The sugar in your yogurt or tea, the sour cream on your taco or that tiny piece of cheesecake you can't say no to? That's what these calories are for. There's no "serving size" to measure here. Instead, keep a running estimate of extra calories. Or you can just eat a few extra servings from other food groups—guacamole with baked chips perhaps? Because splurge calories often come from sugar, see page 70 for the scoop on sugar.

Eating Expectantly Superfoods

Try to make these foods a regular part of your diet!

Super Dairy, Protein and Fats

◆ Yogurt	◆ Milk
◆ Kefir	◆ Eggs
◆ Lean beef	◆ Salmon
◆ Barramundi (sustainable seabass)	◆ Crab
◆ Beans and legumes (including edamame & lentils)	◆ Nuts: all but especially almonds, pecans, pistachios and walnuts
◆ Tofu	◆ Tempeh
◆ Sunflower seeds	◆ Sesame seeds/butter
◆ Pumpkin seeds	◆ Flaxseed/oil
◆ Olive oil	

Super Vegetables

◆ Dark leafy: spinach, kale, Swiss chard, collard greens, arugula, and romaine

◆ Sweet potatoes	◆ White potatoes
◆ Avocado	◆ Mushrooms
◆ Carrots	◆ Artichokes
◆ Pumpkin/Winter squash	◆ Tomatoes
◆ Peppers (especially red)	

Super Fruits

◆ Apples	◆ Apricots (fresh and dried)
◆ Blackberries and raspberries	◆ Strawberries
◆ Pomegranate	◆ Cranberries (fresh and dried)
◆ Blueberries	◆ Cherries
◆ Watermelon	◆ Grapefruit

Super Fruits

- Purple or red grapes
- Orange
- Kiwi
- Cantaloupe
- Dried plums
- Raisins
- Mango
- Guava
- Dates
- Juices: Concord grape, pomegranate, PlumSmart, blueberry, prune, unfiltered apple, grapefruit, orange

Super Grains

- Oats
- Bulgur wheat
- Quinoa
- Wheat germ
- Buckwheat
- Barley

Super Condiments

Even eaten in small amounts, these super condiments pack a powerful punch!

- Dark chocolate
- Garlic and garlic powder
- Miso
- Salsa or hot sauce
- Turmeric
- Basil
- Cloves
- Ginger
- Dried red chilli pepper
- Blackstrap molasses
- Natural cocoa
- Kimchi
- Chiles-all kinds
- Soy sauce
- Oregano
- Cinnamon
- Cumin
- Rosemary
- Thyme
- Honey

Vitamins and Supplements: What You Need to Know

Even if you eat an excellent diet with a lot of variety, such as the Eating Expectantly Diet, it can still be difficult to get some nutrients in the amounts you need from food. Examples include folic acid, iron, choline and DHA. That's why prenatal vitamins and some individual supplements are sometimes recommended. Think of vitamin supplements as a nutrition insurance policy. However, don't depend on them too much. If you learn anything from *Eating Expectantly*, it's that the power of food is much stronger than that of supplements!

Visualizing Portion Sizes

My husband helps me cook a lot (he's also a great cook on his own) but he is usually puzzled when I tell him how much of something to put in a food using "measuring cup lingo." Raised in Europe, where most ingredients are weighed, using a measuring cup is still foreign to him. He's not alone. How many could accurately estimate how many cups of salad are served at a restaurant or the weight of their fish filet or veggie burger? Here are some nifty ways to visualize your portions (To see pictures go to www.webmd.com/diet/healthtool-portion-size-plate):

- ◆ 1 baseball (big tennis ball) = 1 cup / 250 ml
- ◆ ½ baseball (¼ big tennis ball) = ¼ cup / 125 ml
- ◆ 4 dice = 1 oz. (30 g) cheese
- ◆ 1 dice = 1 teaspoon margarine or spread
- ◆ 1 computer mouse = small baked potato
- ◆ 1 golf ball (Ping-Pong ball) = 2 tablespoons of peanut butter
- ◆ 1 golf ball (Ping-Pong ball) = ¼ cup raisins = 120 g
- ◆ 1 poker chip = 1 tablespoon butter, margarine, or mayonnaise
- ◆ Deck of cards = 3 oz. (95 g) meat, poultry or fish
- ◆ Checkbook = 3 oz. (95 g) meat, poultry or fish
- ◆ A closed fist = 1 cup (180 g or 250 ml) of cooked rice, pasta, or cereal

Your Daily BFFFs

In addition to following the Eating Expectantly Diet, be sure to get your daily Bugs, Fluids, Fitness, and Fiber!

- ◆ Bugs: Probiotics that is…Try to eat one probiotic food daily: yogurt, kefir, Yakult, miso, kimchi, etc.

- ◆ Fluid: Ten cups a day, including milk, juice and other drinks. But most should be from filtered water.

- ◆ Fitness: Half an hour minimum, every day, with your health care provider's OK.

- ◆ Fiber: To get your recommended 30 grams of fiber, choose whole grains and eat your fruits and veggies!

"Green" Vitamins

If you prefer a supplement that is vegan and without artificial colors, flavors, or preservatives, there are several choices. However, some have herbal additions such as red raspberry leaf, which is considered "likely safe" during pregnancy. Check the labels to know exactly what you're buying—and research their safety during pregnancy.

Prenatal Supplements: Why Do You Need Them?

A prenatal vitamin is often recommended starting 2-3 months before pregnancy to give your baby a good start. As an added benefit, multivitamin use is associated with a decreased risk of birth defects, and may decrease your risk of having a baby that is low birthweight.[1,2]

In the US, what goes into nutrition supplements isn't regulated—that means you need to be a savvy shopper. Most prenatals have a similar lineup of nutrients—you'll probably see all the B vitamins, C, D, iron, zinc and folic acid. Some brands provide different formulations of iron or calcium to improve absorption or tolerance. Other vitamins contain stool softeners or nutrients that you haven't even heard of! Try to choose one that has these nutrients:

♦   DHA: 200-300 mg; this is often in a separate gel cap.

♦   Choline: 450 mg

♦   Iodine[3]: 220 micrograms

♦   Vitamin D: at least 600 IU

Cutting edge but limited research shows the benefits of other nutrients during pregnancy. You might find these in some high-end prenatals. Discuss with your health care provider.

♦   CoQ-10: In one study, CoQ-10 was shown to decrease the risk of preeclampsia[4] in women at risk. The Natural Medicines Database rates Co-Q10 as "possibly safe" during pregnancy, due to limited clinical evidence.[5]

♦   Inositol: May help prevent folate resistant neural tube defects.[6] Animal studies also show that folate resistant birth defects are linked to reduced levels of inositol.[7] Inositol is often recommended for infertility. However, right now there is insufficient safety information to recommend it during pregnancy.[8]

Comparing Prenatal Supplements

It's a jungle out there with more than 70 types of prenatals. Check out www. prenatalvitamin.com/BuyersGuide/Index.php. You can compare ingredients, vitamins and price (and links to purchase online) on most brands. Check out the National Library of Medicine's Dietary Supplements Label database at dietarysupplements. nlm.nih.gov/dietary. You can search for any type of supplements and find ingredients, nutrients and percentage of the DRIs.

Tips for Taking Your Prenatal

1. Take it on an empty stomach—the iron is best absorbed this way. If it doesn't go down well first thing in the morning, take it before bed. If that doesn't work, have it with a light snack (but not a calcium-rich food—because that can decrease the amount of iron you absorb.) In the end, it's not as important WHEN you take but that you DO take it!
2. If you can't tolerate a prenatal vitamin pill, ask your health care provider about chewable or liquid vitamins. Some health care providers recommend one or two chewable children's vitamin as a last resort—but keep in mind they might not have everything a regular prenatal has. You can supplement your folic acid by eating a fortified cereal.
3. If you do find yourself eating many fortified foods (cereals, snack bars, vitamin waters), take a moment and calculate just how much of each nutrient you are consuming. If several servings of fortified foods per day are the norm for you, it might be wise to cut back on your multivitamin—perhaps taking it every other day—or on the fortified foods.
4. Hard to swallow? Try gummy, liquid, or chewable prenatals. If that's what it takes to get your vitamin down, then go for it! Read the nutrient labels carefully, though, as different brands contain different ingredients—some nutrients may be missing, while others could be excessive.

What About Herbal Supplements?

Herbal supplements may be "natural" but they may not be safe for you during pregnancy. Vitamins as well as herbs are not regulated for quality, contaminants or safety. Buyer beware! A great resource is the Natural Medicines Comprehensive Database, which reviews herbs and supplements for safety, quality, effectiveness and more: naturaldatabase.com. Consumer Labs is a company that independently tests and reviews vitamin and herbal supplements: www.consumerlab.com.

Individual Supplements

With the few exceptions noted below, it's best if you *don't* take individual supplements. So if you're one to take a handful of individual supplements every morning-don't! This includes herbal supplements, which usually have no safety data for use during pregnancy. Many herbs do have drug effects, so use extreme caution and only take herbs if you are working with an experienced herbalist familiar with pregnancy effects.

Individual Supplements that are OK:

♦   Iron—only if your health care provider suggests it.

♦   Calcium—if you don't drink milk or eat other calcium-rich or fortified products: 1,000 mg a day.

♦   DHA—if you don't eat fish or other omega-3-rich foods on a weekly basis: 200-300 mg.

♦   Probiotics—if you don't eat yogurt or another probiotic food on a regular basis. There are times when probiotics are useful.

♦   Vitamin D—it is very possible that you need a vitamin D supplement in the winter, and under some other circumstances too. Some health care providers recommend 1,000 IU per day. See page 59 and page 165 for more info.

The following is general information about the types of calcium and iron available, which applies to what's found in prenatal supplements as well as individual supplements. You'll also find information about DHA and probiotics.

Iron Supplements

Recommendations for routine iron supplements during pregnancy vary by country. The U.S. Centers for Disease Control and Prevention recommend 30 mg of supplemental iron, starting at the first prenatal visit.[9] In Canada, an iron supplement of 16 mg a day is recommended.[10] Some prenatal vitamins contain more than 30 mg, which is OK if your health care provider feels you need more iron. More is not necessarily better—gastrointestinal side effects are more common in doses above 30 mg. Iron absorption decreases with increasing dose, so if your health care provider suggests a large dose, it is better to divide it into several doses.

When shopping for an iron supplement, check the label for the amount of elemental iron, which is the amount of iron in a supplement available for absorption. Different formulations of iron have different absorption rates. For example, ferrous fumerate contains 33% elemental iron, while ferrous gluconate only contains 12%. So on the label, you might see 300 mg of ferrous fumerate, but only 50-60 mg of elemental iron is actually absorbed.[11]

Consider these options if you're not tolerating iron; they boast fewer side effects and better absorption. They're also more expensive. Carbonyl iron (sold as the brand Feosol), a rather recent form of iron used in supplements, is the purest form of iron. Proferrin, contains heme iron, a well-absorbed form of iron found in meat, which can be taken with or without food.

Iron can cause gastrointestinal side effects like nausea, heartburn, diarrhea, dark colored stools and constipation. For individual supplements, starting with half the prescribed dose and building up to the final dose may help with side effects.

Iron can interfere with absorption of calcium and antacids, so it's best not to take them at the same time. Some types of iron can interfere with the absorption of some prescription drugs including antibiotics and thyroid hormones. There may be other interactions depending on the form of iron you are taking. Check with your pharmacist.

Calcium Supplements

Why is calcium such a popular topic in this book? Many women have a diet that comes up short on calcium. Bones don't reach their peak in bone mineral content until 20-30 years of age; after that their density starts a gradual decline. With the added importance of building your baby's bones, you can see why calcium is emphasized here!

Recent research shows another good reason to have enough calcium in your diet: to protect you and your baby from lead. You're exposed to small amounts of lead over a lifetime from drinking water and other sources, and 95% of it is stored in bone. If you don't consume enough calcium, your bones lose calcium at a higher rate and lead stored in your bones is released.[12] Lead is very dangerous for your developing baby—see page 126 for info.

It's best if you try to get your calcium from food first (See page 216 for information on how to sneak calcium into your diet.) If you can't, then you'll need a supplement. Look at the supplement's label for "elemental calcium" to find out how much calcium is in a product. For example, 500 mg of calcium carbonate has only 200 mg of elemental calcium.

There are many types of calcium:

♦ Calcium citrate (Citracal, Solgar): The best absorbed type of calcium, it can be taken on an empty stomach. and is a good choice if you take any acid reducing meds. But, don't take this type of calcium with aluminum containing medications like Mylanta, Maalox, etc.

♦ Calcium carbonate (Tums, Viactive): Not as well absorbed, so you need to take more of it, but it's the least expensive type. Best taken with food.

- Dolomite, Bone Meal or Oyster Shell Calcium: May contain lead or other heavy metals—avoid!

- Coral Calcium: If it sounds too good to be true… it probably is. Beware of claims for this type of calcium—it is mostly calcium carbonate—the same as in Tums. The founder of one brand had actions from the FTC and FDA for false claims. Some brands have been found to contain lead. For more information, see www.quackwatch.org/01QuackeryRelatedTopics/DSH/coral.html

- Calcium lactate and calcium gluconate: These types of calcium are well absorbed BUT contain smaller amounts of elemental calcium than other types, so you would need to take more of them!

Calcium is best absorbed with vitamin D. In general, calcium needs stomach acid to be absorbed so it's best if taken with food. If you take too much calcium carbonate at one time, it can cause "rebound hyper-acidity"—excess stomach acid. If this becomes a problem, consider taking the calcium supplement in several doses during the day, since it is absorbed better that way (Your body can't absorb more than about 500 mg at a time.)

A Sure Sign of Quality:

You've probably heard stories of supplements that don't dissolve or that don't contain what the labels says they do. There's a way to insure that your vitamin is high quality—look for the U.S. Pharmacopeial (USP) Verified Mark:

What does the USP Verified Mark mean? That the product:

- Contains the ingredients listed on the label in the declared potency and amount

- Doesn't contain harmful levels of specified contaminants

- Will break down and release into the body within a specified amount of time

- Has been made according to FDA current Good Manufacturing Processes using sanitary and well controlled procedures

For a list of all USP verified dietary supplements: www.usp.org/usp-verification-services/usp-verified-dietary-supplements/verified-supplements

DHA and Omega-3: Do You Need a Supplement?

There's a lot of discussion in here about DHA and omega-3 fats. You'll get enough DHA+EPA if you eat three-4 oz. (125 g) servings of fish per week that contain at least 500 mg of DHA each. The plant sources of omega-3 listed below should be in addition to the omega-3s from fish, fortified foods or a supplement.

Omega 3 in fish: DHA+EPA in mg per 3 oz. (95 g)	
Salmon, Atlantic	1,800
Herring	1,700
Anchovies	1,200
Rainbow trout	1,000
Salmon, canned	1,000
Sardines	800
Halibut	400
Blue crab	400
Barramundi	375
Shrimp	260
Tuna, canned in water, drained	230
Egg fortified with DHA	100-150
Tilapia	115
Omega-3 in plants: Alpha-linolenic Acid in mg	
Flaxseed oil, 1 Tb	7,200
Walnuts, 1 oz. (30 g)	2,500
Flaxseeds, 1 Tb	2,400
Chia seeds, 1 Tb	2,300
Walnut oil, 1 Tb	1,400
Canola oil, 1 Tb	1,300
Hemp seeds, 1 Tb	1,000
Soybeans, ½ cup (125 ml)	500
Pecans, 1 oz. (30 g)	300

If you don't get enough DHA from food consider a supplement of 200[13] to 300[14] mg. There are a variety of forms of omega-3's available. Some come in prenatal supplements, some are on their own:

♦ Life's DHA: vegetarian source of DHA, produced by micro-algae. This is the type added to all infant formulas and in individual supplements like Finest Natural.

♦ Fish oils: To avoid contaminants, look for highly refined fish oils such as Nordic Naturals Prenatal DHA: tested by a third party for purity and also contains 400 IU vitamin D. If swallowing pills is a problem, consider Coromega.

- Other Omega-3's: Flaxseed oil supplements (as well as ground flaxseed and flaxseed oil) provide an excellent source of alpha-linolenic acid, which is the essential fatty acid that your body can convert to EPA and DHA. However, the conversion process is inefficient, which is why preformed DHA is recommended. EPA is also an omega-3 fatty acid found in supplements along with DHA. EPA is also a long chained omega-3 fatty acid and is converted to DHA. It's fine to have a supplement that has both EPA and DHA.

Probiotics

You'll find that this book is decidedly "pro-probiotic"! I recommend yogurt and other probiotic dairy products as Eating Expectantly Superfoods for their calcium content, ease of digestion and also because of the healthy bacteria they contain. But there are a lot more foods (and supplements) that also contain probiotics.

A probiotic is defined by the World Health Organization as "live microorganisms, which, when administered in adequate amounts, confer a health benefit on the host." The gut contains billions of bacteria—some good and some bad—which create a bacterial balancing act. The balance can be thrown off when you take antibiotics, because good bacteria are killed off with the bad. An overgrowth of "bad" bacteria, yeast or parasites can cause digestive issues and affect your immune health.

Friendly probiotics help keep disease-causing bacteria at bay, help with digestion, aid in nutrient absorption and contribute to immune health. In fact, the first food exposure to probiotics your baby will have is through your breast milk. There is a large body of research showing that probiotics can prevent and treat diarrhea—both antibiotic induced and from rotavirus.[15]

There is some evidence that probiotic use during pregnancy could:

- Prevent atopic eczema in children 2-7 years.[16]

- Reduce the risk of bacterial vaginosis, a bacterial infection that often causes preterm labor.[17]

- Reduce the risk of preeclampsia.[18]

The best way to get your probiotics is from food: yogurt, kefir, Yakult, acidophilus milk, Good Belly as well as fermented foods like sauerkraut, miso (fermented soybean paste), and tempeh (fermented soy beans). Be smart about probiotic supplements because dietary supplements are not regulated as medicine but as food—and it's now a billion dollar business with mainstream supplement companies introducing new brands. Culturelle is a brand that has undergone many scientific studies and doesn't need to be refrigerated. For more information about probiotics, see www.usprobiotics.org.

WEIGHT GAIN: WHAT YOU NEED TO KNOW

What You'll Find:

♦ Where the Weight Goes

♦ How Much Should You Gain?

♦ What's Your Goal?

♦ Having Trouble Meeting Your Goal?

Frequently Asked Questions:

♦ How much weight should I gain?

♦ What if I'm having trouble gaining weight?

♦ How often should I weigh myself?

♦ How can I avoid gaining too much weight?

♦ Is it OK to lose weight during pregnancy?

Gaining weight is part of being pregnant; gaining the right amount of weight for you, and gaining it steadily can help guarantee a normal weight, full term baby. It's especially important for women who were underweight before pregnancy to gain enough; otherwise they are at much higher risk of having a small and/or premature baby. On the other hand, gaining too much could mean trouble during your pregnancy and delivery (large baby at risk for obesity, C-section). It can also lead to weight management challenges later for you—and possibly your baby.

Where the Weight Goes

You have probably seen a life-size picture of a fetus no bigger than a spoon that weighs less than an ounce (30 g). So—why have you gained 5 pounds (2.2 kg)? Since the average birthweight is about 7 pounds (3 kg) and the average weight gain is 30 pounds (14 kg), pregnancy weight gain is obviously more than just baby.

During the first and second trimester, most of your weight gain is a reflection of building your tissue and blood supply necessary to nourish your baby, including development of the placenta, which is important for nutrient transport during your entire pregnancy. In fact, many pregnancy complications including preterm birth, intrauterine growth restriction and preeclampsia are thought to be caused by a problem with development of the placenta. The proper nutrients are necessary for building this important tissue that becomes the lifeline between you and your baby. Your breasts also increase in size and your body builds additional muscle to carry the extra weight. Weight gain at the end of the second trimester until delivery reflects additional placental growth and growth of your baby.

Your body also stocks up on fat. The fat provides additional calories meant for breastfeeding, which is why, if you are overweight, you don't need to gain as much. You already have some extra fat that can be used during breastfeeding. The chart below shows where your weight goes:

Where the Weight Goes	Pounds
Baby	7.5 lb. (3.4 kg)
Breast tissue	2 lb. (0.9 kg)
Placenta	1.5 lb. (0.7 kg)
Amniotic fluid:	2 lb. (0.9 kg)
Uterus	2 lb. (0.9 kg)
Body fluids	4 lb. (1.8 kg)
Blood supply	4 lb. (1.8 kg)
Fat and nutrient stores	7 lb. (3.1 kg)
Total gained	**30 pounds (13.6 kg)**

How Much Should You Gain?

It depends on how much you weigh before pregnancy—and if your weight is considered to be underweight, overweight or normal weight based on your Body Mass Index (BMI.) A discussion about BMI and a link to a BMI calculator is found on page 22

Recommended Weight Gain			
Pre-Pregnancy BMI	BMI Category	Total Weight Gain Range in pounds (kg)	Recommended Average Weekly Weight Gain in 2nd & 3rd Trimester
<18.5	Underweight	28-40 (12-18 kg)	1-1.3 lb. (0.45-0.6 kg)
18.5-24.9	Normal weight	25-35 (11-16 kg)	1 lb. (0.45 kg)
25-29.9	Overweight	15-25 (7-11 kg)	0.6 lb. (0.27 kg)
>30	Obese	11-20 (5-9 kg)	0.5 lb. (0.23 kg)

Recommended weight gain assumes a weight gain of 1 to 4.4 lb. (0.5-2 kg) in the first trimester.

What's Your Goal?

Two things are important to keep in mind about weight gain. First, you need to have a target weight in mind: how much do you want to weigh at the end of your pregnancy? Why? A woman's weight gain is closely related to her goal and on the recommendation about weight gain from her health care provider (which is sometimes inaccurate.) Gaining just the right amount of weight can be difficult: typically only about a third of women gain the amount that's recommended. Women in the overweight and underweight categories are more likely to gain above or below the guidelines.[1]

There's an incentive to gain within the guidelines; you're less likely to have a C-section, hypertension, gestational diabetes or a baby who weighs too little or too much.[2] Start with the right information for your body! Look to the chart above to determine how much you should gain, based on your BMI category.

Second, you need to keep in mind that your pattern of weight gain can be just as important as the total amount of weight you gain. Your weight gain should be gradual. After gaining 1-4 pounds (½-2 kg) during the first trimester, you should strive for consistent weight gain based on your BMI during the rest of your pregnancy, when your baby grows the most. If you are eating healthy foods with just a few splurges, your weight gain will follow the right pattern for you.

Tips for Weighing

Remember that women have fluctuating weights, which vary even more during pregnancy. Here are a few tips for weighing yourself.

♦   Always weigh yourself at the same time of day and under the same conditions. For example, you might weigh yourself first thing in the morning after you use the rest-room, wearing the same nightgown.

♦   Weigh yourself weekly, not daily. Weighing yourself daily could drive you nuts! Since your weight depends on what you've had to eat and drink, the amount of sodium you've consumed, and your bowel habits, you could show a 3-pound (1.4 kg) "weight gain" on Monday and a 4-pound (1.8 kg) "weight loss" on Wednesday.

♦   Compare only weights from the same scale. If your health care provider's scale shows a 4-pound (1.8 kg) weight gain compared to your home scale, don't panic! Scales are often different, so compare only weights from the same scale.

Will You Gain Too Much Weight?

So here's the challenge. You know you shouldn't gain too much weight, but you're not sure how to keep the pounds in check. This quiz should help you identify problems.

1.   Do you regularly drink sugar-sweetened drinks or more than 1 glass of juice at a time?
2.   Do you regularly eat fried or "junk" food?
3.   Do you use a lot of butter, margarine, salad dressing, sour cream, or cheese or regularly eat the skin on chicken, fat on steak, etc?
4.   When you cook, do you pour more than 1 teaspoon of oil per serving into the pan?
5.   Do you sometimes sit down with a box of crackers or cookies and soon find that you've eaten most of the box?
6.   Do you eat a high-calorie desert three times a week or more?
7.   Do you often eat when you're bored, depressed, angry, or happy—but not hungry?
8.   Do you usually eat while doing something else, such as reading or watching TV?
9.   Do you consider yourself sedentary—participating in no regular exercise or do you sit down most of the day?
10. Do you have the mindset of "eating for two?"

If you answered "yes" to four or more questions, your current habits/emotions may cause you to gain too much weight. Keeping an eye on what you eat and how you feel emotionally will help you now—and later, when you are trying to lose your "baby fat."

Having Trouble Meeting Your Goal?

Many women have a difficult time meeting their weight goals during pregnancy. Are you having trouble meeting your goal because you're gaining too much or too fast? Are you not gaining enough? Let's discuss the possible obstacles you may face as you work toward your goal.

Gaining Too Fast or Too Much

Most women fear gaining too much, with good reason. But, regardless of how much you gain, pregnancy is never the time to try to lose weight. For example, if you have reached your goal of a 30-pound (14 kg) weight gain by week twenty, you may need to change your end goal weight, but you still should gain a small amount of weight for the remaining weeks. Discuss with your health care provider.

Here are several explanations for gaining too much weight or gaining weight too fast:

♦ Are you feeling depressed, stressed or overwhelmed with no control over your life? These feelings have been linked to gaining too much weight.[3]

♦ You may be carrying multiple fetuses. If you don't feel that your weight gain is related to eating, consult your health care provider about the possibility of twins or more.

♦ Inaccurate weighing or weighing after eating or drinking. (Weighing after drinking a quart (1 liter) of water, for example, will add 2 pounds (1 kg) to your weight!

♦ Preeclampsia/high blood pressure. If you have rapid weight gain in the second or third trimester of pregnancy, and you also experience swelling of face and/or hands, severe headaches, or vision problems, contact your health care provider immediately! These could be the first signs of preeclampsia, a potentially serious problem. (See page 207 for more information.)

How to Avoid Gaining Too Much Weight

Three factors control your weight gain and how it looks on you: your genes, your activity level, and your diet.

The distribution of pregnancy weight varies among women. You'll hear myths about your weight gain—and how it translates to having a boy or a girl. The truth is your genes control where the weight goes. Check out these ideas to keep a handle on your weight gain.

1. Start a low-impact exercise program approved by your health care provider (such as swimming or walking) or continue an established exercise program. Being active will help you feel better about your expanding waistline and will

decrease your risk of high blood pressure and diabetes. Having a more toned body will get you through labor with no problems with endurance and will help you lose weight after you have your baby.

One mother of two says: "I lost all my weight within a few months after having Brian. I swam regularly right up to delivery. However, with Emily, I was very sick with bronchitis the last six weeks of pregnancy and spent a lot of time in bed. Overall, I was much less active when I was pregnant with Emily, and it took me much longer to take the weight off after she was born."

2. Analyze your eating habits. Keep a food diary: write down everything you eat and drink for a week. Some women don't eat that much—all their extra calories come from what they drink! See how it compares to the Eating Expectantly Diet. Taking the quiz on page 184 will also shed some light on your eating habits.

3. Eat breakfast, and consider having a high protein breakfast. This is one way to help hold the line on weight gain. In general people who skip breakfast make up for the calories (plus more) later in the day. Eating eggs for breakfast can also help you feel full longer, and in general eating breakfast helps you maintain your energy level by keeping blood sugar levels more even.

4. Make sure you're eating plenty of fruits, vegetables and whole grains. These filling foods are healthy for your baby, but also keep you from munching on higher calorie fare.

5. If you're noshing on sweet, fatty foods, check your stress level. It's a fact that when women get stressed, we go for the sweets—and research bears this out. A study of pregnant women found that those who were stressed and anxious ate more carbs, sweets, fats and snack foods.[4] If this describes you, try to deal with your stress and have more health-friendly snacks like raw vegetables available to snack on. If you feel that emotional issues such as stress, self-esteem, depression, lack of control or lack of support are affecting your habits, consult your health care provider for resources to help.

Check Out These Pregnancy "Apps" Which can Help Track Weight Gain and More!

♦ BabyBump Pregnancy Pro (English, Spanish and French)

♦ My Pregnancy Today by Babycenter

♦ Babble.com Pregnancy Tracker

♦ Pregnancy Companion

♦ MommyMD Guide

Not Gaining Enough

There are as many reasons for not gaining enough weight as there are for gaining too much. Though not gaining much weight may seem like a blessing, the deficit could cause major problems for your baby—like prematurity and low birthweight. So, if you're having problems gaining enough weight, try to find the reason below so you can act on it.

♦ **You have a fast metabolism.** Women who were underweight before pregnancy may simply burn calories more quickly. You may need help from a registered dietitian who can closely analyze your diet for ways to increase calories.

♦ **You can't eat much because of nausea, heartburn, constipation, or other physical problems.** First, you need to get to the root of the problem. Tummy troubles often have simple solutions—find them on page 168 and page 223. Psychosocial stress has been known to decrease weight gain. Ask your health care provider for assistance if the usual tips don't help.

♦ **You live a fast-paced life.** Some moms-to-be have very active lifestyles and don't slow down for pregnancy. This could result in burning too many calories or not taking the time to eat. Either scenario leaves fewer calories for baby to grow on. If your lifestyle is interfering with your weight gain, you may need to look at reducing your activities or exercise and/or increasing your calories.

♦ **Psychological factors are interfering.** If you have ever had a weight problem or an eating disorder, you might find gaining weight psychologically difficult. Your overall psychosocial well-being may also have an effect on your weight status. Depression, stress, anxiety, low self-esteem, and lack of social support may all affect your weight gain. Don't hesitate to seek help from your health care provider or a therapist.

♦ **You smoke.** Smoking is associated with not gaining enough weight and also sudden infant death syndrome (SIDS), fetal death, and placenta previa (an abnormal placement of the placenta that may cause complications during delivery.) Do your best to quit or cut down. See www.helppregnantsmokersquit.org for more info and page 112 for resources on quitting smoking.

What To Do If You Aren't Gaining Enough Weight

♦ Make sure your diet is similar to the Eating Expectantly Diet on page 86.

♦ Slow down!

♦ Increase the amount of food you eat. If you are having trouble eating more, increase fat intake—the easiest way to increase calories without increasing bulk. To increase fat intake, the best foods to add are those rich in unsaturated fats, such as flaxseed, and flaxseed oil, walnut, peanut, olive oil, salad dressings, wheat germ, nuts, seeds, avocado, olives, cashew, almond and peanut butter, and margarine with liquid oil as the first ingredient.

◆　Don't forget the snacks. If you're eating only three meals a day, you may not be eating enough. Most pregnant women need a few additional snacks to fit in all the nutrients and calories they need. (See page 199 for snack ideas for high-energy moms.)

◆　Increase what I call "healthy splurges"—foods that have some nutritive value, but have extra calories too—such as milk shakes, frozen yogurt, breads made with fruits or vegetables (like banana bread or zucchini bread), sweet potato or pumpkin pie, pudding, more egg dishes, like egg custard; and foods made with nut butters.

◆　Other ways to add calories:

- Try a snack bar—Luna, Kashi, Gnu, Lara, and Zing Bars all have tasty higher calorie, balanced nutrition snack bars. See a list of recommended snack bars on page 69.

- Try a yogurt smoothie or drinkable yogurt such as Stonyfield Farm Oikos Organic Drinkable Lowfat Yogurt or Stonyfield Farms Super Smoothie.

- Have a protein shake as a between meal snack, like Odwalla Protein Drinks. They contain fruit juice, fruit and extra protein from soy or milk.

- Have a Tex-Mex Parfait: Mash some spiced pinto beans, top with guacamole and plain Greek yogurt (or low-fat sour cream) and garnish with tortilla chips. Now that's high-calorie health food!

- Make it cheesy—whether it's cheese and whole grain crackers or cottage cheese and fruit, low-fat cheese is a great way to boost your calcium, protein and calories.

Keeping Your Baby's Environment Safe

What You'll Find:

- ◆ Bad Habits

- ◆ Environmental Chemicals

- ◆ Bad Bugs and Food Poisoning

- ◆ Water

- ◆ Food Safety

- ◆ Around the House

- ◆ Beauty Care

- ◆ In a Nutshell: Greener Living

Frequently Asked Questions:

- ◆ Is it OK to have just one glass of wine a week?

- ◆ How much caffeine is in dark chocolate?

- ◆ Which fish are safe to eat?

- ◆ How long can food be kept out of the refrigerator?

- ◆ What's safe to use for cleaning and pest control?

SCAN HERE FOR CHAPTER UPDATES

I could have simply called this chapter "The Don'ts"—because it really covers all the things you should try to stay away from to keep your baby healthy. From sushi to smoking; pesticides to pina coladas, the goal of this chapter is to enlighten you about habits and things in the environment that could cause problems for you and your baby. A physician who specializes in high-risk pregnancies once said, "You have only one chance to give your baby what it needs. Why not do everything you can to help your baby along? It's only nine months." Giving advice is certainly easier than following it, right? Hopefully the advice in this chapter will give you the knowledge to keep you motivated.

Bad Habits

The first trimester—or before pregnancy—is a good time to kick some bad habits and pick up some better ones.

Smoking

Quitting smoking is the single most important thing you can do to improve the growth and long-term health of your baby, not to mention improving your own health!

Mothers who smoke or who are exposed to smoke are more likely to[1,2,3]:

♦   Have a miscarriage

♦   Give birth to a premature, small or stillborn baby

♦   Have a baby who is born early or weighs less than 5.5 pounds (2.5 kg)

♦   Have a baby die of Sudden Infant Death Syndrome (SIDS)

♦   Have increased risk of placental abruption and placenta previa; abnormalities which can cause third trimester bleeding, and premature birth.

Smoking early in pregnancy increases the risk of asthma and wheeze in preschoolers.[4] Children exposed to tobacco smoke prenatally are more likely to experience these neurodevelopmental effects of smoking[5,6,7,8]:

♦   Problems with speech processing

♦   Irritability

♦   Attention Deficit Hyperactivity Disorder (ADHD)

♦   Conduct disorder and antisocial behavior

♦   Nicotine addiction

The problems continue for baby if he's exposed to second-hand smoke after he is born, with greater risk of ear and respiratory infections such as pneumonia,[9] and more cold and allergy symptoms.[10] Second-hand smoke is not filtered, and is even more harmful than smoke the smoker breathes. There are over 7,000 chemicals in cigarette smoke, and more than 69 are known carcinogens (cancer-causing). Providing a smoke-free home (and car) for yourself and your family is a life-long gift!

⏰ TAKE ACTION NOW ⏰

BE SMOKE FREE!

✔ Write down your reasons for quitting (or reasons for your partner to quit).

✔ Pick a quit date; write it on the calendar.

✔ Ask a friend or your partner for their help.

✔ Set up rules for smoking—such as only smoking outside.

✔ Stay away from activities, places or people that make you want to smoke or that put you near smokers.

✔ Remove smoking reminders—cigarettes, matches, and ashtrays from your purse, home, work and car and clean everything that smells like smoke.

✔ Talk to your health care provider and your insurance company about tools to help you quit smoking.

✔ Make sure to take your prenatal vitamin daily

✔ Check your dietary intake of these nutrients, which may be needed in larger amounts if you are a smoker: vitamin C and E, Vitamin B6, B12 and folic acid.[11]

✔ Check out these Quit Smoking Resources:

- For pregnant women: www.becomeanex.org/pregnant-smokers.php
- www.smokefree.gov
- www.women.smokefree.gov
- www.helppregnantsmokersquit.org
- 1-800-QUIT-NOW—Your state's quitline (US)
- 1-877-44U-QUIT—US National Cancer Institute
- 1-800-227-2345—American Cancer Society's QuitLine

Alcohol

Think Before You Drink.

Would you give your newborn a sip of your wine? Of course not! But when you drink alcohol (or take drugs), you're sharing—and the problem with that is your baby's liver isn't developed enough to metabolize those substances. The result is that your baby's blood level of alcohol or drugs will be higher than yours, and will remain higher longer. Depending on the amount and frequency of exposure, this can lead to growth retardation, brain damage, birth defects, mental retardation and neurodevelopmental problems, low birthweight, preterm birth, learning disabilities and emotional and behavioral problems.[12]

It's well established that alcohol can harm the unborn. And although one recent study of Danish children reported that light to moderate drinking of 1-8 drinks per week had no significant effect on intelligence, attention or executive function at age 5, don't say "cheers" just yet.[13] A US study showed that light to moderate drinking was associated with having "difficult" babies—attesting to the fact that alcohol can affect behavior from the very beginning.[14] Another recent study of babies whose moms were regular drinkers (2 drinks a day or 4 at one time) showed that growth restriction began before birth and persisted up to age 9.[15] The measurements included head circumference, an indicator of brain growth. The truth is, because susceptibility varies, no one really knows exactly what amount of alcohol is considered safe to a developing fetus. This is why the March of Dimes, the Centers for Disease Control[16], as well as health organizations from Canada, Australia, New Zealand, the UK and France[17] continue to recommend that moms-to-be *avoid* alcohol.

Drugs

All drugs, pharmaceutical or recreational, legal and illegal, prescription or over-the-counter—even those as seemingly harmless as ibuprofen—have the potential to harm your baby. So let your health care provider know if you are regularly taking any kind of drug. Also, ask what's safe to take for a cold, flu, or bad headache. Of course, it's best not to take any medications during pregnancy, especially during the first trimester. But in reality, many women depend on medications for chronic problems such as depression, high blood pressure or allergies. Don't stop taking any prescription medications, however, unless your health care provider instructs you to.

For information about marijuana and other drug use during pregnancy:

◆   www.medicinenet.com/script/main/art.asp?articlekey=51663

◆   www.marchofdimes.com/pregnancy/alcohol_illicitdrug.html

Caffeine

Caffeine, the most widely consumed "drug" on the planet, stimulates the central nervous system, acts as a diuretic, and interferes with mineral absorption. And if you're one of those who can't function without your morning cup of coffee or tea, you're already aware of its addicting properties. What's worse, caffeine **does** affect your baby's growth—by decreasing blood flow in the placenta—and the more caffeine, the greater the effect.[18] Also, the effect of caffeine is greater in women who metabolize caffeine the fastest, which can happen because of genetics or the presence of nicotine.[19] Caffeine intakes above 200 mg are also associated with a higher risk of miscarriage.[20] (There's 140 mg. of caffeine in a cup (250 ml) of brewed coffee; see chart below to find out how much caffeine is contained in a variety of foods and beverages.)

There may be one more reason to can the caffeine; a small double-blind Canadian study suggested that caffeine negatively affects blood sugar and insulin levels in women with gestational diabetes (GDM).[21] If you have risk factors for diabetes (being overweight, a history of large babies, excess pregnancy weight gain) or have been diagnosed with GDM, watch your caffeine intake even more closely.

The best advice: Instead of relying on caffeine, get more sleep and take a brisk afternoon walk for a pick-me-up. Have some bubbly mineral water with a squeeze of fresh lime or simply spritz your face with water. If you *must* have your caffeine, switch to lower-caffeine products and consume as little as possible using these tips:

Here's How to Cap Your Caffeine

♦ Limit your caffeine to 100 mg during the first trimester and up to 200 mg after.

♦ Switch to a lower caffeine drink. A cappuccino or espresso has less caffeine than brewed coffee. Tea has about ⅓ the caffeine of coffee—and a boost of healthful antioxidants.

♦ If it's the ritual of drinking something hot that you crave, try steamed milk with vanilla and honey or other flavoring; hot cocoa, tea, or apple cider.

♦ Try decaf. Some decaffeination processes use solvents to remove the caffeine, which could leave a chemical residue. If the label doesn't specify the method, it's probably done that way. The Swiss Water Method (also called Water Processed), using only water in the decaf process, is the healthiest for you. Caribou Coffee processes their decaf coffee in this way—buy online at www.cariboucoffeee. com. Find local coffee shops that carry water-processed coffee by checking www.swisswater.com/find/. Tea can also be water processed; Lipton is one brand that uses this method.

Experts around the world agree on this: Limit your caffeine to a "moderate" intake of less than 200 mg. So says The American College of Obstetricians and Gynecologists, The March of Dimes, NSW Health (Australia) and The National Health Service (UK).[22,23,24,25] The bottom line: have as little caffeine as you can get by with.

◆ Watch how you caffeinate. Instead of having a large amount of caffeine all at once, try having smaller amount a few times a day. This way you and baby can avoid the big "jolt" of caffeine and you can stay alert throughout the day.

◆ Use caution with anything that claims to give you a boost of energy, like energy shots or drinks. They are most likely full of caffeine or herbal stimulants and could be dangerous. Several recent deaths have been blamed on (but not proven to be caused by) the consumption of energy drinks.

Beverage or Food	Average amount of caffeine in milligrams
Cold Drinks	
Root Beer/fruit sodas 12 oz. (375 ml)	0
Chocolate milk 8 oz. (250 ml)	5-8
Canned/bottled tea 16 oz. (500 ml)	15-40
Fresh brewed iced tea 8 oz. (250 ml)	10-50
Cola drinks 12 oz. (375 ml)	40-50
Mountain Dew 12 oz. (375 ml)	54
Extra caffeine colas 12 oz. (375 ml)	71
Red Bull/Rockstar 8.3 oz. (250 ml)	80
Caribou Coffee Iced tea (small)	108
Monster Energy 16 oz. (500 ml)	160
Hot Drinks	
Hot cocoa 8 oz. (250 ml)	9
Brewed tea 8 oz. (250 ml)	53
Instant coffee 8 oz. (250 ml)	100
Starbucks Frappuccino 9.5 oz. (300 ml)	115
Brewed coffee 8 oz. (250 ml)	140
Starbucks Espresso 2 oz. (65 ml)	150
Starbucks Grande Latte 16 oz. (500 ml)	150
Caribou Coffee Americano, Latte or Cappuccino (small)	180
Starbucks Grande 16 oz. (500 ml)	330

Beverage or Food	Average amount of caffeine in milligrams
Coffee / Chocolate Snacks	
Hershey's milk chocolate 1.55 oz. (43 g)	9
Hershey's Kisses 9	9
2 Tablespoons chocolate chips (semisweet)	13
Scharffen Berger Milk Chocolate ½ bar (43 g)	17
Cadbury Royal Dark 10 squares	18
Hershey's Kisses Special Dark 9	20
Dannon coffee yogurt 6 oz. (190 g)	30
Coffee Ice Cream ½ cup (125 ml)	30-40
Hershey's Special Dark Chocolate bar 1.45 oz (41 g)	31
Scharffen Berger Bittersweet Dark 70% cacao ½ bar (43 g)	42

Sources: Starbucks.com, Center for Science in the Public Interest: cspinet.org/new/ cafchart.htm, www.thehersheycompany.com/nutrition-and-wellness/chocolate-101/ caffeine.aspx, and other company websites.

Beyond Coffee: Other Caffeine-Containing Drinks

Guarana is a small red fruit native to South America; its seeds naturally contain twice the caffeine of coffee beans. A popular addition to energy drinks and shots, (and sodas in South America) guarana should be avoided during pregnancy because not enough is known about the health effects to the unborn. Drinks containing guarana won't have caffeine listed on the label like others do because caffeine isn't added—it's naturally found in the guarana. The dried leaves of the Mate tree (or Yerba Mate) steeped in hot water, is a popular beverage in South America too. Since Mate also contains caffeine and also has unknown effects during pregnancy, it's best to skip it.

Herbal Teas and Supplements

You may be thinking, "How can herbal teas and supplements be a bad habit? Aren't they natural and safe?" Many people turn to herbal teas to avoid caffeine. Others turn to herbal supplements for their medicinal properties because they seem more "natural." But *natural* doesn't necessarily equal *safe*. Your herbals might not be safe at all during pregnancy, and therefore, using them is potentially a bad habit.

According to the Natural Medicines Database (www.naturaldatabase.com), which scientifically evaluates the safety of herbs based on available research, many commonly consumed herbs and herbal teas may not be safe **during pregnancy**. Some common herbal teas, like peppermint, are considered safe during pregnancy. But even though chamomile has been around since the Dark Ages, and there haven't been reports of toxicity, its safety during pregnancy hasn't actually been established. Red raspberry leaf tea (also called or a component of "Pregnancy Tea") is often recommended during pregnancy to help promote uterine health. However, there is some question whether it should be only used in the second and third trimester, since it may increase uterine contractions.

There are probably others that *may be safe*, but there is just not enough information to evaluate them.[26] Also keep in mind that herbal supplements don't have to undergo the same testing as over-the-counter and prescription medications.

You might see some teas on the following list that you commonly drink. You might even see them recommended by others as safe during pregnancy. The truth is that not enough is known about their effects on your baby. As you can guess, women aren't lining up to volunteer to test the effect of herbals on their unborn babies! So unless your health care provider is knowledgeable about herbs, it's best to follow the consumption guidelines below.[27] I always say "better safe than sorry."

Likely Safe:
◆   Red Raspberry Leaf (not first trimester)
◆   Peppermint Leaf
◆   Ginger root
◆   Garlic
Possibly Safe:
◆   Senna (short term)
Insufficient Reliable Information **(Acceptable in amounts commonly found in foods):**
◆   Dandelion
◆   Bitter Fennel
◆   Spearmint
◆   Rose Hip
Insufficient Reliable Information: Avoid
◆   German Chamomile (common in the US)
◆   Lemon Verbena
◆   Roobois (Red Bush Tea)

Possibly Unsafe: Avoid
◆ Aloe
◆ Black Cohosh
◆ Dong Quai
◆ Ginseng
◆ Evening primrose
◆ Feverfew
◆ Hibiscus
◆ Kava Kava
◆ Pau D' Arco
◆ Yohimbe
Likely Unsafe: Avoid
◆ Saw Palmetto
◆ Goldenseal
◆ Ephedra (banned in the US)
◆ Blue Cohosh
◆ Roman Chamomile (common in the U.K.)
◆ Pennyroyal
Unsafe: Avoid
◆ Passion Flower

Environmental Chemicals

We are surrounded by chemicals—both naturally-occurring and those added to products—to make life more beautiful, fragrant or convenient. You're probably aware of the growing concern about environmental chemicals and their effects on health. Infertility, birth defects, cancer, neurological development and immune system problems: these are just a few of the health risks associated with environmental chemicals.

On a typical morning, your body has probably come into contact with at least 20 added chemicals: from the phthalates in your shampoo or air freshener and chlorine in your steam shower, to the pesticide in your fruit, the residues left on your dry-cleaning, along with fragrance, preservatives and coloring in your facial moisturizer. While it's impossible to avoid all chemicals, you **can** limit them—especially those that pose the greatest risk to your baby. In fact, this is important not only when you're pregnant but during your childbearing years, because some chemicals can accumulate in the body over time.

For a summary of this next section see "In a Nutshell" on page 128.

Persistent Organic Pollutants

Persistent Organic Pollutants (POPs) don't easily break down or disintegrate, so they linger in the environment—often decades after people stop using them. POPs know no borders—they can be transported by wind and water around the world and have been found in some of the most pristine areas of the world like Antarctica and the Arctic.

People are mainly exposed to POPs through food. Less common exposure routes include drinking contaminated water and direct contact with the chemicals. POPs biomagnify in the food chain, meaning animals at the top of the food chain (humans, livestock, large predatory fish and birds) accumulate much larger amounts of chemicals than animals lower on the food chain.[28]

Health Effects: POPS negatively affect our environment and the health of humans and animals, and are associated with reproductive, developmental, behavioral, neurologic, endocrine, and immunologic problems.[29] A significant relationship has been found between the amount of POPs in a person's blood and risk of diabetes.[30] During pregnancy, some of your baby's exposure to POPs comes from what's already stored in your body (mostly in body fat). When large amounts of POPs are accumulated in a pregnant woman's body, they are thought to affect neurological and cognitive development in a growing fetus. POPS include PCBs, BPA and dioxin, as well as pesticides such as aldrin, DDT and heptachlor. Some POPS are also endocrine disrupting compounds.

Endocrine Disrupting Compounds

Endocrine Disrupting Compounds (EDCs) also called "endocrine disruptors," are chemicals that may interfere with the body's endocrine (hormone) system and produce adverse developmental, reproductive, neurological, and immune effects in both humans and wildlife.[31] The endocrine system is composed of hormones, hormone receptors and the various glands of the endocrine system (hypothalamus, pituitary, thyroid, adrenals, pancreas, testes and ovaries). EDCs are found in everyday products including plastic bottles, metal food cans, detergents, furniture, food, toys, cosmetics, and pesticides. For more information, see www.epa.gov/endo/pubs/edspoverview/whatare.htm.

Health Effects: EDCs can bind to hormone receptors, particularly estrogen and testosterone, where they can mimic, increase or block hormone action in the body. Thyroid hormone production can also be inhibited by EDCs. Reproductive and sexual development, fertility, and birth defects of the reproductive system have been linked to EDCs.[32,33] Pesticides and other endocrine disruptors are often blamed for decreasing sperm counts around the world.[34]

Did You Know?

Soy beans, soy foods, and other legumes contain isoflavones, plant estrogens which have weak estrogenic activity and thus could be called natural endocrine disruptors. Soy foods and isoflavones have been shown to have positive health benefits and are a large part of the diet in Asian countries and by vegans all over the world. In fact preliminary animal research indicated that soy during pregnancy may have a positive effect on risk of heart disease for children later in life.[35] Whole soy foods as well as fermented soy foods, are nutrient-rich and can safely be a part of the Eating Expectantly Diet. For more information:

◆ lpi.oregonstate.edu/infocenter/phytochemicals/soyiso/

◆ www.soyconnection.com/health_nutrition/index.php

◆ www.ncbi.nlm.nih.gov/pubmed/21418378

Bisphenol A (BPA)

BPA is found in polycarbonate plastic bottles and some plastic food containers (#7 recycling code), dental materials, on the inside of food and beverage cans and on thermal paper used for receipts. The amount absorbed into the skin from thermal paper could be significant if you handle it frequently, such as if you're a cashier.[36] The European Union, Canada, and the United States have banned BPA in baby bottles.

Health effects: BPA has been associated with decreased sperm count, increased cancer risk and neurodevelopmental effects to babies exposed during pregnancy.[37] The US National Toxicology Program at the National Institutes of Health and FDA have "some concern" about the potential effects of BPA on the brain, behavior, and prostate gland in fetuses, infants, and young children.[38]

Dioxins

Dioxins are a group of chlorinated organic chemicals with similar chemical structures. Most dioxin pollution is man-made from burning trash, wood, and other fuels; bleaching paper pulp and from manufacturing chlorinated pesticides. Dioxins in plants come from air, dust and dioxin containing pesticides and herbicides and move up the food chain. According to the World Health Organization, more than 90% of human exposure is through food—mainly animal products.[39] But there's good news about dioxins—industrial emissions of dioxins and PCBs have been cut significantly since 1987.[40] Dioxins in the food supply have also been reduced by close to 50%.[41]

Health Effects: Long-term exposure is linked to impairment of the immune system, the nervous system, the endocrine system and reproductive functions. The developing fetus is most sensitive to dioxin exposure.[42] To cut your intake of dioxins, choose the leanest types of animal protein and eat more plant proteins.

Can the Canned Food?

I'll admit it—I have canned foods in my pantry and you probably do too! Though I eat something made with canned food less than once a week, canned tomatoes, tomato sauce and beans are definitely convenient to have around. So, knowing the potential risks of BPA, should you sweep your pantry of things packed in metal? It depends on what foods you have canned, how often you eat them and if there are alternatives to BPA containing cans. A few studies have shed light on BPA content of canned food: canned fruit contains either no or very little BPA. For other foods, the amounts vary by brand and within manufacturing lots of the same brand, which makes it even more difficult to determine which to choose. For example a study by the Breast Cancer Fund found creamed corn bought in Minnesota had extremely high levels of BPA, while a can of the same brand purchased in New York had undetectable levels.[43] A study of canned foods purchased in Canada found canned fish to contain large amounts, broth based soups and baked beans to contain moderate amounts of BPA while canned apple juice, tomatoes and tomato sauce and soda contained very little. (See the chart at www.ncbi.nlm.nih.gov/pmc/articles/PMC3118530/table/T1/)

If the convenience of canned is a necessity for you, try these tips:

♦ When possible, choose cans that are labeled BPA-free or choose products in glass jars instead.

♦ For broth type soups, choose aseptic packaging like Tetra-pak and instead of canned fish, buy the ones in pouches.

♦ Choosing frozen vegetables in general are a better choice nutritionally so buy those when possible.

♦ Don't worry too much about canned fruit or juices, as they appear to contain very little or no detectable BPA.

PCBs (Polychlorinated Biphenyls)

PCBs are a group of manufactured chemicals (actually a mix of 209 different ones) originally used in electrical transformers, hydraulic fluids and lubricants. US production stopped in 1979 and in other parts of the world by 2001, but PCBs continue to be found in the air, water, soil, fluorescent light fixtures, old well pumps and electrical appliances containing PCB capacitors made before 1979.[44,45]

Health effects: PCBs cause cancer in animals and are considered "probably" cancer causing to humans. They've been linked to problems with nervous system development, which can lead to learning disabilities.[46] They may also affect thyroid hormone levels and cause chromosome abnormalities in sperm.[47] Women with high exposures to PCBs six years before pregnancy and while pregnant had babies who weighed less and had poor short-term memory and children who were more likely to have lower verbal IQ scores, lag behind in reading comprehension and have difficulty paying attention.[48]

Pesticides

Pesticides are hazardous chemicals designed to repel or kill insects, rodents, fungi, and weeds. If you stop to think about it, chemicals designed to kill are not likely to be good for anyone's health! Many pesticides used before 1970 have been found to be harmful to the environment and unfortunately, were used without restrictions— including dumping them into rivers and lakes. Some pesticides are EDCs—and although some have been withdrawn from use (DDT and atrazine), they can still be found in the environment.

Health Effects: Pesticides have been associated with poor semen quality and decreased male fertility, as well as increased risk of hormone-dependent cancers. Some studies show a link between DDE (a breakdown product of the pesticide DDT) and breast cancer, while others do not.[49] A higher prevalence of birth defects as well as long-term effects on intellectual functioning have been linked with exposure to endocrine disrupting pesticides.[50] Choosing organic foods and avoiding pesticide use around the house can help you cut your intake of pesticides. For a full discussion on eating organic and reducing pesticides from food see page 371.

Phthalates

Phthalates describe a group of chemicals used to make plastics more flexible (like water bottles and plastic bags) or sturdy (like PVC), and to make solvents. Also called "plasticizers" they're used in many personal-care products to make scents last longer. ("Fragrance" listed on a label often means a product contains phthalates.) These chemicals are found in many consumer goods like food packaging, cosmetics, detergents, insect repellants, adhesives, nail polish, hair spray, shampoo, vinyl shower curtains, some medications with enteric coating and medical tubing. Phthalates are endocrine disruptors (see info above.) One analysis showed that an average of five different phthalates were found in the bloodstreams of 84% of Americans.[51]

Health effects: Possible DNA damage in sperm[52], reduction in sperm count, sperm motility and abnormalities in sperm shape[53], and increased risk of genital abnormalities of male children.[54] New research shows an increased risk of diabetes in women with higher exposure to certain phthalates.[55] Inspect the label of cleaning products and body care products carefully for phthalates; here are the abbreviations for the most common ones: BBP, DBP, DEHP, DEP, DiDP, DnHP, DnOP. See more info on page 149.

Heavy Metals

Called "heavy" due to their molecular weight, they are both naturally occurring and a product of burning fossil fuels and the smelting of other metals. Heavy metals enter the food supply through the air and soil, through drinking water and fish from polluted oceans. Believe it or not, heavy metals are also additives to some commonly used products like makeup and herbal supplements. Heavy metals are also slow to break down, so like POPs, they continue to linger in the environment.

Arsenic

Arsenic finds its way into the air, soil and water via mining, volcanic eruptions, forest fires and through man-made pesticides.[56] The level of arsenic in soil vary by geographic area. Some plants absorb arsenic from the soil; significant amounts have been found in rice and rice products. Some brands of apple and grape juice have also been found to contain elevated levels of arsenic.[57,58] Avoid drinking those juices on a daily basis. For more information: www.consumerreports.org/cro/consumer-reports-magazine-january-2012/arsenic-in-your-juice/index.htm. Hijiki, a black, shredded seaweed can be very high in arsenic. Arsenic is found in some Asian folk remedies. Although there is a limit to how much arsenic can be in drinking water, there are no limits on the amounts of arsenic in food (or rice) in the US, the European Community or the UK. In Australia and New Zealand, there is a limit for inorganic arsenic of 1 mg/kg for seaweed and mollusks and a limit of 2 mg/kg in shrimp and other fish.[59] If you have a well, make sure to test your water for arsenic (and other contaminants) at least annually—consider testing it again when you confirm your pregnancy.

Arsenic in rice is more of a problem when it's grown where arsenic-laden pesticides were once used, such as cotton fields. Check out this interactive map to see how much arsenic is in the groundwater where you live (or where your rice is grown): www.consumerreports.org/cro/consumer-reports-magazine-january-2012/arsenic-in-your-juice/index.htm#groundwater

Health Effects: Arsenic is known to cause cancer. Higher risk of preterm delivery, miscarriage, stillbirth, low birthweight, and possibly birth defects have been associated with consuming excess arsenic.[60] Some research shows differences in IQ among girls prenatally exposed to arsenic.[61]

Cadmium

A heavy metal often found as a by-product of melting other metals and from the combustion of petroleum and coal. Cadmium is used in the production of nickel-cadmium batteries, as well as some pigments and craft glazes on pottery and food dyes. It's also used to make PVC and vinyl. It can be found in shellfish, liver and kidney meats, but also leafy greens and other plants. Some foods have increased

Should You Eat Rice?

A recent study of pregnant women who ate about ½ cup of rice a day had the same amount of arsenic in their urine as they would after drinking 4 cups (1 liter) of drinking water containing the maximum amount of arsenic allowed by law in the US (10 parts per billion).[62] Should you stop eating rice? Not necessarily, but you may definitely need to cut back! Keep in mind that the bran part of the rice absorbs more arsenic; brown rice and brown rice syrup—a common sweetener in natural foods—both contain more of the metal.[63,64] Rice grown in California (even brown) has less arsenic than from Southern areas of the US, where rice is often grown on arsenic-laden fields that previously contained cotton.[65]

This information about rice underscores the importance of eating a variety of foods and a variety of grains. So far there are no official consumption guidelines for rice or rice products. Follow these suggestions (based on stricter guidelines for children) from a Consumer Report's Study—Arsenic in Your Food.[66]

Limit consumption of rice products to:

♦   Rice: ¾ cup a week OR Rice pasta: 2.5 cups a week, OR rice cereal: 1.5 cups of per week OR rice cakes: 2 per week.

♦   Avoid rice milk.

♦   Instead of using brown rice, choose other whole grains like quinoa or bulgur wheat.

♦   Rice grown in California, India and Thailand; it tends to have the lowest arsenic content. Lundberg Family Farms, a California rice grower, appears to be a good choice.

Other Tips: Rinse rice before cooking and use a ratio of 6 cups water to 1 cup rice and discard the extra water at the end.

levels of cadmium due to use of phosphate fertilizers and sewage sludge on crops.[67] Naturally found in tobacco leaves, cadmium is one of the thousands of chemicals found in cigarette smoke.[68] You may be exposed to cadmium if your hobby is making jewelry, stained glass or if you work in welding or metal plating.

Health effects: Because cadmium can be stored in both the ovaries and testes, it can have an effect on ovulation and female fertility[69], early pregnancy loss[70], and sperm production.[71] It's a known carcinogen, and is toxic to the kidneys, heart and lungs.[72] One study showed that a child's motor skills and perception at 6 years was associated with the degree of exposure to lead and cadmium during pregnancy.[73] Preliminary results of a recent Harvard study linked higher levels of urinary cadmium to a higher risk of having a child with a learning disability or being in special education.[74] To decrease your exposure to cadmium, make sure to have enough iron in your diet because iron deficiency increases your absorption of cadmium.[75] People whose diets are deficient in zinc, copper, calcium and vitamin D may also be at higher risk for health complications of cadmium. Eat a variety of foods and pay attention to seafood consumption guidelines in your area. Oysters in particular are sometimes known to contain high levels of cadmium, so if you regularly eat them, you'll want to cut back.[76] If you live near industrial areas, you may want to have your soil tested before you plant a vegetable garden.

Lead

A naturally-occurring heavy metal that can be found in the air, water, food, leaded paint, some folk remedies (Azarcon, Greta), some imported cosmetics (kajal, surma, kohl) and leaded crystal. Manufacturers in the US and the European Union have voluntarily stopped using lead-based pigments in candy wrappers, but they are still used in Mexico and some other countries.[77] Traditional ceramic ware and folk pottery from China, Mexico and Central America may still contain lead-based paint.[78] Pregnant women and children run the highest risk of problems from lead exposure because the body absorbs more of it during times of growth. Inadequate calcium and iron in the diet can also cause the body to absorb more lead.

Health Effects: Lead can damage the kidneys, the reproductive system and nervous system.[79] Lead exposure can increase rates of miscarriage and stillbirth and decrease male fertility.[80] It can also have long-term effects such as learning disability, brain damage, hyperactivity, high blood pressure, and kidney disease.[81] High blood pressure during pregnancy is also associated with increased blood levels of lead. Various ways to decrease your exposure to lead are discussed later in this chapter on pages 132, 144, 146 and 150.

Mercury

Mercury is a heavy metal that occurs naturally and is also an industry by-product. Methylmercury finds its way into the food supply through some large species of fish. Exposure to mercury can also occur through broken thermometers, fluorescent and high-intensity light bulbs and amalgam dental fillings. Are amalgam dental fillings safe? The US Food and Drug Administration has concluded that dental fillings are safe for pregnant women[82], and research has shown no effect on risk of low birthweight or neurobehavioral outcomes in children whose moms have amalgam fillings.[83,84] However, because controversy still surrounds this topic, you may want to choose a different type of filling if you have a cavity while you are pregnant.

Health Effects: Mercury is extremely toxic to the developing brain and nervous system and can also damage hearing and vision. Children exposed to methylmercury in the womb have had decreases in cognitive thinking, memory, attention, language, fine motor and visual spatial skills.[85]

Fish You Should Eat—Fish You Should Avoid

Eat up to 12 oz. (375 g) (2 average meals) a week of a variety of fish and shellfish that are lower in mercury (Source: www.Fish4health.net)

You can safely eat these fish, cooked, which are low in mercury and other contaminants: *Anchovies, *Barramundi, Catfish (farmed), Clams (farmed), Crawfish (farmed),Cod, Crab, Flounder, Haddock, *Herring, *Mackerel (Atlantic, jack, chub), Mullet, Mussels (farmed), Oysters (farmed), Pollock, Plaice, *Rainbow trout (farm raised), *Salmon (wild or farm raised), *Sardines, Scallops, Shrimp, Sole, Squid, Tilapia, Tuna (Skipjack, Light, canned), Whitefish (*Highest in healthy omega-3 fats)

Avoid these fish due to high mercury or PCB content: Bass (striped), Bluefish, Chilean sea bass, Golden snapper, Jack (Amberjack, Crevalle), King mackerel, Marlin, Orange roughy, Shark, Spanish mackerel (Gulf of Mexico), Swordfish, Tilefish (Gulf of Mexico), Tuna (all fresh or frozen), Walleye (Great Lakes).

Eating Seafood Safely

Fish is good for you; sometimes called "brain food" for adults and the unborn alike. Unfortunately, however, many pregnant women avoid fish altogether while pregnant—sometimes upon the advice of their doctors. That's because there's much confusion about which seafood is good for health (**and** even more about what's good for the environment.) Some waters are polluted with mercury and PCBs, while some fish populations are near extinction due to overfishing. To add to the confusion, many large fish are higher in toxins like mercury, while some don't store any mercury, and some of the smallest seafood species—clams, oysters and other filter feeders—can store heavy metals.

Dr. Charles Santerre, a food toxicologist and seafood expert at Purdue University says, "I advise pregnant women to get their DHA from fish if possible because it's nutrient-rich with trace elements and antioxidants that are good for health and pregnancy." He's created a website, www.fish4health.net and a Fish for Your Health wallet card developed specifically for pregnant women and those of childbearing age. The guide details which fish to eat the get the most omega-3s and the least mercury and PCBs. On the website you can also find links to the EPA for local fish advisories. Free "apps" are available which contain fish information, a food log for you to determine your omega-3 intake, and recipes.

Another great tool is the Monterey Bay Aquarium's "Super Green List"—a list of fish that is good for you and is also classified as a Seafood Watch Best Choice. It can help you choose fish containing low levels of contaminants and at least 250 mg of omega-3's per 8 oz. (250 g). www.montereybayaquarium.org/cr/cr_seafoodwatch/sfw_health.aspx. Calculate mercury in seafood you eat at http://www.nrdc.org/health/effects/mercury/calculator/calc.asp

In a Nutshell

Twenty-One Ways to Reduce Your Exposure to Persistent Organic Chemicals, Endocrine Disrupting Compounds and Heavy Metals:

1. Eat as little animal fat as possible.
2. Choose lean meats, removing the fat and skin from all animal products including fish.
3. Choose skim and low-fat dairy products.
4. Choose smaller seafood species fish (trout, tilapia, shrimp) instead of large predatory fish (tuna, shark, swordfish).
5. Eat up to 12 oz. (375 g) of fish per week of those considered safe choices.
6. Avoid eating oysters, clams and mussels unless you know that they came from a safe area.
7. If you live near an industrial area (or where one used to be), have your soil tested before you plant a vegetable garden.
8. Avoid storing food in crystal and use caution when using handcrafted pottery from other countries, especially those painted with bright colors.
9. Take a close look at your hobbies—they might expose you to paint, adhesives, and metals that contain POPs.
10. If you or someone in your family is a sports or recreational fisherman, pay close attention to consumption guidelines posted at fishing sites and at fishadvisoryonline.epa.gov/General.aspx

11. If you drink water from a well, have the water tested for nitrates, heavy metals and bacteria when you confirm your pregnancy.
12. Make sure you have a good source of iron, calcium, vitamin D, copper and zinc in your diet to decrease absorption of heavy metals.
13. Be very careful about the type of plastic that comes into contact with your food—avoid the #3 and some #7 recycling codes (see page 142).
14. Choose organic food when possible, especially those highest in pesticide residues (see page 371).
15. Avoid exposure to pesticides and herbicides around the house (see page 146).
16. Wash all fruits and vegetables well before eating—even organic, home grown.
17. Limit canned foods or choose brands that are labeled BPA-free or are in alternative packaging (see page 122).
18. Limit rice products to once or twice a week and avoid rice milk.
19. Avoid hijiki, a type of seaweed.
20. Avoid or limit exposure to EDCs in the workplace (by both mom and dad).
21. Carefully read the labels of products that come into contact with skin, hair and lungs avoiding those that contain fragrance, phthalates and other questionable substances (see page 149).

Should You Get a Flu Shot?

One vaccine that's important to get while you are pregnant is the flu vaccine; both the CDC and WHO recommend it with good reason. Pregnant women are more likely to develop serious complications from all types of flu; pregnancy specific problems like premature birth and miscarriage are particularly worrisome. A recent study showed unexpected benefits of the flu shot during pregnancy: reduced risk of preterm birth and stillbirth.[86] However, you may shy away from getting any vaccines during pregnancy, due to fear of a mercury containing preservative called thimerosol. Good news: there are flu vaccines that are preservative-free. Ask your health care provider for more information.

For more information:

♦ Agency for Toxic Substances Registry: www.atsdr.cdc.gov

♦ Persistent Organic Pollutants: A Global Issue, A Global Response: www.epa.gov/ oia/toxics/pop.html

♦ Priority Chemicals in the Waste Minimization Program: www.epa.gov/wastes/ hazard/wastemin/priority.htm

Bad Bugs and Food Poisoning

Food poisoning outbreaks are big news on prime-time TV, and odds are that you've had a case of food poisoning yourself. During pregnancy, you're more susceptible to food-borne illness—and it can hurt your baby too. But, with safe food handling and knowledge about what not to eat, you can keep yourself and your baby healthy.

Food poisoning refers to more than just eating "bad" food. Most food-borne illness is spread through poor hand hygiene, keeping food at room temperature too long or not cooking it to a hot-enough temperature. Many illnesses are passed from hand-to-hand contact (especially in crowded places like cruise ships) and hand-to-food contact—from infected food-handlers, health-care or child-care workers who don't wash their hands properly. Additionally, some illness is spread through contaminated water that you might come into contact with at your local swimming pool, lake or through contaminated drinking water. No surprise: produce or seafood that comes into contact with water containing sewage can also cause serious illness—but this is more of a problem in under- or undeveloped countries.

Illness-causing bacteria, viruses and even parasites—can be killed by cooking to a proper internal temperature—that includes common pathogens like *Salmonella, Campylobacter, E. coli, Clostridium, Staph, Strep, Toxoplasma, Hepatitis A, Rotovirus* and *Norovirus*. Some bacteria are hard to kill—and one bacteria—*Listeria*—can survive refrigeration. Let's begin by discussing two really bad "bugs" to get while pregnant.

Listeria Monocytogenes

Listeria is a stubborn little bacteria that can *grow* and *thrive* in your fridge. While you can get sick from any food you eat raw that's been contaminated with bacteria, it's even more likely to happen with *Listeria*.

Listeriosis causes flu-like symptoms but if *listeria* is passed on to a fetus, it can cause you to have a miscarriage, premature birth, or give birth to a stillborn baby. Prevent *Listeriosis* by following the tips below from the CDC[87]:

Meats and Deli Foods

♦ Do not eat hot dogs, luncheon meats, cold cuts, other deli meats (e.g., bologna), or fermented or dry sausages unless they are **heated** to an internal temperature of 165°F / 65°C or until steaming-hot just before serving.

♦ Avoid getting fluid from hot dog and lunch meat packages on other foods, utensils, and food preparation surfaces, and wash hands after handling hot dogs, luncheon meats, and deli meats.

♦ Do not eat refrigerated meat or vegetable pâté or meat spreads from a deli or meat counter or from the refrigerated section of a store. Foods that do not need refrigeration, like canned or shelf-stable pâté and meat spreads, are safe to eat. Refrigerate after opening. See page 144 for refrigerator storage advice.

Milk and Cheeses

♦ Avoid raw (**unpasteurized**) milk and foods that are made with it.

♦ Soft cheeses made from unpasteurized milk, regardless of whether it's made from cow, goat or sheep milk, are more likely to harbor *Listeria*.

♦ Only eat cheese with PASTEURIZED MILK in the ingredient list.

Smoked Seafood

♦ Do not eat refrigerated smoked seafood, unless it is contained in a cooked dish, such as a casserole, or unless it is a canned or shelf-stable product.

♦ Refrigerated smoked seafood, such as salmon, trout, whitefish, cod, tuna, and mackerel, is most often labeled as "nova-style," "lox," "kippered," "smoked," or "jerky." These fish are typically found in the refrigerator section or sold at seafood and deli counters of grocery stores and delicatessens and should be avoided.

♦ Canned and shelf-stable tuna, salmon, and other fish products are safe to eat.

Melon

♦ Wash hands before and after handling whole melons like cantaloupe.

♦ Scrub the surface of melons with a produce brush under running water. Sanitize brush after use.

♦ For melon that is not eaten right away, refrigerate promptly for no more than 7 days.

International Advice

Canadian women are given similar eating advice regarding how to best avoid *Listeria*. Advice from other countries is slightly different: In Australia, pregnant women are advised to avoid soft white cheeses, like brie and feta, pâté, oysters, pre-packed salads and soft serve ice cream.[88] In the UK, women are told to avoid mold-ripened soft cheeses such as brie, camembert, chèvre (goats' cheese) and others with a similar rind; soft blue-veined cheeses, such as Danish blue, gorgonzola and Roquefort, unless heated to steaming, and all types of pâté,[89] including vegetable pâté. In France, the advice is similar, with the addition of avoiding rillettes, foie gras, the crust of cheese, unpasteurized cheese, tarama (a fish roe salad) and raw germinated seeds.[90]

Toxoplasma Gondii

Toxoplasma gondii is a parasite carried by cats and can also contaminate food. *Toxoplasmosis* may cause mild flu-like symptoms in pregnant women, but if the parasite is passed on to a fetus, it can cause preterm birth and stillbirth and can be the cause of learning, visual and hearing disabilities later in childhood.[91] *Toxoplasmosis* can result from eating undercooked meat and poultry or unwashed fruits and vegetables, from cleaning a cat litter box, or from handling contaminated soil. Severity of the disease may be reduced with antibiotics, but prevention is best:

♦ Avoid cleaning cat litter boxes if possible (or wear gloves.)

♦ Don't let cats on eating or food preparation areas. (Good luck with that one!)

♦ Wash fruits and vegetables well, and cook meat and poultry thoroughly.

♦ Wear gloves when gardening, handling soil, sand or cat litter.

♦ If you have a sand box for children to play in, keep it covered to keep cats out.

♦ Wash your hands after handling animals, especially cats.

For more information:

www.marchofdimes.com/pregnancy/complications_toxoplasmosis.html

Common Sources of Food Borne Illness

For a chart listing of all the "bad bugs"[92,93]—and how to avoid them, scan this QR code or go to www.EatingExpectantly/144

Water

Whether it's the water you drink or the water you swim in, make sure you're keeping it safe during pregnancy. The following substances could be harmful:

♦ Bacteria and other pathogens found in rivers, lakes and oceans, and tap water

♦ Heavy metals

♦ Lead in tap water from lead in pipes or faucets

♦ Excessive amounts of nitrates or pesticides in well water

♦ BPA, phthalates and other chemicals from plastic bottles

Water You Drink

♦ Check your community's annual water report to find out what's in your water.

♦ Have your water tested if you:

- • Suspect you have lead in your tap water or just want to know what's in your water.

- • Have a private well. It should be tested annually—more often if you live close to a landfill or junkyard, or certain activities like farming, manufacturing or oil drilling. (To be on the safest side, have your water tested again when you confirm your pregnancy.) To find a certified lab in the US: water.epa.gov/scitech/drinkingwater/labcert/statecertification.cfm

---

Water Filters

Top-rated for lead removal by Consumer Reports Magazine are the Culligan, Brita and Pur faucet-mounted filters and the Lotus Tersano and Clear20 carafe filters.[94] For More Information:

♦ US EPA: water.epa.gov/drink/contaminants/basicinformation/lead.cfm

♦ National Sanitation Foundation: Certifies and sets standards for water filtration systems: www.nsf.org/consumer

♦ EPA Safe Drinking Water Hotline 1-800-426-4791 water.epa.gov/drink

- Use filtered water; a faucet or under-the-sink-filtration system doesn't involve storing water in plastic, which is a good thing. Water filters may filter out fluoride; if yours does, check with your dentist to see if you should have supplemental fluoride or use a fluoride rinse.

- If you suspect you have lead in your tap water: Before you use water in the morning, let the cold water run for few minutes before using (Save it to water plants or hand wash delicates.) If you usually use hot water to make coffee, tea or for cooking, use cold water instead.

- Buying water in individual bottles may not be any cleaner than what comes out of your tap—and chemicals in the plastic could leach into water. The large water bottles used in water coolers may contain phthalates. Plastic also contributes to pollution and other environmental problems.

- While many refrigerators have built in filters, they are expensive and their ability to remove contaminants vary by brand and type.

- No matter which water filtration system you use, it's important to change the filter regularly!

Filtered Water To Go?

A reusable water bottle with its own built-in filter like The Brita Bottle or the L.L.Bean Katadyn MyBottle Purifier are great ways to have cleaner water in an environmentally friendly way. However, the bottles differ greatly. The more inexpensive bottles filter out sediments and chlorine and definitely make tap water taste better. The pricier ones also filter out microorganisms and chemicals, which may be more of an issue when camping or traveling to foreign countries.

Water You Swim (or Fish) In

When water is clean for swimming, life is good, but it can also be the perfect breeding ground for bacteria, viruses and parasites as well as a gathering place for pollutants. That means when you go swimming, boating or fishing, you have the potential to pick up bugs and other bad stuff that can be harmful to you and your baby.

- Avoid getting water in your mouth when swimming.

- If you go to an out-of-town beach and wonder why no one else is swimming, or to a lake where no one else is fishing, ask why! Beaches and lakes are sometimes closed to swimmers (and other activities) due to high bacteria counts.

- Avoid drinking fresh water from lakes, rivers etc, unless you have a way to clean and filter it.

- Don't eat any fish or shellfish that you (or others) have caught until you check local consumption advisories, which should be posted.

Fishing And Shellfish Harvesting Advisories

Coastal States typically have a shellfish hotline and website to advise the public of biotoxins or algae blooms, and to advise of current shellfish harvesting status. Check your State's Department of Fish and Wildlife.

- US advisories: water.epa.gov/scitech/swguidance/fishshellfish/fishadvisories/general.cfm#goto

- Canadian advisories: www.ec.gc.ca/mercure-mercury/default.asp?lang=En&n=DCBE5083-1

Food Safety

Follow these four basic food safety guidelines and you'll be good to go:

- Clean

- Separate

- Cook

- Chill

Clean

Keeping clean applies to your hands but also many areas in your kitchen and house that are breeding grounds for the "bad bugs".

Hands

While it sounds like common sense, hand washing (especially in the kitchen) is the most important habit to keep you well during pregnancy. Wash your hands in warm, soapy water before preparing food and when you touch raw eggs, fish, meat etc, and after using the bathroom, blowing your nose, petting the dog or cat, changing a diaper, etc. How long does it take to adequately scrub away germs? Twenty seconds, or about the time it takes to sing two verses of "Happy Birthday"—in any language. Make sure to use a nail brush to get the neglected part of your nails clean (which are a magnet for dirt and bacteria.) Wash hand towels regularly. When having a picnic or serving an outdoor buffet, keep alcohol based gel handy! Consider using disposable gloves when handling raw meat, chicken, seafood etc.

Sponges, Dishrags, Towels

Did you know? You may be spreading more germs that you're wiping away with your sponge. For this reason, wash sponges and dishrags often and don't use them to wipe up raw egg or juices from raw chicken, etc.—UNLESS you immediately put it in the laundry basket. (I'm all about using disposable things as little as possible, but when it comes to cleaning up I don't hesitate to use a paper towel!) To keep your sponges clean, put them in the dishwasher or microwave it (when wet) for at least 30 seconds.[95] And wash those brushes used to clean dishes, the sink, or veggies too!

The Sink and Garbage Disposer

Quick—where do the most bacteria live in a typical home? The kitchen sink—yuck! Scrub your sink frequently and then toss the brush or sponge in the dishwasher. You can tell by the smell that the garbage disposer is not the cleanest place either—and sometimes the water from there will splash an unlucky bystander. Keep it clean by sprinkling baking soda (or hydrogen peroxide) down the drain occasionally. I also like to put ice and small pieces of citrus peel to "exfoliate" and keep it smelling fresh.

Sanitizing Solution

♦ To Sanitize Surfaces and Utensils that Come into Contact with Food: Mix 1 teaspoon (5 ml) unscented liquid chlorine bleach + 4 cups (1 liter) water: wipe with solution (or soak). Let stand 2 minutes. Air dry.

♦ To Sanitize Sinks, Toilets and other Non-Porous Surfaces: Mix 1.5 tablespoon (25 ml) unscented liquid chlorine bleach + 4 cups water. Wipe with solution. Let stand 5 minutes. Rinse and air dry.

Produce

Most people associate food poisoning outbreaks with potato salad, chicken or undercooked ground beef. However, raw produce has recently become a major cause of food-borne illnesses—either because it was contaminated somewhere between the field and the market, or it was not cleaned or stored properly once prepared. I'm not suggesting that you cut back on eating produce—you just need to be a bit more careful in how you take care of it! Cleaning your produce is beneficial for two reasons: it removes pesticides and helps remove some bad bugs too. Picking it carefully helps too. When possible, buy lettuce and other produce pre-packaged—I always wonder how many people with dirty hands have picked through and touched all the produce before I get to it!

♦ At a minimum, rinse all fresh produce under tap water at least thirty seconds.

♦ Use a produce brush to clean the skin of firm vegetables and fruits. The mechanical action of rubbing the produce under tap water is an important step in removing pesticide residues and bacteria.

♦ Wash all produce, even if you intend to peel it or cook it.

♦ Soaking followed by rinsing appears to be the best way to decrease bacteria.

• Avoid using dish detergent (or bleach solutions) on produce—they leave their own chemical residues and fragrances.

• Wash your vegetable brush in the dishwasher after using or soak in a bleach or vinegar solution and rinse.

Refrigerator

Clean up all spills in your refrigerator right away with paper towel—especially juices from hot dog and lunch-meat packages, raw meats, poultry and seafood. Follow with some sanitizing solution or a disinfectant wipe.

Clean the inside walls and shelves of your refrigerator regularly with hot water and soap, then wipe clean. Use a sanitizing solution if necessary.

Utensils and Cutting Boards

Wash or sanitize utensils between using for raw meats etc. and ready-to-eat food. This is especially an issue when putting raw food on the grill and taking the cooked meat off—don't use the same utensil!

Sanitize cutting boards in the dishwasher or with a bleach solution. Wooden boards can be sanitized with hydrogen peroxide or by microwaving.

What about Produce Washes?

A study at the University of Tennessee found that soaking in water and rinsing, using a commercial veggie wash or a 1:3 ratio vinegar-water solution were all just as effective at getting rid of bacteria on fresh produce.[96] Another study found that a vinegar-water solution killed most bacteria and viruses on produce.[97] For most fruits and veggies, give a few squirts of the solution, rub for 30 seconds and rinse. For leafy vegetables, immerse in the solution briefly and for foods like broccoli or cauliflower, soak for 2 minutes, then rinse well. The bottom line is, veggie washes are about as effective as soaking with water and rinsing but a homemade vinegar solution seems to work a little better.

Separate

At every step of the food-handling process—from the grocery store to the table, make sure to keep meats and poultry separate from ready-to-eat foods and produce.

♦ When packing your groceries, take care to put produce and raw meats in different bags. In the refrigerator, make sure the juices from raw animal products, deli meats, or hot dogs can't come into contact with fresh produce or other ready-to-eat foods.

♦ If you're using earth-friendly reusable bags to carry raw meats home from the grocery, wash them between uses—they could spread food-borne bacteria to other foods. Or make an exception and use disposable plastic bags only for raw meats, seafood and poultry.

♦ It's best to have a cutting board designated for raw meats, and one for produce; it's easy to keep track of that way—perhaps green for produce and red for raw meats. If not, make sure to wash your cutting board in the dishwasher or sanitize with a bleach solution before using it for produce and other foods you don't plan to cook.

For a full discussion on which type of cutting board is best—and how to sanitize them, see page 359.

Cook

When is it done? When the thermometer says so. Except for shellfish and eggs, you should never judge a food's doneness just by its color. This is especially true for ground meat, which often looks "done" before it is cooked thoroughly. But how to best "take" your food's temperature? Check out this guide: www.fsis.usda.gov/fact_sheets/Kitchen_Thermometers/index.asp#12

Note that Health Canada recommends higher internal temperature of 160° F (71° C) for ALL pork.[98]

Other Foods: Yes—it's a bit awkward to stick that food thermometer in your poached

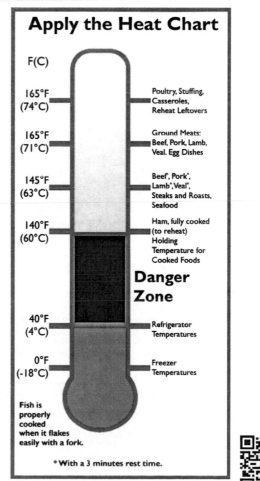

Apply the Heat Chart

F(C)	
165°F (74°C)	Poultry, Stuffing, Casseroles, Reheat Leftovers
165°F (71°C)	Ground Meats: Beef, Pork, Lamb, Veal. Egg Dishes
145°F (63°C)	Beef*, Pork*, Lamb*, Veal*, Steaks and Roasts, Seafood
140°F (60°C)	Ham, fully cooked (to reheat) Holding Temperature for Cooked Foods
	Danger Zone
40°F (4°C)	Refrigerator Temperatures
0°F (-18°C)	Freezer Temperatures

Fish is properly cooked when it flakes easily with a fork.

*With a 3 minutes rest time.

Source: www.fda.gov

egg or your steamed mussel, so for those foods, it's *OK* not to use temperature to find out if it's "done." Here are tips for similar foods:

♦ Eggs: Cook until yolk and white are firm (over hard or hard cooked)

♦ Shrimp, lobsters and crab: Cook until flesh is pearly and opaque

♦ Clams, oysters and mussels: Cook until shells open during cooking. (Discard any that don't open—this means they were not alive to begin with.)

♦ Scallops: Cook until flesh is milky white or opaque and firm.

♦ Deli meats: until steaming

Cookware

Did you know that what you cook your food in is as important as how you cook it? Let's explore all the options to see which cookware is safest to use while pregnant and breastfeeding.[99]

Best:
♦ Cast iron
♦ Glass
♦ Anodized aluminum (also non-stick and scratch resistant)
♦ Earth-friendly nonstick without perfluorooctanoic acid (PFOA) or polytetrafluoroethylene (PTFE)
Very Good:
♦ Enamelware: Contains a baked on enamel coating over either cast iron (Le Creuset) or steel (Crow Canyon or Golden Rabbit). In the US and Canada, the coating is not allowed to contain lead or cadmium. The coating can chip if exposed to drastic temperature changes or metal utensils. Avoid using if chipped.
♦ Stainless steel: storing acidic foods like tomato sauce can increase leaching of metal
♦ Silicone—It can melt above 428°F (220°C)
Good, but:
♦ Aluminum: may leach too much aluminum, especially if used to store acidic foods.
♦ Copper: can leach copper into food, unless coated. However, small amounts of the coating can leach when exposed to acidic foods during long cooking or storage times.

◆ Traditional Non-stick: Can release toxic gases when heated to high temperatures. Questions surrounding the use of non-stick coating revolve around the possible health risks of perfluorooctanoic acid (PFOA), a chemical used in the production of nonstick cookware. However, Consumer Reports found very little PFOA in the air samples taken with new pans and hardly measurable levels among pans that had been used repeatedly.[100]

Avoid if possible:

◆ Plastic: can migrate into food during cooking and storage. If you must use it, use only those labeled "microwave safe" and avoid using plastic with recycling code 3, 6 or 7 or that is visibly damaged, scratched, melted or that smells bad.

Traditional Nonstick Pans

If you're like me, you've got some traditional nonstick pans that you may not want to toss. It may be comforting to know that Teflon itself is completely nontoxic and passes through the body unchanged if ingested. The main problem is that when it's heated to high temperatures, it can emit toxic fumes. If you want to continue to use nonstick, then use these tips to make cooking safer.

◆ Never pre-heat a pan on high, especially when empty.

◆ Cook at the lowest temperatures possible; if your oil is smoking, it's too hot!

◆ Never use a non-stick pan in the oven over 500°F (260°C).

◆ Keep the exhaust fan running.

◆ Never use non-stick pans that are already scratched.

Green Cookware?

Some cookware have various "green" claims—such as using more energy-efficient manufacturing methods or featuring coatings that don't use petroleum-based products like PFOA or PTFE. These include Manpan, ScanPan, Cuisinart Green Gourmet, Starfrit Alternative and EarthPan. EarthPan Hard Anodized Aluminum pans received a Consumer Reports Best Buy rating—which means you won't break the bank when purchasing a set.[101]

Microwave Cooking

I'd be lost without my microwave! But while they're great timesavers, microwaves can be tricky when it comes to food safety, because food doesn't cook evenly and because cooking with plastic is common. Follow these tips for safer cooking in the microwave:

♦ Choose only microwave-safe containers—glass, ceramic or Pyrex is best.

♦ Plastic wrap sure is convenient; the trapped steam helps regulate the food's temperature. If you do use plastic wrap, don't let plastic wrap touch food (especially high-fat or high-sugar foods) and keep an inch between the food and the wrap. Turn back one corner to vent excess heat.

♦ For splatter control, use a paper towel (unbleached), wax paper or (best) a reusable microwave cover.

♦ To help food cook more evenly, make sure your turntable is rotating or turn your food manually ¼ turn halfway through cooking time. Turn large pieces of food over.

♦ When arranging food on a plate, put the foods in a circle, leaving the middle empty. Placing the thinner part of a food—such as the bone of a chicken leg—facing the inside of the plate, will also help it cook thoroughly.

♦ Cook large cuts of meat on Medium (50%) instead of High (100%) power. This allows heat to reach the center without overcooking outer areas.

♦ Food continues cooking after being removed from the microwave, so let it stand for a few minutes before checking the internal temperature.

♦ Take extra care when cooking riskier foods like raw chicken or ground beef in the microwave; cooking them evenly is critical in order to kill food-borne bacteria.

♦ If you defrost food in the microwave, cook immediately to avoid the food staying at a temperature in the "danger zone."

Plastics

This chapter has probably made you think twice about using plastic for cooking and storing food. While plastic may be a big part of your cooking routine right now, consider cutting your dependence on plastic while you're pregnant, nursing and during your child-bearing years. BPA, phthalates, and other chemicals in plastic definitely migrate into food during cooking and storage, especially if the food is fatty, salty or acidic. In fact, just because a plastic is BPA-free doesn't mean it's free of other endocrine disrupting compounds (EDCs). In a recent study 90% of BPA-free plastics leached other endocrine disrupting chemicals.[102] But to be realistic, it's difficult to get completely away from using plastic in the kitchen. Here are some tips to use plastic in a way that's safer, and to move away from plastic!

Moving Towards Plastic-Free & Tips for Using Plastic Safely:

1. Start buying foods in glass jars and bottles instead of plastic. Then re-use the jars to store (and re-heat) leftovers in.
2. Gradually build up a collection of glass storage and microwave safe containers with ventable lids.
3. Microwave only in glass or ceramic.
4. If you buy food in plastic containers or buy plastic disposables, choose safer plastics: with recycling code: 1, 2, 4 & 5. Avoid #3, 6 and 7 (unless it is #7 PLA, which is safe.)
5. If you store leftovers in plastic, let them cool before placing in the container.
6. Hand wash your plastic with a mild soap; hot temperatures can break down plastic more quickly.
7. Avoid using plastic wrap if possible. But if you do, use those made with polyethylene. Saran wraps and Ziploc bags don't contain BPA, pthalates or chlorine.
8. Discard any containers that have an odd smell or look scratched or damaged; that plastic is definitely breaking down (meaning the chemicals are migrating to your food.)
9. Be on the lookout for plant-based plastic, made from corn and other starches, also called Poly Lactic Acid or PLA. It's also labeled #7 but is safe for use and biodegradable. Companies using PLA so far include Whole Foods for produce bags, Walmart for produce packaging and Stonyfield farms for multipacks of yogurt.
10. In the future look for plastic labeled "EA-free", which means the product is free from any compounds that have estrogen-like activity.

What about Freezer Storage Bags?

While I don't recommend *cooking* in plastic during pregnancy, storing in them should be fine if you use brands that are BPA free like Ziploc and FoodSaver. Although it takes a bit more time, the vacuum sealing process of FoodSaver keeps foods fresh longer in the freezer.

This chart summarizes plastic types and recycling codes:

Symbol and Recycling Code (Resin ID)	Type of Plastic	What it's Found In	Cooking / Storing Tips
1 PETE	Polyethylene terephthalate (PET or PETE)	Water and soft drink bottles, cooking oil bottles, packing trays and blisters, peanut butter jars.	Meant for one time use only. Avoid heating because it contains phthalates.
2 HDPE	High-density polyethylene (HDPE or PEHD)	Produce bags, margarine tubs, frozen dinner trays, milk jugs, yogurt containers, some disposable cups.	Safer choice for storage.
3 PVC	Polyvinyl chloride	Commercial food wraps, shampoo bottles, medical tubing, bottles for chemical storage.	Avoid. Contains phthalates.
4 LDPE	Low-density polyethylene (LDPE or PELD)	Produce bags, some food wraps, frozen food bags, grocery bags. Tops for some food storage containers.	Safer Choice.
5 PP	Polypropylene (PP)	Yogurt cups, syrup bottles, Tupperware, reusable storage containers from Glad and Ziploc, water bottles with a cloudy finish.	Safer choice.

Symbol and Recycling Code (Resin ID)	Type of Plastic	What it's Found In	Cooking / Storing Tips
6 PS	Polystyrene	Some yogurt cups, some plastic cups, meat trays, foam food containers and cups.	Avoid. Can leach styrene (a carcinogen.)
7 OTHER	Other: Includes a variety of plastics made after 1987, including Polycarbonate (PC). Also includes poly lactic acid (PLA) a plant-based plastic	Three and Five-Gallon water bottles.	Avoid PC; contains BPA. PLA is plant based and is safe.

Off-Limits Microwave Materials[103,104]

♦ Packaging trays and plastic wraps that meat and poultry are packed in (even when just defrosting)

♦ Commercial plastic wraps (these are usually available at wholesale clubs, not grocery stores)

♦ Plastic storage containers like margarine and whipped topping (Recycling code #2)

♦ Plastic storage containers with recycling code #3, #6 or #7(PC)

♦ Styrofoam cups and takeout containers

♦ Plastic or brown paper grocery bags

♦ Newspaper

Chill

It's a "no-brainer" that keeping hot foods hot and cold foods cold is important, but not doing this remains a primary cause of food poisoning. Some tips for storing food properly:

♦ Keep your refrigerator at 40°F (4° C) or lower and the freezer at 0°F (-18° C) or lower.

♦ Store leftovers in glass, ceramic or stainless-steel. If using plastic is a necessity, **don't** use plastic with a recycling code of 3 (polyvinyl chloride-PVC), 6 (Polystyrene-PS) or 7 (Polycarbonate-PC)—they may contain BPA and/or pthalates.

♦ Keep uncooked ground meat and poultry in the coldest part of your refrigerator, generally the bottom shelf. Take care that blood doesn't drip on produce or ready-to-eat foods.

♦ Don't store food or eat out of pottery with lead glaze. Hot, acidic drinks like coffee can cause lead to leach from lead-glazed mugs.

♦ Fruit juice and acidic foods can cause lead to leach from leaded crystal, so in the off-chance that you consider storing fruit salad in a crystal bowl or your orange juice in a crystal pitcher, don't!

♦ It is safe to refreeze raw food that has been thawed in the refrigerator. However, cooked foods that have been at room temperature too long should not be refrozen.

♦ When refrigerating large quantities of hot food, divide it into smaller containers so it cools more quickly

♦ Thaw food in the microwave or refrigerator—NOT ON THE KITCHEN COUNTER!

♦ Don't keep food at room temperature for more than 2 hours; 1 hour (or less) when it's hot.

♦ For parties and buffets use food warmers/chafing dishes, crock pots and electric skillets for hot foods, and nested bowls with ice or containers made for this for cold stuff.

Is it Still Good?

As a general rule, raw ground beef, seafood, sausage and poultry can be safely kept in the refrigerator 1-2 days; other meats and leftovers 3-4 days.

Scan this QR code or go to our web site www.EatingExpectantly/148, that shows how long you should store food in the refrigerator and freezer.

When Eating Away from Home

The good thing about eating out is—you're not in charge of the kitchen—but in terms of food safety, it's also the bad news. You need to trust that whoever is, follows the rules for safe food handling.

◆ Check out the environment. Skip a place if it doesn't look clean or you notice poor food-handling habits—like staff handling food while handling money (with or without gloves), eating while on the job, touching their nose or hair and then handling or serving food

◆ Ask that your food be cooked thoroughly—avoid medium rare or rare meats, ask for eggs "over hard", "hard poached" or scrambled.

◆ If your food doesn't seem like it's hot enough or appears undercooked, return it or ask that it be heated more. If cold food doesn't seem chilled enough, return it. Speak up; it's your health and that of your children you're talking about.

◆ Before you eat from a buffet or salad bar, make sure "sneeze guards" are in place and that serving utensils are long enough so that the handles (that many previous customers have touched) don't fall into the food.

◆ Remember that raw is risky; avoid any raw fish or shellfish, including raw sushi and all sashimi.

◆ Skip raw sprouts of all kinds.

◆ Forego fresh juices. The hand squeezed juices are lovely, but skip them while you're pregnant.

◆ If you plan to take leftovers home, make sure you will be able to get them to a refrigerator within 2 hours from when they were cooked (not when you left the restaurant/party). If it's warm outside, get that doggie bag to a refrigerator within one hour.

◆ If you get take-out but can't eat it right away, place in a 200°F (95°C) oven to keep it warm.

◆ In all cases, be assertive. Eating out doesn't mean you have to take food safety risks!

Around the House

Painting

You may be doing a room makeover for your baby's nursery, and that will probably involve paint. Exposure to paint fumes during the first trimester may be associated with birth defects[105], which is why historically, pregnant women were told to avoid doing the painting (or to use only latex paint and wear a mask). Now you can easily find low- or no-VOC (Volatile Organic Chemical) paints that are non-toxic and have no nauseating (or dangerous) smells.

Removing paint: Be cautious with any remodeling or paint removal. Paint containing lead was banned in the US in 1978, though it was banned in many European countries in the 1930's. However, Canada (1991) and Australia (1997) were late adopters of lead-free paint. Lead paint is not really a danger unless it's chipping off or if you're trying to remove it. In fact if it's in good condition, it's safer to cover over it! A professional who is certified or licensed in lead safety is the only person who should be stripping lead paint from your home. If not removed properly, fine lead particles can circulate throughout the home where you and your family can inhale or accidentally ingest them. For more information:

♦ www.epa.gov/lead/

♦ www.lead.org.au/lanv6n2/update005.html

Scan this QR Code for "Risk Factors for lead Exposure"[106]

Pest Control: Indoors and Out

Insecticides, pesticides and fungicides are deadly to the pests and weeds, but they can harm your family too, and your unborn baby is the most vulnerable. When animals were exposed to large doses of the common fungicide Vinclozolin, the risk of kidney disease, breast cancer and immune system abnormalities increased, and extended up to four generations later.[107] Keep your family (and future generations) safer by following these tips for healthier pest control:

♦ Exterminating: avoid pest control chemicals––both commercial and do-it-yourself—while you are pregnant, breastfeeding, or trying to get pregnant. Some pest control companies are beginning to use integrated pest management techniques, but it's important to ask them the right questions. If you must use chemicals, only spray on the perimeter of your house, not inside or on lawn or garden, where it can easily be tracked in. And plan to be away from home when the spraying happens.

◆ Roach control: If roaches are your pet peeve, use some integrated pest-management techniques. Observe your pests—where they come in, where they hide. Then cut off their entry access and shut down their food and water supply. Clear out old newspapers, leaf piles and other clutter where they like to nest. Put sticky tape or roach motels in heating ducts and baseboards to trap them. Boric acid is effective against roaches, and although much less toxic than pesticides, you should still keep it away from pets and children.

◆ Use common household products: They can be effective against bugs and weeds alike. Soapy water can be used on ants and aphids. Ants don't like to cross a line of chalk, cinnamon, paprika, lemon juice or soapy water. Vinegar can be used to kill weeds. Keep in mind that the non-toxic route can take more time and patience, but is worth it to the health of your family and the planet.

For more information:

◆ www.beyondpesticides.org/alternatives/factsheets/index.htm

◆ The National Pesticide Telecommunications Network is a toll-free, 24-hour information service that can be reached at 1-800-858-7378

◆ web4.audubon.org/bird/at_home/pdf/HealthierChoices.pdf

Pet Care

Pesticides used in pet care products can migrate into your home and skin. Seek less toxic ways to control fleas and ticks; find a wallet card listing safer options at www.greenpaws.org.

Cleaning

You guessed it—cleaning products are pretty toxic—hence the warning labels. A few common household products can define the "new" clean in your home—vinegar, baking soda, salt, lemon juice, borax and perhaps a touch of hydrogen peroxide. Below are a few green cleaning ideas. If you're not the mix-it-yourself type, there are many environmentally friendly cleaning products available that are made from the same ingredients. Choose a product that is Certified Green by Green Seal or EcoLogo or that meets the EPA's Design for the Environment standards or DfE. Find a searchable list of products at www.epa.gov/dfe/pubs/projects/formulat/formpart. htm#56

Johnson & Johnson Going Green

The company famous world-wide for its "No More Tears" Baby Shampoo is coming clean when it comes to environmental chemicals. They've already taken phthalates and triclosan out of all their baby products, and they're phasing out other chemicals, including some fragrances in baby and adult products. For more information: www.safetyandcarecommitment.com/commitment/faq

Green Cleaning Tips

♦ For whitening the wash: Add hydrogen peroxide as you would bleach.

♦ For grease stains on cloth: Color with white chalk. Let sit 10 minutes and then wash.

♦ For disinfecting: Hydrogen peroxide can be used full strength in the toilet, in sinks and sprayed on to kitchen counters.

♦ For scrubbing: Baking soda and a damp sponge or brush. Or mix baking soda with liquid castile soap.

♦ For stains, mildew or mineral deposits: douse or soak in vinegar or lemon juice.

♦ For windows: Mix 1 tablespoon white vinegar (or lemon juice) with a quart of water. Spray on and dry with newspaper—which provides streak-free cleaning.

♦ To freshen rugs: sprinkle baking soda or cornstarch—about 1 cup (250 ml) for a medium sized rug. Let stand half an hour, and then vacuum.

♦ Wood floors: Mix ¼ cup (65 ml) of white vinegar with 30 oz. (930 ml) warm water.

♦ Oven cleaning: You don't need a gas mask to use this homemade remedy: make a paste of baking soda and water. Coat the inside of your oven with it and let stand overnight. Remove with a moist cloth.

For more tips: idahopublichealth.com/environment/files/healthy-homes.pdf

Nontoxic Disinfectants: Do They Exist?

Baking soda and vinegar have both been touted as adequate household "disinfectants." One study done at the University of North Carolina compared commercial disinfectants; bleach solution, vinegar and baking soda and their ability to kill various bacteria and viruses. Vinegar was effective at killing *Salmonella* bacteria, but it failed at getting rid of *Staph* or *E coli*. Baking soda was only mildly effective at getting rid of *Salmonella*. The researchers concluded that baking soda and vinegar should not be counted on as household disinfectants.[108]

Celebrity Eco-Products

Celebrities around the globe are jumping on the bandwagon for better-for-you-and-the-planet products. One company I'm sold on is The Honest Company, a firm that actress and mom Jessica Alba started "to help moms and give all children a better, safer start." The products, which range from diapers and diaper wipes to facial moisturizers, sunscreen and dish soap, don't contain phthalates, sodium lauryl/laureth sulfates, PVC, parabens, benzene, chlorine, synthetic fragrances and a long list of other "nasties." Check it out at www.honest.com

Hydrogen peroxide is an effective disinfectant and is non-toxic—however, it is more effective at killing germs when used at a stronger concentration than is available at your grocery.[109] You can add it to your white wash instead of bleach. In fact, look for new cleaning products on the market that substitute hydrogen peroxide instead of bleach. The nice thing is you don't need to wear gloves when using them!

The bottom line: Avoid traditional cleaners as much as possible. However, when it comes to killing germs in the kitchen or bathroom, sometimes you do need to resort to a light bleach solution or other disinfectant.

Beauty Care

Smelling Good: Fragrance

Women (and men) around the world like things with fragrance, be it hand lotion, shaving cream, deodorant, lipstick or shampoo. We even put air fresheners in our cars and offices. The problem: fragrance means added chemicals—often hormone-disrupting phthalates like diethyl phthalate (DEP). Phthalates are thought to affect development of the male reproductive system. The Campaign for Safe Cosmetics found DEP in 70% of fragrance products tested in 2010.[110] According to the European Union's Scientific Committee on Cosmetic Products and Non-food Products, up to 1 in every 33 people is allergic to fragrance.[111] These fragrance allergens can cause and trigger asthma attacks. In Europe, potential fragrance allergens must be listed on the label; in the US, fragrance ingredients are considered a "trade secret" and labeling is not required.

Tips for Kicking the Fragrance Habit

♦ Take a quick inventory of fragrances in your home—you'll probably find at least a hundred. Decide which ones you can do without.

♦ Do your best to avoid air fresheners.

- If you must use some synthetically fragranced products, choose one or two and limit/avoid the rest.

- Shop smart. Avoid products with:

  - DEP
  - DEHP (di-(2-ethylhexyl)phthalate)
  - DBP (dibutyl phthalate)
  - BBP (benzyl butyl phthalate)

  In Europe, DEHP, CBP and BBP are banned from use in cosmetics, due to their classification as reproductive toxicants.[112]

- Choose products with no added fragrance, fragrance-free products or those with no synthetic fragrance added. Beware of label claims, though. Recently I was happy to find a deodorant labeled "unscented", but was disappointed to find "fragrance" on the ingredient label! Use the advanced search of the Skin Deep Database (see below) to find products.

Safer Smells

To feed your love of pleasant smells, try these healthier alternatives:

- Saturate a cotton ball with vanilla, almond extract or peppermint extract and leave it in an open dish.

- Simmer cinnamon and cloves with orange slices in a pan with water. See www.theyummylife.com/Natural_Room_Scents for more ideas.

- Burn naturally scented soy or beeswax candles that don't contain a lead wick.

- While it's tempting to use essential oils and products scented with them, the safety of essential oils hasn't been adequately tested during pregnancy.

Looking Good: Cosmetics

Lead in lipstick? Yes, unfortunately. A recent FDA analysis found lead in 400 lip products tested. (Natural pigments in lipstick contain minerals, including lead.) While manufacturers claim the amount of lead you might absorb from lipstick is nothing to worry about, and the FDA agrees, we think lead in lipstick is, well—ugly! For more information www.fda.gov/Cosmetics/ProductandIngredientSafety/ProductInformation/ucm137224.htm#expanalyses

Lead in lipstick may be the tip of the iceberg, however, when it comes to chemicals in cosmetics. That's because the cosmetic industry is largely self-regulated, at least in the United States. Presently the US Food and Drug Agency has no authority to require companies to test products for safety, and it doesn't review the vast majority of products or ingredients before they go to market. In fact there are 500 products sold in the US that contain ingredients which have been banned in Japan, Canada or the European Union.[113] Because ingredients in cosmetics and hair care products can be absorbed through the skin or inhaled if in a powder or aerosol, their safety is of upmost importance, especially while you are pregnant.

How to Choose Safer Cosmetics and Beauty Products

In general, get in the habit of reading ingredient labels on cosmetic and body care products just as you would a food label. According to *Good Housekeeping*, these are 6 ingredients to avoid:

- Petrochemicals including petroleum jelly, isopropyl alcohol or isopropanol, methyl alcohol or methanol, butyl alcohol or butanol, ethyl alcohol or ethanol

- Sodium laureth/lauryl sulfates and other sulfate-based detergents

- Propylene glycol (PG) and polyethylene glycol (PEG), and ingredients formulated with PEGs and PGs

- Formaldehyde & paraben preservatives such as butylparaben, ethylparaben, methylparaben, propylparaben

- Synthetic dyes including anything with F&DC preceding it, usually followed by a color and a number, as well as color ingredients caramel, lead acetate and manganese violet

- Artificial fragrances like those in most beauty products, including your favorite cologne

Read more:

- www.thedailygreen.com/living-green/natural-beauty-cosmetics/toxic-beauty-products

- In the US: Environmental Working Group maintains the Skin Deep Database, which helps consumers check the safety of cosmetic and personal care products www.ewg.org/skindeep/. While some of the recommendations are based on limited data, a little information is better than none. Also see www.safecosmetics.org for more information.

- Around the World: In Australia, a non-government organization, Safe Cosmetics Australia, has a certification program for toxic-free personal care and household products www.safecosmeticsaustralia.com.au/. Health Canada maintains a "Hotlist" of chemicals that are restricted and prohibited from use in cosmetics www.hc-sc.gc.ca/cps-spc/cosmet-person/indust/hot-list-critique/index-eng.php.

Nanotechnology: Smaller is Not Necessarily Better

Nanotechnology involves manipulating particles to a very tiny size—less than 100 nanometers (nm). To put this in perspective, a strand of your hair is 80,000 nm in diameter. We're talking pretty small stuff, of which we don't know the dangers of yet because it hasn't been studied. Environmental groups caution that nanoparticles could cause oxidative stress and DNA mutation—they are especially worried about the effects of breathing nanoparticles, which could happen with powdered cosmetics. No governments currently regulate nanoparticles, though the European Union has noted that a review of the health effects is necessary. For now, stay away from the small stuff—anything that touts nanotechnology.[114]

Nail polish

The smell is a dead giveaway; painting your nails can involve some pretty strong and questionable chemicals including the "toxic trio" of formaldehyde, toluene and dibutyl phthalate (DBP). These chemicals top the list of concerning ingredients in cosmetics. OPI and Sally Hansen brands have removed these ingredients from their products. A recent California study found some smaller brands that advertised chemical-free claims still contained them—so buyer beware.[115] Another option is to use water-based polishes from Suncoat, Honeybee Gardens or Aquarella, which contain no solvents or phthalates.

To be on the safe side, it's best to avoid nail salons, which are often not adequately ventilated and which more than likely use brands that contain toxins. Another reason to stay away from professional manicures and pedicures—the UV drier, which expose your hands to the same cancer-causing light that you'd find in a tanning bed.

Hair Care

Most shampoos and conditioners contain some ingredients you should avoid—especially the phthalates because of fragrance. However, one ingredient released during hair straightening treatments—formaldehyde—is particularly toxic. Formaldehyde is cancer-causing, according to the National Cancer Institute. One brand—Brazilian Blowout—has received media attention for its dangerously high levels. After a warning letter from the FDA, the product is still on the market, but has a warning label. According to its Material Data Safety Sheet, the Acai Professional Smoothing Solution (Brazilian Blowout Original) is classified as a hazardous substance. Ask your salon what type of hair straightening solution they use—and stay away if it has a warning label![116]

Hair products that are in aerosol form are particularly scary because you can accidentally inhale them, as well as get them on your skin and scalp. The long list of ingredients on hair care products are hard to decipher (and too extensive to cover in this book.) The easiest thing to do is to check out the Skin Deep Cosmetics database at www.ewg.org/skindeep.

In a Nutshell: Greener Living

◆ For any product that touches your body, including lotions, sunscreen and makeup, avoid those with fragrance, triclosan, BHA, DEHP, CBP, BBP and oxybenzone.

◆ Use plastics cautiously—don't cook with them and avoid those with #3, #6 and most #7 recycling codes.

◆ Buy products with the least packaging.

◆ Use filtered water.

◆ Use greener cleaners (buy certified green.)

◆ Avoid pesticides, insecticides and herbicides in and around the home.

◆ If you must use toxic cleaners, have someone else do the cleaning or follow safety precautions like wearing gloves and opening windows.

◆ Use paint that is low- or no-VOC.

◆ Avoid air fresheners.

◆ Stay away from nail salons and choose water-based or less toxic nail polish.

◆ Choose organic produce for foods highest in pesticides and for foods you eat daily. See page 371 for more.

◆ Choose organic cotton when possible. (25% of worldwide pesticide use is for growing cotton!)

Finally, here are some resources to help you live the "green" life:

◆ National Geographic: environment.nationalgeographic.com/environment/green-guide/

◆ Green living with a UK point of view: www.greenchoices.org/

◆ Green living tips from "down under": www.livinggreener.gov.au/

7

FIRST TRIMESTER

What You'll Find:

- How Baby Is Growing

- Fueling Your Little Bump: Weight Gain and Calorie Needs

- Eating Expectantly Diet: First Trimester

- Protein Power

- First Trimester Power Nutrients

- First-Trimester Diet Challenges

Frequently Asked Questions:

- Which foods are high in protein?

- Why are antioxidants important?

- Which foods should I eat more of this trimester?

- What can I do for nausea?

- Why am I having weird cravings?

SCAN HERE FOR CHAPTER UPDATES

How Baby Is Growing

During the first three months of pregnancy, good nutrition is vital for your baby's development, but more so for the "infrastructure" that will support your baby in the womb for the next 40 weeks. Building up the placenta and the blood vessels that feed it, is "Job One" during the first trimester. The placenta is the lifeline that brings fuel and nutrients from you to your baby. Although your baby doesn't grow very much this trimester, critical development during this time makes your baby susceptible to birth defects from nutrient deficiencies, alcohol, drugs, infection and radiation. Read on to learn about the many miraculous events taking place within your body during the first trimester.

He or She? The Great Debate

What do you call your baby before you know the sex? Some hoping for a boy or a girl might call it "he" or "she". You might even slip and call the baby "it" or you might just call him "baby". In *Eating Expectantly*, however, you'll see that I chose to call all (or most) references to babies "he". Why? I have two boys of my own, so, naturally I think of fetuses and babies as "he". So for those of you hoping for or knowing you have a girl, please don't take offense!

Developmental Highlights During this Trimester: Below is a very simplified version of how your baby is growing in the first trimester.

1. **Hello! Sperm Meets Egg.** When that one well-shaped sperm, the strongest swimmer of his 250 million siblings, with the best looking tail in the bunch, enters the egg, this new cell is called a zygote. For the next 5-6 days, the zygote takes a romantic cruise up the fallopian tube to the uterus.

2. **Zygote goes cruising.** The zygote contains all the DNA (genetic info from both mom and dad) needed to make a baby. During this cruising time, the cells in the zygote divide, creating an inner group of cells with an outer shell. The inner group of cells becomes the embryo; the outer shell will become a protective membrane. This group of cells is now called a blastocyst.

3. **Blastocyst reaches the uterus.** At about day 5-6, the blastocyst reaches the uterus (also called the womb), where it sticks like glue to the lining. At this point, it's now called an embryo and it begins receiving nutrition from mom's bloodstream.

4. **Embryo divides and conquers.** The hundreds of cells that make up the embryo are multiplying and dividing as well as given specific "jobs" by the DNA. This is called differentiation. From that bundle of cells, some will become bones, others will become organs, others teeth, skin, etc. While your baby "knows" what sex he or she is, you will have to wait a few months for genital formation

Confusing Counting

When you say you are 8 weeks pregnant, it's only 6 weeks after conception! Why? "Pregnancy" is counted from the first day of your last menstrual cycle. So during the first two weeks of your "pregnancy", your body was only getting ready for a pregnancy (building up the uterine lining and such) and your baby was just a twinkle in you and your partner's eyes! The time-frames below correspond to the customary marking of the weeks of pregnancy, keeping in mind that four weeks is actually two weeks after conception!

to occur to be able to find out through ultrasound. All of this happens by week four of pregnancy (or just two weeks after fertilization.)

5. **Week Five to Week Eight: Small but Miraculous.** At just 6 weeks, your baby's neural tube, which becomes his brain and spinal cord, has formed and closed and his heart is pumping blood. Tiny arm and leg buds are visible at 6 weeks and by 8 weeks will become tiny arms and legs. At the end of eight weeks, your baby is about the length of your thumbnail—about half an inch or 12 to 13 millimeters long.[1] He has facial features including eyes, a nose and upper lip. The head area makes up about half of the length of his body.

6. **Twelve Weeks: Lookin' like a Baby!** Lots of things happen this month to make your baby look more human. Eyelids develop and close to protect the developing eyes. Genitals begin to develop, and his body grows a lot in length to make his body look more proportional. His trunk straightens out a bit and his liver begins to make red blood cells. Nipples and hair follicles form. At 11 weeks, your baby is now officially called a "fetus". By 12 weeks, he is now about 2.5 inches or 63 millimeters long and only weighs about half an ounce or 14 grams—yes in 4 weeks he grew about 2 inches![2] Although your baby is tiny and you may be just starting to buy maternity clothes or adjusting your belt to the next notch, your baby's major organs are developed and functioning.

Fueling Your Little Bump: Weight Gain and Calorie Needs

Your bump is hardly visible or non-existent; so are your additional calorie needs! In the first trimester, you should gain very little to no weight—depending on your BMI. As tempting as it is to "go for it" in the food department and eat for two, don't! In fact it's recommended that you don't eat any additional calories the first trimester. You do, however, need greater amounts of vitamins and minerals—choose your foods wisely. Eat to appetite and think QUALITY—not quantity! Check out the chart on the next page. Choosing the foods in the right column will give you fewer calories and more nutrition than the foods on the left.

Instead of This:	Eat That:
Apple Pie	Fresh apple
Fried chicken sandwich	Leftover chicken breast in whole grain wrap
Cream of broccoli soup	Lentil soup
Double Burger	Caesar salad with grilled chicken and milk
French fries	Baked potato
Potato chips	Baked corn or kale chips
Ice cream sundae	Fruit & yogurt parfait
Ramen noodles	Whole grain spaghetti noodles
Iceberg lettuce salad with creamy dressing	Spinach salad with olive oil vinaigrette
Biscuit with egg	Whole grain English muffin with egg

Food Planning for the First Trimester

During the first trimester, cooking and eating can be a big challenge. If you're looking for practical, realistic menus for your eating mood, the menus below (and recipes) are found in the *Eating Expectantly Cookbook*.

Find these menus in the *Eating Expectantly Cookbook*:

♦ Don't Feel Like Eating

♦ Don't Feel Like Cooking

♦ Don't Feel Like Eating or Cooking

♦ Feel Like Staying in Bed, but Can't

♦ Feel Great

♦ Blender Breakfasts (or Snacks to Go)

♦ High-Energy Snack Ideas

Eating Expectantly Diet: First Trimester

What's the best way to eat for a healthy pregnancy? The Eating Expectantly Diet below will help you plan your meals and snacks so that you obtain the nutrients you and your baby need. It provides about 2,000 calories—you may need more, or fewer. It may be helpful to write down what you eat for a few days and compare it to the Eating Expectantly Diet. See more details of the plan in Chapter 4.

Eating Expectantly Diet: First Trimester

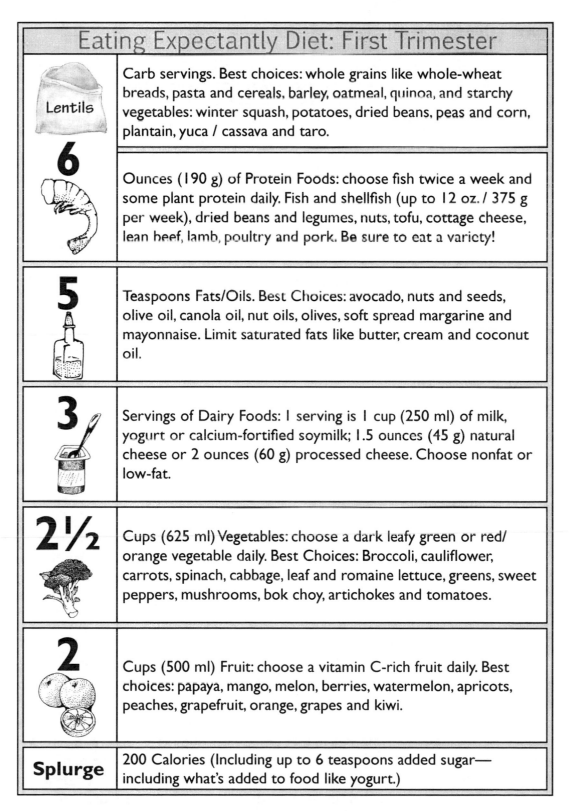

Lentils **6**	Carb servings. Best choices: whole grains like whole-wheat breads, pasta and cereals, barley, oatmeal, quinoa, and starchy vegetables: winter squash, potatoes, dried beans, peas and corn, plantain, yuca / cassava and taro.
	Ounces (190 g) of Protein Foods: choose fish twice a week and some plant protein daily. Fish and shellfish (up to 12 oz. / 375 g per week), dried beans and legumes, nuts, tofu, cottage cheese, lean beef, lamb, poultry and pork. Be sure to eat a variety!
5	Teaspoons Fats/Oils. Best Choices: avocado, nuts and seeds, olive oil, canola oil, nut oils, olives, soft spread margarine and mayonnaise. Limit saturated fats like butter, cream and coconut oil.
3	Servings of Dairy Foods: 1 serving is 1 cup (250 ml) of milk, yogurt or calcium-fortified soymilk; 1.5 ounces (45 g) natural cheese or 2 ounces (60 g) processed cheese. Choose nonfat or low-fat.
2½	Cups (625 ml) Vegetables: choose a dark leafy green or red/ orange vegetable daily. Best Choices: Broccoli, cauliflower, carrots, spinach, cabbage, leaf and romaine lettuce, greens, sweet peppers, mushrooms, bok choy, artichokes and tomatoes.
2	Cups (500 ml) Fruit: choose a vitamin C-rich fruit daily. Best choices: papaya, mango, melon, berries, watermelon, apricots, peaches, grapefruit, orange, grapes and kiwi.
Splurge	200 Calories (Including up to 6 teaspoons added sugar— including what's added to food like yogurt.)

Sample Meal Plan

In a perfect world, this is what your diet might look like in the first trimester. In reality, you may be eating very little due to morning sickness. Don't worry—you'll catch up later.

Breakfast
- Oatmeal with peaches
- Greek yogurt

Snack
- Mini Babybel light cheese
- Celery

Lunch
- Lean roast beef on a whole grain wrap with lettuce, tomato and bell pepper
- Raw carrots and broccoli with dip
- Melon balls

Snack
- Light popcorn
- Vegetable juice

Dinner
- Grilled salmon
- ½ corn on the cob
- Spinach salad with tomato and mushrooms with olive oil vinaigrette
- Fresh orange
- Low-fat milk

Snack
- 1 tablespoon Peanut butter
- Graham crackers
- Low-fat milk

Protein Power

Later in the chapter, we'll discuss the many nutrients your body needs in the first trimester. But first, let's spend some time focusing on protein. Protein is essential during pregnancy; your body uses it to build new cells for your baby. Protein is needed for the placenta—the lifeline that brings nourishment to your baby, and for new blood cells and muscle tissue that support your baby. In addition, protein is used to make all the hormones that wreak havoc in your body when you're pregnant. In the first trimester, however, your protein needs don't increase very much—so don't worry if eating meat (or anything else) is the last thing you want to do!

Protein by the Numbers

If you're into numbers, you can easily calculate the approximate amount of protein your body needs. Take your pre-pregnancy weight in pounds and divide it by half (or weight in kg and multiply by 1.1): that's the number of grams you need at a minimum. Why is that above or below the Dietary Reference Intake (DRI) of 71 grams[3]? That's because the DRI is calculated based on an average weight of 142 pounds (64.5 kg). If you weigh more or less than that your protein needs change accordingly.

Protein: Quantity and Quality

Dietary Reference Intake (DRI): 71 g

Some health care providers recommend a higher amount of protein—about 100 grams—and this is what the Eating Expectantly Diet is based on. Depending on your current diet, you may not actually need to increase your dietary protein at all—most women already eat 75-100 grams per day. See the chart below to see what a day's worth of protein might look like.

Food	Grams
Breakfast:	
Banana, 1	1
Peanut butter, 1 tablespoon	4
Low-fat milk, 1 cup (250 ml)	8
Snacks:	
Greek Yogurt, 6 oz. (190 g)	14
2 Tablespoons hummus, with baby carrots and 1 oz. (30 g) crackers	4
Lunch:	
Lentil soup, 1 cup (250 ml)	28
Grated carrot salad	1
Low-fat milk, 1 cup (250ml)	8
Snack:	
Smoothie, ½ cup (125 ml) fruit, and 1 cup (250 ml) low-fat milk	8
Dinner:	
Stir-fried shrimp, 3 oz. (95 g) and veggies	21
½ cup (125 ml) quinoa	2
Stir-fry veggie mix	2
Snack:	
2 cookies, ½ cup (125 ml) applesauce	2
Total Protein:	103

Protein Content			
Food	**Serving**	**Grams**	**% DRI**
Greek yogurt, fat-free	6 oz. (190 g)	14	20
Beans and peas	½ cup (125 ml)	8	11
Low-fat milk	1 cup (250 ml)	8	11
Aged cheese (Cheddar, Swiss, etc)	1 oz. (30 g)	7	10
Large egg	1	6	8
Meat, poultry, fish	1 oz. (30 g)	7	10
Yogurt, low-fat	6 oz. (190 g)	7	10
American cheese	1 slice (0.7 oz. / 20 g)	4	6
Bread	1 slice (1 oz. / 30 g)	3	4
Cereal	1 oz. (30 g)	3	4
Vegetables	½ cup (125 ml)	2	3
Fruits	1	1	1
Juice	½ cup (125 ml)	1	1
Fat, oil	Any	0	0

Several factors influence your body's protein needs. To enable your body to use the protein you eat for building tissues and cells, you must eat enough calories (energy). This is because your body's first priority is supplying energy. If you eat enough protein but not enough calories, your body will use the protein for energy instead of tissue building and other protein-dependent functions.

Let's say you typically eat 10 oz. (310 g) of fish and/or chicken every day. You don't have much of an appetite for much else, so this fills you up. In this scenario, your calorie intake from fats and carbohydrates is inadequate. Because your body must use the protein for energy, your body will lack the protein it needs for other important purposes.

Also, you won't have enough glucose (blood sugar) to supply your brain with energy, so your body will start breaking down fat into fragments called ketones. The presence of ketones is a sign that your body can't complete the metabolic process. Large amounts of ketones can be harmful to your body and baby. Avoid the production of ketones by getting enough calories and carbohydrates (175 grams per day) in your diet. This may be difficult if you are nauseated. Noodle soups, fruit popsicles and juice like PlumSmart, grape, pomegranate, apple or orange can provide carbs when you don't feel like eating solids.

Consuming a certain amount of protein is not the only goal. The quality of protein also affects how your body uses it. Protein needs are calculated by determining the need for high biological value—also called high-quality or complete—protein. High-quality protein can be efficiently turned into body tissues because they contain all

Eggcellent Nutrition!

For most people, there's no need to shy away from eggs. Egg protein is of the highest quality and is used as a standard to which other proteins are compared. Eggs are the most commonly-eaten source of choline, needed for your baby's brain. Research shows that eating eggs in the morning will also help you stay full until lunch—perhaps keeping you away from the snack machine!

of the Indispensable Amino Acids in adequate amounts. These proteins include eggs, seafood, meat, poultry, milk and dairy products, soy and quinoa. Other high protein foods like beans and nuts, also contain the amino acid building blocks, but are not used as efficiently because of their incomplete amino acid line-up. But don't worry; it's not a problem if you only eat plant proteins, as long as you eat a variety of them.

So, while you may not need to change the quantity of protein you're eating now, you may want to change the type of protein you eat. Eating protein from a variety of sources is important because each type provides different nutrients important for your growing baby. For example, beef is rich in iron and zinc, salmon contains DHA and eggs provide choline, while lentils and other dry beans provide zinc, iron and magnesium but also plenty of fiber.

Why You May Not Get Enough Protein

You might not be able to meet your protein needs if you:

♦ Just don't have the desire to eat protein foods.

♦ Don't drink milk or eat dairy products or don't eat other protein-rich foods like beans.

♦ Have nausea or vomiting that prevents you from eating much of anything.

If you just don't feel like eating meat, you're not alone. Most pregnant women have some food aversion; your stomach may turn at the thought of eating what used to be your favorite food. If your favorite high-protein food turns your stomach, you can eat more dairy or soy foods, which are also good sources of protein—think milk, soymilk and yogurt. Many of the women I've spoken with could tolerate eggs and cheese even if they couldn't eat meat. If you eat or drink four servings of dairy products each day, you'll be meeting ⅓ to ½ of your protein needs. If you don't, you'll need to increase protein from other sources, such as beans and nuts.

Should you supplement your diet with protein powder? Protein supplements provide an easy way to get protein if you aren't a big meat eater or if the smell of protein foods makes you nauseous in the first trimester. But—if you're able to eat a few meals a day, you shouldn't need additional protein supplements. Also, because protein supplements are marketed to athletes, they often have added vitamins, specific amino acids and even herbal supplements that might not be safe during pregnancy. Some contain acesulfame K, an artificial sweetener that the Center for Science in the Public Interest recommends avoiding. As with other products that are processed, choose the "cleanest": the fewer ingredients, the better. Nonfat dry milk powder may actually be the cleanest and safest way to add extra protein to your diet—in smoothies, mashed potatoes, scrambled eggs, etc.

First Trimester Power Nutrients

Make sure to include these important nutrients in your diet this trimester.

Water

Water is one of the most important nutrients in the first trimester—especially if you're suffering from morning sickness. Dehydration can be very serious! Water also helps digestion, which slows down in the first trimester. You need 8 to 12 cups (2 to 3 liters) of total fluid a day—including from food and liquids like milk and juice. Unsweetened coconut water can be a good choice for hydration—it's rich in potassium but does have calories and varying amounts of sodium. This averages out to about 10 cups of fluid you drink; try to drink 4 to 6 cups (1 to 1.5 liters) of filtered water a day. Of course, like everything else, a person's need for fluid varies—according to your size, your climate, and exercise habits.

Building Nutrients

Iron, vitamins B12, B6 and folic acid play key roles in cell division and growth this trimester. (For more on folate, see page 24.) Vitamin B6 has been used to help women who experience morning sickness. Manganese is needed for developing the organs used for hearing. Because of all the metabolic activity as well as development of the placenta, antioxidants like vitamin C and E, found in fruits, vegetables, whole grains and nuts are critical.

Zinc

Dietary Reference Intake (DRI): 11 mg

Zinc performs many functions in a woman's reproductive life; it's necessary for conception, for every phase of growth, and for the developing immune system. It also plays an important role as an antioxidant. Zinc even helps to ensure that your baby is not premature. Unfortunately, zinc is a mineral that women often don't get enough of. High-fiber diets can interfere with absorption of zinc. Beef and shellfish are generally rich in zinc. Women who get most of their zinc from plant-based foods may need to eat more of them because bioavailability from those foods is lower.

Zinc Content			
Food (Cooked when applicable)	Serving	mg	% DRI
Animal sources:			
Oysters, cooked	6 medium	33	300
Beef chuck arm pot roast	3 oz. (95 g)	7.4	67
Crab, Alaska King,	3 oz. (95 g)	6.5	59
Ground beef, 90% lean	3 oz. (95 g)	5.4	49
Lamb chop	3 oz. (95 g)	4.4	40
Breakfast cereal, fortified with 25% of the Daily Value for zinc	¾ cup (190 ml)	3.8	35
Lobster	3 oz. (95 g)	3.4	31
Blue crab	3 oz. (95 g)	3.2	29
Pork chops	3 oz. (95 g)	2.9	26
Chicken, dark meat	3 oz. (95 g)	2.4	22
Yogurt, lowfat	1 cup (250 ml)	1.7	15
Low-fat milk	1 cup (250 ml)	1.0	9
Plant sources:			
Baked beans	½ cup (125 ml)	2.9	26
Pumpkin seeds	1 oz. (30 g)	2.9	26
Wheat germ, plain	2 tablespoons	2.2	20
Cashews, dry roasted	1 oz. (30 g)	1.6	14
Chick peas	½ cup (125 ml)	1.3	12
Edamame	½ cup (125 ml)	1.1	10

Vitamin D

Dietary Reference Intake (DRI): 600 IU

What you eat now can have an impact on what happens in the second and third trimesters of your pregnancy. That's because your body is building a foundation now that's important to preventing problems like gestational diabetes and preeclampsia that can occur later. For example, there appears to be a link between low levels of vitamin D in early pregnancy and gestational diabetes.[4] Many women start their pregnancies deficient; it's best to have your vitamin D level checked now so it can be corrected, if needed, with a prescription level dose. There are three ways to get your D: sun exposure, food (mostly found in milk, mushrooms and salmon) or through a supplement. See page 59 for a full discussion.

Antioxidants

Simply put, an antioxidant is a nutrient that prevents damage to the body caused by oxygen—also called oxidation. When you squeeze lemon juice on apple slices or in your guacamole to prevent browning, you are preventing oxidation. While we would all agree that having oxygen in our body is a good thing, chemically speaking, it can also cause trouble when oxygen "steals" electrons, thus making it more reactive. When there are not enough antioxidants in the diet to combat the free radicals (also called reactive oxygen species or ROS for short), they can damage cell membranes and result in inflammation. In pregnancy, inflammation and oxidative stress is thought to contribute to miscarriage, preeclampsia, intrauterine growth retardation (IUGR), and premature rupture of the membranes (PROM).

An antioxidant-rich diet such as the Eating Expectantly Diet could prevent pregnancy-related problems caused by inflammation. Examples of antioxidants include vitamins C and E, folate and carotenoids such as beta carotene and lutein, as well as minerals like selenium, zinc and copper. A diet containing fruits, vegetables, nuts, lean protein and whole grains is the best way to make sure your body has all the antioxidants it needs.

Vitamin E

Dietary Reference Intake (DRI): 15 mg

Vitamin E is a fat-soluble antioxidant that protects cells from free radical damage. It's also involved in regulation of gene expression, in cell signaling and for the immune system. Most of us don't get enough; it's found primarily in nuts and seeds, oils, leafy greens and fortified cereals.

Vitamin E Content			
Food (Cooked when applicable)	Serving	mg	% DRI
Wheat germ oil	1 tablespoon	20.3	135
Sunflower seeds, dry roasted	1 oz. (30 g)	7.4	49
Almonds, dry roasted	1 oz. (30 g)	6.8	45
Sunflower oil	1 tablespoon	5.6	37
Safflower oil	1 tablespoon	4.6	31
Hazelnuts, dry roasted	1 oz. (30 g)	4.3	29
Peanut butter	2 tablespoons	2.9	19
Peanuts, dry roasted	1 oz. (30 g)	2.2	15
Olive oil	1 tablespoon	1.9	13
Spinach	½ cup (125 ml)	1.9	13

Vitamin C

Dietary Reference Intake (DRI): 85 mg

Vitamin C is important for many reasons during the first trimester. It's needed to make collagen, a structural component for blood vessels, cartilage, tendons and bones. As an antioxidant, it protects cells from oxidative damage and it also helps your body absorb more iron from plant sources. Not having enough vitamin C in the first trimester can be a problem. Women who consumed less than 70 mg of vitamin C early in pregnancy had almost twice the risk of having gestational diabetes later in pregnancy.[5] Lower vitamin C intake from food also appears to be related to preeclampsia[6], a condition which can occur in the third trimester. Eating foods—or drinking juices rich in vitamin C—is a good idea right now. See table below for good vitamin C sources.

Vitamin C Content			
Food (Cooked when applicable)	Serving	mg	% DRI
Green chile pepper-hot	1.5 oz. (45 g)	110	129
Red bell peppers, raw	½ cup (125 ml)	95	112
Guava	1 (3 oz. / 95 g)	80	94
Papaya	¼	75	88
Kiwi	1	70	82
Orange, raw	1	70	82
Black currant juice	½ cup (125 ml)	60	71
Broccoli, cooked	½ cup (125 ml)	50	59
Strawberries	½ cup (125 ml)	48	56
Orange juice, fresh	½ cup (125 ml)	62	73
Orange juice, from frozen	½ cup (125 ml)	47	55
Sweet potato	1 medium	41	48
Pineapple, fresh	½ cup (125 ml)	37	44
Grapefruit juice, from frozen	½ cup (125 ml)	36	42
Mango, fresh	½ cup (125 ml)	30	35
Kale	½ cup (125 ml)	25	29

First Trimester Diet Challenges

The challenges listed here affect or are affected by your diet.

Morning Sickness

A touch of the "queasies" may be your first clue that you're pregnant. If you have morning sickness, you may need to figure out how to survive the day before you can even think about eating. Here's some information to help you through this trying time.

Morning Sickness Myths

Despite the name, only 2% of pregnant women are said to have nausea only in the morning! Most women experience it throughout the day. Even so, in this book, we continue to propagate the myth by calling it "morning sickness", since that's the most commonly-used term for it!

♦ You are not alone. "Morning sickness", also called nausea and vomiting of pregnancy or NVP, is the most common problem in pregnancy, occurring in as many as 90 percent of women. According to the American College of Obstetrics and Gynecology, morning sickness is "clinically significant" in about 33% of women, causing them to miss work or interfere with family life and 10% need medication to control it. Up to 1% of pregnant women experience full-blown hyperemesis-gravidarum, which often results in weight loss and hospitalization.[7,8]

♦ Morning sickness may be a sign that your hormones are at a healthy level. Women with morning sickness have a lower risk of miscarriage—unless they suffer significant weight loss. Researchers believe nausea and vomiting of pregnancy is actually a protective factor against eating things that could cause birth defects.[9]

♦ According to the American College of Obstetrics & Gynecology, women who are regularly taking a multivitamin when they get pregnant are less likely to have severe nausea and vomiting.[10]

♦ While no one knows exactly what causes morning sickness, some have theorized that pregnancy hormones—specifically estrogen and human chorionic gonadotrophin (HCG)—are to blame. Heightened sense of smell has also been blamed as a potential cause.

13 Nausea Survival Tips

If morning sickness is making you miserable, the following tips may help you feel better. The first four tips are from Miriam Erick MS, RD, an international expert on morning sickness, and her book *Managing Morning Sickness*. (Bull Publishing, 2004). (www.morningsickness.net). Note: If you experience severe nausea and vomiting, consult your health care provider. Do not self-treat with medication, vitamins, or herbal supplements without your health care provider's approval.

1. Track Your Environment

Is your environment making you feel worse? Are you sensitive to noise? To light? To heat? Are you more likely to feel sick when you're tired or hungry? Do certain food tastes or textures make you feel better? Make a list of the places and situations that make you more (or less) nauseated and change your environment as needed.

2. Take the Sniff Test

You may have noticed you're a "super-smeller" now that you're pregnant. That heightened sense of smell can make any odor a trigger for nausea. It might be an unpleasant odor like your neighbor's cigarette smoke or the body odor of the person next to you on the train, or it might be a smell you normally love, like garlic, lavender or your partner's cologne. Try to identify and avoid odors you've determined that make you turn green. Experiment with smells that make you feel better.

3. Eat What Sounds Good

Sometimes it's just important to keep something down—no matter what it is. Ask yourself: "What would make me feel better? Something sweet, salty, crunchy, sour, soft, bland, or wet?" I once had a bout of morning sickness on the morning of a TV interview. What sounded good at the moment? Pretzels and diet cola. It definitely wasn't the healthiest breakfast—but after eating it, I was able to get on with my day (and my interview) and eat healthier foods afterward.

4. Drink Enough Fluids

Dehydration can be fatal, and it's the biggest danger of morning sickness. Women with severe morning sickness are often hospitalized to get IV fluids. Most pregnant women need to drink about 10 cups (2.5 liters) of fluids per day. Some women find sparkling water appealing, while others get their fluids from fruits with high water content, like watermelon, cantaloupe, and grapes. Popsicles, slushy drinks, ginger ale, gelatin, coconut water and lemonade may also be appealing. Drinking fluids between meals (35-40 minutes after solids) may also help.

Love Lemon

Both the smell and taste of lemon has been helpful to many women with morning sickness. It may be as easy as having a lemon half nearby to sniff occasionally or a sour lemon candy to suck on. For food that goes down easily, think lemon custard or a Luna LemonZest bar. When life gives you lemons (or in this case, morning sickness) make lemonade!

5. Ask About Medication

In randomized control trials, the combination of vitamin B6 (pyridoxine) and doxylamine, (an antihistamine found in Unisom Sleep Tabs) has been shown to decrease nausea and vomiting of pregnancy by 70%. The American College of Obstetrics and Gynecology (ACOG) recommends either vitamin B6 alone or the combination of B6 and Doxylamine as a first line of therapy.[11] However, it's still best to get the OK from your doctor before using any medications during pregnancy (especially during the first trimester.)

6. Think "Alternative"

Some alternative therapies can also help morning sickness. Motion sickness bands (also called Sea-Bands) have been shown to ease nausea and vomiting of pregnancy; so has acupuncture[12]. Using ginger in various forms has also been shown to help.[13] ACOG recommends you discuss any alternative therapies with your health care provider before trying, however.

7. Never Run on Empty!

Eat small, frequent meals with snacks in between to keep your stomach from emptying completely. This might mean eating a few bites of something every thirty minutes. Some women carry a box of crackers with them to keep nausea at bay.

Help From Others Who've Been There...

Try these remedies that have been helpful for other women:

◆ Eat every two hours—whether you're hungry or not.

◆ Sip on something carbonated and snack on something dry—like club soda with lime and Cheerios or ginger ale and sesame crackers.

◆ Eat candied or crystallized ginger, available at Asian grocers and natural food stores.

◆ Try something sweet, sour and salty—pretzels and lemonade.

◆ Drink ginger ale or ginger beer (not real beer). Let it go a bit flat first.

8. Chill Out!

Nausea can be stressful, especially if it disrupts your usual routine. Steering clear of additional stress can't hurt! Taking a nap—or just closing your eyes a few minutes—especially after meals, helps some women. Try to reduce sensory stimuli too—talking on the phone, loud noises, tight clothing, etc.

9. Add Some Protein, Especially at Bedtime

Research shows that protein-rich foods may have an effect on the mechanics of gastric emptying and thus can decrease the nausea of pregnancy.[14] While you may not feel like downing a full meal, consider adding some low-fat cheese to those crackers, eating some cottage cheese with fruit, adding some Greek yogurt to your smoothie or eating some lettuce wraps filled with leftover chicken. Eating balanced, protein-rich meals also helps control blood sugar; low blood sugar can be another factor that contributes to morning sickness.

10. Avoid Greasy and Spicy Foods

Such foods can aggravate nausea as well as heartburn. However, if this kind of food sounds really good to you, it's worth a try!

11. Eat in Bed

Leave something dry and salty beside your bed at night (crackers, pretzels, nuts) or have your partner bring you a snack in the morning before you get out of bed. (Now there's a fine habit to cultivate!)

12. Eat Cold Foods or Have Your Partner Do the Cooking

The look of raw meat or the smell of strong foods cooking may make you feel sick. Leave the cooking to someone else (or get healthy take-out) and use the time to take a walk or do some shopping. You might also want to eat outside when possible to get more fresh air.

13. Keep your pantry stocked for the "queasies":

♦ Fresh lemon and lemon drop candies.

♦ Greek yogurt or cottage cheese—they're cold, easy to eat and high in protein.

♦ Pasta or quinoa salad—bland and versatile. Add leftover meat or chicken and chopped cucumber.

♦ Crackers or pretzels.

♦ Homemade trail mix: Cheerios, pretzels, chocolate chips and raisins or dried cranberries.

Other First Trimester Challenges Affected by Diet

Frequent Urination

In those first few months, you might feel you're wearing a path in the carpet with all your trips to the bathroom. Having to "go a lot" may be an early hint that you're pregnant. Hormones increase blood flow to the bladder, making it more efficient. As your uterus (and baby) gets bigger, they put more pressure on the bladder: that increases the need to pee. This sensation is strongest in the first and third trimester.

◆ DON'T decrease your total fluid intake! However, if you're getting up several times during the night to urinate, you might want to slightly decrease your intake of fluids a few hours before going to bed.

◆ Sleep on your side; it may help relieve pressure on your bladder.

◆ Start doing Kegel exercises now and continue during and after your pregnancy. These exercises tone up the muscles that hold in urine—you'll appreciate that later in your pregnancy! Keeping these muscles toned during pregnancy can also help you get back in shape and heal more quickly after you have the baby. See page 326 for more information.

◆ If urination is painful, contact your health care provider. Urinary tract infections are more common during pregnancy.

Fatigue

You may feel like you could sleep for the rest of your pregnancy. During the first trimester, when your hormones are playing tag and you're "it", fatigue is common.

◆ Slow Down. Easy to say, right? Accept the fact that you need more rest and say goodbye to non-essential activities. "Just say no" to volunteer jobs, even if it means sitting on your hands when they ask for help with that project!

◆ Choose Quality Foods. While you may not be able to eat much in the first trimester due to nausea, when you do eat, make sure it's of good quality!

◆ Iron Up. During the first trimester, your health care provider will probably check the amount of iron in your blood. Iron-deficiency anemia can cause fatigue and is fairly common in pregnancy due to the greatly increased need for this mineral. If you're up to it, take your prenatal vitamin daily. This will help close any nutrient gaps (including iron.) See page 187 for good sources of iron.

◆ Get Moving. Even though you may not feel you have the energy to exercise, moving more will make you feel more energetic. (See Chapter 14: Fitting Fitness In.)

Cravings and Aversions

We've all heard stories about the husband who runs to the store in the middle of the night to get his wife a pint of Chunky Monkey ice cream—or perhaps the mom who craves pickle and banana sandwiches. What causes that "gotta have it now!" reaction during pregnancy? No one is sure exactly what causes cravings but there are some well-established theories:

◆ Dietary needs: While there is not a Dietary Recommended Intake for chocolate—yet—some cravings may signal that your body needs something. Cravings for some nonfood items like clay, starch, dirt, or ice (called pica), may signal an iron or other mineral deficiency. Taking a prenatal vitamin can fill in many mineral/vitamin gaps in your diet.

◆ Hormones: Other cravings may be due to—you guessed it—those crazy, mixed-up hormones. Altered sense of smell, which in turn changes your sense of taste, is one hormonal explanation.

◆ Drop in Blood Sugar: Cravings for sweets can be explained by a drop in blood sugar, which can happen easily if you don't eat often enough, or you skip meals. In this case, your body needs any carbohydrate food and you may, for example, turn the need into a craving for your favorite high-carbohydrate food, such as ice cream. Cravings for salty foods could signal a need for a little extra sodium because of increasing blood volume.

Cravings can often be healthy. I'm generally not a grapefruit eater, but when pregnant with my second child, I frequently craved grapefruit. I also often wanted a "stick-to-your-ribs" food like a bean burrito or steak. This may have been due to the need for more calories, protein or iron.

What about favorite foods that are suddenly not appealing?

Aversions to certain foods are just as common as cravings, so don't be surprised if your favorite food now turns you off. Sometimes an aversion (to coffee or alcohol, for example) acts to protect your baby. Other aversions are harder to explain. To some women, meat may be unappealing during pregnancy, while eggs, cheese, milk, and beans sound great. (See Chapter 10 for vegetarian eating tips.) Some "almost vegetarians" are surprised when they crave burgers and pork roast! Whatever your particular fancy, rest assured it will probably change during your pregnancy and may be different during your next pregnancy!

Cravings By the Numbers

According to a survey done by babycenter.com, 40% of moms craved something sweet, 33% said "give me salty" and 17% said "picante please". Ten percent craved something sour. [15]

Here are some ways to manage your cravings and aversions:

♦ Keep a Schedule: To keep cravings in check, make sure to eat regular meals and snacks, including a high-protein breakfast.

♦ Eat Small Portions: Gotta have chocolate? Have a chocolate kiss or a few M&M's instead of the whole chocolate bar.

♦ Give Your Craving a Health Halo: Turn your unhealthy craving into something a bit healthier. Want a strawberry cheese Danish? Try low-fat strawberry cream cheese on whole wheat toast. Want a milkshake? Try a fruit smoothie instead. No matter how strong your craving for raw meat, poultry, or fish, cookie dough or other foods that pose food safety hazards, avoid them!

Channel Your Cravings

Hungry for something sweet, or salty, but not sure exactly what? The list below will help you find a healthy option to fit what you crave.

Sweet:

♦ Frozen grapes or bananas

♦ Fruit or chocolate smoothie (recipe in *Eating Expectantly Cookbook*)

♦ Low-fat ice cream or frozen yogurt

♦ Dried raisins or cranberries

♦ Dates & dried plums

♦ 100-calorie packs of cookies

♦ Fruit crisp (recipe in *Eating Expectantly Cookbook*)

♦ Lychee fruit

♦ Mango

♦ Melon

Salty/Savory:

♦ Nuts

♦ Corn Nuts (Original)

♦ Cheese

♦ Tomato or V8 Juice

♦ Baked or regular tortilla chips

♦ Flat bread with sesame seeds

♦ Soy nuts

♦ Anchovies/Sardines

♦ Olives

- Olive tapenade on crackers
- Light popcorn
- Air popped popcorn sprinkled with nutritional yeast
- Edamame with soy sauce

Creamy:

- Greek yogurt
- Dannon Activia yogurt
- Peanut, cashew or almond butter
- Canned low-fat refried beans
- Mashed potatoes
- Guacamole or mashed avocado
- Oatmeal
- Banana
- Fruit smoothie
- Tapioca pudding
- Creamy bean soup (recipe in *Eating Expectantly Cookbook*)
- Creamy butternut squash soup (recipe in *Eating Expectantly Cookbook*)
- Hummus (recipe in *Eating Expectantly Cookbook*)

Juicy:

- Mango
- Orange or grapefruit
- Tangerines
- Pineapple
- Papaya
- Peaches
- Nectarines
- Ripe pear
- Fresh tomato
- Salsa
- Cherries
- Watermelon
- Cantaloupe
- Honey dew
- Grapes

Crunchy:

- Popcorn or popcorn cakes
- Apple slices
- Cucumber with a squeeze of lime
- Carrot sticks
- Caesar salad with croutons
- Celery sticks
- Grated celery root (celeriac) (recipe in *Eating Expectantly Cookbook*)
- Granola & Granola bars
- Chex
- Cheerios
- Pumpkin seeds
- Sunflower seeds
- Triscuits
- Jicama with lime and/or chili powder

Tart:

- Homemade lemonade (recipe in *Eating Expectantly Cookbook*)
- Fresh pomegranate or pomegranate juice
- Kiwi
- Granny smith apple slices
- Fresh cranberry sauce (recipe in *Eating Expectantly Cookbook*)
- Sour cherries
- Kumquat
- Passion fruit
- Plums
- Dried apricots
- Guava

Teeth and Gum Changes

Hormones and increased blood flow affect many areas of your body, including your gums. They can soften, swell and become more prone to infections. Gum disease is also called periodontal disease and if severe, may increase your odds of having a preterm birth![16]

Mild gum disease, called gingivitis, causes the gums to redden, swell and bleed easily: about half of pregnant women have it. A more advanced type of gum disease, periodontitis, includes infection below the gum line which can produce toxins that create an inflammatory response. This response can affect the bone and tissue that support the tooth, leading to tooth loss. Even more dangerous, the body's response to the inflammation has been linked to preterm birth and preeclampsia[17,18], though all studies don't draw the same conclusion. Successful treatment for periodontitis appears to significantly decrease the risk of preterm birth.[19]

According to Dr. Don Callan DDS, a periodontist who researches dental bacteria, "There is definitely a relationship between preterm birth and bacterial toxins that migrate into the rest of the body, which can activate premature labor.[20]" Most dentists are also now aware of research that suggests that harmful bacteria under the gum line can actually damage the heart, increase symptoms of rheumatoid arthritis and damage artificial joints.[21]

These factors increase risk of gum disease[22]:

♦ Smoking

♦ Poor Diet

♦ Plaque

♦ Hormonal changes: pregnancy, puberty, menopause

♦ Diabetes (there is some evidence that uncontrolled gum disease can actually lead to diabetes.)

♦ Stress

♦ Genetics

♦ Clenching or grinding of teeth

♦ Obesity

Here are some tips for taking care of your teeth:

♦ Have a dental checkup and cleaning now if you didn't see the dentist before pregnancy. If treatment is needed, your dentist may postpone it until your second trimester. Make sure your dentist knows that you're pregnant before your visit.

♦ Rinsing with an alcohol-free, over-the-counter mouth rinse containing 0.05% sodium fluoride once a day or 0.02% sodium fluoride rinse twice a day is suggested to help reduce plaque levels and help promote enamel remineralization.[23]

♦ Brush after every meal or snack. If that's not possible, chew sugar-free or xylitol containing gum. Chewing for at least 20 minutes has been shown to prevent tooth decay. Sugar-free gums which decrease the actions that cause tooth decay receive The American Dental Association's Seal of Acceptance. Wrigley's Orbit & Extra, Trident, Stride and Dentyne Ice all have the ADA's Seal of Acceptance.

- If you are vomiting frequently, rinse your mouth with a cup of water mixed with a teaspoon of baking soda and wait an hour before brushing teeth to prevent dental erosion.[24]

- Floss daily. Flossing decreases the amount of bacterial plaque in the mouth, thus decreasing the risk of gum disease. If you have any symptoms of gum disease, such as red, bleeding or swollen gums, receding gums or loose teeth, see your dentist immediately!

- Control blood sugar. If you have diabetes or have a history of gestational diabetes, keeping blood sugar in normal ranges will help prevent gum disease.

- Eat a Tooth Friendly diet. Good nutrition is the first defense against gum disease, so follow the Eating Expectantly Diet with emphasis on dairy and getting enough antioxidants like vitamin C and beta carotene. People who eat dairy foods, including fermented dairy food like yogurt, Yakult, acidophilus milk or kefir, appear to have a lower risk of periodontal disease.[25]

- Eat more whole grains. In a recent study, eating three whole grains a day lowered the risk of gum disease by 23% compared to those that ate less than ½ serving a day.[26]

- Take care when eating cavity-promoting foods; brush or rinse after consuming these:

  - Donuts, potato chips, crackers, cookies, sweetened cereal and similar starchy foods
  - Acidic, sweet drinks like lemonade, sports drinks and cola
  - Sticky sweet foods like caramel, fruit chews and dried fruit

- Eat tooth-friendly snacks such as cheese, nuts and raw vegetables.

Yes to Yakult for Oral Health

Research over the last few years has shown that fermented dairy foods appear to decrease plaque and the risk of periodontal disease.[27] The most recent study, conducted in Germany, tracked a group of people who drank Yakult (a probiotic dairy drink) on a daily basis for 28 days. During the second half of the study, participants did not brush their teeth for 14 days! Plaque index, gingival index and bleeding upon probing the gums was significantly lower in the study group than in the control group, which drank no probiotic drink.[28] The probiotic bacteria are thought to be responsible for the decrease in plaque production.

8

SECOND TRIMESTER

What You'll Find:

♦ How Baby Is Growing

♦ Feeding Your Bump: Weight Gain and Calorie Needs

♦ Eating Expectantly Diet: Second Trimester

♦ Second Trimester Power Nutrients

♦ Focus on Fruits and Vegetables

♦ Choosy Mothers Snack Smart!

♦ Healthier Travel

♦ Second-Trimester Diet Challenges

Frequently Asked Questions:

♦ How much water should I drink?

♦ How many extra calories do I need this trimester?

♦ How can I get enough calcium if I'm lactose intolerant?

♦ How can I possibly eat more fiber?

♦ What are some healthy snacks?

SCAN HERE FOR CHAPTER UPDATES

You've made it through the first trimester—congratulations! The second trimester includes the thirteenth through the twenty-sixth week and it's usually when women feel their best. (Some women continue to have nausea for a few more weeks.) During this time you'll have more energy, especially if you're eating right and exercising. You'll mark the halfway point of your pregnancy and you'll feel your baby move!

How Baby Is Growing

The development of all the major organs and systems is either started or complete. From now on, your baby (and you) will start to gain more weight. Drink up! Hydration is important as you are building your blood supply and to make sure there is enough amniotic fluid for your baby. Try to drink 10 cups (2.5 liters) of fluid per day with most of that coming from water. Continue to keep caffeine to a minimum. As your baby feels more "real" this trimester, let that be a reminder that he depends on you for everything he needs to grow and develop properly, so continue following the Eating Expectantly Diet, which is slightly different for the second and third trimesters.

Developmental Highlights During this Trimester: Below is a very simplified version of how your baby is growing.

1. **At the End of Sixteen Weeks (Four Months):** Baby's movements are more coordinated. Your baby is quite active, and kicking, though you can't feel him yet. He's making facial expressions, swallowing—and even urinating! He starts to develop sucking and swallowing reflexes and may even suck his thumb. His gender becomes apparent this month and he is developing a scalp pattern. His arms have almost reached their final length and bones are forming in his arms and legs. He is growing toenails. He may be 4½ inches[1] or 11 centimeters head to bottom and weighs 3½ ounces[2] or 110 grams—about the size of half a small banana.

2. **At the End of Twenty Weeks (Five Months):** He can hear you; you can feel him move! A growth spurt has occurred this month and as he increases his fat stores, your baby doubles in size. Your baby now measures a little over 6 inches long from head to bottom, and may weigh about 10½ ounces or 315 grams.[3] If you stretched his legs out, he might measure 10 inches or 25 centimeters long! Eyebrows and eyelashes are developing. He's also listening in on your body functions—he can hear your heart beat, the blood in your arteries go wooshing by and your stomach growling, too! A greasy, cheesy covering called vernix covers the skin on his body to protect it from amniotic fluid. Something exciting happens at around twenty weeks—you feel your baby move! (If this is your first pregnancy, it may be closer to 25 weeks.) This is also called "quickening." You baby's muscles are developing and his acrobatic skills are improving; he's turning and rolling like a little gymnast.

3. **At the End of Twenty-Four Weeks (Six Months):** Your baby has hair! Baby is now about 8 inches long or 20 centimeters from head to bottom and weighs about 1⅓ pounds[4] or 600 grams. As your baby begins putting on weight, so will you. The skin on your tummy may begin to feel dry as it stretches to accommodate baby.

Baby is covered with a downy like hair called lanugo—but he also has visible hair on his head and his eyebrows might be visible too! You may find that your baby responds if there is a loud, sudden noise; he can now hear what's on the "outside." Your baby's distinct fingerprints and footprints are formed—and he also has fingernails. (Even identical twins have different fingerprints.)

For boys, the testes begin to descend from the abdomen; for girls, the uterus and ovaries are in place—and they have a lifetime supply of eggs! Taste buds begin to form on your baby's tongue. Did you know that now he may be able to taste some flavors of the food you eat? Eat your veggies and he might too (later)! Don't worry about eating spicy foods, as long as they don't bother you!

Feeding Your Bump: Weight Gain and Calorie Needs

During the second trimester, if you are aiming for a 25-35 pound (11-16 kg) weight gain, you need about 340 extra calories per day—the goal for BMIs in the "normal range." Many things affect your energy needs, including your pre-pregnant weight, your weight gain goal, and how active or inactive you are. Some women are less active; others become more active and need even more calories. You may be in "catch-up" eating mode if you're recovering from nausea from the first trimester. Follow the calorie and weight gain chart on page 183, based on your BMI. The best way to know how much to eat—follow your appetite!

Be Choosy About Calories. Now is the time you may be tempted to "eat for two." But consider that the extra calories you need—350 calories (more or less)—are really not many. And you've got to pack lots of nutrition into those calories because you need larger amounts of almost all nutrients. If you are picky about what you put on your plate, the extra calories will add up to a few extra ounces of protein, an extra serving of whole grain bread or potato and a few more fruits and vegetables. While big splurges should be kept to a minimum, the Eating Expectantly Diet has a 200 calorie "splurge" account that can be used for added sugar and fat.

Eating Expectantly Diet: Second Trimester

Below is a quick and easy guide to the number of foods from each food group you should try to eat.

Eating Expectantly Diet: Second Trimester

9	Carb servings. Best choices: whole grains like whole-wheat breads, pasta and cereals, barley, oatmeal, quinoa, and starchy vegetables: winter squash, potatoes, dried beans, peas and corn, plantain, yuca / cassava and taro.
7	Ounces (220 g) of Protein Foods: choose fish twice a week and some plant protein daily. Fish and shellfish (up to 12 oz. / 375 g per week), dried beans and legumes, nuts, tofu, cottage cheese, lean beef, lamb, poultry and pork. Be sure to eat a variety!
	Teaspoons Fats/Oils. Best Choices: avocado, nuts and seeds, olive oil, canola oil, nut oils, olives, soft spread margarine and mayonnaise. Limit saturated fats like butter, cream and coconut oil.
3	Servings of Dairy Foods: 1 serving is 1 cup (250 ml) of milk, yogurt or calcium-fortified soymilk; 1.5 ounces (45 g) natural cheese or 2 ounces (60 g) processed cheese. Choose nonfat or low-fat.
	Cups (750 ml) Vegetables: choose a dark leafy green or red/orange vegetable daily. Best Choices: Broccoli, cauliflower, carrots, spinach, cabbage, leaf and romaine lettuce, greens, sweet peppers, mushrooms, bok choy, artichokes and tomatoes.
2	Cups (500 ml) Fruit: choose a vitamin C-rich fruit daily. Best choices: papaya, mango, melon, berries, watermelon, apricots, peaches, grapefruit, orange, grapes and kiwi.
Splurge	200 Calories (Including up to 6 teaspoons added sugar—including what's added to food like yogurt.)

How do "Pounds" Translate into "Calories?"

Most recommendations for additional daily calories needed during pregnancy are based on "normal" weight women with a recommended weight gain of 25-35 pounds (11-14 kg). The truth is, many women don't start their pregnancies at a "normal" BMI. The chart below calculates extra calorie needs based on specific weight gains—as warranted by your pre-pregnancy weight or recommended by your health care provider

No one expects you to count calories while you are pregnant—it's best to follow your appetite—and if you want specific advice on how much food to eat, follow one of the Eating Expectantly Diets. But it helps to know the numbers so that you don't splurge too often on high-calorie foods just because you're sporting a big baby bump!

How Many Extra Calories Do You Need?[5]			
Pre-Pregnancy BMI	**BMI Category**	**Recommended Average Weekly Weight Gain**	**Extra Calories per Day**
<18.5	Underweight	1.2 lb. (0.55 kg)	450
18.5-24.9	Normal weight	1 lb. (0.45 kg)	350
25-29.9	Overweight	0.6 lb. (0.3 kg)	210
>30	Obese	0.5 lb. (0.2 kg)	175

How's Your Diet?

Feeling your baby move is a reminder that during these months a healthy lifestyle and good nutrition is Job One. Now is a good time to take inventory of your diet and health habits. See the following survey to find out how your diet compares with the dietary needs of a mom-to-be.

First write down in the appropriate food group everything you've eaten during the last day (or on a typical day) and tally them up. Compare to the Eating Expectantly Diet goal and see how you did.

	Carbs	Protein	Dairy	Vegetable	Fruit	Fats / Oils	Splurge
Breakfast							
Snack							
Lunch							
Snack							
Dinner							
Snack							
Total:							
EE Diet Goals:	9 servings	7 oz. (220 g)	3 cups (750 ml)	3 cups (750 ml)	2 cups (500 ml)	7 tsp	200 calories

How Did You Do: Great! Good! Fair. Oops...

Food-Planning for the Second Trimester

Most women feel their best during the second trimester. Your appetite may be robust, and you may feel like spending more time in the kitchen. The menus listed below and detailed in the *Eating Expectantly Cookbook* are a bit heavier than those I've recommended for the first trimester, and some of the recipes require more prep time.

Find these menus in the *Eating Expectantly Cookbook*:

◆ A Month of Breakfast Ideas

◆ Menus for a Hungry Appetite

◆ I Could Cook All Day

◆ Company's Coming!

Here is a sample day's menu for the second trimester:

Breakfast

◆ Bran flakes with ½ cup (125 ml) blueberries
◆ I cup (250 ml) low-fat milk

Snack

◆ Large apple with
◆ I Tablespoon peanut butter

Lunch

◆ Grilled Chicken Sandwich
◆ Carrot sticks
◆ Caesar Side salad with lite dressing
◆ Water with lemon

Snack

◆ I hard cooked egg
◆ 10 Whole grain crackers
◆ Red pepper strips

Dinner

◆ Chili with beans
◆ Cornbread
◆ Coleslaw with pineapple
◆ Watermelon
◆ I cup skim milk or nonfat soymilk
◆ I oz. (30 g) dark chocolate

Snack

◆ I cup (250 ml) vanilla yogurt
◆ I oatmeal cookie

Lactose Intolerance

About 12% of the population has lactose intolerance[6]—but it's more common in certain ethnic groups—African Americans, Asians, Native Americans, and Hispanics. Lactose intolerance (also called lactose malabsorption), is caused by not producing enough lactase, the enzyme necessary for digesting lactose (another name for lactose is milk sugar.) The result is uncomfortable gas, stomach aches, and in some cases, diarrhea.

If you are lactose intolerant, it doesn't necessarily mean you have to say no to dairy! The U.S. National Institutes of Health (NIH) recently had a Consensus Development Conference on lactose intolerance. Some of the conclusions of the expert panel were[7]:

◆ During pregnancy, the digestion of lactose may improve temporarily.

◆ People with lactose intolerance may tolerate up to 12 grams of lactose at a time—the amount in a cup of milk or yogurt, especially when it's consumed with other foods.

◆ Some research shows that regularly consuming lactose-containing foods may increase the amount of lactose that's tolerated.

◆ People with lactose intolerance may unnecessarily avoid dairy and as a result have a diet deficient in calcium and vitamin D, which can lead to osteoporosis and other negative health outcomes.

Lactase, the enzyme that is lacking in lactose-intolerant people, can be purchased in drops (to put into milk) or in pills (to take right before drinking milk). Lactase is the ingredient in Lactaid, an over-the-counter supplement. Several brands of lactose-free milk are available: Organic Valley, Lactaid and Dairy Ease milk. If you prefer to drink milk fortified with DHA like Horizon, simply use the Lactaid drops.

In general, any factor that slows down the emptying of the stomach—food, fat and fiber—may also improve how well you tolerate milk.[8] Many of my clients say milk is no problem when used over bran cereal, or when it's whole milk. Cocoa may also improve lactose intolerance.[9]

Tips for People with Lactose Intolerance:

◆ Avoid drinking milk on an empty stomach; have it with food instead.

◆ Drink small portions of no more than one cup at a time.

◆ Try naturally low-lactose options: buttermilk, sweet acidophilus milk, aged cheese and yogurt.

- Try drinking milk with different fat contents—higher fat may improve tolerance. (But you'll need to significantly decrease the saturated fat in your diet from other sources.)

- Use a lactase enzyme supplement or use lactose-free milk.

- Try chocolate milk or hot cocoa. (If using an instant cocoa mix, make with milk if dry milk isn't listed on the ingredient list).

- If these tips don't improve your tolerance to milk, consider fortified foods or a calcium-vitamin D supplement.

Q: I can only drink chocolate milk; is that a problem?

A: The only issue with chocolate milk is the extra 55 calories per cup (250 ml) (and extra sugar) it contains. The calcium content of chocolate milk is similar to plain milk (290 milligrams vs. 309 mg per cup) and the amount of calcium absorbed from chocolate milk is similar to that absorbed from whole milk, yogurt, and cheese.[10]

Another concern you may have about drinking chocolate milk is its caffeine content. You'll be happy to know that a cup (250 ml) of chocolate milk contains only five milligrams of caffeine—or about the amount found in 6 oz. (190 ml) of decaffeinated coffee. Remember that *natural (not dutched)* cocoa has a large amount of antioxidants—so you might want to find a chocolate milk mix that contains it.

Second Trimester Power Nutrients

Iron

Dietary Reference Intake (DRI): 27 mg

Sometime between the twenty-fourth and twenty-eighth week, your health care provider will probably test your blood again for iron-deficiency anemia, a somewhat common problem during pregnancy. Because your blood volume increases up to 50%, you need 27 mg of iron per day or almost 50% more iron than you needed before you were pregnant. Most of the iron in your body is found in the hemoglobin—the oxygen-carrying protein in red blood cells. Because of that important role, iron deficiency can make you feel tired, weak, and can decrease your immune system's function. It can also affect cognitive function—which may partially explain the "brain fog" that pregnant women sometimes complain about. Iron deficiency also increases your risk of having a preterm birth and/or a low birthweight baby.

Choose the foods in the right-hand column to pump up your iron intake:

Instead of This:	Eat That:
White rice	Quinoa
Green beans	Spinach or Swiss chard
Onion dip	Hummus/White bean dip
Peanut butter	Tahini (sesame-seed butter)
Chips	Pumpkin seeds/soy nuts
Chicken breast	Chicken thigh
Juice drink	Prune juice
Caramel	Dark chocolate

Iron Enhancers and Inhibitors

Knowing a few things about iron will help improve your iron status, especially if you are anemic. The iron from animal sources (heme iron) is better absorbed than that from plant sources (non-heme iron). Because of this if you are vegetarian, you'll need about twice as much iron than nonvegetarians or about 48 mg.[11] Non-heme iron absorption is more sensitive to both enhancers and inhibitors, listed below. It's also the type of iron added to fortified foods and supplements. Pay attention to the iron enhancers and inhibitors if you're vegetarian or tend to be anemic.

Iron Enhancers

♦   Meat, poultry and fish. Combining just a small amount of animal protein with vegetarian foods will help you absorb more iron. For example, mix a small amount of natural smoked ham with your pinto beans, or slice some leftover steak into your spinach salad, add some fish to your tofu stir-fry or cook some chicken thighs in your lentil soup,.

♦   Vitamin C. Eating a food with vitamin C along with food containing iron enhances the absorption of non-heme iron. The effect is greater at the morning meal, with meals that contain whole grains or beans, and with people who are iron deficient.[12] For example, have berries on your bran cereal, have a kiwi, orange, mango, papaya, pineapple, melon, or berries for dessert after a meal, or have raw or cooked tomatoes, tomato sauce, tomato juice, broccoli, cabbage, greens, cauliflower, or bell pepper as your veggie. Or, drink a half cup of citrus juice, cranberry, blueberry, vegetable or tomato juice, or vitamin C-fortified apple juice with your meal. Check out the Eating Expectantly menus for more ideas!

♦   Cooking with an iron skillet. You can significantly increase the iron content of food by cooking in a seasoned iron skillet. Most foods will double or triple their iron content when cooked this old-fashioned way. Moist, acidic foods

Are You at Risk for Iron Deficiency Anemia?[13]

Just being pregnant increases your risk of being deficient in iron. You are even more at risk if you:

♦ Have a disease that affects nutrient absorption like Celiac or Crohn's disease.

♦ Have a history of heavy periods.

♦ Have been previously diagnosed with iron deficiency anemia.

♦ Are an athlete who does intense workouts.

♦ You are vegetarian.

like applesauce, chili and spaghetti sauce can increase their iron content by ten times or more when cooked in an iron skillet!

♦ Naturally-fermented foods. Fermented foods—which are preserved by friendly microorganisms—contain organic acids which can also help your body absorb more iron.[14] Examples include traditional soy sauce, tempeh, natto, miso, sauerkraut and sourdough bread.

Iron Inhibitors

♦ Tea and coffee. Tea and coffee (even decaf) contain tannins and polyphenols that can decrease iron absorption when drunk with meals. If you're not willing to give those up, have them between rather than with meals, or drink pregnancy-approved herbal teas, such as mint tea.

♦ Calcium. While it's equally good for you, calcium competes with iron for absorption. It's mostly a problem however, when we're talking about supplements. If you take iron supplements, don't take them with your calcium supplements or with milk. Instead, wash your iron down with some orange or other vitamin C-rich juice, which will increase rather than decrease your iron absorption.

♦ Phytates. Phytates are substances found in many Eating Expectantly Superfoods—like whole grains, dried beans, soy foods, nuts and seeds. However, foods with vitamin C counteract the action of phytate, increasing iron absorption up to 400%.[15] Using fermented soy foods like soy sauce, tempeh, natto, miso also cancels out the inhibitory effect.[16]

♦ Chronic antacid use. Use of prescription or over-the-counter medications for heartburn (which frequently contain calcium) can also decrease iron absorption, because stomach acid is needed for absorption of iron. You may need more iron in your diet, and more foods with vitamin C. Let your health care provider know if you are popping antacids frequently—she may be able to prescribe something more effective.

◆ Gastric bypass. Iron deficiency is common in women who have had a gastric bypass—especially for those who've had the Roux-en-Y procedure. The combination of bypass and increased iron needs of pregnancy can sometimes result in severe iron deficiency that requires intravenous iron replacement. Vitamin B12 and folate, necessary for the production of red blood cells, are also common deficiencies after gastric bypass.[17] Check with your health care provider for the amounts of supplemental vitamins you should be taking.

◆ Eating non-food items. Craving clay, dirt or laundry starch? This strange phenomenon called 'pica' is thought to be a result of iron deficiency, but eating them can also affect iron absorption. They may also contain heavy metals like lead that compete with iron (and aren't good for anyone.) Don't be embarrassed to mention this to your health care provider—she can help you brainstorm about possible causes/solutions.

Iron Content			
Food (Cooked when applicable)	Serving	mg	% DRI
Animal Sources:			
Mussels	3 oz. (95 g)	6	22
Beef and vegetable stew *	1 cup (250 ml)	5	19
Deer or elk	3 oz. (95 g)	4	15
Subway Steak and Cheese Sandwich	1 6" (15 cm)	3.6	13
Dark chocolate, 60-85% cocoa	1 oz. (30 g)	1.8-3.3	7-12
Wendy's Chili, small *	1 cup (250 ml)	3.2	12
Egg McMuffin	1	3	11
Small hamburger, Burger King	1	3	11
Lasagna with meat sauce, frozen	1 portion	2.5	9
Ground beef, 95% lean, or fajita meat (skirt steak)	3 oz. (95 g)	2.4	9
Spaghetti & meatballs with tomato sauce *	1 cup (250 ml)	2.3	9
Beef, top round	3 oz. (95 g)	2.3	9
Lamb loin	3 oz. (95 g)	2	7
Beef tenderloin	3 oz. (95 g)	1.5	6
Turkey leg, roasted	3 oz. (95 g)	2	7
Chicken thigh	3 oz. (95 g)	1.2	4
Pork or veal tenderloin	3 oz. (95 g)	1	4
Chicken breast	3 oz. (95 g)	1	4

Iron Content			
Food (Cooked when applicable)	Serving	mg	% DRI
Plant Sources:			
Quaker Oat Bran cold cereal	1 cup (250 ml)	13	48
Kellogg's Raisin Bran	1 cup (250 ml)	7.5	28
Soybeans, mature	½ cup (125 ml)	4.2	16
Lentils	½ cup (125 ml)	3.5	13
Blackstrap molasses	2 tablespoons	2.8	10
Edamame	½ cup (125 ml)	2.3	9
Tomato puree *	½ cup (125 ml)	2.2	8
Pumpkin seeds, roasted	1 oz. (30 g)	2.2	8
Navy, pinto, black, white, garbanzo beans	½ cup (125 ml)	2	7
Tofu, firm	½ cup (125 ml)	2	7
Spinach *	½ cup (125 ml)	2	7
Uncle Sam Cereal	¾ cup (190 ml)	1.8	7
Potato *	1 medium	1.8	7
Quinoa	½ cup (125 ml)	1.7	6
Pumpkin, canned	½ cup (125 ml)	1.7	6
McDonald's Fruit and Maple Oatmeal	1	1.5	6
Prune juice	½ cup (125 ml)	1.5	6
Whole wheat bread	2 slices	1.5	6
Soy yogurt, vanilla	6 oz. (190 g)	1.4	5

*Also contains a significant amount of vitamin C, which helps iron absorption.

Fiber

Dietary Reference Intake (DRI): 28 grams

You may not have thought much about your fiber intake until now. Hormone changes in pregnancy often increase constipation, which becomes a great motivator for learning about and respecting the power of dietary fiber. Most of us don't get enough fiber in our diet; it does a lot more than help digestion:

♦ Adequate fiber intake early in pregnancy (more than 21 grams per day) appears to reduce the risk of preeclampsia later in pregnancy. This may have something to do with its effect on cholesterol and triglyceride levels.

- Fiber-rich whole grains appear to reduce the risk of type 2 diabetes, stroke, heart disease, colorectal cancer and help with weight management. They may also decrease the risk of inflammatory bowel disease, gum disease and help improve blood pressure.

- Soluble fiber has been shown to reduce cholesterol, thus reducing the risk of heart disease.

- Fiber helps control blood sugar, which is particularly beneficial during pregnancy when increased blood sugar and diabetes is more common.

- Fiber fills you up, which makes meals more satisfying; this helps you control your weight gain during pregnancy.

- Fiber keeps your bowels moving, which can help prevent constipation and hemorrhoids.

Fiber Tips

Twenty-nine grams is the recommended daily amount of fiber during pregnancy. However, for simplicity elsewhere in the book, it's rounded to 30 grams. Following are a few simple ways to make sure you get enough fiber every day:

- Fill half your plate with fruits and vegetables—that helps get to the goal of two cups of fruit and three cups of veggies a day. For more information, go to www.fruitsandveggiesmatter.gov and ChooseMyPlate.gov.

- Choose whole-wheat bread, crackers, and pasta. The Eating Expectantly Diet recommends whole grains at every meal.

- Eat bulgur, barley, whole grain couscous or quinoa instead of white rice. If you're not a fan, gradually get used to them by mixing whole grains half and half with white rice.

- Start your day with a high-fiber cereal. Choose cereals with at least 5 grams of fiber per serving.

- When baking, replace part of the white flour with Hi-Maize high fiber flour (www.kingarthurflour.com), whole-wheat flour, wheat bran, oat bran, or oatmeal.

- Add some flax to your cereal, yogurt or smoothie. Flax has been referred to as "Nature's Scrub-Brush" when it comes to keeping your colon clean, and it has a great nutty taste. Buy it ground or grind your own, but refrigerate it because it oxidizes quickly once ground.

- Snack on high-fiber foods such as fresh or dried fruits, vegetables, and whole-grain crackers. Look for snack bars that have added fiber like Gnu, Kashi, Zing, Lara and Luna bars. I especially like Gnu bars for their fiber content—12 grams per bar. (www.GnuFoods.com)

♦ If your diet is normally low in fiber, increase the fiber in your diet gradually. Adding a lot of fiber to your meals all at once can result in bloating and gas. Also, remember to drink plenty of fluids while eating high-fiber foods. Without enough fluids, high-fiber foods can cause constipation.

If you follow the advice above, you'll be sure to get the 29 grams of fiber currently recommended during pregnancy. But if you want to know the numbers, see the chart below.

Dietary Fiber Content			
Food	Serving	Grams	% DRI
Fruits:			
Figs	5	9	32
Guava	1	5	18
Apple, fresh with skin	1 medium	4	14
Blackberries, raw	½ cup (125 ml)	4	14
Pear, fresh with skin	1	4	14
Papaya	1 cup (250 ml/ 145 g)	3	11
Prunes	5	3	11
Banana	1 medium	3	11
Orange, fresh	1	3	11
Grapes	½ cup (125 ml)	0.5	2
Most other fruits contain 1–3 grams (3-10% of DRI) of fiber per serving.			
Vegetables:			
Artichoke	1 medium	6	21
Potato with skin	1 medium	5	18
Avocado	½ medium	4	14
Green peas	½ cup (125 ml)	4	14
Pumpkin, canned	½ cup (125 ml)	3.5	12
Spinach, cooked and drained	½ cup (125 ml)	3	11
Broccoli, cooked and chopped	½ cup (125 ml)	3	11
Sweet potato, baked in skin	1 medium	3	11
Rhubarb, cooked	½ cup (125 ml)	3	11
Corn, Green beans, canned	½ cup (125 ml)	2	7
Lettuce, any type	1 cup (250 ml)	1	4

Dietary Fiber Content			
Food	Serving	Grams	% DRI
Legumes:			
Black beans	½ cup (125 ml)	8	29
Split peas	½ cup (125 ml)	8	29
Baked beans, canned	½ cup (125 ml)	7	25
Hummus	½ cup (125 ml)	7	25
Refried pinto beans	½ cup (125 ml)	6	21
Green peas	½ cup (125 ml)	4	14
Edamame (green soy beans)	½ cup (125 ml)	4	14
Vegetarian burger crumbles	½ cup (125 ml)	4	14
Vegetarian burger	1 patty	3	11
Nuts and Seeds:			
Almonds, cashews, pine nuts, pistachios, pecans, sunflower seeds	1 oz. (30 g)	3	11
Sesame seed butter, (tahini)	2 tablespoons	3	11
Flaxseed	1 tablespoon	3	11
Peanuts, Walnuts	1 oz. (30 g)	2	7
Grains:			
Uncle Sam Original Cereal	¾ cup (150 ml)	10	36
Kashi Go Lean High Protein/ Fiber Cereal	1 cup (250 ml)	10	36
Kashi Go Lean Crunch	1 cup (250 ml)	10	36
Kashi Good Friends Cereal	1 cup (250 ml)	8	29
Raisin bran	1 cup (250 ml)	7	25
Nature's Path Organic Flax Plus Pumpkin Raisin Crunch	¾ cup (190 ml)	7	25
Wheat germ or wheat bran, unprocessed	¼ cup (65 ml)	6	21
Nature's Path Organic Instant Hot Oatmeal	1 packet	5	18
Nature's Path Organic Flax Plus Waffles	2 waffles	5	18
Kelloggs All-Bran Multi-Grain Crackers	18	5	18
Nature's Path Organic Pomegran Plus Granola with Cherries	¾ cup (190 ml)	4	14
Bulgur or quinoa	½ cup (125 ml)	4	14
Triscuits	7	4	14
Corn tortillas	2	4	14
Oat bran	¼ cup (65 ml)	3	11

Dietary Fiber Content			
Food	**Serving**	**Grams**	**% DRI**
Barley	¼ cup (65 ml)	3	11
Cheerios	1 cup (250 ml)	3	11
Whole wheat tortilla, 8 inches (20 cm)	1 (45 g)	3	11
Mission Artisan Style tortilla, any type	1	3	11
Nutri-Grains waffle	2	3	11
Bran muffin	1	3	11
Popcorn	3½ cups (875 ml)	2	7
Oatmeal	¼ cup (65 ml)	2	7
Whole-wheat bread	1 slice	2	7
Brown rice	½ cup (125 ml)	2	7
Tortilla chips, baked or fried	20 chips (1 oz. or 30 g)	2	7

Focus on Fruits and Vegetables

The Centers for Disease Control and Prevention use the slogan "Fruits and Vegetables-More Matters" to encourage Americans to eat more fruits and vegetables each day. Why? Besides being great sources of vitamins, minerals, and fiber, they also contain phytochemicals—biologically active substances that have positive effects on health. These benefits include the prevention of cancer and heart disease. As discussed earlier, the antioxidants found in produce are believed to be super-powered when it comes to health—especially during pregnancy.

The great thing about fruits and vegetables is that when you fill up on them you're less likely to eat chips, cookies, and other nutrient-poor foods which can also be high in sugar and fat. Try to eat a variety of fruits and vegetables from day to day—whether it's fresh, frozen, canned or juice. (But limit fruit juice to half a cup (125 ml) at a time.)

How to Get More Produce on Your Plate

In chapter 4, we discussed the elements of MyPlate. Now that you're in the second trimester and eating well, hopefully "Your Plate" matches MyPlate for fruits and veggies. It's easy—half your plate should be fruits and veggies!

Here are some easy tips for adding fruits and vegetables to your meals. Many of them are found in the *Eating Expectantly Cookbook*:

Breakfast

♦ Whip up a fruit or veggie smoothie.

♦ Add mashed banana, dried fruit, or applesauce to muffin or pancake batter.

♦ Top whole grain waffles with blueberries, strawberries or other fresh fruit or make a homemade sauce using berries and a little honey.

♦ Add fresh or dried fruit to your cereal.

♦ Eat a fruit before you have anything else. (While fruit juice is a suitable way to get ½ cup (125 ml) of fruit in the day, avoid having it at breakfast during the second and third trimester.)

♦ Add tomatoes, mushrooms, fresh herbs, spinach, onions, garlic, olives and red or green peppers or chiles into your eggs or make a breakfast salsa.

Which Fruit are Healthiest?

The Center for Science in the Public Interest, publisher of Nutrition Action Healthletter, has compiled a list of the healthiest fruits, based on their vitamin C, carotenoids, folate, potassium and fiber content.[18] Here are their "Gold Medalists." Don't despair if your favorite fruit isn't on this list; just try to include these fruits more often to get the most nutrition.

♦ Guava
♦ Watermelon
♦ Grapefruit
♦ Kiwifruit
♦ Papaya
♦ Cantaloupe
♦ Apricots
♦ Orange
♦ Strawberries

♦ Blackberries
♦ Raspberries
♦ Tangerine
♦ Persimmon
♦ Mango
♦ Honeydew melon
♦ Star Fruit
♦ Peaches, dried

Lunch

♦   Always start with a veggie—be it carrot or celery sticks, salad, slaw or some vegetable soup.

♦   Add apple, raisins, grapes, pineapple, mango, or mandarin orange slices to your chicken, tuna, or tossed salad.

♦   Use darker greens, such as romaine, kale or spinach, for your salads.

♦   Sauté some kale, spinach or other greens with a little olive oil and seasonings to accompany your meal.

♦   Bean and lentil soups are a great way to get your veggies, carb and protein at lunch.

♦   Drink vegetable or tomato juice with your meal. There are all kinds of tasty juice combinations of fruit, veggie, or both on the market now. Find what tastes good to you but watch the sodium levels.

♦   Add chopped veggies (carrots, peas, broccoli) to your rice, pasta or quinoa.

♦   Have a salad ON your sandwich! Add leaf lettuce or spinach, thinly sliced cucumber, avocado, finely shredded cabbage, grated carrot, and tomatoes to your sandwiches. In New Zealand, sandwiches with corn on them are a favorite!

♦   Stuff a potato with fajita beef or chicken, or barbecue.

♦   Stuff leftover veggies or salad in a pita pocket with cheese.

♦   To save time, buy ready-to-eat salads, carrots, and broccoli. It's best to wash them one more time before using.

Dinner

♦   Have a stir-fry for dinner; buy the vegetables cleaned, chopped, and ready to go!

♦   Zip up your spaghetti sauce or chili with bell pepper, zucchini, carrots, or eggplant. Shred or chop these vegetables finely and they will cook quickly. If you have a picky partner or children at home, you can purée the cooked vegetables into your sauces. They'll never know they're there if you don't tell them!

♦   Try snacking on bites of frozen peas and corn—and they're lots of fun for toddlers in the house to eat too.

♦   Use puréed roasted red pepper, pumpkin, or carrots as the base for a sauce.

♦   Start dinner with a vegetable-based soup, such as minestrone or gazpacho.

- Make a fruit salsa to accompany your grilled chicken or seafood.

- Make an appetizer of oven-fried zucchini sticks or eggplant slices.

Snacks

- Add a handful of berries or dried cranberries to your cup of yogurt.

- Snack on any fresh fruit or veggie.

- Have some fat-free bean dip with your baked chips.

- Keep some fruit cups on hand for easy snacking.

Dessert

- A mixed fresh-fruit salad makes a great finish. In the winter, you can incorporate more canned or frozen veggies.

- Top a tiny slice of pound cake with fresh or frozen berries or canned peaches.

- Make a fruit smoothie with your favorite frozen fruits.

- Try a fruit sorbet.

- Have a frozen yogurt layered with fruit.

- Munch on a frozen banana or frozen grapes.

- Top off a grilled dinner with grilled fruit kebabs.

- Dip strawberries in a yogurt dip or chocolate sauce. (Everyone needs an occasional splurge!)

- Savor some dark chocolate-covered prunes, raisins, strawberries or banana.

- Have a fruit "sparkler"—mix club soda or Perrier with a dark red juice like pomegranate or berry and add a squeeze of lime. This is a fun "mocktail", especially if you are the designated driver.

Choosy Mothers Snack Smart!

When I ask my clients if they snack, they usually look embarrassed. Most people think of snacking as eating foods they shouldn't, or "cheating." Actually, snacking can be healthy, and it's a must during pregnancy. Snacking helps you get all the nutrients you need when you can't eat much at a meal. It also gives you more energy during those times when baby seems to be sapping all of it. Being choosy about snacks can also help you control your blood sugar (whether you have diabetes or not) and help you get to (but not over) your goal weight.

The best snacks offer the most nutrition per calorie. Fruits and vegetables are tops; they offer lots of nutrition, virtually no fat, and few calories. Their fiber and fluid content are additional benefits.

Stay Away From These Fruit & Veggie Snacks:

♦ Potato chips and French fries. Yes, they're made of potatoes and contain significant potassium—but don't eat them because of that!! (Ok—except for sweet potato fries—they are worth a very occasional splurge!) If you bake your own fries from scratch, however, they're great.

♦ Packaged fried veggies—from peas to okra, these snacks, which are sometimes baked, still add up to about 150 calories and eight 8 grams of fat. Yikes!

♦ Yogurt-covered raisins have 3-4 grams of saturated fat per ounce (30 g). Ouch.

♦ Smoothies—not homemade: the amount of fruits and juice (and sweetener!) contents varies, so ask about the ingredients before ordering. They have a minimum of about 300 calories for 20 oz. (620 ml).

Pack a Snack Stash:

It's not a matter of if, but when you will suddenly need to EAT RIGHT NOW! Keep these snacks in your purse, car or desk drawer for that sudden urge:

♦ Dried fruit or trail mix

♦ Dry cereal mixed with dried fruit

♦ Nut or seed butter. Dip out a spoonful and eat with crackers or fruit.

♦ Fruit cup packed in juice

♦ Whole grain crackers

♦ Snack bars (see page 69 for a list of the healthiest)

♦ Soy nuts

♦ Milk (Keep single-serve boxes of Horizon milk on hand)

Healthy Snacks

Many of these recipes can be found on the *Eating Expectantly Cookbook.*

High-Carbohydrate Snacks:
◆ Taste of Nature, Zing, or Lara bars
◆ Bean soup (watch the sodium)
◆ Raisin bran or other high-fiber cereal with milk or yogurt
◆ Popcorn (Choose the one with the least fat, or air pop your own.)
◆ Whole grain crackers: Look for those with the fewest ingredients
◆ Fig Newtons
◆ Baked tortilla chips, or other baked chips with salsa
◆ Bean dip

Dairy Snacks (these also have protein):
◆ Milk
◆ Smoothie
◆ Yogurt
◆ Drinkable yogurt/smoothies
◆ Kefir
◆ Low-fat cheese
◆ Dip made with cottage cheese or fat-free cream cheese

High-Protein Snacks:
◆ Nut or sunflower seed butter on whole grain crackers or with banana or apple
◆ Ants on a Log—peanut butter on celery sticks with raisins or Craisins
◆ Whole-grain cereal with milk
◆ Edamame
◆ String cheese and with fruit
◆ Whole grain tortilla or baked tortilla chips with refried beans and cheese
◆ High protein cereal like Kashi GoLean
◆ Cottage cheese and fruit
◆ Fat-free cream cheese dip with celery, carrots, and broccoli

Healthier Travel

Chances are that during the ten months of your pregnancy, you **will** travel–maybe a lot. Traveling while pregnant may be "business as usual," but it could wreck your plan for eating, weight gain and fitness. If you have a choice, traveling during the second trimester is ideal just because you feel better and thus you can better tolerate the rigors of travel. Here are some tips:

♦ Plan ahead for eating—make layovers lengthy enough to grab a healthy bite—or bring your own from home.

♦ Plan for the unexpected—delays, time waiting on the tarmac, no time to find food. Bring your own snack stash.

♦ Avoid drinking gas-producing foods and carbonated drinks before your flight.

♦ Drink plenty of water to stay hydrated—and bring a refillable water bottle.

♦ Whether you are flying, driving or traveling by train, do some isometric or get up to walk around at least every hour to prevent blood clots in your legs.

♦ Keep alcohol-based hand sanitizer with you to prevent picking up "bugs" along the way.

If traveling internationally, check which immunizations are required and if it's safe to take them while pregnant.

Scan this QR code for more information about traveling while pregnant:

Second Trimester Diet Challenges

You may breeze through this trimester with no issues at all, or you may experience one of these:

Constipation

Progesterone, a pregnancy hormone, slows down the movement of food in your intestine, causing more water and nutrients to be absorbed, and constipation is often the result. The pressure of the growing baby on your intestines and rectum can add to this problem. An iron or calcium supplement can further worsen it.

"Constipation" means different things to different people. Some people say they're constipated if they don't have a bowel movement daily. Actually it's defined as three or fewer bowel movements in a week or if stool is hard, dry, painful, or difficult to pass.[19] Some people with constipation lack energy and feel full or bloated.

Here's what you can do:

◆ Check the amount of iron in your prenatal supplement. If it's significantly over 30 mg, ask your health care provider if this amount is appropriate for you. Don't take an extra iron supplement unless recommended. Carbonyl iron, the form of iron in CitraNatal Harmony, Prenate Mini, and PreferaOB are reported to be easier on the digestive tract and less likely to cause constipation.

◆ Drink up—at least 10 glasses daily, more than half should be from filtered water. It's especially important to drink plenty of fluids when you're eating more fiber. You might try drinking something warm in the morning—hot tea or decaf coffee—to get things moving.

◆ Move to get things "going". Lack of exercise is actually a risk factor for constipation. Exercise can help make the muscles of the large intestine work better, which decreases constipation. But timing is important—wait an hour after a meal to exercise. Just taking a 10-15 minute walk twice a day may keep constipation away.

◆ Eat plenty of high-fiber foods. Eat at least five cups (1,250 ml) of fruits and vegetables per day, as well as five servings of whole grains. Prunes, figs, apples and bran cereal are top foods for constipation. Consider eating one serving of food a day that contains eight grams of fiber (See page 191, "Focus on Fiber.")

◆ Go for the good bugs. Probiotics—whether in yogurt, a probiotic drink like Yakult or Good Belly, or as a supplement, may help your digestive system work better.

◆ "Flaxitize" your food. Add 2-3 teaspoons of ground flaxseed to your cereal or smoothie every day.

◆ Relax. Sometimes constipation happens because we are just too busy to "go" when nature calls. And the longer stool is held in the intestines, the more water is removed and the harder it becomes. Stress can also play a role in constipation—see section below for dealing with that.

◆ Avoid foods that cause constipation. Some people are constipated when they eat certain foods, such as cheese, white rice or bananas.

◆ Avoid caffeine, since it can cause a loss of even more fluid, which can make the stools hard.

◆ Consider trying a fiber supplement like Benefiber or Metamucil. They need to be used on a regular basis to work, however. Benefiber has no flavor or texture so it can be stirred into just about anything.

◆ Bring in the reinforcements. If constipation is a problem despite following the above advice, discuss with your health care provider—there may be an underlying medical cause. Also ask about using a stool softener, (active ingredient: docusate), which works by drawing fluid back into the stool to make it softer. Some prenatal vitamins contain a stool softener, but don't advertise it. Or you can take a separate stool softener, which goes by brand names Colace, Correctol and Dulcolax. Don't use a laxative unless your health care provider approves.

Stress

We all live with stress. And the truth is, being pregnant can add an extra element of stress. Worrying about doing everything right, how you're going to manage financially, or just dealing with the physical changes of pregnancy can add extra anxiety to a life that may already have its fill of stress. Pregnancy hormones can cause mood swings, which may leave you even less able to cope with the pressures of life in the fast lane.

There's bad news about stress and its effect on pregnancy. Research has shown that stress and anxiety could affect the physical, behavioral and cognitive development of your baby.[20,21] It could affect your baby's growth now, as well as future immune health[22], and cognitive development.[23] According to the March of Dimes, severe or long-lasting stress as well as single catastrophic events may increase the risk of having a preterm birth. Just as diet may "program" a child's development for future health problems, a woman's emotional state during pregnancy could also program a child for behavioral problems. One study shows that anxiety at a vulnerable time in brain development could increase the risk for hyperactivity and anxiety later in childhood.[24]

Research shows that stress causes inflammation in the body that can promote disease. During pregnancy we know that inflammation is the cornerstone of some pregnancy problems like preeclampsia. While this may give you yet one more thing to worry about, hopefully it will help motivate you to slow down or make changes to lessen your stress.

Stress can affect your diet in several ways; you may eat more to calm yourself, you may lose your appetite, or stress may make you indifferent to the quality of your diet.

Here's what you can do:

- Eat anti-inflammatory foods like fruits vegetables and omega-3 fats. Consult previous lists of the healthiest fruits and veggies and eat them often. Eat cold water fish, walnuts and flaxseed. Take your DHA supplement.

- Get Support. Research shows that partner support during chronic stress may decrease the risk of preterm delivery.[25]

- Get Outside. There's nothing like a little nature time to decompress. (The extra vitamin D from sunshine can't hurt.) If you live in a snowy climate, visit an indoor botanical garden for some nature time.

- Take time to reflect on the positive. Whether this is practiced thru prayer, deep-breathing, quiet music, meditation or making a list of things you are thankful for, it may help put things in perspective.

- Move more. Exercise is one of the best ways to ease tension and anxiety. Try taking a stroll whenever you feel stressed. Some yoga or Tai Chi may quiet the mind as well as strengthen your muscles.

- Learn to say no. You may not be able to do what you did before pregnancy—either physically or emotionally. Cut out unnecessary commitments, and make sure there's enough "you-time" on your calendar. Take more time for rest, exercise, and planning and preparing healthy meals.

- Use relaxation techniques such as biofeedback and meditation. Many DVD's with relaxing music and scenery are available, and these can help you take a mental vacation. Download podcasts with guided relaxation exercises.

- Find support outside the home through friends and coworkers or on the web. Other new moms or moms-to-be should be especially empathetic. At the same time, avoid those who are not supportive or cause you stress. Remember that your partner will also be feeling stress and will likely need support, too.

- Below are some internet pregnancy resources, including bulletin boards and chat rooms you may find helpful. Just remember, don't believe everything you read on the internet!

  - Lots of topics to choose from: www.whattoexpect.com/groups/
  - Find a due-date buddy: forum.baby-gaga.com/forum-9.html
  - Find a birth club or topic: community.babycenter.com/post

THIRD TRIMESTER

What You'll Find:

♦ How Baby Is Growing

♦ What Could Happen This Trimester

♦ Feeding Your Big Bump: Weight Gain and Calorie Needs

♦ Eating Expectantly Diet: Third Trimester

♦ Third Trimester Power Nutrients

♦ Third Trimester Diet Challenges

♦ How's Your Diet?

Frequently Asked Questions:

♦ How many extra calories do I need this trimester?

♦ What if I've gained too much weight?

♦ What can I do for heartburn?

♦ Is there anything I can do to prevent high blood pressure?

♦ Which foods will help my baby's brain?

SCAN HERE FOR CHAPTER UPDATES

During this trimester, your baby hits his stride for growth and gains a significant amount of weight to prepare for his grand entry. Your quickly expanding baby bump makes it harder to move around like you used to; you might find it difficult to do simple things like getting out of bed! But luckily, you can also see the light at the end of the tunnel for this adventure called pregnancy. You'll be getting ready for your baby's arrival—whether it's preparing your baby's room, shopping for baby clothes and gadgets, celebrating the upcoming birth or spending more time visualizing what life will be like with a new baby. As busy as you'll be, it's still important to take time for yourself—to eat well, keep stress low and get enough rest.

How Baby Is Growing

Your baby is now rapidly filling your uterus. All that's left for him to be "done" is to put on more body fat and weight, and further develop his lungs and brain. As your due date gets closer and there is less elbow room, your baby may be turning flips less often. You might, however, feel a different type of rhythmic movement—hiccups!

The brain and nervous system grows tremendously this trimester. Make sure the fat you eat is healthy—and that you get enough DHA, a major building-block of brain tissue.

Developmental Highlights during this Trimester: Below is a very simplified version of how your baby is growing in the third trimester.

1. **At the End of Twenty-Eight Weeks (Seven Months): Upside Down.** Your baby grew a lot over the past month and should weigh about 2¼ pounds (1 kg) and be about 10 inches (25 cm) from the top of his head to the end of his bottom[1] or close to 16 inches (40 cm) from head to toe.[2] Baby is now storing calcium, and his bones are hardening. Not only does your baby hear the vibrations of your music, he may even move to their rhythms! Brain patterns in utero show that at this stage, your baby may even be dreaming! Many babies now find they fit better upside down and start to position themselves for birth. Your health care provider can determine if your baby is positioned head-down.

2. **At the End of Thirty-Two Weeks (Eight Months) Eyes Wide Open and Brain Expanding.** Although your baby still needs to develop lung surfactant (an oily substance which enables the lungs to inflate and deflate properly), he'll start to practice breathing. His kicks are strong and vigorous, and many women can feel (or even see) a heel, fist, or elbow through their abdomens. Your baby now weighs almost 4 pounds[3] (1.8 kg) and is up to 18 inches long (46 cm) from head to toe. He is now controlling his own body temperature—a big physiological milestone—which also allows him to start shedding some body hair. His hearing is more fine-tuned and he can hear sounds more distinctly. From now on, your baby will put on about a half pound (225 g) a week—which explains why your tummy is expanding so much! His

brain is growing quickly too. As baby gets bigger, you may feel less comfortable. Drink plenty of fluids, put your feet up from time to time and lie on your left side—also consider support hose. Let others pamper you—you're doing the most important job of your life!

3. **At the End of Thirty-Six Weeks (Nine Months) He Sees the Light!** Your baby is considered full term at 37 weeks, but it's still best if he gets a few more weeks in the "oven". "Opt out" of an early scheduled delivery, if possible. He measures close to 21 inches (53 cm) and weighs about 6 pounds (2.7 kg).[4] His pupils can open and close, so he's able to detect light. The bones in the head are flexible and ready to squeeze through the birth canal. Lanugo, the fine body hair, and vernix, the waxy covering, are disappearing. Fat deposits under the skin help fill out his body and make him look less wrinkled. Baby has his own sleep-wake cycle—but you may find he's very awake (and active) about the time you are trying to sleep. It's a good time to get a few power naps in, to practice "sleeping when the baby sleeps"—advice you'll get once your baby is born. You'll still feel your baby move plenty, but as it gets more crowded in there, he may move and punch less. Some doctors recommend doing "kick counts"—ask your health care provider for more info.

4. **At the End of Forty Weeks (Ten Months) Meet Your New Baby!** Your baby will be born any day (or week) now. Don't be surprised to deliver a week or two past your due date, especially if it's your first pregnancy! It's a good lesson that babies don't always follow your schedule; it's also true for sleeping and eating once your baby is born. These last few weeks can be tiring as your very large baby bump sometimes gets in the way of doing the simplest things like fastening your seat belt (but do so anyway!) Take it easy and take good care of yourself as you wait for the arrival of your new little one. Your life is about to be turned upside down—be ready!

What Could Happen This Trimester

During the third trimester, a few special health conditions could develop: high blood pressure, preeclampsia and gestational diabetes. These are discussed fully in Chapter 11. Research shows that there are some nutrition and lifestyle choices that may decrease your risk of these conditions:

High Blood Pressure/Preeclampsia

High blood pressure and its more serious cousin, preeclampsia, are related to several factors—including nutrition. The DASH (Dietary Approaches to Stop Hypertension) dietary pattern is a healthy plan that's been shown to lower blood pressure.[5] The Eating Expectantly Diet is similar in that it recommends 5 cups (1,250 ml) of fruits and vegetables, 3+ servings of dairy, is rich in magnesium and fiber and lower in

Just What the Doctor Ordered? Chocolate

Several studies have shown that eating chocolate regularly in the third trimester (as little as once a week) is associated with a 50% decrease in the risk of preeclampsia.[6,7] While there isn't enough evidence to declare chocolate a superfood, I do call it a "super condiment"—something you can add to your diet in small amounts to give it a nutritional boost! And who couldn't use a bit of chocolate to brighten the week? Choose natural cocoa and dark chocolate for the greatest polyphenol content.

saturated fat and sodium. Following the Eating Expectantly Diet and eating more potassium, calcium and magnesium-rich foods *could possibly* help lower your risk of high blood pressure.

B vitamins—including folate and vitamins B6 and B12 have been associated with several factors that increase the risk of preeclampsia. Folate, highlighted for its importance in pre-pregnancy and in the first trimester, is also important in the last trimester. A lower intake of dietary folate is associated with inflammation, which is associated with preeclampsia and preterm delivery.[8,9] Keep getting plenty of folate in your diet!

Low serum levels of calcium, vitamin D, zinc and magnesium have been linked to a higher risk of preeclampsia.[10] In fact, vitamin D deficiency (defined as serum 25OH-D of <23 ng/mg) is associated with preeclampsia, insulin resistance and gestational diabetes.[11] Consumption of dairy-based foods containing probiotics[12] has also been shown to decrease the risk.

Most of the research for calcium has been done with calcium supplements rather than food, but they showed that intake of at least 1,000 mg per day cut the risk of preeclampsia in half. Most participants in the studies had a low dietary calcium intake to begin with.[13] Getting your calcium from dairy products gives you more than just calcium—you also get vitamin D, potassium, and magnesium—nutrients linked to lower blood pressure.[14]

Gestational Diabetes

As hormones produced in the placenta make your body less sensitive to insulin, your body may have a problem controlling blood sugar, which can lead to Gestational Diabetes Mellitus (GDM). Your health care provider will probably check for this by giving you a special test called a Glucose Tolerance Test or GTT, between 24 and 28 weeks. You have a lower risk of GDM if you had a healthy weight at the start of your pregnancy and have not gained too much weight. Exercising regularly can help insulin work better and possibly prevent GDM. Eating mostly "smart carbs"—as outlined on page 62—foods that are high in fiber and have a low glycemic index have been shown to cut the risk of GDM. In fact, women who eat a diet with a "high glycemic load" and little cereal fiber are twice as likely to be diagnosed with

GDM.[15] A higher fat diet, as well as saturated and trans fat intake, are also linked to GDM.[16,17] Vitamins may also play a role in prevention of GDM; vitamin D deficiency and a vitamin C intake of less than 70 mg is associated with nearly a double risk of having GDM.[18,19]

Here's how you can help prevent future problems:

♦ Tally up your fiber; the goal is about 30 grams a day.

♦ Eat 2 cups (500 ml) of fruit and 3 cups (750 ml) of vegetables a day.

♦ Eat a dark green leafy veggie at least 3 times a week.

♦ Make sure you still have a significant source of folic acid in your diet—either through a prenatal supplement or fortified cereal.

♦ Make sure your calcium intake is at least 1,000 mg per day, preferably from food.

♦ Watch your weight gain.

♦ Exercise daily (with health care provider's OK).

♦ Get enough vitamin D.

♦ Eat smart carbs: skip the sweets.

♦ Eat healthy fats: limit saturated, avoid trans fats.

Weighing In

Are you in the habit of weighing yourself daily? Don't! During the third trimester you are more prone to water-retention and weight fluctuations. So when you panic, thinking you've gained a pound in two days, the weight gain may simply be a result of water retention. Weigh yourself just once or twice a week at the same time of day under the same conditions. This will give you a truer idea of how your weight gain is progressing.

Note: If you do feel you have suddenly gained two or more pounds (1 kg) in a few days and notice some of these symptoms; extreme swelling in your hands, face, or eyes; persistent headaches or vision changes, belly pain on the right side, nausea or vomiting, notify your health care provider immediately. This may be a sign of preeclampsia.[20]

Feeding Your Big Bump: Weight Gain and Calorie Needs

During the last trimester, continue to keep an eye on your final goal weight, as well as paying attention to weekly weight gains. Women with pre-pregnant weight in the normal range should continue to gain about a pound (450 g) a week; women in the overweight range should gain about a half-pound (225 g) per week. If you were underweight before pregnancy you need to gain more than a pound (450 g) a week.

If you find that you've already exceeded your goal weight, discuss this with your health care provider. She will probably still want you to gain weight, but at a slower rate. It's never a good idea to try to lose weight while pregnant, no matter how much weight you've gained. If you find that you're much less active now that you were pre-pregnancy, you may not need as many extra calories. However, you still need all the added nutrients.

In the third trimester many women find that their "get up and go has got up and went." Between feeling really big and uncomfortable and getting kicked in the ribs in the middle of the night, you may have a hard time getting enough sleep!
On the other hand, you may find that with your baby's arrival just around the corner, you have renewed energy! Some women begin "nesting"—they get a burst of energy to get everything ready for the baby's arrival. If you find that you're significantly more active, you may need to increase your calories. (See page 199 for high-energy snack ideas.) Continue to eat a balance of complex, high-fiber carbohydrates from grains, fruits and vegetables and a variety of protein sources. Watch out for the bad fats: saturated and trans fats!

Eating Expectantly Diet: Third Trimester

How many extra calories do you need this trimester? That depends on how much you want to gain. The Eating Expectantly Diet above is calculated for about 1 pound (450 g) of weight gain per week. If your goal is more—or less than that—use the chart on page 183. Below is a quick and easy guide to the number of foods from each food group you should try to eat.

What's Different Between the Second and Third Trimester Diet?

Your baby's bones are getting stronger—and that requires more calcium and other minerals. Calcium may lower your risk of high blood pressure and preeclampsia, so I've recommended an optional extra serving of milk or calcium-rich food in the third trimester. This additional dairy serving is particularly useful for women who previously had a low intake of calcium, or are at risk of high blood pressure.

Eating Expectantly Diet: Third Trimester

9 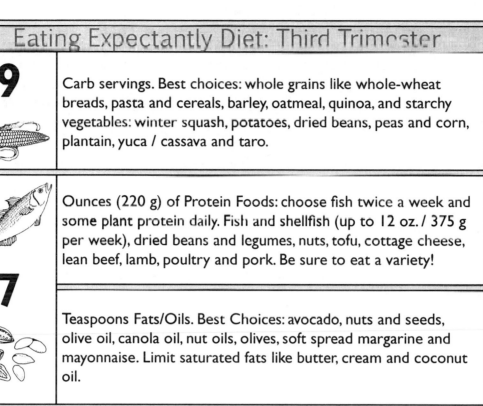 Carb servings. Best choices: whole grains like whole-wheat breads, pasta and cereals, barley, oatmeal, quinoa, and starchy vegetables: winter squash, potatoes, dried beans, peas and corn, plantain, yuca / cassava and taro.

Ounces (220 g) of Protein Foods: choose fish twice a week and some plant protein daily. Fish and shellfish (up to 12 oz. / 375 g per week), dried beans and legumes, nuts, tofu, cottage cheese, lean beef, lamb, poultry and pork. Be sure to eat a variety!

7 Teaspoons Fats/Oils. Best Choices: avocado, nuts and seeds, olive oil, canola oil, nut oils, olives, soft spread margarine and mayonnaise. Limit saturated fats like butter, cream and coconut oil.

3-4 Servings of Dairy Foods: 1 serving is 1 cup (250 ml) of milk, yogurt or calcium-fortified soymilk; 1.5 ounces (45 g) natural cheese or 2 ounces (60 g) processed cheese. Choose nonfat or low-fat.

3 Cups (750 ml) Vegetables: choose a dark leafy green or red/orange vegetable daily. Best Choices: Broccoli, cauliflower, carrots, spinach, cabbage, leaf and romaine lettuce, greens, sweet peppers, mushrooms, bok choy, artichokes and tomatoes.

2  Cups (500 ml) Fruit: choose a vitamin C-rich fruit daily. Best choices: papaya, mango, melon, berries, watermelon, apricots, peaches, grapefruit, orange, grapes and kiwi.

Splurge  200 Calories (Including up to 6 teaspoons added sugar—including what's added to food like yogurt.)

Sample Meal Plan for the Third Trimester

This menu is different from the other trimesters in that the carb count is a bit lower in the morning. During the third trimester, placental hormones work against insulin, sometimes causing elevated blood sugar in the morning. You can counteract this by eating a high protein breakfast and limit simple carbs until lunchtime.

Breakfast
- Omelet with spinach , pesto and Swiss cheese
- ½ Whole grain English muffin

Snack
- Hummus with jicama

Lunch
- Entrée salad with mixed greens, shrimp, tomatoes, asparagus, corn, black olives
- Lite balsamic vinaigrette
- Whole grain roll
- Mango
- Low-fat milk

Snack
- Berry smoothie with flaxseed

Dinner
- Lean beef fajitas with peppers in corn tortillas
- Chopped tomatoes with cilantro (or pico de gallo)
- Grilled zucchini
- Fresh orange

Snack
- Whole grain cereal or fiber bar with milk

Slashing Your Sugar

If you are "mostly" following the Eating Expectantly Diet you've probably already cut your sugar intake. But by now, you may be getting a bit more lax about your diet. Check out these tips to cut your sugar (for more info, see page 72):

Instead of This:	Eat That:
Juice drink	Fruit juice mixed with club soda
Sports drink (for refreshment)	Water with lemon, or agua fresca (Recipes in *Eating Expectantly Cookbook*)
Sports drink (for electrolyte replacement)	Milk

Instead of This:	Eat That:
Candy bar	Raisins, dates, or dried plums or cranberries
Milk chocolate	Dark chocolate
Sandwich cookie	LU Petit Beurre cookies
Ice cream or yogurt	Sugar-free ice cream or yogurt
Pancake syrup	Reduced calorie pancake syrup (not sugar-free) or all fruit syrup (Recipes in *Eating Expectantly Cookbook*)
Bottled sweetened tea	Brewed tea with fresh mint and an orange slice

Food-Planning for the Third Trimester

The main problems with eating during the last months of pregnancy are:

1. You get full quickly.
2. You may be too tired to cook.
3. Heartburn may restrict the variety or amount of foods you eat.
4. You may be so busy getting ready for the baby that you neglect your diet.
5. You may be trying to cut food expenses to buy necessities for your baby.

The third trimester menus in the *Eating Expectantly Cookbook* are designed with the above in mind. Look over the list below for ideas.

Now is a good time to prepare some foods to freeze for those first days or weeks with your new baby. This would be an excellent opportunity to enlist the support of family, friends, neighbors and co-workers who want to help but aren't sure how. Sort of like a pre-baby pot-luck for the freezer! Just ask—most folks are glad to contribute. Let them know what you have in mind so you don't end up with stuff you don't/won't eat. Giving them healthy ideas (or recipes from *Eating Expectantly Cookbook*) for what to cook for you may help them too!

Find these menus in the *Eating Expectantly Cookbook*:

♦ Using Leftovers with Flair

♦ Meals in Minutes

♦ Feel Full Menus

♦ Best Bite Snacks

♦ Vegetarian Budget Menus

Third Trimester Power Nutrients

Although your need for vitamins and minerals during the third trimester remains essentially the same as during the second trimester, some nutrients are more critical.

Calcium

Dietary Reference Intake (DRI): 1,000 mg

If you think of bones as a calcium bank, approximately ⅔ of the calcium "deposits" you'll send your baby will be during this trimester. Three to four servings of calcium-rich foods daily are recommended. If you don't have enough dietary or supplemental calcium, *you'll* be the loser because calcium will be drained from your bones to supply your baby's needs for it. Besides dairy products such as milk, yogurt and cheese, you'll also find calcium in kale, collard greens, mustard greens, soybeans, bok choy, and tahini.

Calcium is a vital mineral for your baby's bone development, but it also plays a critical role in maintaining a healthy blood pressure. Unfortunately, it's a mineral that adults often delete from their diets if they cut down on dairy. The DRI for calcium is 1,000 milligrams. This is the amount found in about 3.5 cups (875 ml) of milk. Milk and dairy products also provide protein, magnesium, vitamin D, and riboflavin. If you don't consume dairy products or lots of calcium-rich veggies, make sure you make other calcium-rich foods or calcium-fortified foods part of your everyday diet. Some substitutes for milk like soy, almond, flaxmilk and rice milks, as well as some juices may contain added calcium and vitamin D, but check the label to be sure. Shake those beverages well because calcium may fall to the bottom. Rice milk is not recommended in the Eating Expectantly Diet due to its arsenic content. See page 125 for more info.

If possible, get your calcium from food—nutrients in food generally work together to help the body use them more efficiently. DO consider a calcium/vitamin D supplement if you don't get enough from your diet.

You may wonder, "Doesn't my prenatal vitamin have enough calcium?" Nope. If it did you really wouldn't be able to swallow it! Most prenatal vitamins contain only a small percentage of the DRI for calcium. You must obtain the majority of calcium you need from your diet, or if needed, from a separate calcium supplement. See page 99 for info about calcium supplements.

Calcium Content			
Food (Cooked when applicable)	Serving	mg	% DRI
Animal sources:			
Milk: any fat, lactose reduced, buttermilk or chocolate	1 cup (250 ml)	300	30
Yogurt, fruit-flavored, nonfat	6 oz. (190 g)	300	30
Taco Bell Bean and cheese burrito	1	229	23
Swiss cheese	1 oz. (30 g)	220	22
Wendy's Frosty	Jr. size	200	20
Thin crust cheese pizza, small	1 slice	210	21
Salmon, canned with bones	3 oz. (95 g)	203	20
Kraft American cheese made with 2% milk	1 slice	200	20
McDonalds Fruit n Yogurt Parfait	1	150	15
Taco Bell Pintos 'n Cheese	1	150	15
McDonalds Reduced fat ice cream cone	1 small	120	12
Part skim mozzarella	1 oz. (30 g)	120	12
Sardines, canned in oil, with bones	2	92	9
Vanilla ice cream, light, no sugar added	½ cup (125 ml)	92	9
Cottage cheese (1% fat)	½ cup (125 ml)	80	7
Cream cheese, fat-free	1 tablespoon	63	6
Plant sources:			
Blackstrap molasses	2 tablespoons	400	40
Silk soymilk, chocolate or vanilla	1 cup (250 ml)	300	30
Orange juice, calcium-fortified	1 cup (250 ml)	300	30
Firm tofu made with calcium sulfate (a processing agent)	4 oz. (125 g)	200+ (varies)	20+
Collard greens	½ cup (125 ml)	178	18
Rhubarb	½ cup (125 ml)	174	17
Tahini (sesame seed butter)	2 tablespoons	128	13
Turnip greens	½ cup (125 ml)	125	13
Nopales (prickly pear cactus)	½ cup (125 ml)	122	12
Almond butter	2 tablespoons	110	11
Kale	½ cup (125 ml)	90	9
Beet greens	½ cup (125 ml)	82	8
Mustard greens	½ cup (125 ml)	75	8
Almonds	22 (1 oz. / 30 g)	75	8
Okra	½ cup (125 ml)	68	7

How To Be Sneaky with Calcium

Even if you don't like milk, there are ways to sneak it in so you can get the calcium you need. Here are just a few ways to increase the calcium in your diet; many of these recipes can be found in the *Eating Expectantly Cookbook*:

Dairy-Based Tips	
1.	Make creamy soups (homemade or canned) with milk or evaporated milk.
2.	Use evaporated milk, which has twice the calcium, when preparing food like mashed potatoes, pudding, and cream sauces. Shake well before opening the can to get all the nutrients that may settle on the bottom.
3.	Eat dairy-based desserts such as pudding, yogurt, egg custard and fruit smoothies. But don't overdo! Check out the recipe for Berry Mousse Parfait
4.	Add low-fat or fat-free cheese to your mashed potatoes, vegetables, pasta, sandwiches, and sauces. Instead of meat, use low-fat cheese or tofu in your lasagna or Spinach-Stuffed Shells.
5.	Add nonfat milk powder to prepared soups, muffin and pancake mixes, milk shakes, and cream sauces. Add milk instead of water to pancake and other mixes.
6.	Add some calcium-rich veggies, milk and cheese to your entrees, such as Broccoli Quiche both of which contain milk.
7.	Use plain yogurt or cottage cheese as a base for salad dressing or dip, or use fruit-flavored yogurt as a sauce for fruit salad or as a dip for fresh fruit. Greek yogurt has the benefit of being extra thick and rich in protein, too.
Non-Dairy Tips	
8.	Add molasses to homemade quick breads, cookies, and pancakes (or add it to your mix). It contains 200 mg per tablespoon!
9.	Use more sesame seeds and tahini (sesame-seed paste). They're high in calcium and can be added to snack bars, cakes, vegetables, and dips. (See Recipe for Favorite Snack Cake in *Eating Expectantly Cookbook*).
10.	Eat fish with small bones. Salmon Pâté contains both salmon and fat-free cream cheese—both calcium-rich foods. (Make sure to leave the skin off the salmon.) If a salty snack is what you're craving, 2 sardines pack a whopping 92 mg of calcium and are also rich in Omega-3 fats.
11.	Eat Green! Collard, turnip and mustard greens, as well as kale, okra and bok choy contain well-absorbed calcium. The greens also contain lutein, an antioxidant important for your baby's brain and visual development.
12.	Instead of buying regular orange juice, buy calcium-enriched orange or apple juice, which usually contains 300 milligrams of calcium in 1 cup (250 ml).

13. Add soy to your diet, but if it's soymilk make sure it's calcium-fortified. Use silken tofu as a base for dips, puddings, and salad dressings; use firm tofu as a meat substitute in lasagna and "meatloaf". Even edamame provides a good source of calcium—about 50 mg in half a cup (125 ml).

14. Eat more almonds. An ounce of almonds contains 75 mg of calcium; Two tablespoons of almond butter provide 112 mg.

Vitamin D

Dietary Reference Intake (DRI): 600 IU

Vitamin D is needed to help your body absorb and use calcium to strengthen your baby's bones. It also plays critical roles throughout pregnancy as noted earlier. Good sources of vitamin D include regular exposure of the skin to sunshine, milk, salmon and mushrooms exposed to UV light. See page 59 for full discussion.

Mushrooms: A Surprising Source of Vitamin D

When you think "Vitamin D", your mind may not automatically think "mushrooms", but they can be an excellent source! All mushrooms contain some D—though it varies greatly by type—and growers can naturally raise the vitamin D content by exposing mushrooms to some UV light. Look for a Vitamin D or UV light exposure label on the next container of mushrooms you buy.

Vitamin D Content of Mushrooms		
Variety (Serving size of 3 oz. (85 g))	IU	% DRI
Maitake, raw	943	157
Portabella, exposed to UV light	493	82
White button mushrooms, exposed to UV light	400	67
Chanterelle, raw	178	30
Morel, raw	173	29

Magnesium

Dietary Reference Intake (DRI): 350 mg

Magnesium works in partnership with calcium for muscle contraction. It's also a structural component in bone, making it important in the third trimester. Low serum magnesium has been linked to increased risk of hypertension and an increased risk of heart disease in women. Magnesium deficiency is also implicated in preeclampsia. Consumption of soft water and other competing minerals may also increase the risk of not having enough magnesium.[21] Women generally don't get enough, consuming only 70% of the recommended amount.[22]

Magnesium Content			
Food	Serving	mg	% DRI
Pumpkin seeds	1 oz. (30 g)	156	45
100% Bran Cereal (e.g., All Bran)	½ cup (125 ml)	121	35
Trail mix with nuts, seeds and chocolate chips	½ cup (125 ml)	117	33
Chili with beans, canned	1 cup (250 ml)	115	33
Brazil nuts	1 oz. (30 g)	107	31
Oat bran, dry	½ cup (125 ml)	96	27
Wheat germ, toasted	¼ cup (65 ml)	90	26
Brown rice	1 cup (250 ml)	84	24
Almonds	22 (1 oz. / 30 g)	80	23
Spinach, frozen, chopped	½ cup (125 ml)	78	22
Swiss chard, chopped	½ cup (125 ml)	75	21
Shredded wheat, spoon size	1 cup (250 ml)	65	19
Legumes, (black, white, lima)	½ cup (125 ml)	60-70	17-20
Peanuts	1 oz. (30 g)	50	14
Molasses, blackstrap	1 tablespoon	48	14
Tofu, firm	½ cup (125 ml)	47	13
Milk 1% fat, with nonfat milk solids	1 cup (245 ml)	34	10
Banana	1 medium	32	9
Whole wheat bread	1 slice	26	7

Potassium

Dietary Reference Intake (DRI): 4,700 mg

Potassium is a mineral that keeps fluids and other electrolytes (like sodium and chloride) in balance. Being an electrolyte means it conducts electrical impulses to keep your muscles (including your heart) moving, which of course, is pretty vital! Research shows that adequate potassium is linked to lower blood pressure[23] and reduced risk of stroke. It also appears to play a role in maintaining bone density.[24] If you get muscle cramps, some people blame it on a lack of potassium—but it could also be from not getting enough magnesium or calcium or from being dehydrated.[25]

Try to eat five cups (1,250 ml) of fruits and vegetable a day, but if you can't, focus on those that are potassium-rich!

Potassium Content			
Food	Serving	mg	% DRI
Beet greens, cooked	½ cup (125 ml)	654	14
Baked potato (white or sweet)	1 medium	610	13
Halibut	4 oz. (125 g)	610	13
White beans, canned	½ cup (125 ml)	594	13
Yogurt	8 oz. (250 g)	579	12
Edamame	½ cup (125 ml)	485	10
Tomato, raw	1 large	430	9
Cantaloupe	1 cup (250 ml)	427	9
Spinach, cooked	½ cup (125 ml)	420	9
Tomato sauce	½ cup (125 ml)	405	9
Other legumes	½ cup (125 ml)	350-400	7-9
Banana	1 medium	362	8
Avocado	¼	354	8
Molasses	1 tablespoon	293	6
Potato	½ cup (125 ml)	239	5
Watermelon	1 cup (250 ml)	170	4

Here in the home stretch, when you have more things to do than hours in the day, you might find it more difficult to eat all your fruits and veggies. Here are some tips.

Quick and Easy Ways to Eat More Produce:

♦ Grab an apple or banana on your way out the door to eat in the car.

♦ Keep a bunch of washed grapes handy for snacking.

♦ Keep a bag of Cuties (Clementines) at work. Easy to peel and sweet to eat!

♦ Use mashed avocado instead of mayo on sandwiches. Yum!

♦ Purchase pre-chopped veggies for stews, stir-fries etc, or buy frozen mixes.

♦ Keep raisins or prunes in your desk drawer to snack on.

♦ Keep a bag of prepared lettuce or spinach on hand for a quick salad. Wash before eating.

♦ Dip into some salsa or hummus dip.

♦ Keep some fruit cups on hand at work or in the car for when you need a snack.

Nutrients for Brain Development

Several nutrients are more important this trimester for brain growth:

Iodine

Dietary Reference Intake (DRI): 220 micrograms

Iodine is needed in larger amounts in late pregnancy so your baby can make thyroid hormone, required for the nervous system. An iodine deficiency during pregnancy is dangerous, causing birth defects and other serious problems. Use iodized salt to make sure you meet your requirement for iodine; half a teaspoon contains 200 mcg. The WHO recommends 250 mcg iodine daily during pregnancy: the DRI is 220 mcg.[26] Iodine-rich foods include cod, milk, potatoes, shrimp and seaweed. Keep in mind that sea salt may have iodine—and it may not—check the label! Sea salt/seaweed condiment combinations are also a good way to get your iodine (find it at www.seaveg.com). Seaweed provides an excellent source of iodine—but some contain TOO much, which can cause hypothyroidism. So use with caution.

DHA

DHA (an omega-3 fat) is also important for brain development and is primarily found in cold-water fish like salmon, herring and anchovies. Try to eat fish at least once or even better, twice a week. Flaxseed, flaxmilk and walnuts are good sources of omega-3 too. (For a full discussion of omega-3's see page 79 and page 101.)

Choline

Dietary Reference Intake (DRI): 450 mg

Choline is a B vitamin critical for the memory center of the brain. A small study done at Cornell University indicates that women who eat more Choline (940 mg a day) in the third trimester may decrease the risk of their baby developing metabolic and chronic stress-related diseases like high blood pressure and diabetes later in life.[27] (The tolerable upper intake is 3,500 mg.) Eggs and lean beef are good sources; eat them regularly to make sure you get enough because not all prenatal vitamins contain choline. Liver—both chicken and beef—are the best sources, but should be eaten with caution due to high vitamin A (and possible heavy metal) content.

Lutein

Lutein, an antioxidant, plays a key role in the developing retina by protecting the cell membranes from free radical damage and by filtering out damaging blue light.[28] It's also been found in key areas of the brain. Lutein is not a standard ingredient in most prenatal vitamins; focus on dark leafy greens like spinach, kale, Swiss chard and romaine lettuce[29]—as well as eggs[30]—to get enough.

Vitamin B6

Dietary Reference Intake (DRI): 1.9 mg

Vitamin B6 is essential for the use of protein—necessary for the building of tissues, including brain and muscle tissue. It's also used in the metabolism of carbohydrates and fats and is used in 100 enzyme reactions in the body—clearly an important vitamin! B6 is needed in proportion to the protein in your diet; the more protein you eat, the more B6 you need. (See chart below for vitamin B6-rich foods.) Folic acid (another B vitamin) as well as vitamin B6 and vitamin B12 are also key players in keeping the amino acid homocysteine at a healthy level. Increased homocysteine levels have been linked to neural tube defects, preeclampsia and pregnancy loss. Make sure to continue having a source of synthetic folic acid in your diet such as from your prenatal vitamin or fortified cereal.

Vitamin B6 Content			
Food	**Serving**	**mg**	**% DRI**
Animal sources:			
Turkey, white meat	3 oz. (95 g)	0.7	37
Salmon, sockeye	3 oz. (95 g)	0.5	26
Chicken breast	3 oz. (95 g)	0.5	26
Pork tenderloin	3 oz. (95 g)	0.4	21
Rainbow trout / halibut / light tuna	3 oz. (95 g)	0.3	16
Ground beef / roast beef	3 oz. (95 g)	0.3	16
Plant sources:			
Baked potato, with skin	1 medium	0.6	31
Chickpeas	½ cup (125 ml)	0.55	29
Breakfast cereals fortified with 25% DV for B6	1 cup (250 ml)	0.5	26
Banana	1 Medium	0.4	21
Brown rice	1 cup (250 ml)	0.29	15
Prune juice	1 cup (250 ml)	0.27	14
Sunflower seeds	¼ cup (65 ml)	0.25	13
Potatoes, white or sweet, boiled	½ cup (125 ml)	0.2	10
Winter squash	½ cup (125 ml)	0.2	10
Avocado	¼	0.1	5

Other B Vitamins

The need for water-soluble vitamins such as thiamin, riboflavin, and niacin depends on your calorie intake. Since the calorie requirements increase in the third trimester, make sure your diet contains foods rich in these vitamins. Women who follow strict vegetarian diets (no animal protein) should either take a vitamin B12 supplement of 2.6 micrograms a day or eat fortified food containing that much.[31]

Third Trimester Diet Challenges

Fatigue

At this point, you're carrying around at least an extra 15-20 pounds (7-9 kg). This can put a strain on your back, the ligaments in your abdomen and pelvis, and on your legs and feet—to name a few. That's enough to make anyone feel tired, but toss in a few sleepless nights due to heartburn, baby's kicks, or worries, and it's enough to make any mom-to-be crave a power nap! Fatigue can cause you to slack off on the quality of your diet or even skip meals. Follow these tips to keep up your energy!

♦ Eat smaller meals with snacks in-between instead of large meals—definitely don't skip meals. Including protein at breakfast like eggs, cottage cheese, Greek yogurt, nut butters or high protein cereals will help keep you going. Snacks also help lift afternoon energy. Keep a snack stash in your drawer: peanut butter. crackers, raisins, dried figs, apricots dried plums, graham crackers, and granola bars. See recipe in the *Eating Expectantly Cookbook* for healthy trail mix.

♦ Put your feet up whenever you have a chance. Some swelling in the feet and legs is considered normal during the last few months—that puts extra pressure on your legs and feet and makes them tired. You may have already figured out that your 5-inch (12.5 cm) stilettos don't work for you anymore. Check out flat, supportive shoes; consider shoe inserts for those flats that don't have any arch support. Support hose are sometimes recommended to help circulation and help prevent varicose veins. Ask your health care provider for more info.

♦ Take it easy at work: Don't stand for more than 4 hours at a time, avoid working more than 40 hours a week and don't lift a lot of weight—these have all been associated with problems like low birthweight, premature birth and preeclampsia.[32]

♦ Take powernaps! An afternoon snooze has been shown to decrease stress, improve productivity, increase learning, and improve health. Can you think of a reason why you shouldn't take a snooze? (except for perhaps your boss...) I remember taking several naps at work during lunch when I was pregnant. That, and a walk at lunchtime got me through the day.

- Let the housework go! It's good practice for the first few months with baby. Start putting your health first and the housework second. Do only what has to be done (laundry, for example) and delegate the rest! Give yourself permission to *not* be Super Woman!

- Keep Moving! Exercise may be the last thing you want to do when you feel tired, but it really helps in the long run because it improves circulation and increases your endurance. You may need to rethink your exercise strategy if your size or ligament pain is getting in the way. Consider exercises that put less stress on your joints and ligaments: water exercise, swimming, spinning or yoga. I learned to love the water when I was pregnant. You feel weightless in the water, and that's great when you feel so big! After a long workday, being in the water can be very refreshing and relaxing. It's no-impact!

Heartburn

As the baby grows, he compresses your stomach, leaving minimal space for food. The hormones that slow down your digestion also relax the lower esophageal sphincter, a muscle that keeps food in your stomach. These changes cause stomach acid to back up into your esophagus, causing a burning sensation that feels as though it's around your heart.

- Portion Control. It's not just what, but how much you eat that can cause heartburn. Since there is less room for the stomach, eating or drinking too much at a time will leave stomach contents with nowhere to go but up. Eating smaller meals will keep you more comfortable.

- Sip, don't Gulp. Drinking too much liquid at a time bloats your stomach, which can also bring on the burn. Instead, have more of your liquids between meals.

- Don't Rush it! Slow down and chew your food well—this is where digestion starts. Gobbling food or not chewing it well makes it take longer to digest. Chewing your food well slows down your eating, so may help you eat less if weight gain is a problem.

- Track Your Triggers. While these triggers are different for every person, the most common ones are coffee, tea, cola, carbonated drinks, chocolate, caffeine, citrus, tomato products, vinegar, chile, garlic, onion and other spicy foods. High fat and fried foods can be problematic, as well as some acidic foods like barbeque sauce, ketchup and sports drinks. Peppermint, though not spicy or acidic, can also be a trigger.

- Don't Take it Lying Down! That is, don't lie down immediately after eating. Instead wait two to three hours after eating before reclining. If this isn't possible, eat your largest meal at lunch.

- Chew Gum. Research shows that chewing sugar-free gum after a meal may significantly reduce the severity of heartburn.[33] Choose a non-minty flavor.

- Put Gravity to Work. Try to avoid activities that require bending forward after eating—such as gardening. Elevate your upper body when sleeping by propping the head of your bed on wooden blocks, or slipping something between your bed and box springs. Propping your head up on pillows, however, doesn't help heartburn and may make it worse unless you raise your head *and* shoulders. At this point, you shouldn't be lying on your back—lying on your left side is better for digestion and circulation.

- Question Natural Remedies. While natural remedies are abundant in stores and on the internet, use them with caution. Apple cider vinegar, for one, seems to work for many. In amounts typically used as a food, vinegar is safe. However, apple cider vinegar tablets are a completely different substance, as are the enzymes found in papaya.

- Why not milk? Historically, people used to drink milk for heartburn. Now we know that it helps temporarily but eventually stimulates more acid production. If you want to try milk as a remedy, use skim milk, or try some plain yogurt.

- Avoid exposure to cigarette or cigar smoke (you want to do this anyway!) Chemicals in smoke make it easier for stomach acid to travel vertically.

- Bring in the reinforcements: If the diet approach isn't helping your heartburn, discuss antacids or prescription meds with your health care provider. Antacids work by neutralizing acid, but they only work briefly. Tums (calcium carbonate) is commonly recommended for heartburn—many women are already taking it as a calcium supplement. Talk with your health care provider before using other over-the-counter or prescription antacids you took before pregnancy; some are not recommended.

Are Natural Remedies For Heartburn Safe During Pregnancy?

A number of natural remedies are recommended for heartburn—and they may or may not work. But when you're desperate, it's tempting to try just about anything. Keep in mind that not all natural remedies are safe, whether you are pregnant or not. Take extra caution now during pregnancy Here's the lowdown:

Remedy	Safe During Pregnancy?	Why/Why Not
Yogurt/Probiotic	Yes	Improves function of digestive tract
Papaya Fruit	Yes	Has an enzyme (papain) that may help digestion
Apple Cider Vinegar	Yes	Vinegar is generally recognized as safe
Aloe Vera	No	May be associated with miscarriage, birth defects[34]
Licorice	No	May be associated with miscarriage or early delivery[35]
Papain (papaya) supplement	No	Could be toxic to baby[36]

Hemorrhoids

Hemorrhoids are swollen (actually varicose) veins in the rectum caused by increased blood flow to the pelvic area as well as pressure from your growing baby bump. They can be extremely painful. Being constipated—and subsequent straining during a bowel movement—can also be a cause or a contributing factor.

♦ Prevent constipation (see page 201 for tips.)

♦ Take a load off. Lying on your side from time to time, floating weightless in a swimming pool and sitting on a "donut" pillow can relieve the pressure.

♦ Avoid heavy lifting, pushing, and sitting or standing for long periods of time, which can put pressure on your bum.

♦ Using witch hazel soaked pads (Tucks) and cold compresses can help ease the pain. Pre-moistened, alcohol-free wipes instead of toilet paper can be a relief.

♦ Discuss all hemorrhoid and constipation treatments with your health care provider. If your health care provider recommends a stool softener; keep in mind that it can take as long as three days to work.

How's Your Diet?

Research data shows most pregnant women's diets do not meet the DRIs for power nutrients such as vitamin B6, vitamin D, vitamin E, folate, iron, zinc, calcium, and magnesium. How does your diet stack up?

	Health Habit	Answer	
1.	I eat a variety of foods daily.	Yes	No
2.	I eat an orange or dark green vegetable daily.	Yes	No
3.	I eat a citrus fruit or another fruit or vegetable high in vitamin C daily.	Yes	No
4.	I eat two to three servings of protein food daily.	Yes	No
5.	In one week, I eat many types of protein; beef, poultry, fish, soy, beans, nuts, grains, seeds, dairy.	Yes	No
6.	I eat at least four servings of whole grains almost every day.	Yes	No
7.	I eat at least 5 cups (1,250 ml) of fruits and vegetables on most days.	Yes	No
8.	I eat at least three servings of dairy products or calcium-rich foods daily.	Yes	No
9.	I'm gaining the right amount of weight for my size.	Yes	No
10.	I avoid caffeine, alcohol, and drugs.	Yes	No
11.	I get enough unprotected sun for Vitamin D production, or I take Vitamin D supplements or eat Vitamin D-fortified foods.	Yes	No
12.	I have a source of DHA in my diet to meet recommended amounts—food or supplement.	Yes	No
13.	I know which foods have trans fat and try to avoid them.	Yes	No
14.	I have a healthy balance of fat in my diet; mostly mono-unsaturated and polyunsaturated with adequate omega-3 fats and as little saturated fat as possible.	Yes	No
15.	I avoid skipping meals and try to eat small meals with snacks between.	Yes	No
16.	I eat as many unprocessed foods as possible.	Yes	No
17.	I try to eat "smart carbs" and limit concentrated sweets like soda, candy, and sweet tea.	Yes	No

If you answered "yes" to at least seven questions, you're doing pretty well. Fewer than that? Well, you know what you need to work on.

10

VEGETARIAN EATING

What You'll Find:

♦ Vegetarians: The Healthy Minority

♦ The Pregnant Vegetarian

♦ Vegetarian Meal Planning Tips

♦ Questions You May Have

Frequently Asked Questions:

♦ Can my baby get all the nutrients he needs if I don't eat meat?

♦ How can I get enough calcium if I'm vegan?

♦ What are some healthy vegetarian choices to order at a restaurant?

♦ What nutrients should I try to eat more of?

♦ How can I find vegan prenatal supplements?

SCAN HERE FOR CHAPTER UPDATES

Vegetarian eating is on the rise as more people realize the benefits of eating plant proteins. Even if you just "lean" toward vegetarian eating, you can receive many of the same health benefits.

Most people eat some vegetarian foods without even thinking about it. Whether you choose a bean burrito or lentil soup, make scrambled eggs with cheese, or you eat no animal products at all, you are practicing some level of vegetarian eating. People eat vegetarian for a variety of reasons: sustainability or humane treatment of animals, religion, because eating vegetarian is healthy, because they're concerned about the environment, or simply because vegetarian food is tasty and cheap.

The Dietary Guidelines for Americans, American Institute for Cancer Research, the World Cancer Research Fund, the Heart and Stroke Foundation of Canada, The UK Food Standards Agency and The American Heart Association all recommend a diet which emphasizes vegetables, whole grains, legumes and fruits. Why? Because eating more of those foods are associated with optimum health and reduced risk of major chronic diseases.

Complementary Proteins: An Old Myth

Years ago, vegetarians were advised to "combine" their proteins to provide a complete balance of amino acids: legume with grain, grain with dairy, or nut with grain to have a "complete protein." According to the position of the Academy of Nutrition and Dietetics on Vegetarian Diets, complementary proteins do not need to be consumed at the same meal if an assortment of plant proteins are eaten throughout the day and energy needs are met.[1]

Vegetarians: The Healthy Minority

Many people would like to have the health records that vegetarians have. Vegetarians generally have a lower body mass index (BMI), lower cholesterol, lower blood pressure, and lower risk of heart disease, cancer and type 2 diabetes than non-vegetarians.[2] They may also have lower risk of constipation, diverticular disease (an intestinal condition), gallstones, and appendicitis.[3]

Research shows that a low-fat vegetarian diet along with stress management and exercise can actually reverse coronary heart disease.[4] A pooled analysis of more than 76,000 men and women showed the largest risk reduction for ischemic heart disease in lacto-ovo vegetarians and in those who ate some fish but no other meat.[5] This sounds a lot like "Flexitarian" eating, an eating style that incorporates the best of vegetarian eating with some animal protein, summarized in the book *The Flexitarian Diet* by Dawn Jackson-Blatner RD.

The specific features of vegetarian diets that are responsible for the many health benefits include eating less saturated fat and cholesterol and eating more fruits and vegetables. Vegetarians may also have beneficial lifestyle habits that contribute to good health, such as regular exercise and not smoking. Maintaining ideal body weight can reduce the risk of heart disease, high blood pressure, and diabetes.

The position of the Academy of Nutrition and Dietetics states, "Appropriately planned vegetarian diets are healthful, are nutritionally adequate, and provide health benefits in the prevention and treatment of certain diseases. Well-planned vegetarian diets are appropriate for individuals during all stages of the lifecycle."[6] The key word here is "well planned". But—not *all* vegetarian diets are healthy—they too can have too much fat and sugar or not include a variety of foods. If you are currently a vegetarian, your diet is probably on its way to meeting the dietary guidelines. If you are contemplating becoming vegetarian, you can become part of the healthy minority, too!

Comparing Diets: Vegan vs. Non-Vegetarian

The table below is from an analysis of 13,000 men and non-pregnant women. It gives a general idea of how a vegan diet stacks up nutritionally[7]—Expressed in percentages of the Dietary Reference Intakes (DRIs).

Comparing Diets		
Nutrient	**Vegans**	**Non-vegetarians**
Calcium	91%	71%
Magnesium	83%	68%
Zinc	93%	112%
Iron	99%	88%
Potassium	63%	60%
Folate	183%	136%
Vitamin A	89%	69%
Vitamin B6	112%	112%
Vitamin B12	158%	221%
Vitamin C	141%	106%
Vitamin E	59%	48%

The Pregnant Vegetarian

Some pregnant women turn to vegetarian foods when they find they can't tolerate meat. Sometimes eggs, cheese, or black beans go down a lot easier than a pork chop. Of course, many women are practicing vegetarians before they become pregnant. How does being vegetarian affect pregnancy? Most pregnant vegetarians can expect to meet or exceed their nutritional needs, with a well-planned diet.

Vegetarians should pay particular attention to a handful of nutrients: vitamin B12, iron, calcium, and zinc, as well as vitamin D. On the other hand, vegetarians are more likely to have higher magnesium, folate, vitamin C and E, carotenoids and phytochemicals than meat eaters.

Vegetarian Meal Planning Tips

Follow the tips below for a nutritionally adequate vegetarian diet.[8]

1. Choose a variety of foods.
2. Eat the minimum number of servings listed in the Eating Expectantly Diet; the range of servings provides 2,000-2,400 calories.
3. Make sure to get adequate dairy or calcium-fortified foods, or take a calcium supplement.
4. Include one or two servings every day of these omega-3-rich foods. Each provides about 2 g of ALA, an omega-3 fat.

    *   1 teaspoon flaxseed oil
    *   1½ tablespoons walnut oil
    *   2 tablespoons canola or soybean oil
    *   2 tablespoons ground flaxseed
    *   ¼ cup (65 ml) walnuts
5. Take a DHA supplement that totals 200-300 mg per day or eat DHA-fortified foods.
6. Eat other healthy fats: nuts, pumpkin, hemp and sesame seeds; avocado, olives and olive oils also provide healthy fats.
7. Have enough vitamin B12—either from a supplement, fortified foods, or from dairy products or eggs.
8. Get adequate vitamin D from regular unprotected sun exposure, or through fortified foods or supplements. Cow's milk, some brands of plant "milks" and breakfast cereals are fortified with vitamin D. See page 59 and page 234 for the full story.
9. Get enough iron—from your prenatal supplement and iron-rich foods. Take your prenatal vitamin with vitamin C-rich juice to increase its absorption.
10. If you eat sweets, eat them in moderation

The Everything Vegan Pregnancy Expert

Over the years, when I've needed advice on vegetarian eating, I've turned to Reed Mangels PhD, RD, who I consider the authority on vegan eating, especially during pregnancy. I recommend Reed's newest book, *The Everything Vegan Pregnancy Book: All You Need to Know for a Healthy Pregnancy that Fits Your Lifestyle*.

Nutrients That May Be of Concern

Protein

Plant protein can meet your protein needs for pregnancy, if you eat enough calories. Dairy and egg-eating vegetarians seem to have adequate protein intakes, while some vegan women's protein intakes are marginal. Vegetarians who eat a large proportion of grain based foods for their protein may not be getting enough protein because most grains don't have the right mix or amount of amino acids. Grain-based proteins may not be as efficiently utilized. This underscores the importance of having a variety of protein foods, including some legumes, quinoa and soy, which contain high quality protein.

The list of foods below will give you an idea of foods that can contain 10 grams of protein per serving; protein needs increase by 25 grams per day during pregnancy. Eat a variety of protein foods throughout the day and day-to-day.

Vegetarian Foods That Contain about 10 Grams of Protein
◆ Beans (white and most other beans), ⅔ to ¾ cup (165-190 ml)
◆ Cashews, ½ cup (125 ml)
◆ Cottage cheese, 1% low-fat, ⅓ cup (85 ml)
◆ Edamame, heaping ½ cup (125 ml)
◆ Miso, ⅓ cup (85 ml)
◆ Peas, 1¼ cup (315 ml)
◆ Peanut butter, 2¼ tablespoons
◆ Pistachios, ⅓ cup (85 ml)—about 100 kernels
◆ Quinoa, 1¼ cup (315 ml)
◆ Milk or Soymilk, 1% low-fat, 1¼ cup (315 ml)
◆ Tempeh, cooked ⅓ cup (85 ml)
◆ Tofu (extra firm), 3.5 oz. (110 g)
◆ Veggie burger, 1 patty (71 g)
◆ Walnuts, 35 halves or ⅔ cup (165 ml)

Vitamin B12

Vitamin B12 is vital during pregnancy, but is not found in plant foods. If you drink an average of 2 cups (500 ml) of milk and eat 1 egg a day, you'll meet your daily need for B12. However, if you're vegan you must get a "reliable" source—such as from Red Star Vegetarian Support Formula nutritional yeast, fortified foods like commercial breakfast cereals, some plant milks or a supplement.

According to Suzanne Havala, DrPH, M.S., R.D., Clinical Assistant Professor, School of Public Health, University of North Carolina at Chapel Hill, "Some vegetarian specialty foods thought by many to be good sources of vitamin B12, such as tempeh and spirulina, are in fact not reliable sources. Food labels listing the vitamin B12 content of these foods include forms of the vitamin that are not active for humans and may compete for absorption with cyanocobalamin, the form we use."

Because product formulations often change, be sure to check labels. It's best to look for the word "cyanocobalamin" on the label when looking for a reliable source of B12. If you don't eat any fortified foods or dairy, make sure your prenatal supplement has enough B12. Ask your health care provider for more info.

Iron

Although anemia is no more common among vegetarians than meat eaters, anemia is common for many pregnant women due to the high iron requirements of pregnancy. The type of iron in plant foods (non-heme iron) is not as well absorbed as the iron in meat (heme iron), so the recommended intake for vegetarians is 49 mg instead of 27 mg.[9] Even with the 30-40 mg of supplemental of iron usually found in prenatal supplements, vegan women may have to plan well to get enough iron from foods or choose a supplement with a little more iron. The type of iron found in plant foods is more sensitive to both foods that enhance and inhibit its absorption.

Foods That Inhibit Iron Absorption:
♦ Phytates: found in grains and legumes are thought to have a small effect.
♦ Tea, including some herbal teas.
♦ Coffee and cocoa: Make sure to drink them between meals instead of with meals.
♦ Calcium: both calcium-rich foods and calcium supplements can decrease iron absorption.
♦ Fiber: has a small effect.
Foods And Processes That Enhance Iron Absorption:
♦ Vitamin C: helps increase the absorption from plant foods. Vitamin C can also counteract the effect of phytate.
♦ Cooking in an iron skillet: especially with an acidic food.
♦ Leavening: breaks down the phytate in bread, and enhances iron absorption

- ◆ Fermentation: miso and tempeh are fermented and this may enhance iron absorption. The iron in sourdough bread may also be better absorbed.
- ◆ Soaking and sprouting: of beans, grains and seeds can also break down phytate. But remember that raw sprouts are also a potential source of foodborne bacteria and are not recommended during pregnancy.

Calcium

Calcium can be a challenge if you are vegan. However, plant-based beverages like soy, flax or almond milk are likely to have added calcium. A specific recommended intake for calcium has not been established for vegetarians, so it's best to follow the Dietary Reference Intake (DRI) for calcium, which is 1,000 milligrams. If you have lactose intolerance, see page 186. See page 215 for sources of calcium.

Sea Vegetables

Sea vegetables can be good sources of calcium and iodine. But they could contain TOO much iodine as well as heavy metal pollutants. Make sure your seaweed comes from a controlled source, such as a sea vegetable farm.

Oxalates and phytates, substances found in leafy green vegetables and whole grains, can affect absorption of calcium. The high oxalate content of vegetables like spinach, Swiss chard, rhubarb, and beet greens make the calcium in these vegetables largely unabsorbable. But overall, calcium from low oxalate vegetables (broccoli, bok choy, kale, mustard and turnip greens) is absorbed as well as the calcium from milk. High-fiber foods, especially wheat bran, are high in phytates—which can decrease the absorption of calcium from milk. Almond butter, almonds, tahini (sesame seed butter) and molasses also provide a good source of calcium. If you are concerned about your calcium intake, talk to a registered dietitian about increasing the calcium in your diet or ask your health care provider about a supplement. See page 99 for more information on supplements.

Are all Milks Created Equally?

Can you swap rice or almond milk for soymilk or dairy milk and expect the same nutritional package? No. Calcium is found naturally in dairy products, while plant beverages must be fortified. The added calcium can fall to the bottom of the container, even after shaking. Soy beverages are the closest to dairy milk for protein; almond, flax, rice, coconut and hemp milk have only 1-4 grams per cup (250 ml), compared to 8 grams in soymilk and dairy milk. Many plant milks contain added sugar. Rice milk has been found to contain arsenic, and is not recommended during pregnancy.

Vitamin D

Few foods are naturally high in vitamin D; milk, some brands of soymilk and almond milk, and some cereals are fortified with it. In recent years, researchers have discovered that many of us don't get enough vitamin D—whether you are vegetarian or not. Some researchers believe that the current DRI for vitamin D is inadequate.[10] Exposing the hands, arms, and face for five to fifteen minutes of sun per day is believed to provide enough vitamin D from sunshine for light skinned people during the summer at 42 degrees latitude. In the US: at and south of Providence RI, Hartford CT, Boston, Des Moines, Cleveland, Medford OR. In Europe: Corsica, France, Girona, Spain, and through the Mediterranean. In the Southern Hemisphere north of the South Island of New Zealand and Chiloe Island, Chile. People who use sunscreen, have dark skin, or live at higher latitudes or in cloudy or smoggy areas may need increased exposure or may need to get their vitamin D from fortified foods or a supplement, especially in the winter.

Vitamin D insufficiency appears to occur in a wide variety of latitudes. In one Australian study of mostly Caucasians, 40% of women from southeast Queensland (27 degrees South) and 37% of the women in a region close to Melbourne (38 degrees south) had vitamin D insufficiency. It is thought that outdoor behavior (avoiding the outdoors in the summer heat and wearing sunscreen to prevent skin cancer) are both factors that affect the decline in blood levels of vitamin D, even in sunny climates like Florida where 40% of women studied had low vitamin D levels at the end of winter.[11]

If you don't eat enough fortified foods or get enough unprotected access to sunshine, especially in the winter, you should consider a supplement. Keep in mind that Vitamin D2, (ergocalciferol), the vegan form of vitamin D is less bioavailable than vitamin D3, so if you depend on that form of vitamin via a supplement, you may need more than usually recommended.[12] If you suspect you may not have had enough vitamin D in the past, have your vitamin D level tested. A vitamin D deficiency usually requires a prescription-sized dose to correct. See page 59 for more info.

Vegan Ingredient Watch

Vitamin D2 is the vegetarian source for supplements; D3 is generally made from sheep wool, however some D3 is not from animals. Foods like milk and cereal fortified with Vitamin D can be either D2 or D3. Also many Vitamin D supplements contain gelatin. Many DHA supplements are from fish but Life's DHA is a source from algae. For an excellent resource on vegetarian food ingredients, see the Vegetarian Journal's Guide to Food Ingredients at www.vrg.org/ingredients/index.php#vitamin_d

Vitamin B6

All women seem to have a problem getting enough vitamin B6. Your body needs this vitamin in proportion to your protein intake, so if your diet is especially high in protein foods, you may need even more B6. (See page 221 for a list of vegetarian sources of B6.)

Iodine

Some studies suggest that vegans who don't use iodized salt or eat sea vegetables may not get enough iodine.[13] Also vegetarians may eat more goitrogens—foods that interfere with iodine uptake by the thyroid gland like soybeans, cruciferous vegetables and sweet potatoes. Sea salt and kosher salt are not reliable sources of iodine, and some sea vegetables have excessive amounts. See page 220 for more information.

Shopping for a Vegan Supplement

Several companies make vegan vitamins:

♦ www.veglife.com

♦ www.freedavitamins.com

♦ www.country-life.com

♦ www.rainbowlight.com

Zinc

Zinc is a very important nutrient for a developing fetus. It is abundant in such foods as legumes, shellfish, whole grains, and cheese. Many people don't have enough zinc in their diet.

Factors that may affect absorption of zinc include fiber, phytates, and some minerals. You can obtain an adequate amount of zinc by making careful food choices. Consult the list on page 164 to see how much zinc your diet supplies.

Omega-3 Fats

Omega-3 fats are long chain polyunsaturated fats important for fetal brain and eye development. Alpha-Linolenic Acid (ALA) is an essential omega-3 fat—our bodies can't make it, yet it's required to produce two other important fats: docosahexanenoic (DHA) and Eicosapenaenoic Acid (EPA). Vegetarian diets are low in DHA and EPA, because those fats are found primarily in cold water fish and fortified foods such

---

Just the Facts: Optimum Omega-3's from a Vegetarian Diet

♦ Eat foods rich in ALA on a daily basis: flaxseed oil, ground flaxseed, walnuts, canola and soybean oil (found in salad dressings and mayonnaise.)

♦ Use olive oil and canola oil for cooking.

♦ Eat less omega-6-rich oils—corn, sunflower, safflower and cottonseed, which can interfere with the production of DHA.

♦ Limit intake of saturated fat and avoid trans fats as they interfere with DHA production.

♦ Consider taking a DHA supplement of 200-300 mg while you are pregnant and breastfeeding.

---

as eggs and milk. Vegetarians also have a much higher intake of Linoleic Acid (LA)—another essential fat that can decrease the conversion of ALA into DHA and EPA. Because the conversion of ALA to DHA is not very efficient, increasing these fatty acids in the diet do not result in increases of DHA in either Mom or baby, suggesting that more preformed DHA and EPA is needed.[14]

Going Veggie During Pregnancy

Sharon Palmer, RD

Plant-based eating is my life. Not only am I a registered dietitian and writer specializing in plant-based diets, I've been a vegetarian most of my life. I believe that there are so many health benefits to be gained—for both people and the planet—by switching from eating animals to eating more plants. My foray into vegetarianism started as a child, as I was raised in a semi-vegetarian home. This is before celebrities touted this eating style and soy foods were available at every supermarket. Today I'm a vegan-vegetarian; I eat mostly vegan meals when I'm at home and switch to a vegetarian diet, including dairy products and eggs, when I travel or dine at someone's home. But when I was pregnant, I followed more of a semi-vegetarian diet, eating animal flesh only occasionally. People always think you need so much protein in order to be healthy—especially when you're pregnant. But the fact is that Americans get way more protein than they really need. The great thing about being vegetarian is that it's not just about what you're not eating—animal foods filled with saturated fats and dietary cholesterol. It's about what you are eating—fruits and vegetables in every color of the rainbow, whole grains, beans, lentils, nuts, and seeds. These foods are filled with vitamins, minerals, and fiber. But even more significant may be the multitude of phytochemicals found only in plant foods—the greater your volume and variety of these foods, the greater the volume and variety of phytochemicals that enter your body. Now scientists are learning that various phytochemicals, from anthocyanins in blueberries to lycopene in tomatoes, offer important health protection. It's funny, I craved fruits and veggies when I was pregnant, I just couldn't get enough of them. Even when I had morning sickness, the only thing that sounded good to me was a tart, fruit smoothie. My body was telling me that I needed all of these delicious, nutritious plant foods to feed my baby. And I think my fetus was swimming in an antioxidant, anti-inflammatory bath during his time in my tummy. My blood levels must have been sky high with these health-promoting chemicals, which may have provided my son special health protection for years to come.

Sharon is the author of *The Plant Powered Diet: The Lifelong Eating Plan for Achieving Optimal Health, Beginning Today* (The Experiment, 2012) and the editor of *Environmental Nutrition*. For more information: www. sharonpalmer.com

Eating Expectantly: The Vegetarian Way

You can follow the Eating Expectantly Diet on page 86. However if you don't drink cow's milk or soymilk, you will need to eat other calcium-rich foods and you may need a few extra servings from the protein group, depending on the rest of your diet.

Sample Vegan Menu

This menu contains between 2,200-2,400 calories and exceeds the Dietary Recommended Intakes for all nutrients.

Breakfast
- ◆ I cup (250 ml) Cheerios
- ◆ ½ cup (125 ml) blueberries
- ◆ I cup (250 ml) low-fat organic soymilk

Snack
- ◆ ½ cup (125 ml) calcium-fortified orange juice
- ◆ ⅓ cup (85 ml) hummus on 5 whole grain crackers

Lunch
- ◆ I cup (250 ml) lentil soup with I piece corn bread, 2 teaspoons olive oil margarine
- ◆ Broccoli and tofu stir-fry with 2 teaspoons canola oil, ½ cup (125 ml) tofu, ½ cup (125 ml) broccoli, ¼ cup (65 ml) mushrooms
- ◆ ½ cup (125 ml) quinoa
- ◆ I cup (250 ml) low-fat organic soymilk
- ◆ I tangerine

Snack
- ◆ I large apple

Dinner

- Spinach salad with walnuts, 2 tablespoons dried cranberries, ¼ avocado, and vinaigrette dressing made with flaxseed oil
- Stuffed bell pepper with ½ cup (125 ml) couscous, ½ cup (125 ml) black beans, and ½ tomato, ½ cup (125 ml) corn
- 1 cup (250 ml) low sodium vegetable juice

Snack

- Smoothie with ½ cup (125 ml) low-fat organic soymilk and ¾ (190 ml) cup frozen strawberries

Sample Lacto-Ovo Vegetarian Menu

This menu, which contains eggs and dairy products, contains approximately 2,400 calories and exceeds all of the DRIs for pregnancy.

Breakfast

- 1 piece whole wheat toast with 1 tablespoon sunflower seed butter and 2 teaspoons honey
- 1 cup (250 ml) nonfat organic milk
- ½ grapefruit

Snack

- 1 oz. (30 g) string cheese
- 6 whole wheat crackers
- 3 dates

Lunch

- 1 cup (250 ml) split-pea soup
- 1 cup (250 ml) spinach salad with candied walnuts, dried cranberries, tomato, vitamin D mushrooms, ¼ avocado, and vinaigrette dressing made with flaxseed oil
- 2 pieces corn bread with 2 teaspoons olive oil margarine
- 1 kiwi

Snack

- 2 cups (500 ml) light popcorn
- 1 large hard cooked egg
- ½ cup (125 ml) low sodium vegetable juice

Dinner

- 1 Veggie burger on whole-wheat bun
- ½ cup (125 ml) sautéed red pepper
- 2 teaspoons mayonnaise, mustard
- Lettuce and tomato
- 1 cup (250 ml) grilled zucchini
- 1 cup (250 ml) nonfat organic milk

Snack

- 6 oz. (190 g) Greek yogurt
- ½ cup (125 ml) sliced peaches

Vegetarian Burger in Paradise?

Burger King offers the BK Veggie Burger in the US, Canada, and the UK; the BK Veggie Bean Burger is available in the UK, Europe and Asia. They are considered vegetarian but not necessarily vegan, depending on sourcing for the mayonnaise and bun. Although I applaud Burger King for offering vegetarian options, both sandwiches have more than 1,000 mg of sodium. The Veggie Bean Burger is deep-fried, and it still manages to have less fat and saturated fat than most burgers on the menu, but the saturated fat still adds up to 5 grams! Keep in mind that if cooked in the microwave, the Veggie Burger is considered vegan, but if grilled, it may come in contact with meat cooked on the same grill.

Shopping Vegetarian: A to Z Guide

If you're considering turning to more vegetarian fare, you may wonder about some of the terms used for vegetarian foods. Here's a glossary:

- **Agar:** an odorless, tasteless sea vegetable used as a thickener to replace gelatin.

- **Edamame:** green or immature soy beans becoming popular at chain restaurants like Pei Wei. You can buy edamame frozen in the bag and they make a great snack. See recipes in the *Eating Expectantly Cookbook*.

- **Egg Replacer:** a vegetarian substitute for eggs made out of a variety of flours and vegetable starches.

- **Hydrolyzed Vegetable Protein (HVP):** a protein obtained by acid hydrolysis from any vegetable, including soy. HVP is used as a flavor enhancer in broths, sauces and gravies.

- **Meat Analogue:** a generic word for a vegetarian meat substitute. A meat analogue is often made of soy but can also be made from wheat gluten or seitan.

- **Miso:** a nutrient-rich, salty condiment made from fermented soy beans, rice, buckwheat or barley. Miso comes in a paste form in light and darker varieties; the lighter varieties tend to be less salty and more mellow in flavor—the intensity and flavor increases with the color. Miso soup is a staple in Japanese cuisine.

- **Nutritional Yeast:** a yellow, nutty, cheese flavored inactive yeast that is extremely nutrient-rich. In Australia, it's sometimes called "savoury yeast flakes," while in New Zealand it's called "Brufax." (Vegemite, though made from brewer's yeast extract, contains no vitamin B12.) Tasty when sprinkled over popcorn or on garlic bread, in a soup or in mashed potatoes. Red Star Vegetarian Support Formula Nutritional Yeast provides a reliable source of vitamin B12. Just 1 tablespoon provides more than 100% of your daily needs for Vitamin B12, B1, B6, Riboflavin and Niacin. It also provides an excellent source of zinc, selenium and 4 grams of protein in 1 heaping tablespoon of large flakes.

- **Seaweed/Sea Vegetables:** There are thousands of types of seaweed—we only eat a few of them. Seaweed is technically part of the algae family and can be found in oceans as well as fresh water. In general, seaweed is very nutrient-rich—especially iodine and vitamin K. But—some seaweed like arami, hiziki and kombu should be limited because they can have too much iodine, which can also pose a problem. Some sea vegetables may also contain heavy metals.

- **Seitan:** a meat substitute made from wheat protein or gluten. It has a texture similar to meat and also called "wheat meat". It can be homemade by making wheat dough and rinsing and kneading to remove the starch. It can also be bought—check out Arrowhead Mills Seitan Quick Mix. Seitan is also the basis of some deli favorites like "lunch meat", "not dogs" and "fajita strips" and can be found often in Asian cuisine.

- **Tahini:** made from toasted and ground sesame seeds, it's very high in absorbable calcium. Often used in Middle Eastern cooking, as in baba ganoush and hummus (recipes in *Eating Expectantly Cookbook*).

- **Tempeh:** made from whole soybeans and is made into a type of "cake" through a culturing and fermentation process. It can be grated and used as a substitute for ground beef, or in chunks or slices, can be used in a sandwich, stir-fries or stews. Its taste has been described as nutty, meaty or mushroom-like.

- **Textured Vegetable Protein (TVP):** also called Textured Soy Protein or TSP. Made from soy flour, TVP is a high fiber, high protein dehydrated meat substitute. It comes in many forms, from flakes, to nuggets and must be rehydrated before being put into recipes. It works well in chili, soups and tacos. TVP is an ingredient in many processed foods including veggie burgers.

- **Tofu:** made by coagulating soymilk and pressing the curds into blocks. When the coagulating agent contains calcium, it makes the tofu calcium-rich. Tofu is almost tasteless on its own, so it takes on whatever flavor you give it in cooking. There are two types of tofu—silken and regular. Though they both come in firm and extra firm textures, they are not interchangeable in recipes.

- **Silken tofu:** also called soft, silk or Japanese style and has a softer consistency than regular tofu. It is often found in aseptic packaging, so you can keep a couple in the pantry. Silk tofu is fragile and can easily fall apart in your hand, thus it's most often used in recipes for sauces, pies and salad dressings. Silk tofu also comes in firm and extra firm textures.

- **Regular tofu:** also called bean curd or Chinese-style tofu, it comes in a plastic container in water in the refrigerated section of the store. Firm or extra firm regular tofu is perfect for stir-fries, and other dishes where you want the tofu to retain its shape, whereas medium or soft texture is better for substituting for ricotta cheese or to make scrambled tofu. Freezing tofu makes it have a spongier texture and it absorbs marinades better.

Resources

- *The Everything Vegan Pregnancy Book: All You Need To Know For A Healthy Pregnancy That Fits Your Lifestyle* by Reed Mangels PhD, RD, 2011

- *The Plant Powered Diet* by Sharon Palmer RD, 2012

- *Simply Vegan: Quick Vegetarian Meals* by Debra Wasserman with Reed Mangels, PhD, RD, 2006

- *The New Becoming Vegetarian: The Essential Guide To A Healthy Vegetarian Diet* by Vesanto Melina and Brenda Davis (Aug 2003)

- *Vegan for Life: Everything You Need to Know to Be Healthy and Fit on a Plant-Based Diet* by Jack Norris and Virginia Messina (Jul 12, 2011)

Eating Out Vegetarian-Style

As more people eat meatless, restaurants are adding vegetarian and vegan options to their menus. Some restaurants are very accommodating and will put together vegetarian meals that aren't even on the menu. Below are some healthy vegetarian entrées you're likely to find at various kinds of sit-down restaurants. Not all meatless entrées are vegan, so if you are concerned about animal-derived ingredients, you should consult the restaurant manager.

Vegetarian Entrées by Cuisine

Asian/Chinese

Any tofu (also called bean curd) dish

Egg foo young

Noodle or curry dish with vegetables and/or tofu

Bistro/Continental

Veggie burger

Vegetable platter

Spinach-and-artichoke dip

Veggie wrap

Roasted vegetable sandwich

Quiche

Ratatouille

Vegetable risotto

Vegetable soup

Bean soup

Stuffed potato

Indian

Vegetable curry

Lentils

Spinach paneer

Italian

Cheese- or vegetable-stuffed ravioli or manicotti

Eggplant parmesan

Pasta primavera

Pasta e fagioli (pasta-and-bean soup)

Cheese or veggie pizza

Vegetarian lasagna

Mexican

Bean burrito

Huevos rancheros

Cheese or green chile enchilada

Bean Tostadas

Vegetable Caldo

Middle Eastern
Falafel (ground chickpea fritters often served in pita bread)
Hummus (chickpea dip)
Tabouli (bulgur salad)
Baba ganoush (eggplant dip)
Ful medames (fava bean and chickpea dish)
Cucumber and tomato salad
Yogurt salad
Steak House
Vegetable or bean soup
Salad bar
Baked potato bar
Steamed vegetables
Thai
Vegetarian basil rolls
Vegetable boat
Curried Tofu

For more general information about dining out, see chapter 16. Check these websites for specific information about vegan fair at chain restaurants:

♦   www.peta.org/living/vegetarian-living/chain-restaurants.aspx

♦   www.vegansociety.com/lifestyle/travel/

Eating Vegan at the Ball Park

Vegetarian options are now offered at least 30 Major League ballparks across the US. Some, like the Houston Astros, Chicago White Sox, New York Mets, and Seattle Mariners stadiums offer Veggie Dogs—after all, what's a baseball game without a hot dog? To find out more specifics about vegetarian offerings at pro sports venues as well as zoos, amusement parks and airports, see www.soyhappy.org/venue.htm

Questions You May Have

Q: I just found out I have gestational diabetes. How can I fit vegetarian foods into my meal plan?

A: Actually, a vegetarian diet is a good way to control your blood sugar. A vegan diet, which is usually fiber-rich, has a lower glycemic index. A randomized control trial of people with type 2 diabetes following a vegan diet had improved blood sugar control and many were able to decrease their diabetes medications.[15] Visiting with a registered dietitian can help in planning a vegetarian diet to meet your specific needs.

To Find a Registered Dietitian

You can find a registered dietitian by location and areas of expertise. See www.eatright.org/programs/rdfinder/.

Q: Is a vegetarian diet lower in fat than a diet containing meat?

A: Generally, yes, but not always. A diet that is not well planned can have as much fat (including saturated and trans fat) as a typical Western diet. The important feature for any type of diet is to eat the right kind of fats, limiting saturated fat and avoiding trans fats. For example, a lacto-ovo diet can have a lot of cheese, and full-fat dairy products, which raise the saturated fat content of the diet. A vegan diet can also be high in fat, although most of the fat would be unsaturated (unless it contains coconut, palm or palm kernel oil). For example, nuts, tahini, avocado, and nut butters, staples for some vegetarians, are very high in fat, but the fat is healthy fat. Other hidden fats can find their way into the diet through such goodies as soy or rice milk frozen desserts and carob or deep fried foods like tempura, and falafel.

11

HIGH-RISK PREGNANCY

What You'll Find:

- ◆ Expect the Unexpected

- ◆ Problems with Blood Sugar: Diabetes

- ◆ Keys to Controlling Gestational Diabetes

- ◆ High Blood Pressure

- ◆ When You're Expecting Twins or More

- ◆ Coping with Bed-rest

- ◆ Older Moms

- ◆ Pregnancy After Gastric Bypass Surgery

Frequently Asked Questions:

- ◆ What kind of diet should I follow if I have gestational diabetes?

- ◆ Should I cut my salt intake if I have high blood pressure during pregnancy?

- ◆ How can I prepare and eat healthy meals if I'm on bed-rest?

- ◆ How much weight should I gain if I'm expecting twins?

- ◆ Should I eat differently if I'm over thirty-five?

SCAN HERE FOR CHAPTER UPDATES

Expect the Unexpected

The unknown can be scary—especially when you're pregnant! To equip you for the unexpected, this chapter tells you how some special conditions may affect you and your baby and how to best deal with them. There are other complications associated with pregnancy, but this chapter will discuss only those that can affect or be affected by your diet. Being informed is the key to taking charge of your health and having the healthiest pregnancy possible.

Dealing with Your Emotions

When you discover that you have a high-risk pregnancy, you'll probably find yourself on an emotional roller coaster. You may experience guilt, fear, anger, denial, depression, or loneliness. Emotions are sometimes helpful in getting you through rough times, but emotions can be unhealthy if they prevent you from taking care of yourself.

For example, guilt and fear may motivate you to change your lifestyle to protect your baby, and denial may give you time to get used to the idea of a high-risk condition. But, being stuck in denial can keep you from making the right choices to help you and your baby. Depression and loneliness may alienate you from people who can help you. Depression and anxiety may also have long-term effects on your baby. Identifying your feelings can help you adjust and seek support from others. If any of your emotions hinder you from dealing with your situation or significantly affect your sleeping or eating patterns, speak with your health care provider.

When I was put on bed-rest for eleven weeks during my second pregnancy, I had many of the emotions mentioned earlier. At one point I got so upset that I was ready to walk out the front door and away from my problems. Of course that wasn't possible, but it did give me an emotional release. (Looking back, the idea of walking away from my own belly is pretty funny!) What helped me the most was the support I received from others and reading about the experiences of women on bed-rest.

Whatever happens, and whatever you have to do to carry out your pregnancy, it will be worth it when you see your healthy baby!

You Are Not Alone

One of the hardest aspects of a high-risk pregnancy is feeling like you're the only person with your problem, at least in your neighborhood. But—you're not alone; many women have been there or are facing the same challenges right now. Below (and throughout this chapter) are some places to find support and information:

Resources

♦ Sidelines National Support Network is a national, nonprofit network for women and families experiencing high-risk pregnancies. Sidelines offers phone or e-mail support through a volunteer who has experienced a similar high-risk pregnancy. You can contact them by visiting www.sidelines.org, or calling 1-888-HiRisk-4 (888-447-4754)

♦ The American Diabetes Association is the best resource for information on all types of diabetes. On this website you can find many resources, including a consumer and professional magazine. Visit www.diabetes.org or call 800-DIABETES (800-342-2383).

♦ The American Association of Diabetes Educators (AADE) can help you find a Certified Diabetes Educator in your area that can help you: www.diabeteseducator.org 800-338-3633.

♦ Medline Plus, a service of the US National Library of Medicine, has an excellent resource about high-risk pregnancies: www.nlm.nih.gov/medlineplus/healthproblemsinpregnancy.html

♦ Health Link British Columbia has information on a variety of high-risk conditions: www.healthlinkbc.ca/kb/content/special/uf9705.html

Problems with Blood Sugar: Diabetes

When you eat, the body breaks down the starches and sugars into glucose, which is the basic fuel for all cells in the body. Insulin, a hormone made in the pancreas, is necessary for glucose to get into cells where it can be used for energy. When you have problems with insulin—either your body doesn't produce enough insulin, or your body ignores the insulin, it causes blood sugar to build up in the blood. This leads to a condition called diabetes.

Type 2 diabetes (formerly called Adult Onset) is the most common form of diabetes. Being overweight is a risk factor for diabetes. Because more people are becoming overweight, there has also been a worldwide increase in the number of people with diabetes. Unfortunately, diabetes often goes undiagnosed—as many as 40% of people in the US with diabetes don't know they have it.[1] In fact, if you have Polycystic Ovary Syndrome (PCOS), you may have impaired glucose tolerance or even type 2 diabetes and not know it.

Check out your risk for diabetes here: www.diabetes.org/diabetes-basics/prevention/diabetes-risk-test/

Pre-existing Diabetes

If you had diabetes prior to pregnancy, it's critical to have well-controlled blood sugar *before* and during pregnancy. It's a good idea for you to be working with a health care provider who is a maternal fetal specialist. In fact, the American Diabetes Association recommends you see your health care provider before pregnancy. If you are pregnant and haven't seen your health care provider yet, make an appointment NOW. Some medications you are taking may not be safe during pregnancy; however, don't stop any medications without first talking to your health care provider. For more information: www.diabetes.org/living-with-diabetes/complications/pregnant-women/prenatal-care.html

Gestational Diabetes

Gestational Diabetes Mellitus or GDM is a type of diabetes that occurs in women who have high blood sugar (glucose) levels during pregnancy. According to the American Diabetes Association, due to recently changed diagnostic criteria, up to 18% of pregnancies may be affected by GDM.[2] GDM is a type of diabetes that usually disappears after delivery, but ⅔ of women will be diagnosed with type 2 diabetes later in life. Keeping a healthy weight, exercising regularly and eating a proper diet can prevent type 2 diabetes.

How Will You Know if You Have Gestational Diabetes?

Since most women don't have typical symptoms associated with diabetes such as blurred vision or weight loss, it's standard practice to test all women for diabetes between their 24th and 28th week of pregnancy. Oral Glucose Tolerance Tests (OGTT) are done after an overnight fast. A 2-hour OGTT is now recommended by the American Diabetes Association, though some health care providers still use older diagnostic methods which include a 1-hour screening test followed by a three-hour OGTT if needed.[3] However, if you have some of the risk factors for diabetes, such as being overweight, having a family history of diabetes, previous history of GDM or impaired glucose tolerance, your health care provider may decide to screen you at your first prenatal visit.

The 2-hour OGTT involves checking your fasting blood sugar and drinking a **really** sweet drink containing 75 grams of glucose and then checking your blood sugar one hour and two hours later to see how your body processed the sugar. If one or more of the blood tests are abnormal, you'll be diagnosed with GDM.[4]

Effects on Baby

♦ Larger Size: The most common problem is that your baby could be larger (also called macrosomia) which can lead to trauma during delivery and increased need for a C-section.

♦ Low blood sugar during the first few days of life

♦ Breathing Problems

Previously it was thought that having GDM increases the risk of having a child who is overweight later in life. Newer analyses indicate that a mom's pre-pregnancy weight and blood sugar level during pregnancy are more strongly associated with childhood obesity than just a diagnosis of GDM. This means that keeping tight control of blood sugar may make it easier for your child to have a healthy weight later in life.[5]

What to Expect

♦ Checking your blood sugar daily, at least 3 times and often 4-6 times a day

♦ Changing your current diet and lifestyle

♦ Closer monitoring by your health care provider and possibly a referral to a diabetes specialist

♦ Meeting with a Registered Dietitian or Certified Diabetes Educator for instructions on eating and managing your diabetes

♦ Possibly requiring insulin injections or oral medications to control blood sugar

Check out this podcast about GDM by the Centers for Disease Control and Prevention www2c.cdc.gov/podcasts/player.asp?f=11504&loc=WhatIsGestational

---

Just the Facts

You are at greater risk of GDM if you[6]:

♦ Have a parent, brother, or sister with diabetes.

♦ Are African American, American Indian, Asian American, Hispanic/Latino, or Pacific Islander.

♦ Are 25 years old or older.

♦ Are overweight.

♦ Have had gestational diabetes before, or have given birth to at least one baby weighing more than nine pounds.

♦ Have been told that you have "prediabetes", a condition in which blood sugar levels are higher than normal, but not high enough for a diagnosis of diabetes. Other names for it are "impaired glucose tolerance" and "impaired fasting glucose."

Diabetes Around the World: Ethnicity and Other Factors

There are definite differences in the risk of diabetes depending on your ethnicity. In the US, Native Americans, Asians, Hispanics, and African-American women are at higher risk for GDM than non-Hispanic white women. In Australia, GDM prevalence was higher in women whose country of birth was China or India than in women whose country of birth was in Europe or Northern Africa. GDM prevalence was also higher in Aboriginal women than in non-Aboriginal women. In Europe, GDM has been found to be more common among Asian women than among European women. Apparently, the proportion of pregnancies complicated by GDM in Asian countries has been reported to be lower than the proportion observed in Asian women living on other continents. In India, GDM has been found to be more common in women living in urban areas than in women living in rural areas.[7]

Keys to Controlling Gestational Diabetes

♦ Keep your weight in check. Make sure to keep weight gain to what's recommended for your pre-pregnancy weight. See page 105. Keep in mind that your health care provider may suggest you gain less weight than what's on the chart.

♦ Count Your Carbs: Make it a priority to learn the carbohydrate content of foods once you are diagnosed with GDM. The amount and type of carbs you eat, as well as what you eat with them, will directly affect your blood sugar levels. If you have been following the Eating Expectantly Diet, with its emphasis on smart carbs, you most likely won't have to change your diet very much!

♦ Eat balanced meals at regular intervals and eat a consistent amount of carbohydrates at each meal. Generally three small meals plus two or three "balanced" snacks are recommended. A balanced snack contains carbohydrate and protein. See a registered dietitian for a personalized meal plan.

♦ Start, or Keep Moving! More than likely, regular exercise will be a cornerstone for treatment of your diabetes—and it may keep you from taking insulin. Talk to your health care provider about recommending a daily exercise program; most health care providers approve of walking or swimming. Inquire if there are any situations when you should *avoid* exercise. (See Chapter 14, "Fitting Fitness In", for more information on exercise during pregnancy.)

♦ Keep a handle on weight gain; some women find their weight gain slows down once they are controlling their blood sugar.

♦ Choose foods low in saturated fat and try to avoid trans fat.

♦ Avoid emotional eating, such as eating when you are sad, angry, or stressed-out.

- Eat more whole-grain foods and legumes.

- Avoid concentrated sweets such as cookies, candy, pie, sugar, honey. (If you must have a sweet, choose dark chocolate, but limit to a one-half ounce serving—about two Hershey's kisses.) Also, limit or avoid fruit juices, even unsweetened. They contain concentrated amounts of fruit sugar, which can raise blood sugar.

- Keep your diet high in fiber. Fiber helps stabilize blood sugar. So stay away from foods made with only white flour as much as possible. Try to eat raw (instead of cooked) fruits and vegetables. Eat high-fiber cereal with milk as a snack. (See page 191, "Focus on Fiber.")

- Smile! You have a unique opportunity to improve your family's diet! Try to make the changes permanent.

Be Choosy about Carbs

You do need carbohydrate foods. In fact, the Academy of Nutrition and Dietetics recommends eating at least 175 grams of carbohydrates per day to insure proper fetal brain development.[8] (To give you an idea, a piece of bread or fruit contains 15 grams of carbohydrate.) Carbohydrates are found in starchy foods like bread, crackers, cookies, cereals, rice, potatoes, pasta, corn, milk, yogurt, dried beans, fruit, and fruit juice. Carbohydrate is also found in smaller amounts in non-starchy vegetables like green beans, carrots, and tomatoes.

However, it's recommended that you eat smaller quantities of carbohydrates than you did before your diagnosis. For example, typically it's recommended that during pregnancy 50-55% of calories come from carbohydrates, but if you have diabetes, less than 45% is recommended.[9] Also, the timing of carbohydrate foods can make a difference to your blood sugar. Because your body is more resistant to the action of insulin in the morning, it's generally recommended that you limit carbohydrate foods to 1-2 servings before noon.

The Sweet Success Program in California recommends staying away from fruit juices and processed and refined starch products such as instant potatoes, instant noodles, instant hot cereals, cold processed cereals, canned soups, and packaged stuffing. It also recommends avoiding sugar-containing sauces such as teriyaki and barbecue. On the other hand, it encourages eating whole-grain breads, non-instant oatmeal, legumes and lentils because of their small effect on blood sugar. Of course, any food containing concentrated sugars also provides concentrated sources of carbohydrates and should be limited. Read the food label carefully to find grams of carbohydrate. The grams of total carbohydrate listed are based on one serving. If two servings are eaten, the total carbohydrate needs to be doubled, three… tripled and so on. For more information on label-reading see page 346.

The Food Pyramid for Gestational Diabetes is from the California Diabetes and Pregnancy Program. It's at: www.lomalindahealth.org/common/legacy/llumc/sweetsuccess/pdfs/foodpyramid-eng.pdf

For more information including other diet tips:

◆ www.cdph.ca.gov/programs/cdapp/Pages/SweetSuccessMaterials.aspx

◆ www.cdph.ca.gov/programs/NutiritionandPhysicalActivity/Documents/MO-NUPA-MyPlateforGestationalDiabetes.pdf

What About Glycemic Index?

If you're familiar with some popular diets, like *South Beach*, you are probably familiar with the Glycemic Index or GI. Choosing more foods with a low GI may help you control your blood sugar. See page 63 for a full discussion of Glycemic Index.

The Scoop on Sweeteners

There are three types of sweeteners: nutritive sweeteners, which contain calories; sugar alcohols, which contain fewer calories; and nonnutritive sweeteners (also called artificial sweeteners), which contain no calories. The different types of sweeteners and their use during pregnancy (and as they relate to diabetes) are described below.

Sucrose and Other Sugars

If you have diabetes while pregnant, you should limit or avoid foods with concentrated sugars. You can find the different types of sugars on food labels by looking for these words: sugar (brown, confectioner's, invert, raw, cane, crystallized cane, turbinado), honey, corn syrup, dextrin, fruit juice concentrate, maple syrup, corn sweetener, malt, and molasses. Less-processed sugars like honey, molasses, and brown sugar have the same calories as processed sugars and can have the same effect on your blood sugar. Small amounts of sugar are common in many foods. That's okay; simply choose foods with the least amount of sugar. Keep in mind that 4 grams of sugar is equivalent to 1 teaspoon. If you are counting your carbohydrates, you will have to include sugars in the count.

Sugar Alcohols and Artificial Sweeteners

Sugar alcohols may or may not have calories. The ones with calories can affect your blood sugar and some can have a laxative effect if eaten in excess. Artificial sweeteners should be used in moderation. For more information see page 72.

For a list of resources about all types of sweeteners, visit snap.nal.usda.gov/professional-development-tools/hot-topics-z/artificial-sweeteners and a link to info about additives including artificial sweeteners: www.cspinet.org/reports/chemcuisine.htm

What about "Diet Foods?"

It's not just sugar and calories that "diet" products may be lacking; they're usually processed and lack vitamins and minerals, which are so important for you and your baby. One thing that many diet drinks and processed foods (diet and regular) *do* have is phosphorus-containing preservatives. These preservatives (which contain "phos" in the name) appear to have a negative effect on bone density of the hip[10] and to increase risk of cardiovascular disease.[11] Bottom line? In the last couple of years, diet soda drinkers have been shown to have an increased risk of depression, heart disease and of being overweight. Some researchers say it's premature to drastically change behaviors until there are larger, more thorough studies. Bottom line: If you crave the calorie-free bubbly stuff, it's healthier to develop a taste for sparkling mineral water with a squeeze of lemon or lime instead. If you can't overcome the craving, limit to 1 serving a week..[12]

Keeping Track

It's easier to be motivated to keep a daily log of blood sugar, etc, if you have a system that works for you. Here are a few options:

My favorite paper log is called Health Cheques by Jane Stephenson RD. It's a checkbook-sized journal that includes places to record food, activity and blood sugar. There is also a mini booklet that lists Diabetic Exchanges. Find them at www1. appletree-press.com/detail.php?prod_id=2517

Online Tools and Phone "Apps"

♦ www.personaltracker.com: a free online tool for tracking your blood sugar, food and exercise. A large database computes your calorie and nutrient intake; meal and exercise plans are also available. A similar website from the same company, www.nutrihand.com, allows your dietitian, diabetes educator or health care provider to log in and access your information, with your permission. Both sites also have mobile "apps". 1-877-Nutrihand.

Most of these "apps" have similar functions: logs for blood sugar, food, medication, exercise and even blood pressure, pulse and weight:

♦ OnTrack Diabetes

♦ Glucose Buddy

♦ Glooko Logbook and MeterSync cable lets you download data directly from your meter. You can also add carb intake, insulin dose and activity. It also allows you to email reports. While the logbook is a free iPhone "app", the cable or infrared adapter will run you from $14.95 to $39.95. It's available through www.amazon. com/s/ref=nb_sb_noss_1?url=search-alias%3Daps&field-keywords=glooko

Exercise: A Shot in the Arm

Imagine something that makes you feel more energetic and relaxed, makes your body muscular instead of flabby, and reduces your long-term risk of heart disease and cancer. This "something" may help you avoid taking insulin. Would you go out and buy it by the bucketful? Exercise is this wonderful "something", and it is strongly recommended for people who have diabetes.

Regular physical activity is recommended for those with diabetes to help control blood sugar.[13] However, you should talk to your health care provider to see what specific guidelines he or she has for you. Regular exercise improves the efficiency of your body's insulin, which can help control blood sugar levels so that you may not have to take insulin. If you are taking insulin, be sure to always have glucose tablets and a snack with you while you are exercising, in case you experience low blood sugar. Also, exercise with a water bottle at hand to avoid getting dehydrated.

Words of Wisdom from Judy Simon MS, RD, CD, CHES

I have been privileged to work in the area of women's health my entire 30-year career as a dietitian. I have worked with women from conception through lactation by helping them optimize their diets for healthy conception, pregnancy and to feed their babies! After my own 8-year journey with infertility I took an even stronger interest in reproductive nutrition. I am so happy to have had two healthy babies (now teenagers)!

Many of the women I work with who have struggled to conceive also end up with a high-risk pregnancy due to being overweight, or having PCOS, insulin resistance, type 1 or 2 diabetes, or a past eating disorder. I've worked with many women who need individual medical nutrition therapy during their pregnancy and find themselves changing their diet drastically. It's not always easy to change your diet, but find strength in knowing that your diet can make a critical difference to the health of your baby and to you. For the best care, I suggest you ask lots of questions of your health care team. It's important to understand your medications, your diet and any exercise recommendations or limitations.

I love what I do and smile regularly when my patients let me know they are pregnant and when they deliver!

 Judy is Clinic Dietitian and Faculty Member at University of Washington Medical Center. She also has a private practice specializing in reproductive nutrition. Food for Fertility is her program for overweight women struggling to conceive: www.mind-body-nutrition.com

Questions You May Have

Q: Will I have to take insulin?

A: If your blood sugar can't be controlled by diet and exercise, you will probably take insulin via a self-administered shot. You may take one or more insulin shots a day. Blood sugar monitoring is a great way to see how your insulin is working as well as how you are doing with your diet. Keeping a log of your insulin, blood sugars, exercise and diet can help you and your health care team decide on the best insulin regimen for you.

Q: What else can affect my blood sugar besides carbohydrates?

A: Many other factors can affect your blood sugar or blood sugar level:

- The amount of protein and fat you eat at a meal.

- How much fiber is in your diet. Fiber slows down digestion, causing slower release of glucose into the bloodstream.

- Your activity level. Exercise uses up extra glucose and causes insulin to work more efficiently, thus keeping your blood sugar down and reducing the likelihood that you will have to take insulin.

- Your overall health. Infection and illness can increase blood sugar levels.

- Your stress level. Emotional stress can also increase your blood sugar level.

Q: What are the effects of hyperglycemia (high blood sugar)?

A: High blood sugar can cause your baby to have increased body fat, which could cause delivery problems. High blood sugar can also increase your baby's risk of being overweight and having impaired glucose tolerance when older. If a baby has low blood sugar at birth caused by the mother's hyperglycemia, it could affect brain development and function.[14]

Q: I have gestational diabetes. Will I still have diabetes after my baby is born?

A: Most women's blood sugar levels go back to normal shortly after delivery. Only a small number of women continue to have glucose intolerance—sometimes because the diagnosis of gestational diabetes actually uncovers undiagnosed type 2 diabetes.

However, it's estimated that ⅔ of the women who have gestational diabetes will be diagnosed with type 2 diabetes five to fifteen years later. Women who have GDM with one pregnancy will more than likely have it with other pregnancies, too. The American Diabetes Association recommends having your blood sugar tested six to twelve weeks postpartum and at least every three years thereafter. Women diagnosed with prediabetes should be treated with lifestyle changes or metformin and should be monitored annually.[15]

Can you avoid the diabetes that sometimes follows GDM? Very possibly. Losing weight, making healthy food choices and exercising regularly can all help you avoid developing type 2 diabetes.[16]

Q: Will my baby have diabetes?

A: Not at birth. However, having diabetes (either preexisting or gestational) does increase your child's risk of being overweight and of having impaired glucose tolerance, which are risk factors for diabetes. Breastfeeding is the first line of defense, since it decreases the risk of diabetes and obesity. Your family should also practice a healthy lifestyle, including regular activity, a healthy diet with plenty of high-fiber foods, and keep body weight close-to-ideal.

High Blood Pressure

Sarah was surprised when she went to her health care provider's office at 30 weeks and found that her blood pressure was too high. She felt fine! No one in her family had high blood pressure (hypertension), and she had never had a problem with it either. Fortunately, her health care provider wasn't taking any chances. He told her to reduce her work hours, sit down more often, lie down several times a day on her left side, and monitor her blood pressure at home. She went into labor at 38 weeks and delivered a healthy 6½ pound (3 kg) baby boy. Because her blood pressure was normal after delivery, and because her hypertension didn't worsen during her pregnancy, Sarah was finally diagnosed with "gestational" hypertension.

Hypertensive Disorders of Pregnancy

The most common and least understood of pregnancy complications, occurring in about 1 in every 12 pregnancies (8%).[17] The following list of definitions will help you understand high blood pressure during pregnancy[18]:

Chronic hypertension: High blood pressure occurring before pregnancy OR before the 20th week of pregnancy OR that lasts more than 12 weeks after delivery.

Gestational or Transient Hypertension: High blood pressure that develops after 20 weeks of pregnancy (formerly called pregnancy-induced hypertension or PIH.) Women with gestational hypertension usually have no symptoms, and their blood pressure returns to normal after delivery. They may also develop chronic hypertension later in life.

Preeclampsia: Both chronic hypertension and gestational hypertension can lead to preeclampsia, a serious disorder that includes high blood pressure and protein in the urine. Swelling of the face and hands, headaches, vision changes, sudden weight gain (generally over 5 lb or 2.3 kg in a week or less) and stomach pain can be symptoms. Preeclampsia can lead to eclampsia, which can be very dangerous (even fatal) to both mom and baby. For more information about preeclampsia: www. preeclampsia.org.

Are you at Risk for Preeclampsia[19,20]?

♦ First pregnancy

♦ Carrying multiple fetuses

♦ Preeclampsia in a previous pregnancy

♦ History of chronic hypertension, kidney disease, or diabetes

♦ Age under 18 or over 35

♦ Overweight

♦ Family history (mother or sister) who had preeclampsia

♦ Partner's mother had preeclampsia

Treatment

♦ Sometimes prescription drug therapy is needed to keep blood pressure at a healthy level. However, angiotensin converting enzyme (ACE) inhibitors and angiotensin receptor blockers (ARBs) are toxic to a fetus and if taken before you were pregnant, should be discontinued and replaced with a medication safe during pregnancy—there are several commonly used ones.

♦ Women with certain risk factors for preeclampsia may be told to take baby aspirin as a preventative measure after the 12th week of pregnancy. Discuss this with your health care provider.[21]

♦ The only "cure" for preeclampsia/eclampsia is delivery of the baby, which is why the risk of delivering prematurely is so high for women who have a hypertensive disorder. Other treatments include hospitalization and intravenous medications.

Crunching the Numbers:

♦ High blood pressure during pregnancy: 1 in 12

♦ Women with chronic hypertension diagnosed with preeclampsia: 1 in 4

♦ Pregnant women diagnosed with preeclampsia: 1 in 20

♦ First pregnancies with preeclampsia: 1 in 10

High Blood Pressure Problems

High blood pressure can cause some serious problems[22,23]:

♦ **Low Birthweight Baby:** Blood pressure affects the diameter of blood vessels, and thus, the amount of oxygen and nutrients that travel through them to your baby.

♦ **Premature Birth:** Delivering a baby early is the only "cure" for preeclampsia and the main cause for preterm deliveries.

♦ **Placental Abruption:** When the placenta separates from the uterus wall, it can decrease the amount of nutrients and oxygen your baby receives.

What You Can Do To Improve Your Blood Pressure

No matter where you fall on the spectrum of hypertensive disorders of pregnancy, a healthy diet could make a difference—and it definitely won't hurt! And, there's good news when it comes to diet for high blood pressure.

The National Heart Lung and Blood Institute research has found that the Dietary Approaches to Stop Hypertension (DASH) diet, an eating plan that is lower in sodium, low in saturated fat, cholesterol and total fat which emphasizes fruits, vegetables, and fat-free or low-fat milk and dairy products, can reduce your blood pressure.[24] The DASH eating plan also includes whole grains, fish, poultry and nuts and has less red meat, sweets, and added sugars compared to the typical American diet. It is rich in potassium, magnesium and calcium. For ideas on how to eat with more DASH, check out The DASH Diet Action Plan: Proven to Boost Weight Loss and Improve Health by Marla Heller MS, RD (Grand Central Life & Style, 2011). Don't use the book for weight loss while you are pregnant: for now, just use the ideas to eat healthier.

More recently, the Beef in an Optimal Lean Diet (BOLD) diet, which includes four ounces (125 g) of lean beef a day, has shown similar heart-healthy results.[25] And there may be one more benefit to a DASH-like diet—a small study in Australia found it also improved mood and decreased depression in postmenopausal women.[26] Although there have been no studies on the effect of the DASH diet on pregnancy outcomes, the DASH diet is similar to healthy eating guidelines all over the world.

Just the Facts: Salt and Sodium

◆ Sodium needs increase during pregnancy because of the extra fluid your body retains to cushion your baby.

◆ The Adequate Intake for Sodium during pregnancy (in Canada and the US) is 1,500 mg; the Tolerable Upper Limit is 2,300 mg.[27,28]

◆ In Australia, the Adequate Intake is set at 460-920 mg.[29]

◆ The average sodium intake in the US is 3,400 mg.[30] This means that some people eat *more* than that.

◆ Some swelling is a normal part of pregnancy; cutting your sodium below what's recommended won't help and may hurt.

◆ If you frequently eat out or eat many convenience foods, you probably do want to reduce your intake to one that more closely matches the recommended intake of 1,500 to 2,300 mg.

Make Sure Your Eating is BOLD and has DASH

1. Increase the potassium in your diet: Make sure to have at least 5 cups (1,250 ml) of fruits and vegetables daily including one or two servings of legumes, nuts or seeds so that total potassium equals 4,700 mg (which is the DRI for pregnancy). See chart of potassium-rich foods on page 218.
2. Incorporate magnesium-rich foods into your diet including a daily serving of nuts or seeds. The DRI for pregnancy is 350 mg. See page 217 for a chart of magnesium-rich foods.
3. Include adequate calcium-rich foods; aim for 3-4 servings of low-fat dairy or calcium-rich foods daily. If you don't eat enough calcium-rich foods, consider a supplement. This has been shown to significantly reduce the risk of preeclampsia in a data review of 11 studies and close to 15,000 women.[31]
4. Eat a variety of protein sources including one vegetarian source of protein daily.
5. Reduce saturated fat intake by eating only very lean cuts of beef and pork, and using reduced-fat or fat-free cheese and low-fat or skim milk. Trim extra fat from all meat, poultry and fish before eating. Lean cuts of beef include those that include "Round" and "Sirloin" in the name, as well as 95% lean ground beef.
6. Continue taking your prenatal vitamin. They contain the right balance of antioxidant vitamins (vitamin C and E, folic acid) and minerals like zinc and selenium.

The DASH Diet vs. the Eating Expectantly Diet: They are actually very similar!

DASH Diet	Eating Expectantly Diet
Fat-free or low-fat milk products	
2-3 cups (500-750 ml)	3-4 cups (750-1,000 ml)
Fruit Servings per day	
2 to 2.5 cups (500-625 ml)	2 cups (500 ml)
Vegetable servings per day	
2 to 2.5 cups (500-625 ml)	3 cups (750 ml)
Lean protein	
6 oz. (175 g) or less	6-7 oz. (175-200 g)
Nuts, seeds and legumes	
4-5 days per week	Daily
Saturated fats and sugars	
Limited	Limited
Potassium-rich foods	
Encouraged	Encouraged
Magnesium-rich foods	
Encouraged	Encouraged
Sodium	
Limited to 1,500-2,300 mg	Moderation encouraged; 2,300 mg is upper limit during pregnancy

Vitamins and Antioxidants: Could They Make a Difference?

Research using individual, large doses of vitamin C and vitamin E has shown positive as well as very negative results.[32] Low serum levels of vitamin D increase the risk of preeclampsia. Research also shows an association between hypertension, preeclampsia and C-reactive protein (CRP), a marker for inflammation in the body.[33] Since we know that antioxidants help control oxidative damage that can lead to inflammation[34], an antioxidant-rich diet, as recommended throughout this book, could help fight high blood pressure during pregnancy. Even though preeclampsia is a late pregnancy occurrence, most of the preventative measures are recommended early in pregnancy. See page 207 to find out more.

Lead and Hypertension

Chapter 6 discusses some of the health pitfalls of lead. A recent review found a link between blood lead levels and gestational hypertension and preeclampsia. This underscores the importance of a calcium-rich diet which reduces your exposure to lead, both from dietary sources and from lead that may be stored in bone.[35]

Reducing Your Risk for the Next Pregnancy

There are several strategies that can cut your risk of high blood pressure and preeclampsia:

♦ Get as close to your ideal body weight as possible. A very large, multi-hospital study in the US confirmed that the higher your BMI over normal, the greater your risk for having transient hypertension and preeclampsia during pregnancy.[36] White women with a BMI over 25 had an almost double risk, and women with a BMI over 30 had a more than triple risk of developing severe preeclampsia compared to women with a BMI of 20.

♦ Take a multivitamin-mineral supplement before you become pregnant.

♦ Get moving—exercise is good for maintaining your body weight, stress relief and blood pressure.

♦ Make sure you have adequate exposure to sunshine or an adequate source of vitamin D in your diet.

♦ Follow the DASH or BOLD diets above.

When You're Expecting Twins or More

One way to have an instant family is to have a multiple pregnancy! In the United States and other countries that have increased the use of fertility treatments, carrying multiple fetuses is much more common. Twin births have increased 42% from 1990-2005; Pregnancies with triplets or more increased 400% between 1980 and 1989, but since have been decreasing slightly.[37] The likelihood of having a multiple birth rises with age; a woman who is between thirty-five and forty is three times more likely to have fraternal twins than a woman who is twenty to twenty-five years old. Contrary to urban legend, your husband's family history of twins has nothing to do with your chance of having multiples!

Multiple (also called multifetal) pregnancies are considered high-risk, and here's why: Newborn multiples are much more likely to be preterm, low-birth-weight, and small for their gestational age. During a multiple pregnancy, a woman is more likely to have preeclampsia, iron-deficiency anemia, hyperemesis gravidarum (persistent, excessive nausea and vomiting), placenta previa (abnormal placement of placenta), and kidney problems. Many women carrying multiple fetuses are given medication to stop labor—also called tocolytic agents—and put on bed-rest.

Does this mean that you'll have all the problems listed above? No. You have more control over your pregnancy and the health of your babies than you may think. Some of the small daily choices you make—like eating the right foods, resting when your body tells you to and following the advice of your health care provider—can significantly affect your babies' well-being.

Many women at the University of Michigan Multiples Clinic have beaten the odds. They follow a special nutrition program developed by Dr. Barbara Luke—who is both a registered nurse and a registered dietitian—and have great results. Two-thirds of the moms at this clinic deliver at thirty-six weeks or later—compared with only two-fifths nationwide. Triplets born in this clinic's program weigh 35 percent more than the national average birthweight for triplets. Twins are usually 20% heavier than average. Two-thirds of the clinic's newborns weigh more than 5½ pounds (2.5 kg), and one-fourth of the clinic's newborns weigh more than 6½ pounds (3 kg).[38]

What do all these numbers mean? It bears repeating: Careful attention to your health while you're pregnant can significantly affect your babies' well-being. The University of Michigan Multiples Clinic emphasizes the importance of diet as well as specialized recommendations for supplements.

What Can You Expect?

◆   To be monitored more carefully, including more health care provider visits and more ultrasounds

◆   To eat more in order to gain extra weight

◆   To be put on a reduced work schedule or bed-rest

Factors Affecting Birthweights of Multiples

◆   Your prepregnancy weight and height: shorter and lighter mothers are more prone to having smaller babies.

◆   How much weight you gain.

◆   The pattern of your weight gain: weight gain in early pregnancy is important.

◆   How long your pregnancy lasts: gestation.

◆   Your diet: quality counts!

◆   Whether the babies are identical or fraternal: Identical twins—produced from one egg that splits—generally weigh less.

◆   Sex: girls tend to weigh less.

The Most Important Factor: Weight Gain

The amount of weight you gain when pregnant with multiples directly affects how much your babies will weigh. And because multiples often don't go to term, weight gain needs to occur at a greater rate in the first 24-28 weeks of pregnancy.

Recommended Weight Gain for Twins		
Pre-Pregnancy BMI	BMI Category	Total Weight Gain Range in pounds (kg)
18.5-24.9	Normal weight	37-54 (17-25 kg)
25-29.9	Overweight	31-50 (14-23 kg)
>30	Obese	25-42 (11-19 kg)

Provisional Guidelines from the US Institute of Medicine, partially based on Dr. Barbara Luke's research.[39]

Recommended Weight Gain for Supertwins

There is not a lot of data about weight gain for women pregnant with supertwins (triplets or more.) Dr. Barbara Luke recommends that moms of triplets gain 58 to 75 pounds (26-34 kg) (at estimated term delivery of 34 weeks.) One study found that a weight gain of 35 pounds (16 kg) by 24 weeks was associated with reduced frequency of small for gestational age triplets.[40] An estimated 70 to 80 pound (32-36 kg) weight gain may be required for a healthy quadruplet pregnancy (with an estimated delivery at 32 weeks.)[41]

Also Important: Gaining Consistently

The pattern of your weight gain also affects your risk of preterm delivery and low birthweight. That is gaining weight consistently throughout pregnancy is related to a healthier outcome. In underweight women, a weekly weight gain of 1.1 pound (0.5 kg) a week before 20 weeks and 1.9 pounds a week (0.85 kg) from 20 weeks to delivery was associated with both twins weighing at least 5.5 pounds (2.5 kg). For normal weight women, gaining 1.5 pounds (700 g) a week was associated with giving birth to both twins weighing at least 5.5 pounds (2.5 kg).[42]

How much weight you should gain, as well as the specific amount of nutrients you need, depend on many factors, which can't be addressed in detail here. I highly recommend that you purchase *When You're Expecting Twins, Triplets or Quads; Proven Guidelines for a Healthy Multiple Pregnancies* by Dr. Barbara Luke (Harper Resource. 3rd Edition 2011). I also suggest that you visit with a registered dietitian, who can help you with any individual eating challenges you have. Remember to keep your eye on the prize: healthy babies!

Your Diet

Even more vitamins, minerals and calories are needed to fuel more than one growing baby. One thing we do know is that nourishing twins and supertwins takes **a lot** of good quality food!

The Need for Supplements

When you're pregnant with more than one baby, it's impossible to get all the nutrition you need from food alone. Here's a roundup of supplements recommended by Dr. Barbara Luke in the book *Expecting Twins, Triplets and Quads*. Check out the book and her website www.drbarbaraluke.com/vitamin.aspx for specific amounts and rationale.

♦ Multivitamin with folic acid (but not with minerals)

♦ Individual Supplements:

- Calcium
- Folic acid
- Vitamin D

- Magnesium
- Vitamin C
- Fish oil

- Zinc
- Vitamin E

Essential and Omega-3 Fatty Acids

Essential fats (discussed in detail in Chapter 3), are important for development of the nervous system (including the brain) and retina. This development occurs at the end of pregnancy and throughout the first two years of life. The amount of essential fatty acids in the bloodstreams of multiple fetuses is significantly less than in a single fetus. Also because many multifetal pregnancies don't go to term, DHA is especially important for now—and later. Some of the fat in your current diet is stored for breastfeeding, so you need to consume more essential and omega-3 fats, especially DHA. Dr. Luke recommends 1,000 mg of fish oil per day.[43] Ask your health care provider for specific advice. See for some good sources of essential fatty acids.

How Can I Possibly Eat More Food?

While some women have no problem putting on the pounds, others have trouble eating all that extra food needed to gain the right amount. What to do?

First, make sure your diet has all the essentials, then add extra foods to boost your calorie intake and to meet your specific needs, which have hopefully been worked out by your dietitian. The foods most concentrated in calories are fat and sugar, the usual no-nos. However, to get all the calories you need with what seems to be an ever-shrinking stomach, you might need to choose higher calorie foods more often.

Ways to Put On Extra Pounds

1. Eat your way through the day. Call it grazing or munching, just do it! Eat three meals and three to four snacks per day. Balanced meals and mini-meals that contain protein are best.

2. Where's the beef? Hopefully in your fridge and freezer. Dr. Luke recommends eating lean meat regularly for the iron. See page 188 for iron-boosting tips.

3. Dip it. From refried beans, to hummus to baba ganoush, these dips provide a high protein, high fiber snack that is easy to eat.

4. Eat a daily "extra" like a milk shake, flan or peanut-butter chocolate chip cookies.

5. Drink, drink, drink! Dehydration can bring on preterm labor, so drink often. Eight 16-ounce (500 ml) glasses of water per day is recommended. (Yes, you read that right—that's a lot of fluid!)

6. Get in the slow lane. Since it's important to slow down to allow your body to nurture your babies, you may need to let some things go, such as cleaning, and cooking. Use the quick and easy menus in the *Eating Expectantly Cookbook* Encourage your partner to go crazy in the kitchen (and with the vacuum cleaner). Let your good-hearted friends fill your freezer with ready-to-eat meals. Treat yourself to gourmet takeout or restaurant delivery, remember that you may need to fill in some fruits and veggies when eating out.

Chewing the Fat: Ways to Increase Your Weight

The easiest extra to add extra calories is by adding fat. Concentrate on adding vegetable fat. You may need to eat as much as 40 percent of your calories from fat to gain enough weight, rather than the 20-35% that's normally recommended.

♦ Sprinkle ground flaxseed on your cereal or in your smoothies.

♦ Munch on nuts and seeds, especially walnuts, pecans and sunflower seeds.

♦ Use salad dressing made with flaxseed oil or walnut oil—or make your own!

♦ Put nuts, olives, and avocado in your salads and sandwiches.

♦ Eat guacamole!

♦ Eat more salmon: it's a rich source of DHA important for your babies' brain and eye development.

♦ Use more mayonnaise; say yes to potato and egg salad!

♦ Add olive oil to your pasta and vegetables, more salad dressing to your salads, and extra oil when cooking. Try dipping oil for your bread instead of butter.

♦ Choose full-fat dairy products.

♦ Keep healthy snack bars in your purse and car for easy munching on the go. See page 69 for a chart of healthy ones.

Drink Your Way to Weight Gain

Another easy way to get more calories with added protein and a balance of vitamins and minerals is to drink a nutrition supplement drink. (You know the ones—often advertised for those your parents' age!) There are plenty of choices to choose from like Boost, Ensure, and Carnation Instant Breakfast. They contain from 15-20 grams of protein per serving, which can really help you meet your protein needs. Also check out the Naked Protein Juice Smoothies—a clean choice—but drink just half a bottle at a time due to high carb content.

There are liquid and powdered forms that you can add to milk. There are also a few non-creamy options like Ensure Clear and Boost Breeze. If you have gestational diabetes, try Boost Glucose Control or Glucerna, or find one made with an artificial sweetener. Have a goal of drinking 1 or 2 a day, depending on the rest of your energy intake and weight gain.

Resources for Parents of Multiples

Books:

♦ *When You're Expecting Twins, Triplets, or Quads: Proven Guidelines for a Healthy Multiple Pregnancy.* Barbara Luke and Tamara Eberlein. New York: HarperCollins, 2011. See DrBarbaraLuke.com for more information including consulting services and a line of maternity clothes for multiples!

♦ *Oh, Yes You Can Breastfeed Twins!* April Rudat RD, April Rudat Registered Dietitian LLC. 2007.

♦ *Mothering Multiples: Breastfeeding and Caring for Twins or More!* by Karen Kerkhoff Gromada, La Leche League International, 2007

♦ *It's Twins: Parent-to-Parent Advice from Infancy Through Adolescence.* Susan Heim Hampton Roads Publishing Company. 2007

On-line Resources:

♦ Sidelines (support group for women with high-risk pregnancies)

  • 1-888-HiRisk-4 (888-447-4754)

  • www.sidelines.org

♦ www.twinstalk.com: parent to parent advice for raising multiples.

♦ www.marvelousmultiples.com: reliable information from a registered nurse. You can also find a list of Marvelous Multiples Prenatal Education classes by state.

- www.justmultiples.com: from books to birth announcements to feeding/nursing tools and strollers, It's one stop shopping!

- www.doubleupbooks.com: The Premier Bookstore for Twins, Triplets and More.

- www.eatright.org/programs/rdfinder/ : The Academy of Nutrition and Dietetics (Can refer you to a registered dietitian in your area.)

- MOST (Mothers of Super Twins)

  - 516-434-MOST
  - www.mostonline.org

- National Organization of Mothers of Twins Clubs

  - 800-243-2276
  - www.nomotc.org

- The Center for Study of Multiple Birth

  - 312-266-9093
  - www.multiplebirth.com

- The Triplet Connection

  - 209-474-0885
  - www.tripletconnection.org

- Twins Magazine On-line www.twinsmagazine.com

- www.multiples.about.com/parenting/multiples/

Coping with Bed-Rest

We all dream of having just one day in bed to sleep, watch TV, or catch up on our reading. But spending several weeks in bed may seem more like a nightmare—believe me—been there, done that!

Bed-rest is prescribed for multiple reasons, including hypertension or preeclampsia, multiple gestation (twins or more), premature labor, or poor growth of baby (also called intrauterine growth retardation, or IUGR). Some women are put on bed-rest for several months, which can really give a person "cabin fever".

Following is a guide to help you make the most of your "cocooning time". Much of the information is from talking with others and also from personal experience. I was on bed-rest for eleven weeks for preterm labor. It was all worth it in the end. My son Robert was born healthy and weighed 7 pounds, 7 ounces (3.5 kg). My labor even had to be helped along a little!

At first, the days seemed to go on forever. But once I got into a routine and my health care provider gave me the okay to get up a little more, time became much more bearable. I wrote most of the following information before I was on bed-rest, so I was able to follow my own advice. And it worked! I hope it helps you, too.

Welcome to "Club Bed"

Setting Up the Room

You will probably want to set up a makeshift bedroom near the place where your family gathers. A family room off the kitchen works nicely. Here are the basic living supplies with which you'll want to furnish your new room:

- Bed or comfy couch with plenty of pillows (Or rent a hospital bed.)

- Phone or cell phone with charger within arm's reach.

- Free long distance—either add a plan to your home phone that includes long distance or get more minutes on your cell phone for all the long distance phone support you'll need. Alternatively, try www.skype.com to connect visually over the internet.

- Notebook (paper or electronic) for making all kinds of lists—things to do, things for others to do, things to buy, things to make, bills to pay, what's on sale where, and so on. A notebook or laptop is also perfect for keeping in touch, watching movies, skyping or working.

- Ice chest or mini fridge for your bedside.

- Microwave.

- Large bedside table or a hospital-type table that can be raised or lowered to your level. (This can be rented from a medical supply company. Several TV trays work well, too.)

- Any vitamins and medication you are taking, including those taken occasionally for heartburn, constipation, etc.

- Large pitcher, filled with fresh water daily, and an ice bucket.

- Water bottles or light weights for doing arm exercises (if your health care provider approves.)

- An intercom system (invest early in one for the baby; it will save your voice and save your family lots of trips back and forth fetching for you.) Alternatively, keep a little bell by the bedside and ring it when you need help. (Your honey will just **love** that!)

Eating and Dietary Considerations

Yes, eating is a whole new challenge when you spend all your time in a horizontal position! Should you eat more—or less while you are on bed-rest? That really depends on *why* you are on bed-rest! If it's because your baby is too small, you are on bed-rest to devote more of your energy to his growth and you should eat more. On the other hand, you may be on bed-rest to stop preterm labor and you may have gained excess weight—then you might need to watch your food intake more carefully. Let your health care provider, weight gain and appetite be your guide.

A potential problem of sedentary life is a possible increase in blood sugar, which could lead to gestational diabetes. To help control your risk, avoid concentrated sweets and fruit juices and watch your carb intake before noon. (See page 208 for more about gestational diabetes.)

Your Guide to Bedroom Cuisine

◆ Make shopping lists and menus so your family or friends can shop (and cook) for you.

◆ Keep snacks next to you:

  • A fruit bowl filled with fresh and antioxidant-rich dried fruit such as apricots, dates, raisins, cranberries blueberries, figs, and prunes

  • A jar of peanut or sunflower seed butter

  • Individual portions of cheese: String cheese, Light Laughing Cow cheese or Mini Babybel Light

  • Whole grain crackers, rye crisps, graham crackers, baked tortilla chips

  • Prepared raw veggies

  • Nuts

  • Sunflower and pumpkin seeds

◆ Beware—convenience foods that need no refrigeration are often high in fat and salt, not to mention preservatives and coloring. (Think individually wrapped peanut butter cheese crackers.) Eat sparingly or make your own in your spare time!

◆ Keep a microwave next to you, as well as low-fat popcorn and decaffeinated tea, cans of hearty single-serving soups such as split pea, chunky chicken-vegetable, and lentil. (Pick the reduced sodium versions, as soup tends to be very salty.)

◆ White or sweet potato. Pop one in the microwave. All you need to add is a little butter and/or a sprinkle of cheese or cinnamon sugar.

◆ If you are allowed to get up briefly to make a meal, the following can be prepared in six to seven minutes from scratch or with leftovers:

- Scrambled or poached eggs with toast; they can be made in the microwave in a minute or two.

- Frozen microwave dinners

- Refried vegetarian beans, on tostada shell with avocado

- Salad with prepared lettuce in the bag—you just add the tomato, cheese, leftover chicken, fish or beef, and veggies

- Hummus wrap with lots of salad greens

- Chicken or roast beef-English-muffin with melted cheese

- Tuna or salmon salad on whole grain bread

◆ Get it delivered: besides the usual pizza or Chinese food delivery, most big cities have services that bring you food from any restaurant.

Exercise and Activity

Your activity level is a very individual matter that should be discussed with your health care provider. Ask about doing stretching, isometric exercises and/or arm exercises using light weights, 16 oz. water (500 ml) bottles or 12 oz. / 33 cl cans. Such exercises will help you keep some muscle tone and help you avoid feeling sore from lack of movement. Also ask about turning from side to side often during the day and about getting a massage. Massage therapy helped me with back and hip pain when I was on bed-rest.

Other Survival Tips

◆ Make a schedule of what you'll do during the day. This will make the day seem shorter and less monotonous.

◆ Enlist others' help. If you have children, make a poster of chores for them to do.

◆ This may be a good time for your children to learn to do laundry, dishes, and even how to cook, depending on their ages. If you don't have children, you'll need to depend on your partner, family (if they live close by), or friends. Although asking others to do things for you may be difficult, make a list of all the little things that need doing and delegate them to different people. Hire a maid service if you can afford it.

◆ Remember it's okay to let the housework go. (In your case, it's a must!)

Bed-Rest Joke

The best and worst thing about bed-rest: You aren't the cook and you aren't the cook! (From Sidelines newsletter.)

♦ You have only one priority: for your little one to grow as much as possible for as long as possible. Whether the floor is mopped or the carpet is vacuumed really isn't important. Investigate getting household help from a home-care agency. My insurance covered this benefit, which improved the quality of our life immensely. A home-care assistant can take care of your children, cook, clean, run errands, and so forth.

♦ Think positive. You might want to invest in a "positive thought for the day" type of book. Though the time in bed might be rough, having a premature or sick baby would be much worse. Make the most of your time.

♦ Find other women who've lived or are living the "horizontal life." When I was on bed-rest, Norma, a friend of mine who had been on bed-rest, called regularly for support. That helped a lot. Get the word out among friends and coworkers or at your place of worship, and folks who have been where you are will likely step forward with a comforting word or a helping hand.

You can also check out the support groups and websites listed below:

♦ Sidelines (support group for women with high-risk pregnancies)

  • 1-888-HiRisk-4 (888-447-4754)

  • www.sidelines.org

  • The site also has live chats and message boards.

♦ StorkNet's Bedrest Survival Guide at http://www.storknet.com/complications/bedrest/index.html

♦ *Pregnancy Bed Rest, Complications and Postpartum Depression* from Judith A. Maloni, PhD, RN at Case Western Reserve University: fpb.case.edu/BedrestPPD/

Older Moms

In the past, most women started their families in their early twenties. Not anymore! In the US Between 1990 and 2008, births to women over 35 increased from 9% to 15%.[44] Waiting to start a family can have both advantages and disadvantages. Some women find that thirty- or forty-something is the perfect time for them. They are financially stable, have spent time developing a career, and are ready to start on the "mommy track." On the other hand, they may be more set in their ways and may be less physically ready for pregnancy and motherhood.

What Can You Expect?

Compared to women in their 20's, pregnant women over 35 have an increased risk of hypertension, diabetes, placental abruption or placenta previa, preterm birth, and small for gestational age births.[45] However, recently it was questioned whether some of these risks were truly due to older age, or as a result of diabetes and hypertension of pregnancy (which is more common in women over 35). A large study of women at the University of Oslo found that there was no significant difference in the above mentioned risks in women over age 35 over vs. younger than 35. The only difference was that older women were more likely to have C-sections or instrumental vaginal deliveries.[46] The authors concluded that for older women without pre-existing conditions pregnancy appears to have fewer problems at delivery than once thought.

As a woman gets older, and especially if over age 35, her risk of having a baby with Down syndrome and other genetic defects increases. This is due to the age of the eggs, since a woman is born with all her eggs and as she ages, so do her eggs.

What You Can Do

The most important thing you can do to reduce your risk of diabetes, C-section, and other complications is to achieve a body weight as close to your ideal weight as possible **before** you get pregnant. Gaining the right amount of weight can also help, as can practicing a healthy lifestyle, exercising regularly and eating a well-balanced diet. Start your prenatal care as soon as possible and follow your health care provider's advice about everything.

Preventing Age Related Pregnancy Problems: What May Help

Gestational Diabetes

The risk of gestational diabetes (GDM) increases with age beginning at age 25. One researcher estimates that women over 35 are 10 times more likely and women over 40 are 15 times more likely to develop gestational diabetes[47], which may be due to the fact that as we age, we tend to gain weight. In general, an overall decline in physical activity and adoption of a "modern lifestyle" are thought to be contributing factors. What you can do to cut your chances:

♦ Gain the right amount of weight for your BMI. This is critical.

♦ Get moving! Regular exercise can help control weight gain and control blood sugar. See the chapter 14 titled "Fitting Fitness in."

♦ Limit your saturated and trans fat intake and don't smoke—this may also increase risk of GDM, and in any case, is not healthy for pregnancy!

♦ Since the risk of GDM increases so much with age, and it's possible to have undiagnosed type 2 diabetes, consider following the eating tips for Gestational Diabetes on page 250. Also, limit foods that score high on the glycemic index—see page 63 for more info.

Hypertension

The risk of high blood pressure and preeclampsia also increases in women over 35. Sometimes chronic hypertension is also diagnosed in pregnancy. Here's what you can do:

♦ Consider your calcium intake—adequate calcium is important for blood pressure control.

♦ Maximize other minerals; potassium and magnesium also affect blood pressure. See page 217 and page 218 to find out how.

♦ Eat plenty of fresh fruits, vegetables, legumes and whole grains. Dietary sources of antioxidants and vitamin E (but not supplements) may decrease the risk of diabetes in general.

♦ Get enough vitamin D. Many people have low serum levels; limited research shows vitamin D levels in early pregnancy could impact risk of preeclampsia. See page 59 for a complete discussion on vitamin D.

Pregnancy After Gastric Bypass Surgery

Women who never dreamed they could become pregnant are often surprised with a positive pregnancy test; losing weight increases fertility.

Eating for pregnancy might be challenging for you depending on when your surgery was. Weight gain may pose a problem if you become pregnant within six months of your surgery, because food intake is limited due to pouch size, food intolerances and possible surgical complications. The usual gastrointestinal problems of pregnancy like morning sickness and heartburn may also be worse than usual. Pregnancy after bariatric surgery is considered a high-risk pregnancy; expect to be monitored more closely.

Nutrition Tips

This is based on advice developed by Jeanne Blankenship MS, RD, CLE, formerly of the University of California, Davis Medical Center and the guidelines that she contributed to: The American Society for Metabolic and Bariatric Surgery Allied Health Nutritional Guidelines for the Surgical Weight Loss Patient.[48]

◆ Meet with your bariatric surgery RD; she can create a specific meal plan to insure adequate calorie and nutrient intake.

◆ Procedures with the greatest risk of nutritional deficiencies include the Biliopancreatic Diversion (BPD), Biliopancreatic Diversion Duodenal Switch (BP-DS) and the Roux-en-Y (the most common procedure). The Adjustable Band (ABG), Vertical Banded Gastroplasty (VBG) and Vertical Sleeve Gastrectomy (VSG) (BP) are purely restrictive and thus don't seem to cause as many nutritional deficiencies as other procedures.[49]

◆ The need for additional nutrition supplements will depend on the type of surgery you had. Most all procedures call for a high potency multivitamin-mineral supplement, plus additional vitamin B12, calcium citrate, iron, and a B complex. Malabsorptive procedures like Biliopancreatic Diversion (BPD) and Duodenal Switch also require supplemental fat-soluble vitamins Vitamin A, D and K.[50] DHA is recommended for all pregnant women; ask your health care provider if you need to take more than 200-300 mg. Because malabsorptive procedures require more intense and extreme nutrition supplements, check with your health care provider on specific supplements and exact amounts.

◆ Iron deficiency anemia and vitamin D deficiency are common in patients **before** they have gastric bypass surgery. Therefore, the best practice is to have labs drawn for iron, vitamin B12 and Vitamin D to determine if you are deficient, regardless which procedure you've had.[51]

◆ Avoid supplements that are timed-release or with an enteric coating; chewable or liquid vitamins are best. Supplements and medications should dissolve within 30 minutes of soaking in room temperature water to be well absorbed in your body.[52]

◆ You may be asked to monitor your urine for ketones.

◆ Consider a high protein liquid supplement or a whey or soy protein powder supplement to insure adequate protein in your diet.

CONSIDERING BREASTFEEDING

What You'll Find:

♦ Breastfeeding: 100% Natural

♦ Why Choose Breastfeeding?

♦ Possible Obstacles

♦ Going Back to Work

♦ Nutrition during Breastfeeding

♦ Drugs and Breastfeeding

♦ Breastfeeding for Special Groups

♦ Questions You May Have

Frequently Asked Questions:

♦ How can I convince my partner that breastfeeding is best?

♦ How can I tell if I'm making enough milk?

♦ Can I go back to work and still breastfeed?

♦ Who can help if I have problems breastfeeding?

♦ How much weight should I lose while breastfeeding?

SCAN HERE FOR CHAPTER UPDATES

Breastfeeding: 100% Natural

My Experiences: Stick with It for Success

When my first son, Nicolas, was born, I never wondered how I'd feed him. In fact, this decision had been made long before I even met my husband! As a health professional who knew all the physical benefits of breastfeeding and had recommended breastfeeding to thousands of women, I had to breastfeed.

The pressure was on! The most difficult week of my life was that first week after Nicolas was born. I had a long labor and a difficult delivery. Nicolas and I didn't catch on to the fine art of breastfeeding right away. When Nicolas did not breastfeed for twenty-four hours, I felt guilty and gave permission for him to have a bottle. It was a big mistake!

Nicolas continued to receive bottles in the hospital. At home, our breastfeeding attempts failed again; during a feeding, he would latch on and pull away more times than I could count (or bear). As a last resort I called our pediatrician, who referred me to a certified lactation consultant, who saved the day!

We had two problems, Nicolas and I. He had nipple confusion. (Sounds like the making of a good joke!) That explained his frequent latching on and pulling away. He had gotten used to a plastic nipple in the hospital, so he couldn't get the hang of mine. And I wasn't positioning him correctly. Within a day, we were doing much better. One week after seeing the lactation consultant, we were pros!

If I hadn't known about the benefits of breastfeeding, recommended it to so many women, and been under financial pressure from quitting my job, I would surely have quit breastfeeding that first week. That's why I literally do "feel your pain", if you want to breastfeed but are having problems.

Looking back, I'm so glad I persevered and nursed Nicolas. The time we spent together was wonderful. And Nicolas was never sick while I was nursing him. One of my most memorable nursing sessions took place at an outdoor jazz concert that my husband Frank, Nicolas, and I attended when he was three months old. I felt perfectly comfortable feeding him under the privacy of a blanket. Actually I felt proud, because we were enjoying our own little routine. I didn't feel embarrassed about breastfeeding in public, as I had at first, and I liked feeling self-sufficient: no packing up bottles, trying to keep them cold, or looking for a place to warm them.

When my second son, Robert, was born, we had a totally different experience. I nursed Robert very soon after delivery, and he caught on immediately! I made it clear that Robert was not to have any artificial nipples while in the nursery, so he never had nipple confusion. At home, Robert continued to eat very well. Because I felt like a pro, I was comfortable breastfeeding him anywhere. Breastfeeding was especially convenient when we traveled overseas to visit family; we didn't have to worry about buying formula in a foreign country or hassling with bottles on the plane or train.

I would never trade the experiences of nursing my children—both were special. More and more studies are citing the benefits of breastfeeding, so I urge you to give it a try!

The Right Choice: It's Up to You

Breastfeeding undoubtedly offers the most benefits for baby and mom. However, whatever method you decide to use, make it a decision you feel good about.

Keep in mind that because of increased workplace lactation programs, it's easier to continue breastfeeding after you go back to work. Some women find that using a stockpile of frozen breast milk or combining breastfeeding with some formula also works.

Even if you breastfeed for a short time, your baby will benefit. If you do decide to combine breast- and bottle-feeding, introduce the bottle only after breastfeeding is well established, to avoid nipple confusion. Limiting artificial nipples, bottles, and pacifiers the first six weeks not only helps avoid this problem but it's recommended to help establish a good milk supply.

Because this is a nutrition book for moms (not babies), this chapter will be primarily devoted to breastfeeding. However, combining breastfeeding and formula feeding is an option that also works for many. (You can find everything you need to know about feeding your baby in my book *Baby Bites: Everything You Need to Know about Feeding Your Infant and Toddler in One Handy Book*.)

Babies were born to Breastfeed

Health organizations around the world recommend breastfeeding. In 2012, the American Academy of Pediatrics reaffirmed its recommendation of exclusive breastfeeding for about six months, followed by continued breastfeeding as complementary foods are introduced, with continuation of breastfeeding for one year or longer as mutually desired by mother and infant.[1] The World Health Organization: Exclusive breastfeeding is recommended up to 6 months of age, with continued breastfeeding along with appropriate complementary foods up to two years of age or beyond.[2]

Why Choose Breastfeeding?

There is no doubt that breastfeeding is recognized as the preferred form of nutrition during the first months of life because it conveys significant health benefits for both mom and baby. Those benefits are listed below. But here's the bottom line in my opinion—breastfeeding is the ultimate gift of health to your baby. It's the most empowering feeling in the world to be able to provide nature's best to your baby, without depending on anyone or anything. The outside world stops when it's just you and your baby, if only for just a few minutes.

Breastfeeding: Benefits to Baby[3]

♦   Colostrum, the earliest breast milk called "liquid gold", is made in small amounts, which matches the size of your newborn's stomach. Colostrum is baby's first immunization because it's rich with antibodies, hormones and disease fighting immune factors including immunoglobulins, antibodies, lymphocytes, and immune enhancers. It not only protects the newborn from viruses, bacteria, allergens and toxins, but also serves to activate or "jump start" baby's own immune system.[4] It's also rich in the antioxidant lutein, which is important for your baby's developing vision.[5]

♦   Breastfeeding reduces the risk of middle ear infections, nonspecific gastroenteritis, upper and lower respiratory tract infections, atopic dermatitis, asthma, obesity, type 1 and 2 diabetes, leukemia, and sudden infant death syndrome. Breast milk also postpones and may prevent the development of allergies and asthma. Premature babies who aren't breastfed are more at risk for necrotizing enterocolitis, a very serious condition.

♦   Breastfeeding stimulates growth, and promotes very rapid healing, which is very important to consider after the ordeal of birth and the trauma it can cause.

♦   The skin-to-skin contact promotes bonding and attachment and gives babies emotional security.

♦   Breastfeeding is made specifically for your baby and his needs. It changes as he grows. Premature babies gain even more positive health benefits: better ratings for intelligence, motor and behavior and larger brain size.

♦   Breastfeeding decreases the risk of overweight in adolescence and adulthood; and promotes good jaw, oral muscle and facial development.

♦   Breast milk decreases the risk of gluten intolerance, when baby is breastfed at the time of gluten exposure.

Breastfeeding Celebs

If you're a celebrity watcher, you know of many "A" list moms who think "Breast is Best" for their babies too. Like you, these women have demanding schedules; they obviously don't have any financial obstacles to buying formula. Angelina Jolie, Julia Roberts, Gwyneth Paltrow, Victoria Beckham, Christina Aguilera, Brooke Burke, Mariah Carey, Kourtney Kardashian, Beyonce, Sarah Jessica Parker, Pink, Jennifer Garner, Alyssa Milano, Madonna, Jada Pinkett-Smith, Kate Beckinsale, Maggie Gyllenhaal, Gisele Bundchen, Mary-Louise Parker, Salma Hayek, Naomi Watts, Elizabeth Hasselback and Gwen Stefani are just a few that have chosen to give their babies the gift of good health. Won't you join them?

Breastfeeding: Benefits to Mom[6]

- May improve your mental health. Research has shown a link between breastfeeding and a lower risk of postpartum depression.[7]

- After delivery, reduces the risk of blood loss after delivery, helps shrink the uterus and delays the return of your menstrual cycle.

- Stimulates the release of oxytocin, which enhances mom-infant attachment by decreasing anxiety and causing a feeling of calm and contentment.

- Saves time and money. No formula, bottles or nipples to prepare or buy. Convenient and ready to feed your baby anytime, anywhere.

- Reduces a mom's risk of type 2 diabetes, rheumatoid arthritis, hypertension, heart disease, breast, and ovarian cancer.

- Improves bone density and decreases risk of hip fracture later in life.[8]

- Results in less work missed due to having sick babies.

- Uses more calories and helps you return to your pre-pregnancy size.

Possible Obstacles

There are only two main obstacles to breastfeeding—the people around you, and the idea that you can't do it. If you get prepared and plan ahead, you can get around those issues and enjoy the successful nursing experience of a lifetime. Following are some barriers and ideas on how to overcome them:

Lactation Lingo: Terms You Should Know

♦ **Baby Friendly Hospital Initiative:** A UNICEF and WHO effort to insure that hospitals certified as "Baby-Friendly" do not accept any free or reduced cost formula, bottles or nipples and also meet ten specific steps to support breastfeeding in their facility.

♦ **Expressed milk:** Milk you take from your breast, either with your hands or a breast pump.

♦ **International Board Certified Lactation Consultants (IBCLC).** A health care professional who specializes in the clinical management of breastfeeding. IBCLCs are certified by the International Board of Lactation Consultant Examiners, Inc. under the direction of the US National Commission for Certified Agencies.

♦ **Lactation Specialist—** This certification is completed after taking a 40 hour course in breastfeeding management and passing an exam. It's a stepping stone to becoming an IBCLC.

♦ **La Leche League International.** An International, nonprofit, nonsectarian organization dedicated to providing education information, support and encouragement to women who want to breastfeed. Their website www.llli.org is a great resource for information and can help you find a local support group. La Leche League is found all over the world. A La Leche League Leader is a mother who has had a specific type of breastfeeding and parenting experience, meets the prerequisites for leadership, and has finished the extensive written training curriculum.

♦ **WIC Breastfeeding Peer Counselors—**Peer counselors are mothers who have breastfeeding experience and are trained to provide basic information and support to other mothers with whom they share various characteristics, such as language, race, and socioeconomic status. They work in a WIC program, the supplemental nutrition and education program for Women, Infants and Children in the US.

Unsupportive Family and Friends

How can the people you care about the most not be on "your side?" It's not their fault really; it's mostly due to lack of *accurate* information. Here's what you can do:

♦ Point out the benefits of breastfeeding that would most interest the unsupportive person. For example, your partner might be interested in saving money or in learning about the scientifically proven benefits of breastfeeding. Be assertive in your beliefs.

◆ Let your partner know that he'll be in the loop. When women start talking about breastfeeding, some men feel completely left out, and this may explain their opposition. Let him know there are plenty of ways for him to be included by:

- Having a positive and supportive attitude. Let him know that this is his "job one." He can do that without spending time, money or energy.

- Bringing you snacks, water and whatever else you need while nursing.

- Spending time with you while you are nursing. You can watch TV together or discuss the latest in politics.

- Spending one-on-one quality time with your other children so that they don't feel left out either.

- Feeding your baby expressed milk once breastfeeding is well established (after six weeks).

- Feeding your baby solid foods when he is about six months.

◆ Find friends or relatives who have breastfed and are willing to help you bring your family around to your way of thinking. Knowing someone who can share your experience and offer support may also make learning to breastfeed easier.

◆ Invite your partner, family member, or friend to go to a breastfeeding class or La Leche League meeting. Attend a La Leche League meeting while pregnant and continue throughout your breastfeeding experience for support.

Unsupportive Hospital or Staff

Unsupportive hospital staff can be quite a problem for women who are still undecided about breastfeeding. Even in our pro-breastfeeding society, overworked hospital staff who have no personal experience with breastfeeding may unintentionally discourage you from breastfeeding rather than trying to help you. Be assertive and trust your instincts.

Try to be proactive, because you may have your baby at a time a lactation consultant is not on duty. Look for a Baby Friendly Hospital or one that employs International Board Certified Lactation Consultants (IBCLC). Ask about their services before you go into labor, including how to get help after hours. Contact a La Leche Leader, local lactation consultant or your breastfeeding peer counselor from WIC for support and encouragement. Sometimes even a long-distance call with a friend or relative can provide the support you need! (Find breastfeeding hotlines later in this chapter.)

Difficulties at the Hospital: Advice from Kelli, Mom of Three

Spencer, my oldest, and I had great difficulty breastfeeding for the first 2 months due to an unsupportive nurse providing me with misinformation after delivery (i.e., feedings must occur every 2 hours for 20 minutes on each breast). When I asked for help due to difficulties with latching and keeping him awake while still in the hospital, she simply reinforced her instructions. I trusted that the information given to me was accurate since it came from a nurse and for some reason I never discussed our problems with his physician. I finally gave into the advice of my mom and just did what felt right. Turns out, all it took was for me to switch to an on-demand schedule (which I didn't know was a "technique"). Unbelievably I received the same "feed on a schedule" advice after delivering my second son Carson. Inaccurate information given to me with both babies caused me countless tears and immense feelings of inadequacy as a mother. Only because of strong family support, determination and trusting my instincts did I finally succeed.

Fast-forward to a much different experience with Brody, my third child. I was fortunate enough with Brody to have a nursery nurse who was also a lactation specialist. She was incredibly supportive and informative. She allowed me to nurse Brody within the first half hour of birth, (with the other two it was several hours later), helped me to get back in the swing of positioning the baby, and reinforced that on-demand feedings were recommended and that the information given to me with the other two was considered outdated. With Brody, we have not had any problems, and for the first time, I have not had feelings of inadequacy as a mother!

My advice to other moms-to-be: find out about the hospital's lactation consultant services *before* you go into labor and consult with them *before* problems arise. If no services are available after hours (which of course is when most babies decide to come), find a certified lactation consultant outside of the hospital that could be available to you whenever you deliver. Paying the hourly fee is well worth it considering how much you could spend on formula if breastfeeding doesn't work (as well as the anguish, inadequacy and disappointment you may feel).

Unsupportive Pediatrician or Staff

Before you have your baby, find a pediatrician (or family health care provider) who supports breastfeeding. Ask nursing moms or the local La Leche League Leader—word usually spreads quickly about who the most supportive health care providers are. Call the prospective pediatrician's office while you are pregnant. Breastfeeding questions may be delegated to his office nurse or medical assistant—also quiz them on their breastfeeding knowledge. Research shows that some pediatricians lack knowledge and training on breastfeeding topics. That's OK as long as they understand their lack of knowledge, support your determination to breastfeed and refer you to someone who *is* knowledgeable.

If you plan to interview prospective pediatricians, you can ask about his practice's approach to breastfeeding during the interview:

♦ In what situations would you recommend formula feedings, interruptions of breastfeeding or weaning from the breast?

♦ Does your office have a written protocol for breastfeeding moms that other staff can refer to if you are out of the office?

♦ If I have trouble breastfeeding, who in your office can help, or which lactation consultant can I be referred to?

♦ Which over-the-counter medications or antibiotics are safe to take while nursing?

Unfortunately, you won't really know how supportive or knowledgeable your pediatrician's office is regarding breastfeeding unless you have a problem. When in doubt, do seek a second opinion!

The Idea that You Don't Have Enough Milk

Once a mother is breastfeeding her child, her biggest concern is usually whether she is producing enough milk. Sometimes friends, family or even health professionals unfamiliar with breastfeeding may plant seeds of doubt in your mind. Know this! You **can** make enough milk; it's a simple process of supply and demand. Your breasts never completely empty—with continuous stimulation the mammary glands continue to make milk. The more often you nurse your baby, the more milk your body makes. Here are some tips to help you make sure your baby is getting enough breast milk:

♦ Feed your baby on demand. Put your baby to the breast shortly after birth or within 2 hours, if at all possible. Baby will be sleepy at first and you may need to wake him to feed. Let your baby determine the length and frequency of feedings. You should nurse eight to twelve times in a twenty-four-hour period during the first six weeks to help establish your milk supply. Pay attention to early hunger signs such as rooting, activity, sucking on hands, etc.

♦ Make sure you have positioned your baby properly: baby and mom should be comfortably positioned (tummy to tummy).

♦ Put your feet up, prop you and baby up with pillows and relax! Baby should be also be comfortable, with a good grasp of your nipple to successfully empty your milk glands. "Asymmetric latch" is the best way for your baby to comfortably empty the milk ducts. When putting your baby to the breast, point your nipple towards the roof of your baby's mouth; his mouth will cover more of the bottom part of the area around the areola. When your breasts are emptied, they'll make more milk to fill the demand.

- ◆ Look for the physical signs that your baby is getting enough breast milk:
  - Weight gain:
    - » It is normal for baby to lose a small amount of weight after birth. He should regain it by 2 weeks.
    - » Once your milk comes in, your baby should gain about 6 oz. (190 g) per week
  - Diapers: After the first week, 5-6 very wet diapers per day and 3-4 dirty diapers after day 4.
  - After feeding, your breasts feel softer and baby seems content, often falling asleep at the end of the feeding.

- ◆ Your baby's stomach can only hold ½ an ounce (1 tablespoon) of colostrum the first few days of life, and usually is feeding every 2 hours. Your baby's stomach on Day 1 is the size of a shooter marble and does not stretch; feeding more than this amount causes spit-up. Day 3 it is the size of a ping pong ball. Day 10 it is the size of a large chicken egg. (www.ameda.com/ages_and_stages_list)

- ◆ Keep in mind the timing of growth spurts, usually 2 weeks, 6 weeks, 3 months, 6 months and 9 months. These are crucial times to breastfeed on demand or keep pumping to increase milk to meet the demand. *This is the time when you might doubt your ability to make enough milk.* Your baby is nursing more often so that your body makes more milk for him to grow. Don't be surprised if you are feeding *very often* during this time.

Do take care of yourself. It's important to take it easy, especially the first few weeks. Relax at home, take a nap when the baby does and eat well. (Note: this advice will be repeated by many!) Life with a new baby isn't always easy. Stay committed and develop a strategy to get through the rough times.

Reaching Out for Help

Most breastfeeding experts agree that the first six weeks (but especially the first two weeks) are crucial for long-term breastfeeding success. If you have trouble at any time, but especially the first few weeks, seek help from a breastfeeding specialist, whether that is your health care provider, lactation consultant, La Leche Leader, WIC peer counselor, a lactation specialist, WIC nutritionist, or a breastfeeding educator. Here are a couple of ways to get free help:

- ◆ La Leche League International: You can reach La Leche League International at www.lalecheleague.org or 800-La Leche, or 847-519-7730 to find a Leader by zip code. In Canada, 800-665-4324 or 514-LaLeche to find a French speaking Leader.

- Office on Woman's Health, US Department of Health and Human Services: support line. English and Spanish speaking peer counselors available. 800-994-9662, www.womenshealth.gov/breastfeeding/why-breastfeeding-is-important/

- Feeding Expert: Nurses, dietitians and lactation consultants offer free advice at 800-986-8800. The hotline is a service of Similac; lactation consultants are provided by a third party.

My Experience as a Breastfeeding Mom and Lactation Consultant by Marisa Van Dommelen, MS, IBCLC.

During my first four years as a WIC nutritionist, I learned to listen to mothers and became fascinated with the reasons women became mothers and the reasons they chose to breastfeed or give formula to their children. So, when I started my Master's program, I had a mission: to bring awareness to the community I worked in, to support mothers who were lacking information and to improve government involvement about the crucial topic of breastfeeding.

When I became a mother, there was no doubt my child would take nothing but breast milk. Labor wasn't what I expected; but that made me more determined to stick with my commitment to breastfeed. Nursing didn't come as naturally as I expected; many new mothers often experience the same thing. For me, it was about learning how to handle obstacles and tackling them one at a time. It was overwhelming at times—but life is full of detours and obstacles; and about how you handle them. It's about the right choice you make that instant. Many of my essential choices came long before my pregnancy, as I learned about the benefits of breastfeeding. I knew that my children would be as healthy as I could make them both during pregnancy and after, with proper nutrition and with breast milk as long I could provide it. As an International Certified Lactation Consultant for 9 years, it's been my honor to help many mothers who have committed to nursing their children. I've worked with many mothers of children with special needs whose breast milk has made the difference between life and death. I'm blessed to have earned the respect of my community and health professionals in helping bring awareness to health and the gift of life—"breast milk."

Marisa works as a nutritionist and lactation consultant at an Early Childhood Intervention Program in Southern New Mexico and is an active volunteer in her community.

Going Back to Work

Due to economic necessity or for personal fulfillment, most women go back to work after having a new baby. But this should not be a barrier to breastfeeding.

Back to Work Checklist

Breastfeeding after going back to work is a great way to continue to provide your baby with the best nutrition while you're away. And it's good for your employer, too. Since breast milk protects against infection, a woman who breastfeeds misses fewer days of work because of her baby's enhanced immune system. Breastfeeding while working does take a bit of planning, though, hence another checklist:

◆ Check out breastfeeding support at work while you are pregnant. Your supervisor and Human Resources are good places to start. Become familiar with state laws protecting pumping in the work place.

◆ Start a lactation room or program if your employer doesn't have one. Corporate lactation programs are becoming more popular as the business world realizes the benefits of breastfeeding. A lactation program usually includes a mother's room for pumping, an electric breast pump available for use, and attitudes and policies that are supportive of breastfeeding. For more information on starting a workplace lactation program: www.cdc.gov/nccdphp/dnpao/hwi/toolkits/lactation/index.htm and www.corporatevoices.org/lactation

◆ Find a day-care provider close to your workplace. This will enable you to feed your baby during your lunch hour. Or if you hire a provider that comes to your home, make it an agreement that she will bring the baby to you.

◆ Rent a hospital grade electric pump if your workplace doesn't provide one. (The WIC program loans out high quality pumps to moms returning to work or school.) Breast pumps can be rented from hospitals, lactation consultants, and health departments.

◆ Be sure to establish a good milk supply before you begin giving your baby breast milk from a bottle. Give your baby plenty of time to learn how to drink from the bottle before you go back to work.

◆ Nursing your baby on demand when he or she is with you is crucial to maintain your milk supply.

Real Life Stories from Women Like You

Going back to work can affect your feeding decisions. While some women view going back to work as an insurmountable obstacle to breastfeeding, many women feel "where there's a will, there's a way!" See how these women fit breastfeeding into their work life:

◆ Madiha was determined to breastfeed her daughter Inaaya. Her company supported breastfeeding. She rented a breast pump from the hospital and used it at work. (She used the Medela Double Pumping Kit, which allowed her to empty both breasts at the same time and still have time to run errands or eat lunch. For more information on electric pumps, contact your hospital, a lactation consultant, or www.medela.com.) Madiha found that breastfeeding Inaaya was just the contact she needed after being away most of the day. I admired Madiha for her determination. She carried on this routine for nine months, until she started daycare in her home and was able to nurse on demand.

- ◆ Alicia was a teacher. Luckily, she had her baby in May, which gave her almost 4 months home with Cristian. During her time at home, she stockpiled her milk and at the end of the summer, starting cutting back on her breastfeeding times, and gave her son breast milk that had been frozen. By the time she was back at work, she was able to feed him in the morning and at night; her mom gave him breast milk from a bottle during the day. He started solids at 6 months and that also decreased his milk intake. With a carefully timed pregnancy and advance planning, Cristian was exclusively breastfed for 6 months.

- ◆ Sarah had a high-stress job. Her boss and company were not very supportive of motherhood, yet Sarah wanted to breastfeed. She learned that breastfeeding didn't have to be done full-time. She established a good milk supply while she was home with Erin, then she gradually figured out the routine that worked best for her family. She nursed Erin in the morning, Erin's daycare fed Erin two bottles of formula in the afternoon, then Sarah nursed Erin in the late afternoon while her husband prepared dinner and again before she went to bed. Sarah had arranged a reduced work schedule (9-3) for her first 3 months back. Her boss had been against it, but she told him either that or she was going to take her 12 weeks of Family Medical Leave off. Over time, her boss saw the flexible arrangements as a long-term investment which he later "sold" as an employee benefit. Sarah's milk supply adjusted to Erin's feeding schedule. On the weekend, Erin's dad helped out with the midday bottles.

- ◆ Nicole didn't want to have to pump at work, but she wanted to breastfeed. By planning ahead, she and her husband saved some money so that she could work part-time after Frank was born. (She put together a job-sharing arrangement.) While at home for ten weeks after her delivery, she built up her milk supply and arranged her schedule to be away five hours each morning. By working part-time, Nicole had the best of both worlds.

- ◆ Karen loved breastfeeding and wanted to continue once she went back to her job as a hairstylist. Like many women who work in service professions, Karen found that the work environment was not conducive to pumping. Her solution was to get a car adapter for her electric breast pump and a windshield sun shade for privacy; she pumped a few times a day in the privacy of her car. She kept a picture of Eli, her son there, which made it easier to pump.

Achieving Work-Life Balance

Regardless of how you feed your baby, you'll want to find a way to balance work and quality time with your new baby—and the rest of your family. Balancing work and family life will also help you successfully breastfeed. Consider the following options:

Parental Leave Time

If you're lucky, your company (or your country) allows an extended maternity leave: if you're even luckier, you get paid for it. The U.S. Family Medical Leave Act requires companies with at least 50 employees to allow new parents 12 weeks of unpaid leave. Other countries allow 52 weeks off. Regardless of how much time you get, it's important to find out what you're entitled to and take full advantage of it.

Work-Related travel

If your job requires you to travel frequently, you might want to cut your travel time to a minimum whether you breastfeed or not. If you can't cut your travel time, spending more time with your baby—and nursing—still won't be impossible, but it will require diligent planning. Kristen arranged daycare with a national franchise when she traveled so she could take Katie with her.

Flexible Work Arrangements

Many companies offer programs to help with work/life balance. Options like flex-time, part-time, telecommuting, compressed work weeks, and job-sharing are useful in many ways to parents, especially new ones. Maximize your maternity leave and check out flexible work schedules or a gradual phase-back to work.

Supportive Boss and Coworkers

Going back to work while your child is an infant may be emotionally difficult. Seek out supportive coworkers—perhaps those who also have children. A supportive boss will understand if you need to take time off to take your child for her check-ups or need extra breaks to pump. Assure your boss that as a result of her flexibility, your productivity will not slip and you won't miss as much work as other new moms might due to taking time off to take care of a sick baby.

Supportive Company

If your current job doesn't provide a family-friendly environment, consider finding one that does. For many companies, work-life balance is an employee benefit often considered more valuable than salary, vacation or other benefits. Check out these resources to find a family-friendly company:

- ◆ www.jobsandmoms.com/: developed by career coach Nancy Collamer, the website offers articles, advice, a blog and home based job ideas.

- www.workingmother.com to find the annual list of top family-friendly 100 companies to work for.

A Special Note To Guys by Dave Grotto RD, LDN

Support your loved one with her decision to breastfeed or not. It is a big decision and one that requires lots of thought, researching and planning. I was surprised to find out that breastfeeding isn't always second nature for most women. It requires practice and patience and guys can help in this area too. There's lots of great research and resources that support the decision to breastfeed. Nutritionally speaking, it is the most tailored food that money can't buy! Not only are there all the nutrients present in breast milk to support health and growth, but there is a bit of mom's own natural immunity that gets passed along to baby—and that simply can't be found in infant formula. And nutrition is only one of the many benefits of breastfeeding. But sometimes it's not as simple as to breastfeed or not to breastfeed. In my own life, one of our daughters had difficulties expressing enough milk during a feeding so we supplemented her feedings with infant formula. Results? Baby, mom AND dad were happy. Total win!

Dave Grotto is a Registered Dietitian and Author of *101 Optimal Life Foods and 101 Foods That Could Save Your Life!* **You can find more of his nutrition humor on his blog: davidgrotto.wordpress.com/**

Nutrition during Breastfeeding

Eating well while nursing is important, but you can relax a bit because unless you have an absolutely horrible diet, your body will still be able to make good quality breast milk. Your body uses stored nutrients so you, not your baby, will have a deficit if you don't eat right. However, there are several nutrients that you should strive to get more of; they're crucial for your baby's continued brain and visual development.

There's more good news: An extra benefit of breastfeeding is the one time in your life when you'll have a full plate and still lose weight! Enjoy but don't go overboard—I've also known women who continued to *gain* weight while breastfeeding. Also, regardless of what you hear, there's really NO food you need to stay away from *just because you are breastfeeding*. More on this later!

Eating Expectantly Diet: Best for Breastfeeding

Below is a quick and easy guide to the number of foods from each food group you should try to eat. The Best for Breastfeeding Diet contains a range of 2,100 to 2,300 calories and meets the needs of the average breastfeeding woman—100-300 calories above pre-pregnant needs. (It's about the same as the Eating Expectantly Second Trimester Diet.) Keep in mind that you may need more or fewer calories.

Eating Expectantly Diet: Best for Breastfeeding

9 Carb servings. Best choices: whole grains like whole-wheat breads, pasta and cereals, barley, oatmeal, quinoa, and starchy vegetables: winter squash, potatoes, dried beans, peas and corn, plantain, yuca / cassava and taro.

7 Ounces (220 g) of Protein Foods: choose fish twice a week and some plant protein daily. Fish and shellfish (up to 12 oz. / 375 g per week), dried beans and legumes, nuts, tofu, cottage cheese, lean beef, lamb, poultry and pork. Be sure to eat a variety!

Teaspoons Fats/Oils. Best Choices: avocado, nuts and seeds, olive oil, canola oil, nut oils, olives, soft spread margarine and mayonnaise. Limit saturated fats like butter, cream and coconut oil.

3 Servings of Dairy Foods: I serving is I cup (250 ml) of milk, yogurt or calcium-fortified soymilk; 1.5 ounces (45 g) natural cheese or 2 ounces (60 g) processed cheese. Choose nonfat or low-fat.

Cups (750 ml) Vegetables: choose a dark leafy green or red/orange vegetable daily. Best Choices: Broccoli, cauliflower, carrots, spinach, cabbage, leaf and romaine lettuce, greens, sweet peppers, mushrooms, bok choy, artichokes and tomatoes.

2 Cups (500 ml) Fruit: choose a vitamin C-rich fruit daily. Best choices: papaya, mango, melon, berries, watermelon, apricots, peaches, grapefruit, orange, grapes and kiwi.

Splurge 100-300 Calories (Including up to 6 teaspoons added sugar—including what's added to food like yogurt.)

Calorie Needs

First let me say that there is really no need to count calories. Your calorie needs during breastfeeding can vary a lot and there is much debate among the scientific community about how many extra calories you actually need while breastfeeding. It depends on how much body fat you accumulated during pregnancy, how much milk you're producing and how active you are. For example, you may need just 200 extra calories above your pre-pregnant needs, if you only nurse a few times a day and you're not very active. However, if you're exclusively breastfeeding, you have very little body fat and you are active, you might need 500 calories more than before you were pregnant.

The bottom line: follow your appetite—eating like you did in the second trimester with 6 small mini-meals a day may be ideal. Your body will definitely tell you when you need more food. The first weeks with baby are often chaotic, and you may have a hard time getting in sync with your new schedule. In fact, many new moms (including me) have found it difficult to squeeze in a shower. And some women rely on high fat snack foods to get them through—which can pack on pounds instead of help lose them! So be sure to keep some easy–to-eat-with-one-hand foods, (fruits, vegetables, fruit and nut bars, healthy sandwiches and wraps) and take advantage of all those friends who offered to cook for you.

Losing Weight and Breastfeeding

◆ You'll probably lose some weight without even trying. But… some moms don't lose weight while nursing and actually gain weight. But that has more to do with food choices and sedentary lifestyle than the calorie burning of breastfeeding.

◆ Don't actively try to lose weight until about 6 weeks postpartum—you will lose weight but it will be mostly fluid weight. Instead, focus on eating a well-balanced diet to nourish yourself and your baby.

◆ Losing 1 to 1.5 pounds (500 g to 1.5 kg) per week is generally safe. Losing more than that can mobilize environmental chemicals stored in body fat. So, keep your calories to at least 1,800 calories per day (1,500 if you are very petite.). Monitoring the growth and general health of your baby is also a good way to check the quality and quantity of your milk.

◆ In general, it's tough to lose the last 5 or 10 pounds (2.5 to 5 kg) . This is when you should bring in the reinforcements: aerobic exercise and weight resistance. These exercises help you lose more body fat while keeping muscle and are more effective at helping you lose postpartum weight than just diet alone.[9] More muscle means burning more calories all the time!

Fluid Needs

For fluid, drink to thirst. However, if the weather is hot or if you are exercising, drink more fluids rather than just relying on your thirst. You'll know if you aren't drinking enough if your urine becomes darker than usual (or if you become constipated.) Sometimes it's easy to ignore thirst if there is nothing close by to drink of if you're just too busy, so it's a good idea to sit down with a glass of something, preferably filtered water, when you nurse. But other fluids can hydrate you too. More than likely drinking 12 cups (3 liters), including all types of fluids, will meet most women's needs.[10]

One thing you do need to know about fluid—drinking more will not necessarily increase milk production. Drinking less will not help with engorgement, either.[11]

Other Nutrient Needs

Overall, your nutrient needs are similar to those in the second trimester, with a few exceptions.

Protein

You'll need about 71 grams of protein per day, which is the same as during pregnancy. Strive to have different types of protein each day from beans, nuts, eggs, seafood, lean beef, poultry, and pork, and low-fat dairy. They all have something good to offer, but when it comes to animal protein, choose the leanest possible and trim visible fat.

Fat

It's one nutrient that changes in your milk according to your diet. Note that it's the *type* of fat rather than the *amount* that's important. Continue to keep saturated fat to a minimum and avoid trans fats. The fat you packed away during pregnancy is now used to make milk, so your previous diet also affects your milk now. Besides supplying calories, DHA (an omega-3 fat) is the building block of brain and eye tissue, which both continue to grow—a lot—during the first year. Continue to have a source of DHA in your diet, either through cold water fish (see list on page 127 and page 101) or from a DHA supplement of 200-300 mg as recommended by the American Academy of Pediatrics.[12]

Although alpha-linolenic acid (an essential fatty acid found in walnuts and flaxseed) is also important in the diet, a DHA supplement or eating adequate DHA-fortified foods is necessary if you are vegetarian. See page 235 for a full discussion.

Carbohydrates

About half your calories should come from carbohydrate-rich foods. As during pregnancy, choose smart carbs and eat a variety of fruits, vegetables and whole grains.

Vitamins and Minerals

While you need less of some nutrients compared to pregnancy, you need more of these: Vitamin A, C, B6, B12, pantothenic acid, biotin, choline, chromium, copper, iodine, manganese, selenium, zinc and potassium, which you should be able to obtain through a healthy diet.

Should You Continue Taking Your Prenatal Vitamin?

While many health care providers advise that breastfeeding moms continue taking their prenatal vitamin, it can also make you constipated due to its high iron content. If you choose to take a multivitamin other than your prenatal, look for one that contains choline.

Iron

Unless you had significant blood loss during delivery or you are anemic, your need for iron decreases significantly. In fact, you need less iron now than before you were pregnant because you aren't having menstrual periods. However, if you had a tendency to be anemic during pregnancy, ask your health care provider about getting your iron status checked postpartum. Iron deficiency anemia is linked to postpartum depression.

Vitamin D

You should strive to get adequate vitamin D through exposure to the sun, food or a supplement. (See page 59 for full discussion.) However, because vitamin D is so critical to the health of your baby, and the fact that many women are vitamin D deficient, the American Academy of Pediatrics recommends that all infants who are breastfed (either exclusively or combined with formula), should receive a supplement of 400 IU of vitamin D, beginning at hospital discharge.[13]

Calcium

Many women slack off on calcium-rich foods after delivery. However, calcium is as important—or even more important—while breastfeeding. If you don't have calcium from your diet (or supplements), it will come from what's stored in your bones, which can contribute to osteoporosis later. Unfortunately, heavy metals like lead are also stored there, and can be released into the bloodstream too. Research shows that women who breastfeed have a significantly lower risk of hip fracture post-menopause—and the longer a woman breastfed, the lower her risk.[14]

Choline

Another "brain" nutrient, it's found in large amounts in breast milk and also in your baby's hippocampus—the memory center of the brain. Most women don't have enough choline in their diet.[15] Eggs and lean beef are rich sources. See page 220 for more info.

Lutein

New research keeps pouring in on this super-antioxidant! It protects your baby's eye from damaging blue light and also protects cell membranes (and DHA) found in the retina. Lutein has also been found in the areas of a baby's brain important for language, hearing and memory. The amount in your breast milk is determined by the lutein in your diet. Best sources are leafy greens like kale and spinach. See page 220 for more information.

Iodine

It's a mineral you might not think too much about, but it's critical for your baby's brain. Use iodized salt and try to find a multivitamin with iodine.

Zinc

It's something women often don't get enough of, and you need more of it now than while you were pregnant to help with growth and development and the immune system. Sources include seafood, lean red meat, poultry, eggs, nuts and beans, yogurt and whole grains.

Fiber

Between the effects of anesthesia and the hormones of pregnancy, your digestive system may feel a bit sluggish the first week or two after delivery. Don't forget to eat fiber-rich fruits and vegetables, whole grains, a daily probiotic and plenty of water to keep things moving. See tips for easing constipation on page 201.

Food Sensitivities in Breastfed Babies

Contrary to what you may have heard, most babies are not bothered by any foods in their mom's diet. That's why there's no list of "foods you should avoid while breastfeeding" in this book! That means that you don't need to stop eating gassy, spicy or garlicky foods for the sake of your baby, because he might like the taste of those foods as much as you do! In fact, research shows that flavors in breast milk actually help babies accept more new foods when they start eating solids.

So here are the facts: a certain amount of fussiness is normal for young babies, especially in the evening. However, if fussiness is accompanied by other symptoms such as excessive spitting up or vomiting, colic, rash or persistent congestion, greenish or bloody stools, these might indicate a food allergy or sensitivity. Reactions can happen immediately up to many hours after you eat a food. If your baby seems to be reacting to something you ate, take a look at these foods:

♦ Common allergens: cow's milk products, soy, wheat, corn, eggs, and peanuts

♦ Foods that you have eaten for the first time since nursing

♦ Foods that you have recently eaten in large amounts

♦ Food that another family member is allergic to

Cow's milk protein is a common cause of sensitivity among babies. It can cause colic-like symptoms, eczema, wheezing, vomiting, diarrhea (including bloody diarrhea), constipation, hives, and/or a stuffy, itchy nose. If you suspect a dairy protein sensitivity, remove all dairy protein from your diet including milk, cheese, sour cream, yogurt etc. Many babies outgrow milk sensitivities and allergies by the age of 3, but often before 1 year.

Gas happens too, because of an infant's immature digestive system. Both of my babies had problems with gas—but Nicolas had it bad! I started limiting foods in my diet—first dairy, then many fruits and vegetables. In the end, my diet was *extremely* limited and he *still had gas*! On the advice of our pediatrician, we tried an over-the-counter remedy—simethicone drops—which helped a lot. If your baby has gas, talk to your health care provider.

Should You Avoid Allergenic Foods While Nursing?

Allergies, also called "Atopic disease", includes asthma, allergy related skin inflammation (atopic dermatitis) and food allergies, has increased dramatically in the last few decades. Asthma has increased 160%, atopic dermatitis has increased 2-3 times[16] and peanut allergy has doubled.[17] Family history can be a big factor. If one parent has allergies, a baby's risk of allergies is about 48%; the risk can increase to 70% if both parents have allergic or atopic disease.

This is an issue where the research pendulum swings back and forth. Here's what we know:[18]

♦ Breastfeeding exclusively for at least four months prevents or delays atopic dermatitis, cow milk allergy and wheezing in early childhood, compared to feeding with regular cow's milk formula.

♦ Some intact proteins, which are common allergens, such as from peanut, egg and cow's milk have been found in breast milk. However, studies looking for an association between allergens in breast milk and atopic disease have shown mixed results. Until more randomized, controlled studies are done, we don't know for sure if avoiding those foods during pregnancy or breastfeeding will help or not. Right now, this is not a recommendation of the American Academy of Pediatrics[19] or the Australasian Society of Clinical Immunology and Allergy.[20] However, if you do decide to avoid allergenic foods, consult with a registered dietitian to help develop a meal plan for you that contains all the nutrients you need.

♦ Some studies have shown that probiotics given in late pregnancy (and to infants during the first 6 months of life) may reduce the incidence of eczema, but other studies have shown no effect.[21] Probiotics are generally not a recommended action to prevent allergies, but due to their general positive health benefits, they are recommended in this book!

♦ If you supplement with formula and your infant is at high risk of allergies, choose a hydrolyzed or partially hydrolyzed formula, which has also been shown to prevent or delay the occurrence of atopic disease.

♦ One thing that *is* universally recommended and proven to reduce the risk of allergies: avoid letting your baby be exposed to tobacco smoke.

♦ Probably the best advice for women who have allergies or a family history of allergies is to breastfeed as long as possible (exclusively for six months) and to eat a large variety of foods so that specific food proteins will not be passed in large amounts to the baby through the milk. For an excellent discussion on this topic see: kellymom.com/health/baby-health/food-sensitivity/

Peanut Allergies

Protein from peanuts is one of the most potent allergens, sometimes causing fatal reactions. Some infants have reacted upon the first known exposure to peanut protein. Two possibilities explain this. Peanut protein has been found in breast milk of moms who ate peanuts. That's not to say that if you eat peanut butter sandwiches while breastfeeding your baby will develop an allergy. Understanding the cause of allergic diseases is very complicated. Another hypothesis of peanut exposure is through topical skin preparations; peanut oil, also called oleum arachidis, is frequently used in the pharmaceutical and cosmetic industry. In the past, oils and creams with peanut oils were used in the treatment of very dry and damaged skin such as eczema. When peanut oil products are used on skin that is dry or damaged, the absorption into the body is easier; and thus so is "sensitization" to the microscopic amount of protein. (Refined oils contain 100 times less peanut protein than unrefined oil and usually cause no reaction in people with peanut allergies.)

Food Sensitivities?

If your baby does appear to be having food sensitivities, ask your lactation consultant or registered dietitian familiar with breastfeeding about trying an elimination diet.

Drugs and Breastfeeding

If for some reason you need to take a prescription (or over-the-counter) medication while you're breastfeeding, it doesn't mean you have to stop breastfeeding! (However, I've heard horror stories of women whose health care providers told them to stop nursing when they didn't need to!) Many medications are compatible with nursing because they do not enter breast milk. Your pharmacist may be the most knowledgeable in this area. Do ask before you take anything! There is also an excellent book on the subject called Medications and Mother's Milk 2012: A Manual of Lactational Pharmacology by Thomas Hale. Certified lactation consultant Kelly Bonyata has a list of medications and their safety category on her website at kellymom.com/bf/can-i-breastfeed/meds/aap-approved-meds/. You can also find information at www.motherisk.org/women/breastfeeding.jsp.

Breastfeeding for Special Groups

Moms of Multiples

If you have given birth to multiple babies, can you still breastfeed? The answer is an enthusiastic "Yes!" As you may have guessed, breastfeeding multiples is a bit more complicated than nursing one baby. But since multiples are often born premature and smaller (low birth\weight, small for gestation) than single babies, your breast milk is vital to give your babies a healthy boost and prevent a serious illness called necrotizing enterocolitis.

Resources: Breastfeeding Multiples:

♦ *Oh Yes You Can Breastfeed Twins!* by April Rudat RD.

♦ kellymom.com/ages/newborn/bf-basics/bf-links-multiples/

♦ www.twinstuff.com/breastfd1.htm

♦ Info about breastfeeding twins and triplets, with pictures of positions: multiplebirthsfamilies.com/category/breastfeeding/

> ### Yes, You can Breastfeed Triplets!
>
> I'm happy to say that as a Lactation Consultant I've had the honor of meeting a mother who breastfed and pumped for her triplets for 7 months straight! A breastfeeding mother from Las Cruces, NM did what her pediatrician advised her to do—provided breast milk for her special needs premature girls.
> **Marisa Van Dommelen, MS, IBCLC, RLC**

Vegetarians

Vegans (vegetarians who eat no animal products) need to plan their diets a little more carefully to make sure their breast milk contains everything their babies need. Vitamin B12 must be consumed from a reliable source such as fortified breakfast cereal or a supplement; the DRI for breastfeeding is 2.8 micrograms. If you don't have a reliable source of B12 in your diet, it's recommended that your baby be given a supplement—a deficiency can lead to severe and permanent neurological damage.[22] While you need much less iron while breastfeeding, if your intake was marginal during pregnancy, you may need to catch up. Calcium and zinc may also be harder to find in a vegan diet. See page 214 and page 164 for food sources.

Preemies

If your baby was born prematurely, breastfeeding will give him a unique nutritional boost. Your baby's gestational age, strength of suck, and other health issues may require that you need to pump exclusively for a while. Depending on their gestational age, preemie babies can't usually coordinate breathing, sucking and swallowing; and will have to be fed through a tube until their suck is strong enough to give them adequate nutrition. While it may be disappointing not to be able to nurse your baby "in person," just remember what a special gift you are giving. As soon as a baby can be held, breastfeeding should be initiated. A baby uses less energy to breastfeed than bottle feed, according to Marisa Van Dommelen MS, IBCLC so feeding at the breast will help him conserve energy that he needs to grow.

New research indicates that breastfeeding the premature infant may provide even more health benefits than feeding a full-term infant[23]; it has been shown to improve short-term and long-term health. Benefits include drastically reducing the risk of necrotizing enterocolitis, reducing the severity of retinopathy of prematurity, improving gastrointestinal function and neurological development. Preterm infants who receive breast milk have fewer hospital admissions during the first year of life. The antioxidant lutein, (found in breast milk depending on mom's dietary intake) has been shown to decrease inflammation and cellular damage in premature infants, which could reduce vision complications associated with prematurity.[24]

Preemie Colostrum

Here's the cool thing about nursing a preemie; the first milk you make—colostrum—will contain more nitrogen, calories, vitamin A, zinc and sodium than the milk of a mom of a term infant. Your colostrum is also higher in anti-infective properties like immunoglobulin A (IgA), lysozyme, and lactoferrin, which protect your baby from bacterial and viral infections. These extra nutrients help your baby catch up in growth and development. Your body will make the transition from colostrum to breast milk at a slower pace, so your baby will receive even more "liquid gold." Your breast milk will continue to change to meet *your* baby's needs. Because of this, breastfeeding is really a lifetime gift for your baby!

Long term studies of preemies fed breast milk suggest that they have a lower risk of metabolic syndrome, improved insulin metabolism and have lower blood pressure later in life. In fact, the American Academy of Pediatrics recommends that all preterm infants receive breast milk, whether fresh, frozen or donated.[25]

Brain and eye development take place in the last trimester, which your baby missed some of, so the essential fatty acids are very important. Check your intake of essential fatty acids and make sure you eat a good daily source of them. If you don't, consider a supplement.

Preterm infants sometimes have higher nutrient needs than breast milk can satisfy, so your pediatrician or neonatologist may prescribe a special vitamin supplement and/or a Human Milk Fortifier. Don't worry—it doesn't mean there's anything wrong with your breast milk. It's just that due to a baby's small size, prematurity or need for catch up growth, he may need something extra. Consult the Lactation Consultant on staff; she may be able to provide alternative ways to increase calories without having to use milk fortifiers. Some hospitals offer donor milk to use while mothers get breastfeeding and pumping established.

Words of Encouragement from Helene, the Mom of Five:

"The bond between mother and child while the child is being nourished in the womb is not over when the umbilical cord is cut. The bond continues and grows as the mother breastfeeds and holds that new miracle of life in her arms. It is not just a nutritional need that is being met for the baby; it is a psychological, emotional, and physical need for both as well. No sensation compares with nursing your child. Nothing is as satisfying and fulfilling as nursing. I would tell every new mother who is considering breastfeeding to do it."

Questions You May Have

Q: Can I start drinking coffee again?

A: For you and the other caffeine starved moms out there—yes! However, your baby will be sharing your coffee (and any other caffeinated beverages and foods) receiving about 1 percent of the caffeine kick that you get. Your baby metabolizes the caffeine slower than you do—and the younger he is, the longer it takes—so take it easy on those double espressos when you have a newborn! The equivalent of two to three cups (500 to 750 ml) of coffee, or 300-500 mg of caffeine should be OK, according to the American Academy of Pediatrics.[26] However, caffeine can accumulate and cause your baby to be irritable and to have trouble falling asleep—it can also affect the let-down (the action that releases milk from the glands to the milk ducts)—good reasons not to overindulge. See p[age 116 for a listing of caffeine sources, some of which may surprise you!

Q: My mother says I should drink a beer before I breastfeed to increase my milk supply. Will it? And is it safe for my baby?

A: Another urban legend disproven! Drinking a beer before you nurse won't increase your milk supply and may hurt it. Alcohol lowers levels of the hormones needed for the production and flow of breast milk (prolactin and oxytocin). As a result, alcohol slows let-down and decreases milk production. But, must you continue to be the designated driver for the next year too? Not necessarily. An occasional drink here and there, if timed right, is just fine. Here are a few tips to keep in mind:

- The younger the baby, the more immature the liver and the slower his body can deal with alcohol. Be extra cautious drinking when you have a newborn.

- Alcohol peaks in breast milk ½ to 1 hour after drinking. So don't drink immediately before or during a nursing session.

- Wait 2-3 hours after you drink to nurse. Lactation consultant Kelly Bonyata notes on her website, www.kellymom.com "if you're sober enough to drive, you're sober enough to breastfeed."

- Daily exposure to alcohol is a developmental concern for babies, possibly causing gross motor delay and effects on growth. It has also been shown to affect a baby's sleep patterns. So, it's best to drink in moderation—one or two drinks, once or twice a week.

- Alcohol metabolism in adults can vary a lot depending on your weight, food intake, etc—use common sense.

- Ask your health care provider for more information.

Q: If I breastfeed, will my baby have a smaller risk of being overweight when he gets older?

A: Yes. Breastfeeding does decrease your baby's chances of becoming overweight or obese as he or she gets older.[27] In fact a large meta-analysis estimated that breastfed babies are 22% less likely to be overweight in later childhood or as adults.[28] The longer you breastfeed, the less your child's risk of becoming overweight.[29]

Q: I've heard that PCBs can be in breast milk. Can this affect the safety of my breast milk?

A: Over a lifetime, a person is exposed to environmental pollutants that accumulate in small amounts in the body—mostly in fat. The chemicals of greatest concern are organochlorines, a group of synthetic compounds persistent in the environment. Examples of these are polychlorinated biphenyls (PCBs), a family of industrial chemicals, and dichlorodiphenyl trichloro-ethane (DDT), an insecticide. Chemical treatment for termites is often associated with these residues. Although some of these chemicals have been banned in the United States for years, they persist in the environment and are still used in other parts of the world.

During pregnancy, a fetus's exposure to chemicals is much higher than during breastfeeding, but since body fat stored during pregnancy is used during breastfeeding, your diet during pregnancy can affect the amount of pollutants in your breast milk.

Should this information affect your decision to breastfeed? No. Chemicals in our environment are an unfortunate reality. The commonsense solution is to try to limit your present and future exposure to chemicals by following the tips on page 128.

Q: If I get food poisoning, should I avoid nursing my baby?

A: No. If a mom gets food poisoning, the bacteria usually doesn't pass into the breast milk. It's actually recommended that you continue breastfeeding, because this will help protect your baby from getting sick with the same bacteria. Just be sure to drink more fluids to avoid becoming dehydrated.

Q: I'd like to start a vigorous exercise program. Can I still successfully breastfeed?

A: Yes. Exercise doesn't change milk production or nutrient content. Exercise will help you get your "before-baby" body back and can also improve your mental outlook. See page 333 "Fitting Fitness In" for more information.

More Information on Infant Feeding

For more information on infant feeding, see my next book—*Baby Bites: Everything You Need to Know About Feeding Infants and Toddlers in One Handy Book*, the follow-up book to *Eating Expectantly*. *Baby Bites* is written in the same easy-to-read style, contains information about feeding kids from birth to three, and also contains delicious recipes. To review an excerpt from *Baby Bites*, visit www.healthyfoodzone. com. For even more information on making your own baby food, see *Super Baby Food* by Ruth Yaron.

First Weeks With Baby

What You'll Find:

♦ What to Expect after Delivery

♦ The Baby Blues

♦ Losing That Baby Fat

♦ Eating Expectantly Diet: Lose That Baby Fat

♦ Your Next Pregnancy—WHAT?

Frequently Asked Questions:

♦ What are some quick meals I can make the first week after delivery?

♦ What's the difference between the "baby blues" and postpartum depression?

♦ How soon can I start exercising after giving birth?

♦ What's the best way to lose weight?

♦ How quickly can I expect to lose my baby weight?

SCAN HERE FOR CHAPTER UPDATES

What to Expect after Delivery

Exhausted and overjoyed—but not hungry: that may describe how you feel after delivery. However, some women are so famished, they call out for pizza! If eating doesn't sound good, you should drink—fruit juice or lemonade can replenish energy as well as hydrate. Personally, I rarely drink sweetened drinks, but after eighteen hours of labor with my first son, I quickly slurped down a can of lemon-lime soda!

Labor and anesthesia slow down your digestion immensely. You may also have hemorrhoids from pregnancy or labor. Eat high-fiber foods like bran cereal, flaxseed, whole grain bread and cereal, fruits and vegetables and plenty of water to get your digestive tract back to normal. Prunes, dates and figs are tiny fruits that pack concentrated energy and fiber. Your health care provider may even recommend a stool softener to get things moving.

Concentrate on getting your strength back and taking care of your baby those first few weeks. Hopefully you cooked some meals ahead of time and froze them. If not, let your partner or other family members cook. See below and the *Eating Expectantly Cookbook* for healthy, fast, and convenient menu ideas.

Menus for the First Week with Baby

That first week, it's sometimes too tiring to decide what to eat!

Stick-to-Your Ribs Breakfasts
Start the day with a protein and fiber rich dish at breakfast and you'll get through the day with less temptation to nibble.
Whole grain waffles with nut butter, sliced fruit and a drizzling of honey
High protein whole grain cereal with milk, whole grain toast
Cottage cheese with pineapple, half a cinnamon raisin English muffin
Banana rolled up with peanut butter and a sprinkling of mini chocolate chips in a whole grain wrap
Boiled or microwaved eggs, whole grain bread
Greek yogurt parfait with fresh fruit and granola
Shrimp and crab omelet with fat-free cream cheese
Greek yogurt smoothie with berries
French toast with melted ham and cheese

Here's a week of quick dinner menus that take about 10 minutes to prepare. OK we cheated, there's some takeout here too.

Day 1
Chinese Takeout: Chicken and Snow Peas, Moo Shoo Shrimp
Steamed brown or white rice
Fresh fruit
Day 2
Omelet with chopped spinach and cheese
Whole grain English muffin
Grapes
Day 3
Boca Burger on whole-wheat bun with lettuce, tomato and pickles
Baked tortilla chips and salsa
Shredded carrots with pineapple, raisins and a dab of mayonnaise
Strawberries with yogurt dip
Day 4
Minute steaks on whole grain roll
Mixed vegetables
Spinach salad with candied walnuts and cranberries
Yogurt with blueberries
Day 5
Hummus dip with veggies
Poached salmon with dill (in the microwave)
Microwave oven baked sweet potato
Cantaloupe or canned peaches
Day 6
Bean tostadas or burritos on whole grain tortillas with lettuce, tomatoes and cheese
Jicama sticks
Guacamole
Frozen bananas dipped in chocolate syrup
Day 7
Mixed green salad with cooked salad shrimp, artichoke hearts, tomatoes, sunflower seeds and carrots
Garlic bread
Mixed Berry Smoothie
Dark chocolate kiss

The Baby Blues

Having a baby, especially your first, is probably the biggest life change you'll ever experience. In fact, it can literally turn your world upside down. Changes in work and social relationships, lack of sleep, having less time for yourself, new-mom worries and hormonal changes can all make your changing moods feel like a roller coaster ride. If you have times when you feel anxious, irritated, overwhelmed, restless or teary-eyed, these are absolutely normal symptoms of the "baby blues". Those feelings should subside in a few weeks or so—if they don't, you could be developing postpartum depression (also called postnatal depression).[1]

The symptoms of postpartum depression are the same as depression diagnosed at other times in a woman's life. Besides the symptoms mentioned above, if you have deep sadness, changes in appetite, insomnia, feel worthless and find little joy with previously favorite activities or if you have thoughts of harming yourself or your baby, you could be experiencing postpartum depression. About 15% of women who have given birth develop depression, which often goes away within a year but sometimes stays on as chronic depression.[2] Having depression in the postpartum period can affect your ability to care for your baby and yourself, so it's important to get help. Sometimes just getting some emotional and practical help can be enough, but professional counseling or a visit to a psychiatrist may also be needed. However, it may be hard to recognize when you have a problem and when your moods have stopped being "normal." Please talk with your health care provider or a friend if you suspect you are having symptoms of depression.

Eating well and being active can also help your mental health. Sufficient omega-3 fats, especially DHA, are important; low levels have been linked to anxiety and depression. Vitamin D insufficiency is related to an increased risk of postpartum depression, especially among African-American women.[3] So, getting outside and exposing your skin to a little sun can help your mental health in more ways than one! (See page 59 for more vitamin D info.) Adequate intake of zinc, selenium[4], magnesium, and iron and may also have protective effects against postpartum depression.[5]

For more information and resources:

◆   www.nlm.nih.gov/medlineplus/postpartumdepression.html

Losing That Baby Fat

Are you ready to get rid of the extra pounds you gained during pregnancy? Silly question, right? I'll never forget how disappointed I was after my first son Nicolas was born. To me it was very demoralizing to have to put on the maternity clothes that I actually felt like burning! I had to learn to be patient, and I suggest you try to do the same. It took ten months to gain the weight; it's not going to come off in a month. The key to lifetime weight control is a healthy diet combined with exercise.

However, you'd best not exercise vigorously the first six weeks. (Personally, I didn't have to worry about that; I was too tired!) Remember those hormones discussed in Chapter 9: The Third Trimester (the ones that caused your joints and pelvis to become more elastic)? Well, they haven't quite returned to normal yet, so take it easy for a while or you could damage some joints or ligaments. A simple walking regimen is a good start. It's a great way to show off your new baby to the neighbors or meet other new moms at the mall.

Women who started pregnancy close to their ideal weight, and gained the recommended 25-35 pounds (12-17 kg) may not need to work too hard at losing the weight, but they will still have to work to get their pre-baby body back—with exercise! On the other hand, up to 20% of women retain 11 pounds (5 kg) after pregnancy[6] and women who are overweight have a higher risk of keeping some weight on and even gaining some weight postpartum.[7] If you are nursing, you shouldn't reduce your calorie intake below 1,800 calories, unless you are very petite. You may just need to consciously cut back on extras (no more middle-of-the-night snacks!) and start moving more. The weight will come off gradually.

Chew Away Stress and Save Calories with Gum

Personally, I like to chew gum—always sugar-free. It helps me stay away from dessert when I really don't need it, improves my breath after eating garlic bread, and it's a tasty substitute for tooth brushing when I'm away from home. I'm happy to report that research backs up some of the benefits of chewing gum.

♦ Initial research in the journal *Appetite* shows that chewing gum before snacking helps diminish cravings for sweets and decreases snack intake. Imagine, saving yourself from that apple cobbler a-la-mode, just by popping in a stick of gum.[8,9]

♦ When life throws you stress—chew gum! A self-perception test showed more than half of "gum chewers" agreed that chewing gum helps them cope with everyday stress; others who were not habitual gum chewers reported that chewing gum made them feel more relaxed.[10]

Here are other ways that chewing gum might help you lose or maintain your weight:

♦ Chew gum while you're cooking to suppress the urge to nibble.

♦ If stress is an eating trigger for you, pop in a piece of gum when you feel tense.

♦ Chew gum when everyone else is chowing down on the chips and salsa.

♦ When all that's available to drink is high calorie soda, chew a stick of gum to keep your mouth moist.

Disordered Eating: Are You at Risk?

Dieting and trying to lose weight can often be the "tipping point" that brings on disordered eating, which can lead to an eating disorder. Do you feel that you don't have control over the amount of food you eat? Does food dominate your life? Do feel desperate about losing weight? If you answered yes to any of those questions or if you find yourself following abnormal eating patterns like very restrictive eating, binging, purging, taking laxatives or anything else extreme to lose weight, this may signal a disordered eating pattern. You may need help. For more information, contact the National Eating Disorders Association Information and Referral Helpline at 800-931-2237 or visit www.nationaleatingdisorders.org. It's best to work with a team of health professionals who specialize in eating disorders, such as a physician, psychologist or therapist and registered dietitian. Remember, modeling healthy eating behaviors with food and feeling OK with your body will help your child have a healthy relationship with food.

Moving Away from the "Diet" Mentality

Most nutrition professionals will tell you that "Diets" don't work. That's because a "diet" is a usually short-term, sometimes extreme, change in habits. (OK, so we called the eating plans in this book "Diets"—but only because it's a term everyone is familiar with and it's easier to say than "eating plan"!) While a diet may cause you to lose weight, it's often temporary, which leads to discouragement, decreased self-esteem, disordered eating, weight gain and—another diet. Yo-yo dieting can be much harder on the body and the psyche than just keeping your weight where it is.

So, instead of discussing "diet rules", this section will focus on changing behaviors. Calorie intake is discussed for frame of reference only. For example, eating too few calories can impact breastfeeding. Also you've got to know a little about calories to understand weight loss. To be successful, you'll need to commit for the long-term.

Changing Habits

From my years of experience in counseling women to lose weight, I've found that the women who take the slow but steady approach are the most successful.

According to some experts, people need almost six months to truly change their habits, perhaps because it actually involves changes in the brain. Yet many expect to do a major over-haul of diet and lifestyle in two weeks!

When people change their diets drastically (and adopt quick weight loss diets), they may at first drop pounds quickly. Much of that weight loss is water. Then, when weight loss tapers to 1 pound (0.5 kg) or less per week, people feel they're failing and give up. What they forget is that 1 pound (0.5 kg) per week adds up to 52 pounds (24 kg) a year! That's a lot of weight!

If you were not overweight prior to pregnancy and are happy with your eating habits, you can probably skip the rest of this chapter and move on to "Fitting Fitness In". However, if you also have pre-pregnancy pounds to shed, you are contemplating pregnancy and need to get thinner or you need to reign in some not so great habits, read on. We'll discuss how to get started, making goals and evaluating weight loss programs and books.

Learning from Others: Habits, Not Diets

The key to losing weight permanently is determining which eating or lifestyle habits need changing, and then altering those eating habits, setting realistic goals, and adopting an exercise program that you can stick with for life.

Temporary changes result in temporary weight loss!

Following are some of the characteristics I've observed in people who are most successful in losing weight. Many of my personal observations have also been confirmed in research studies, such as the National Weight Control Registry (NWCR,) an ongoing, university-based study which tracks over 5,000 people who have lost 30 pounds (14 kg) or more and kept it off for at least one year.[11]

People who lose weight successfully...

♦ Exercise regularly. Ninety-four percent of participants report increasing their physical activity; the most frequent activity being walking. Ninety percent exercise, on average, about an hour a day.[12] (See the next chapter, Fitting Fitness In for more about exercise.)

♦ Set realistic goals. When participants don't meet their goals, they learn from their experiences and set achievable goals instead of giving up.

♦ Work at self-monitoring. This may mean keeping a food diary, tracking the amount of fat eaten in a day, weighing themselves regularly, or logging their exercise hours each week. Seventy-five percent of NWCR participants weigh themselves at least once a week.[13] In the first week of my weight loss classes, participants are asked not to change their eating habits, but just to write everything down. Without exception, everyone loses some weight that week, just by being more aware of what they eat. And, knowing you have to write it down keeps you honest!

♦ Have social support. People who complete a weight-loss program with friends or family lose more weight and are more likely to keep it off. Research confirms that people who have the support of friends or family, or that of a support group are more likely to lose weight.[14]

- Work on liking themselves (or already do).

- Are motivated to lose weight for internal reasons rather than external reasons. For example, Judy used to lose weight to fit into her old size-ten jeans. Now she is losing weight to make sure she sticks around long enough to see her baby graduate from college.

- Concentrate not just on the bathroom scale, but on some positive outcome, such as having more energy, being able to bend over to tie a child's shoe lace, or climb up a flight of stairs without being out of breath.

- Eat breakfast. Some people say they don't eat breakfast, because if they do it makes them hungry all day. However, breakfast has been shown to have a large effect on weight control. Seventy-eight percent of NWCR participants report eating breakfast every day[15]! What you eat can also make a difference. Some enlightening research showed that starting the day with eggs can contribute to weight control by reducing calorie intake, prevent snacking between meals and keep you from getting hungry when mealtimes are delayed.

- Have conquered emotional eating (eating when bored, angry, depressed, or stressed) or are working on it.

- Have learned to eat sensibly at restaurants, at parties, while traveling, and so on.

- Control their diet; they don't let their diet control them! They make educated, conscious choices about the food they eat. If they want to splurge for a special occasion, they do. They are honest with themselves about the reasons they eat.

- Reward themselves. In my weight loss classes, participants always had a weekly reward planned for small goals. It could be something tangible or intangible. For example, if your goal is to walk 5 days this week and you do it, you could reward yourself by giving yourself an hour to browse in the library, or perhaps a movie rental (NEVER food)! Rewards are also a recommended habit by the National Institutes of Health, along with many of the things listed here.[16]

An Unlikely Ally in Weight Loss: Sleep!

Could the amount of shut-eye you get affect your weight? Yes! Researchers have recently uncovered the association between lack of sleep and increased risk of heart disease, obesity and diabetes. New research shows that it also makes a difference to postpartum weight loss. Women who slept less than 5 hours in 24 hours at 6 months postpartum were more than twice as likely to retain at least 11 pounds at 1 year postpartum. Also, women whose snooze time decreased between 6 months and 1 year postpartum were also twice as likely to hold onto a significant amount of pregnancy pounds.[17] Sounds like a good excuse for a nap to me!

Goal Setting

Lose 100 pounds (45 kg) in 4 months! Fit into my high school prom dress in 2 months! Lose 10 pounds (4.5 kg) by next week! Sure, we see people attain those kind of goals on TV, but it's their full-time job and they have an entourage of consultants. But for the "rest of us", goals like these may be unachievable and are more likely to be tossed aside with shame and disappointment. While these goals may be doable, they may take longer than you think! So, while it's good to have long-term goals, you should have a lot of smaller, short-term goals that you can actually accomplish in the near future. Remember, one underlying goal should be to feel better about yourself.

When possible, goals should be SMART:

♦   Specific

♦   Measurable

♦   Attainable

♦   Realistic

♦   Timely

Here are some examples of good short-term goals:

Exercise Goals:
♦   Walk one mile three times this week, on Tuesday, Saturday and Sunday.
♦   Buy good quality walking shoes (this could also be a reward for walking consistently for a month, or it could be an incentive to get you walking.)
♦   Join a gym by Wednesday.
♦   Go to the gym—every other day.
♦   Practice isometrics at your desk for five minutes daily.
♦   Take the stairs instead of the elevator twice a day.
Food Goals:
♦   Eat 3 fruits today.
♦   Eat 4 vegetables today.
♦   Eat 3 whole grains today.
♦   Choose a calorie-free drink instead of soda when you go out to eat this week.
♦   Choose grilled instead of a fried chicken sandwich.
♦   Try a healthy new food three times each week. (lowfat milk, sugar free yogurt, veggie burger, you name it)

Behavior Goals:

- Write down everything you eat five days this week.
- Don't skip any meals for one week.
- Eat only when sitting at the table.
- Keep a tally of your daily exercise.
- Make a list of things to do instead of eating when you're bored.
- Weigh yourself regularly, but no more than once a week.
- Give yourself permission to eat a small amount of a splurge food and enjoy every bite once a week.
- Grocery shop with a list.

Rewards

Don't forget to reward yourself, perhaps for reaching 3 out of 5 of your short-term goals. Or maybe give a reward for just one of them, if it's a tough one. Don't let mommy guilt settle in when rewarding yourself. Remember if you don't take care of yourself, you can't take care of your family. Try to get the support of a friend, spouse or other family members—it can make a difference!

Sample rewards:

- A long bath
- Fifteen minutes for yourself—to read, craft, send email or just think
- Exercise ball
- Yoga DVD
- A new book
- Something to make you look or feel pretty—new earrings, perfume, eye shadow, a new haircut or color
- A movie or music download
- Manicure or pedicure

Evaluating Weight-Loss Plans

Do you really NEED a weight loss plan or diet? Probably not, but many find more motivation with structured systems. And because diet programs and diet books are abundant, you won't have any trouble finding one. But beware! Many of them promote quick weight loss. Others may recommend unbalanced diets, which leave out one or more foods or food groups. Some can be downright dangerous.

The steps below can help you evaluate a weight-loss plan:

1. Does the plan promote balanced eating, allowing all foods in moderation? Does it omit certain foods or food groups? A balanced plan should allow all foods, even the so-called "bad" ones, at some point in the program.

2. Does the plan include exercise? Exercise is so important to weight loss—and even more important for keeping it off. Most people who lose weight lose some muscle along with fat. However, if you exercise, you will lose little or no muscle mass. Maintaining muscle mass helps you lose more weight, since muscle uses more calories than fat, even when you are sitting in front of the TV! A combination of aerobic and weight resistance exercise is very effective for losing weight and shaping up.

3. Does the plan include behavior modification (changing current behaviors)? For long-term weight loss, you must identify your problem behaviors so you can work to change them. Some tools used for behavior modification might include self-monitoring (keeping a food record) or exercises that promote an awareness of eating patterns.

4. Does the plan use trained professionals as counselors, or people whose only qualifications are that they have lost weight? Many plans use people who have lost weight or are good salespeople as counselors. Though these people may be good motivators, they may unintentionally give out inaccurate information. There are many people out there trying to make a quick dollar (or Euro). Beware of anything that sounds too good to be true; it probably is. Look for counselors who are licensed, registered, or have a degree from an accredited college or university.

5. Does the plan involve buying special foods or supplements? Personally, I feel that learning how to eat "real" food is better for long-term weight loss. However, some people like the convenience of packaged foods, and they have been shown to help people lose weight.

6. Does the plan provide a foundation for healthier eating habits? Hopefully, the plan teaches you how to cook healthfully, plan menus, and eat sensibly in social situations, and how to keep from slipping back into bad habits (and weight gain).

Postpartum Weight Loss—What To Expect?

The amount of time it takes to lose the weight and get your old body back is probably a big surprise to every mother. Much to my disappointment, I needed almost nine months to return to my normal weight. I thought I'd be back to my old self within just a few. Doing aerobics three times a week made the biggest change in the way my body looked and helped me lose those stubborn last 5 pounds (2.2 kg).

The recommended post pregnant weight loss is about 1 to 1.5 pound (0.5 to 0.7 kg) per week. You're probably thinking, "A pound (0.5 kg) a week! I'll never lose this weight!" Consider the importance of long-term success, which means keeping the weight off. People who lose weight slowly seem to keep it off the longest.

Here are some things you should expect:

◆ Very few people go back to wearing their "skinny" clothes right after delivery. Expect to wear your maternity clothes for a few more months, even though you probably feel like trashing them!

◆ You may need to buy a few outfits one size bigger than you wore before pregnancy to wear until you get your shape back.

◆ Your body may have reproportioned itself. For example, Kate weighs the same as she did before pregnancy, but her hips are a few inches wider. Most of us continue to have a little tummy unless we diligently practice abdominal exercises. Some women find their rib cages permanently expanded and need to wear a larger bra size. Believe it or not, some women even wear a larger shoe size after pregnancy.

◆ If you are breastfeeding, you may feel as though you are bursting out of your blouses.

◆ Many women lose the last few pounds after they stop breastfeeding.

◆ Exercise can't be emphasized enough. It will help you lose baby fat and tone up some of the muscles you haven't used in quite a while.

Overall, be patient. I clearly remember asking my aerobics teacher how fast I could get into shape after the baby came, if I worked out regularly. I wanted real numbers. She said it could be done in six to eight weeks, but I might need time for recovery. "Not me," I thought. I was going to be Supermom! Well, after a tough labor and delivery and a long adjustment to motherhood, months passed before I had the time and energy to restart my exercise program. After my second son was born, I didn't have a problem losing the weight. I breastfed him longer and I was much more active chasing two kids around.

The Calorie Equation

To lose 1 pound (0.5 kg) per week, you can cut your food intake by 500 calories per day, use more calories by exercising, or combine eating less and exercising more. For example, Colleen walks about an hour every evening, which uses approximately 240 calories. She has also cut 300 calories of extras out of her diet—basically eating fruit instead of a bowl of ice cream. Colleen's diet-and-exercise approach works best for long-term weight maintenance. Besides being good for muscle tone, cardiovascular health, and endurance, exercise is also good for your mental health! Following is an example of a good fitness program. Most of these activities can be done with a baby nearby or in a front pack. Postnatal exercise programs often encourage baby participation. As you can see, fitness doesn't have to be boring!

Walk Your Way to Weight Loss

Can you walk your way to lower weight and better health just by using a pedometer? Yes says one study, in which women were told to use a pedometer and record their steps each day. The women were to increase their steps by 500 each week until they got to the goal of 10,000 a day. The more steps the women walked, the more their BMI and waist circumference went down.[18]

Suggested Activity Program for Colleen:

♦   Height: 5'4" (1.62 m)

♦   Weight: 160 pounds (72 kg)

♦   Goal Weight: 120 pounds (54 kg)

Activity Goals: Aerobic activity 5 hours per week, strength training or yoga ½ hour, three times a week

♦   **Monday:** 1 hour of postnatal exercise class

♦   **Tuesday:** 30-minute walk at lunch, 30 minutes of strength training after dinner

♦   **Wednesday:** 1 hour of postnatal exercise class

♦   **Thursday:** 30-minute walk with baby in front pack, 30 minutes of strength training

♦   **Friday:** Colleen's day off

♦   **Saturday:** 1-hour hike with baby in front pack

♦   **Sunday:** 1 hour of gardening, ½ hour of yoga

By following this activity program, Colleen burns over 1,700 calories! To lose 1 pound (0.5 kg) per week, she also needs to reduce her diet by 1,800 calories per week or about 250 calories per day. (Please note that the numbers of calories burned are calculated specifically for Colleen.)

Depending on your weight, height, and activity level, you will probably want to eat between 1,200 and 1,800 calories per day to lose 1 pound (0.5 kg) each week. Eating under 1,200 calories is usually not advised unless you have a petite build. (If you are breastfeeding, it's best not to go below 1,800 calories unless you are petite.)

How Much Exercise?

You begin looking at food in a whole different way when you think how much activity you need to do to burn off the calories:

- **Potato chips 1 oz. (30 g):** 20 minutes biking

- **Medium size French fries:** 32 minutes jogging

- **Blue Cheese dressing, 2 tablespoons:** 1 hour vacuuming

- **Biscuit with egg and sausage:** 1 hour + 22 minutes brisk walking

- **Onion rings (9):** 27 minutes of swimming

- **Chicken Nuggets (6):** 48 minutes of dancing

- **Soda 16 oz. (500 ml):** 1 hour stroll

Calories based on a 150 pound (68 kg) person. Source: www.cancer.org/healthy/toolsandcalculators/calculators/app/exercise-counts-calculator

Eating Expectantly Diet: Lose That Baby Fat

(If you're breastfeeding, see page 290 for the Best for Breastfeeding Diet)

This meal plan has about 1,600 calories and is meant to be a rough guideline for healthy weight loss. While some women prefer a structured plan, many women do well just concentrating on eating more fruits and vegetables and cutting back on extra fats. This meal plan does not contain enough calories or nutrients for breastfeeding moms.

Eating Expectantly Diet: Lose That Baby Fat

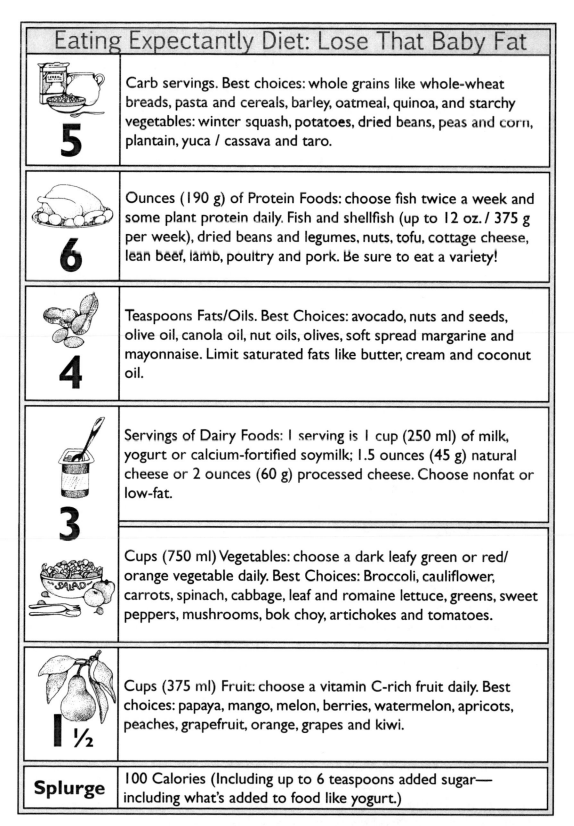

5 Carb servings. Best choices: whole grains like whole-wheat breads, pasta and cereals, barley, oatmeal, quinoa, and starchy vegetables: winter squash, potatoes, dried beans, peas and corn, plantain, yuca / cassava and taro.

6 Ounces (190 g) of Protein Foods: choose fish twice a week and some plant protein daily. Fish and shellfish (up to 12 oz. / 375 g per week), dried beans and legumes, nuts, tofu, cottage cheese, lean beef, lamb, poultry and pork. Be sure to eat a variety!

4 Teaspoons Fats/Oils. Best Choices: avocado, nuts and seeds, olive oil, canola oil, nut oils, olives, soft spread margarine and mayonnaise. Limit saturated fats like butter, cream and coconut oil.

3 Servings of Dairy Foods: 1 serving is 1 cup (250 ml) of milk, yogurt or calcium-fortified soymilk; 1.5 ounces (45 g) natural cheese or 2 ounces (60 g) processed cheese. Choose nonfat or low-fat.

Cups (750 ml) Vegetables: choose a dark leafy green or red/orange vegetable daily. Best Choices: Broccoli, cauliflower, carrots, spinach, cabbage, leaf and romaine lettuce, greens, sweet peppers, mushrooms, bok choy, artichokes and tomatoes.

1½ Cups (375 ml) Fruit: choose a vitamin C-rich fruit daily. Best choices: papaya, mango, melon, berries, watermelon, apricots, peaches, grapefruit, orange, grapes and kiwi.

Splurge 100 Calories (Including up to 6 teaspoons added sugar—including what's added to food like yogurt.)

Tales from the Trenches: How Dietitians Lost Their Baby Fat

Sure, we've all heard about or seen those moms who don't look like they've just had a baby (or 2 or 4.) And we know many Olympic athlete moms that have no fat whatsoever around the waist, so getting your pre-baby body back can be done, with the right motivation. I took a poll of other registered dietitians, people who know food and fitness, to tell us their postpartum weight loss stories, which may sound very familiar. Here they are:

Elizabeth Ward, MS, RD

I gained 33 pounds (15 kg) with my 3rd child. I was most surprised at how long it took to lose the weight—9 months to lose 7.5 pounds (3.5 kg)! Yes, I was counting. Once I stopped breastfeeding—when she was about 9 months old—the last five or so pounds came off easier.

Motivating advice: I weighed myself once a month only, so I took it a month at a time to limit frustration. I gave myself one night a week to splurge—ate whatever I wanted, no questions asked, no guilt. That helped me through the rest of the week. Another piece of advice: the weight will come off if you truly keep trying; if you don't try, you'll probably gain. Take small steps and you'll get your body back (well, not really back... but mostly!)

 Elizabeth Ward is a registered dietitian, freelance writer and former media spokesperson for the Academy of Nutrition and Dietetics. She is a contributor to webmd.com and USA Today and is the author of several books, including her latest, *MyPlate for Moms, How to Feed Yourself & Your Family Better.*

Carrie Zisman, MS, RD

I have two children, 5 years and 18 months. Having had children later in life (I'm 40), my metabolism had already started to slow down so postpartum weight loss was especially difficult and frustrating. For background, I'm 5'2" (1.57m) and had always had an easy time maintaining a petite 110 pound (50 kg) frame. I think I was born to be a dietitian—being a health nut and foodie who gets as excited about kale as I do a great quality cookie, and being active my whole life, I never had to worry too much about my weight. That said, I gained a healthy 36 and 32 pounds (16 and 14 kg) respectively.

For my first, I had also been on bed rest for 9 weeks and lost a lot of muscle. For the first baby, I also made the mistake of thinking if I'm nursing, I can eat anything I want. Wrong! I realized this was not how my body was going to work and went back to watching what and how much I ate. I also started to exercise to build back my lean body mass. It took me 11 months to finally take it all off (more than it took to put on). Once I got there, I soon realized that taking off excess weight and keeping it off are two totally different things. Not having as much time to exercise as I did before and nibbling a bit too much from my daughter's "kid" food, I quickly realized I was actually going to have to join the millions of people out there and work at staying trim. It was a battle, but humbling and educational for this dietitian.

Fast-forward to 2011 and I had my 2nd baby just shy of my 39th birthday. Now, with a full house and full-time job, I had even less energy and time to exercise. Nibbling was also a constant struggle and detrimental to any attempt to lose excess weight or stay at a healthy weight. Once my baby was sleeping and I went back to work, I committed to getting back to my former 5 AM exercise routine. I had to step up my routine to include metabolism-boosting plyometrics, total body cardio strength training, and jogging. It's not been easy and I struggle every day to keep it off. I'm not quite down to the scale weight and clothing size I was before, but I'm at a healthy BMI and have more lean body mass now. Though my stomach is a little softer than before, I'm fit and healthy and a good role model for my children.

Carrie Zisman is a corporate wellness dietitian in Bethesda, MD. She enjoys cooking, eating, traveling, anything active outdoors, and hanging out with her husband, daughter, son, and Rhodesian Ridgeback.

Ann Dunaway Teh MS, RD

I was so excited for my 6-week follow-up appointment with my doctor to ensure that all was well after giving birth to my second child, but more importantly I couldn't wait to get the green light to start exercising again! Once I got permission, reality set in—how do I find time to work out while taking care of my now family of 4, enjoying my new baby girl as well as breastfeed every 2-3 hours? Some days it feels like an accomplishment to just get out of my pajamas! Ultimately, I remember that if I do not feel good and am not happy, then everyone suffers. Getting back in shape and losing my pregnancy weight is key for me to feeling good, especially if I want to keep up with my 3 year-old son. So I started slowly—rather than feel overwhelmed about how much weight I had to lose, I just focused on moving and feeling better now that I actually have more mobility.

Involving my baby in safe exercises is a great way to spend time with her while I get back in shape. She is my own personal set of weights that gets heavier as I get stronger! Squats really soothe her bubbling tummy. I have a postpartum yoga DVD that encourages baby involvement. My 3 year-old likes joining in on some of the exercises and walking around the neighborhood with me—we make a fun game of counting mailboxes and fire hydrants. There are times though when I walk by myself too for some "me" time. Eventually I'll work up to running again, but when my body feels ready.

Since I am breastfeeding, I am often ravenous. I keep a bottle of water with me at all times and the refrigerator and freezer stocked with fruits and vegetables. While I love fresh produce, the convenience of frozen is perfect for this period in my life—so quick and easy to prepare when I don't have much time in the kitchen.

My daughter is now almost 8 months old and I'm already within 5 pounds (2.5 kg) of my pre-pregnancy weight. I gained just over 50 pounds (23 kg) during both of my pregnancies. Despite eating well, I was unable to exercise during either pregnancy due to high-risk complications: spent the last 8-10 weeks on bed-rest with both. I attribute my weight loss success so far to eating plenty of fruits and vegetables, breastfeeding, and staying as active as I can.

While it's easy to be anxious about losing weight, I remind myself that it took 10 months to put on the weight and for lasting weight loss it can take that long if not longer to lose it all. I counsel my patients with the same advice I follow myself. There are some days when exercise doesn't happen or I don't eat enough fruits or vegetables. Rather than getting down on myself, I just start each day anew and stay positive. Getting back to my pre-pregnant self will come in time and meanwhile I am finding creative ways to be active with my baby and my son, while making sure we are all eating well, most of the time!

Ann Dunaway Teh is a registered dietitian, mom, athlete and avid cook who enjoys sharing her passion for nutrition and good living with others. Through her business, Dunaway Dietetics, Ann specializes in weight management, sports nutrition and wellness for individuals, families, schools and businesses. www.dunawaydietetics.com

Smart Substitutions

Losing weight doesn't mean depriving yourself totally, it just means making better choices. Check out the calorie savings these changes provide:

Food	Calories	Action	Calories Saved
I tablespoon margarine	100	Butter Buds or Molly McButter	100
I 12 oz. (375 ml) cola drink	150	Club soda with lime	150
2 chocolate-chip cookies	140	I peach	100
I cinnamon roll	230	I Quaker Caramel Corn Cake	180

Food	Calories	Action	Calories Saved
3 cups (750 ml) whole milk	450	3 cups (750 ml) 1% milk	150
2 tablespoons Litehouse Original Bleu Cheese dressing	150	Litehouse Lite Bleu Cheese	80
2 tablespoons Wishbone Creamy Caesar	170	Wishbone Caesar Delight Salad Spritzer 20 sprays	150
Starbucks Grande Iced peppermint white chocolate mocha, 16 oz. (500 ml)	500	Starbucks Skinny Cinnamon Dolce Latte, 16 oz. (500 ml)	380
McDonald's Angus Mushroom & Swiss Burger	770	Premium Grilled Chicken Classic Sandwich	420

Lose Weight by Leaning toward Vegetarianism

Cutting down on animal protein is one good way to cut calories and fat, which can lead to weight loss. Leaning toward vegetarianism, or even becoming vegetarian, might be a good idea. While testing meatless recipes for the book *Make the Change for a Healthy Heart*, I was losing weight without even trying. I had to consciously eat extra snacks to avoid losing weight! (See Chapter 10 for more on vegetarian eating.) Research shows that a vegetarian diet can be a very effective way to lose weight.[19,20]

For more information: Weight Control Vegetarian Style—website by Ginny Mesina RD: www.vegnutrition.com/weight/index.html

Your Next Pregnancy—WHAT?

Sometime after your labor anesthesia wears off and before you send out birth announcements, someone will ask, "So when are you going to have another baby?" You may not be ready to answer that question for a long time—at least I wasn't! On the other hand, you may want another baby right away. If possible, wait at least eighteen months before you become pregnant again. A study of more than 11 million births around the world revealed that babies conceived 6 months after birth were 40% more likely to be born prematurely and had a 61% increased risk of being low birthweight.[21]

The most important thing you can do before your next pregnancy is to lose all your "baby fat" plus more if you need to, because your weight at the start of your pregnancy can have a significant effect on your pregnancy and on the long-term health of your next baby (and you). Keeping extra weight on between pregnancies is a risk factor for still being overweight 15 years after pregnancy[22]! Also, continue to follow a cleaner diet and lifestyle.

Most importantly, enjoy that baby of yours! The time passes quickly! When you are ready to think about getting pregnant again, turn to Chapter 1: Contemplating Pregnancy to learn what you can do for a healthy pregnancy before you conceive.

No matter when you decide to have another baby, or even if you decide not to, don't lose the good habits you established during pregnancy. A healthy diet is one of the most important things you can do to ensure good health for you and your children. Your baby is watching you, and good or bad, he will take on the habits he sees you practicing. Teaching your children good eating habits by setting good examples is one of the most precious gifts you can give them. For more advice on feeding your baby and older children, see my other books, *Baby Bites: Everything You Need to Know about Feeding Infants and Toddlers in One Handy Book* and *Healthy Food for Healthy Kids* at www.healthyfoodzone.com.

14

FITTING FITNESS IN

What You'll Find:

- Why Exercise?

- Two All Star Pregnancy Exercises

- Ten Tips for Smarter Exercise

- Fitting Fitness into Your Busy Lifestyle

- Exercise After Pregnancy

- Questions You May Have

Frequently Asked Questions:

- I've never exercised before: why should I start now?

- Should I exercise differently while I'm pregnant?

- What if I don't have time for exercise?

- When should I NOT exercise?

- What are some good yoga poses for pregnancy?

SCAN HERE FOR CHAPTER UPDATES

Why Exercise?

Throughout this book I've mentioned exercise again...and again! I'm hoping repetition will bring home the message that exercise is one of the most important things you can do for your present and future health. Regular exercise can bring you numerous benefits with just a small time investment. So whether you're planning a pregnancy, already pregnant or are trying to lose your baby fat, consider getting moving!

Before you thought about having a baby, you may have exercised (or had a goal to start) to help you lose weight or fit into your skinny jeans. Now that a baby is in the picture, your fitness goals have probably changed. Sure, you may be exercising to avoid gaining too much weight, but now you're most likely interested in bumping up your fitness level for one reason; to improve your and your baby's health.

The benefits of exercise are nothing new. In fact, around 65 BC, Cicero was quoted as saying "It is exercise alone that supports the spirits and keeps the mind in vigor." And that was way before we had clinical trials to prove it!

Just the facts: How Much Exercise is recommended during Pregnancy?

Experts around the globe agree: exercise during pregnancy is a good thing. Here is a summary of recommendations from America, Canada, the UK and Australia.[1,2,3,4,5]

♦ Moderate exercise for healthy pregnant women is safe and 30 minutes of exercise on most if not all days of the week is recommended.

♦ In general, women can continue a previous exercise program or start exercising if they haven't before.

♦ During the third trimester, more vigorous exercise should be limited to three times a week.

♦ Developing core muscle strength can be helpful to deal with the changes of pregnancy.

Why You Should Exercise

♦ It helps you manage your weight.[6] Whether you want to lose weight before you get pregnant, keep weight-gain under control during pregnancy or lose weight after you have your baby, exercise is your solution. Muscle burns more calories than fat, so increasing the muscle you've got is a no-brainer! Exercise during pregnancy even helps decrease the amount of weight you keep on after pregnancy.[7]

◆ It helps manage your mood. A brisk walk can help you blow off steam after a stressful day or help you energize after a long night up with a sick baby. Physical activity may even reduce your risk of depression, or aid in managing it.[8,9,10] A boost of brain chemicals explains this psychological perk.

◆ It may help with lower-back and pelvic pain. Weight gain and a change in your center of gravity plus those pesky pregnancy hormones often means low-back or pelvic pain in mid to late-pregnancy. Regular exercise can fight those common complaints, says an ongoing study of more than 34,000 women in Norway.[11]

◆ Research shows that women who practice yoga have lower perceived stress, improved sleep and psychological health and decreased pregnancy-related discomforts.[12,13]

◆ It strengthens muscles, including your most important muscle, your heart. And yes, it is possible to increase muscle strength and aerobic fitness during pregnancy—even if you were inactive before pregnancy.[14] Improving muscle-tone gives you more stamina—which you'll need for the months ahead—and helps you feel better about your expanding body.

◆ It helps you sleep better.[15] Whether you're struggling with sleep in the last trimester or stressing about trying to get pregnant, sleep is sometimes elusive. But, regular exercise can help you fall asleep and stay asleep.

◆ It can supercharge your mind. Running low on brainpower? Exercise increases blood circulation, bringing glucose and oxygen to the brain. Physical activity can have a protective effect on the aging brain, including possibly preventing dementia and Alzheimer's disease.

◆ It fights chronic disease. With regular exercise you reduce your risk for all these diseases: high blood pressure, stroke, heart disease, osteoporosis, type 2 diabetes, metabolic syndrome, breast and colon cancer.

◆ It boosts the immune system—just taking a 30-minute walk temporarily increases immune cells, which attack bacteria and viruses.[16]

◆ It can help you normalize your menstrual cycle. A structured exercise program has been shown to help normalize ovulation in women who have Polycystic Ovary Disease.[17]

◆ It can put a spark in your sex life. Whether you're trying to get pregnant, or not thinking about the next baby for a long while, exercise helps you look better and feel better, which can lead to…well, you know. But there's more—physical activity can also help with erectile dysfunction.[18] So when you go on your daily walk, grab your guy to go with you.

- For women with normal pregnancies, regular exercise may shorten labor and decrease your risk of having a Caesarean section. It may also help reduce muscle cramps and swelling in the legs.[19]

- Exercise can be...fun! Whether it's water exercise, dancing or ping-pong, exercise doesn't have to be drudgery. Make it fun and you'll be more likely to do it. Bocce ball, anyone?

Two All Star Pregnancy Exercises

No discussion of pregnancy/postpartum fitness would be complete without mention of the Pelvic Tilt and Kegel exercises. The nice thing about these exercises is that they can be done anywhere!

Pelvic Tilt

The pelvic tilt is the go-to pose for strengthening abdominals—needed for pushing through delivery—and to help relieve that pesky back pain that often rears its ugly head in the second and third trimester. It can be done while lying down (in your first trimester only), squatting on your hands and knees, sitting on an exercise ball or standing against the wall. The point of the exercise is to use your abdominals to tilt your pelvis forward so that it stretches and strengthens your lower back muscles. Do it often.[20]

How to Do a Pelvic Tilt Standing

- With your feet shoulder-width apart, stand straight with your head, tailbone and feet touching the wall. With your hand, feel the small gap between the small of your back and the wall. Take a deep breath and as you exhale, push the small of your back into the wall. You may feel the need to bend your knees slightly as you inhale, resume starting position.

- Repeat five to ten times.

Kegels

Strengthening the muscles of the pelvic floor is the aim of the Kegel exercise. The pelvic floor muscles support your urethra, bladder, uterus and rectum, which are all under pressure as your baby gets heavier. Kegels are known for helping to keep away hemorrhoids, and also prized for helping keep urine inside your bladder when you cough or sneeze! After delivery, the increased circulation that Kegels promote will help speed healing if you've had an episiotomy or tear.

How To: Do a Kegel[21]:

Tighten the muscles around your vagina—as if you are trying to stop the flow of urine. But don't do them while you are urinating.

♦ Hold it for five to ten seconds and release.

♦ Repeat ten to twenty times.

♦ Do three or more times a day.

Risks of Not Moving

According to the Society of Obstetricians and Gynecologists of Canada, **inactivity** during pregnancy also has its risks[22]:

♦ Loss of muscular and cardiovascular fitness

♦ Excessive maternal weight gain

♦ Higher risk of gestational diabetes

♦ Higher risk of pregnancy-induced hypertension

♦ Development of varicose veins and deep vein thrombosis

♦ Shortness of breath and low back pain

♦ Poor psychological adjustment to the physical changes of pregnancy

---

Are You at Risk for Gestational Diabetes?

You can lower your risk by exercising—before and during pregnancy[23]!

When Exercise is NOT Recommended:

There are some situations when exercise is to be avoided during pregnancy.[24,25] These include significant heart disease, restrictive lung disease, incompetent cervix/ cerclage, growth restricted fetus, multiple gestation at risk for premature labor, persistent second or third trimester bleeding, placenta previa after 26 weeks, premature labor, ruptured membranes and preeclampsia / pregnancy-induced hypertension. A few other situations where exercise is questionable include: severe anemia, poorly controlled type 1 diabetes, and poorly controlled chronic disease. Check in with your health care provider if you have any questions about exercising.

Ten Tips for Smarter Exercise

For the most part, these guidelines apply to exercise during pregnancy.[26]

1. Take it Easy

Your resting heart rate is higher than it was before you were pregnant, and it also rises more quickly during exercise, so watch the intensity of your exercise. Also, don't be surprised if your exercise stamina is lower than usual. If you're new to exercise, start out slowly with ten to fifteen minutes a day, three times a week and build up to at least 30 minutes on most days.[27] Use the "talk test": make sure you can comfortably hold a conversation (without getting out of breath) while exercising, to make sure you don't overdo it.

2. Don't Jolt Your Joints

Hormones cause your joints and connective tissue to relax in preparation for delivery—this can make joints susceptible to injury. Use gentle stretching to cool down, but avoid overstretching. Exercise that involves lots of bouncing, jerky movement, jumping, or quick changes in direction could cause joint pain or injury—so avoid or do with caution. So if Zumba is your thing, you'll need to lower the impact and keep the twisting to a minimum. In general, it's best to stick to walking, swimming, spinning or the elliptical, treadmill or low impact aerobics. Exercise that's geared just for pregnant women, such as prenatal yoga or water aerobics, is an especially good idea if you are new to exercise.

3. Watch Your Balance and Skip the Stilettos

And this doesn't only apply to exercising! Your increasing (and lopsided) weight gain changes your body's center of gravity and puts more strain on your feet, so make sure your shoes support your posture instead of adding to problem. Exercise on a wooden floor or a securely carpeted surface to reduce shock and to provide sure footing.

4. Be Consistent

Regular exercise is best, even if it's only a few minutes per day; being active regularly makes it a habit that's easier to continue. I've found that the road to poor health is paved with good intentions. Millions of homes are full of treadmills, stationary bikes, rowing machines, and weight sets that serve as dust-collectors and clothes racks. Their owners would be much better off if they simply set aside thirty minutes a day to go for a walk.

> ### First trimester and don't feel like exercising?
> Don't worry, whenever you start will be just fine! Better ever, than never!

5. Warm Up and Cool Down

Always begin with five to ten minutes of low-intensity exercise, such as slow walking, cycling, or water walking for swimmers, to warm up your muscles. During the warm-up, also do some gentle stretches. End your exercise with ten to fifteen minutes of cool-down and stretching.

Get off your back. Avoid exercising flat on your back after the first trimester. Your uterus is more likely to be compressing the inferior vena cava, the main blood vessel returning blood to your heart. This could interfere with blood flow to your baby.

Go Slowly. Get up from the floor slowly to avoid dizziness caused by a sudden drop in blood pressure.

6. Hydrate Healthfully!

Drink plenty of water before, during and after exercise to prevent dehydration and overheating. Unsweetened coconut water can be a good choice in hot weather.

7. Keep Cool

Be careful how hard and how long you exercise and to keep from getting overheated, avoid vigorous exercise in hot, humid weather and when you have a fever.[28]

8. Eat Enough

During pregnancy, blood sugar levels are usually lower than nonpregnant levels, and your body uses carbohydrates at a faster rate. You might experience low blood sugar during exercise, (especially if you're taking medication for diabetes) so make sure you don't exercise on an empty stomach. You may want to have some fruit and low-fat cheese, a yogurt, or some trail mix with dried fruit before your workout for more energy. Milk is a great post-exercise drink for muscles due to its mix of protein, carbs, potassium and other minerals. Regular exercise can help you avoid gaining too much weight—but to make sure you are eating enough, check that your weight gain is on track.

9. Support Yourself

Wear a bra that fits well to support growing breast tissue and good shoes to absorb the impact of exercise on your feet, legs and back.

10. Save the Competition for Post-Pregnancy

Olympic swimmer Dara Torres swam during her pregnancy at age 39 and went on to qualify for the Olympics just a few months postpartum. But—for those of us who aren't in Olympic condition and don't have a stable of trainers and consultants on hand—it's recommended that competitive training and competition be avoided.[29]

A Nutritionist and Personal Trainer Shares Her Pregnancy and Post-Pregnancy Fitness Routine
Tammy Lakatos Shames, RD, LD, CDN, CFT

As a registered dietitian and personal trainer, my friends, family and clients frequently ask me what I did to stay fit while I was pregnant with my twins, and what I did after they were born to get back in shape.

I always start by explaining that exercise was my saving grace when I was pregnant—and I mean that in every sense of the word. Although I had to scale back compared to what I typically would do when I wasn't pregnant, exercise helped me to clear my head, feel better about myself, boost my confidence and boost my mood. (Yes, even a pregnant personal trainer doesn't always feel so attractive during pregnancy. My ankles swelled to the size of large grapefruits and at the end of the day I often felt like I could have popped the pressure in my swollen legs with a pin—definitely not an attractive feeling!) It also made me feel like I was being proactive so that I would be strong and have an easier time in the delivery room (I wound up having my twins via an emergency C-section, but while I was pregnant this helped to give me peace of mind.)

As for specifics of my exercise program, I was sure to get some activity in every day. Low-impact was what the health care provider recommended for me since I'm only five-foot-two (1.57 m) (and that's including the curls and some frizz that stand above my head that make me appear taller) and was carrying twins. So for ten months I kissed goodbye to my long runs. Luckily for me, I really enjoy long walks and the health care provider approved of them, so I put my headphones on with my favorite music (anything from Journey to Rhianna to Nirvana) and just started walking. Inside or outdoors didn't matter to me, as long as I was moving. Most days I would walk for about an hour, but I always listened to my body and occasionally the round ligament pain caused by my growing babies was too intense to finish my walk.

Strength training is another important aspect of a good fitness program. Once again, I was limited in the level of intensity I was permitted since I was carrying twins. I had to refrain from intense training and stick to doing mild to moderate strength work. I was determined to try to maintain as much strength as possible so that I would be as fit as possible for delivery and caring for the babies. I tried to do something to build my strength at least four to five days a week. I know this is a lot, but remember, fitness and health is my job! So I invested in small hand weights so at times when I couldn't make it to the gym, I could at least lift weights while watching my favorite TV show. I did shoulder presses above my head, bicep curls, triceps presses and lunges. I even did push-ups against the wall—they're good for building strength. If you're someone who doesn't want to spend the money on hand weights, canned soup works well for weights, as well as water bottles and shampoo bottles. I also started doing bicep curls when I would carry my groceries back from the store. (I live in NYC so we walk to our stores). I highly recommend trying to build strength at least three days a week, even if it's just for 15- 20 minutes. It makes it a lot easier to carry all of the extra baby weight and fluid when you're strong.

I felt I was fairly prepared physically for the delivery of my twins. Well, that was until I had a C-section at 31 weeks which took me by surprise. Although I was a bit disappointed that I had spent time preparing to have my body fit and ready for a natural delivery that I didn't get to put to use, I knew that the exercise would be good for helping me get back into shape.

I wasn't allowed to do any intense exercise for the first six weeks after giving birth (C-section protocol), but I did slowly (and I mean very slowly—in the beginning it was a crawl due to the pain from the C-section) walk the 12 city blocks back and forth to the NICU to visit my twin daughters twice daily. By the end of the six weeks, my pace to the hospital was beginning to quicken and the pain from the C-section wasn't preventing me from wanting to exercise. After clearance from my health care provider, I returned to doing my long walks and my strength training and adding an occasional day of running a couple of times a week. This and the nursing definitely helped me to lose the baby weight.

Although I lost the baby weight fairly soon after birth, my stomach remained distended for quite a while after birth. It seemed to be a lifetime, but was definitely several months. I know I did everything I could to get my stomach to flatten sooner—I ate healthfully, exercised, nursed and drank plenty of water, and this was my genetics working against me. To this day, I am still in awe of any woman whose stomach quickly flattens after childbirth. When I know that I did all that I could to stay fit and to get my body back after pregnancy and knowing that I had genetics working against me in that regard, I'm happy to know that I did what I could to stay fit and to maintain my strength. I realize it would have been a sad state of affairs had I not taken such good care of myself and this serves as a good reminder for me to encourage my clients to do the same.

Tammy and her sister Lyssie Lakatos, RD, CDN, CFT, make up the The Nutrition Twins. They are the authors of *Fire Up Your Metabolism: 9 Proven Principles for Burning Fat and Losing Weight Forever* **(Simon and Schuster) and** *The Secret to Skinny* **(HCI Books). They were named Top Nutrition Experts to follow by Huffington Post and they blog at www.modernmom. com. You can find more about them at www.nutritiontwins.com**

Exercise Warning Signs[30]

Stop exercising immediately and call your health care provider if you have any of these symptoms:

- Vaginal bleeding
- Dizziness or feeling faint
- Increased shortness of breath
- Chest pain
- Headache

- Muscle weakness
- Calf pain or swelling
- Uterine contractions
- Decreased fetal movement
- Fluid leaking from the vagina

Avoid these Exercises[31]

- Sports which involve a higher risk of falling like downhill skiing, skating, horseback riding, gymnastics, some racquet sports, hiking on uneven terrain and skateboarding.

- Contact sports, such as hockey, soccer and basketball.

- Scuba diving—large amounts of water pressure put your baby at risk for decompression sickness.

- Exercise at altitudes above 8,250 feet (2,500 meters)—unless you are in good shape and have appropriate acclimatization.

Target Heart Rates

You've heard about increasing blood volume during pregnancy—the extra blood supply makes your heart beat faster, both at rest and during exercise. Increasing your heart rate too much during exercise could cause you to become overheated, which could lead to developmental problems for your baby. Also, a fast–beating heart may beat less efficiently, and may not circulate enough nutrient-rich blood throughout the whole body.

The "talk test" is one way to make sure you're not pushing yourself too hard. That is, if you can carry on a conversation without gasping for air while you exercise, your intensity is most likely fine. Another way is to monitor your heart rate. Check in with your health care provider to see if she has an individual goal for you. The American College of Obstetricians doesn't recommend a specific target heart rate. The Society of Obstetricians and Gynaecologists of Canada recommends[32]:

- Under age 20 years old: 140-155 beats per minute
- 20-29 years old—135-150 beats per minute
- 30-39 years old—130-145 beats per minute

Michelle F. Mottola PhD, Exercise Physiologist and Director of the F. Samuel McLaughlin Foundation Exercise and Pregnancy Lab at the University of Western Ontario has developed guidelines for specific groups of moms-to-be:

For medically screened, low risk, very fit women who are used to more intense workouts, these guidelines may be more appropriate[33]:

♦ 20-29 years: 145-160 beats per minute

♦ 30-39: 140-156 beats per minute.

For overweight or obese women, these guidelines may be more appropriate[34]:

♦ 20-29 years old: 110-131 beats per minute

♦ 30-39 years old: 108-127 beats per minute

Fitting Fitness into Your Busy Lifestyle

For most people, (and by "most people," I mean *me*—and maybe you too?) time is the biggest barrier to exercise. Even so, most of us probably have fifteen to thirty minutes a day to squeeze in a walk. Here are a few ideas for fitting fitness into your lifestyle:

♦ Walk whenever and wherever you can. Take a walk every morning before work, or every day after work. If you have shops, restaurants or other services walking distance from your house, save gas and let your feet carry you. Keep tennis shoes in the car so you're always prepared for a good walking spot.

♦ Use half your lunch break to take exercise—even if it's only 10 minutes. This was my strategy on days I didn't go to aerobics. The funny part of it was that I turned down so many rides. Everyone must have felt sorry for the big pregnant woman walking down the street! When it was too cold or raining, I walked in the basement of the hospital where I worked. I've also used the video "Walking Away the Pounds" with co-workers. It's fun and not so intense that you feel the need to shower afterwards.

♦ Take the Stairs. In your two-story home, unplug the downstairs phone so that every time the phone rings, you need to go up and down the stairs once. You'll also be more efficient at work if you take the stairs instead of the elevator.

♦ Wear a pedometer and track your daily steps, challenging yourself to increase your daily or weekly steps.

Overweight?

It might be harder to get motivated to exercise. However the payoff is big—research shows exercise during pregnancy helps keep weight gain to recommended levels—and helps you take the weight off after pregnancy.[35]

- Write your exercise times on your calendar and keep them! Set the alarm on your phone so you don't forget!

- Find an exercise partner! It's more fun and harder to be a no-show when you know someone is counting on you.

- Dance! In communities large and small there is dancing to be had, and it's a fun way to exercise without "exercising." From Tango to Waltz to Contra-dancing and Country-Western, you're sure to find a style that fits, and you can find events for the whole family. Don't worry—if you seriously doubt your abilities, most groups are very beginner-friendly. Remember the African saying: "If you can walk, you can dance." Check out www.cdss.org (country dance and song society) for information about folk, English and contra dance events in the US.

- If you travel for work, book a hotel with a fitness facility. See more tips for healthier travel on page 201.

Speedy Exercise

Squeeze in more activity with these 1-5 minute exercise breaks:

- While you talk on the phone, pace back and forth or do arm exercising by doing curls with a full 16 oz. (500 ml) water bottle

- Instead of fast-forwarding through the commercials, mute them and march or dance in place during every commercial, (or if you're feeling energetic, during the whole show!) This might be a good time for stretching and strength training using water bottle weights too.

- While you wash your hands, do shoulder rolls, knee bends or a pelvic tilt.

- Instead of emailing a co-worker, walk to his or her desk.

- Take the stairs whenever you can.

- When you're on the phone and sitting, march your legs in place or do leg lifts. Or keep a "pedal exerciser" under your desk and pedal away!

- Take the "long way" when going to the restroom, mailroom or to meetings.

- Instead of a work break, indulge in a fitness break and take a short walk or stretch.

- If it's safe, park a little farther away or get off a stop or two early from the bus or subway and walk.

- Walk the dog; your pooch will love you for it! If you don't have a dog, borrow one from a neighbor.

- Purchase an exercise video just for pregnant women. Collage Video has a large selection or pregnancy fitness, yoga and Pilates videos. I love that you can view clips online before you buy. www.collagevideo.com. If you are on bed-rest or limited activity, another video might be right for you—*Bedrest Fitness*—(also available in Spanish) developed by Darline Turner-Lee, a Physician's Assistant and Personal Trainer. Find it at www.nextstepfitness.com

My Personal Exercise Schedule

If you want to get it done, you need to schedule it!

My goal is to exercise _____ times per week, for _____ minutes each time.

My Exercise Schedule:	Time / What Exercise
Monday	
Tuesday	
Wednesday	
Thursday	
Friday	
Saturday	
Sunday	

Twelve Sneaky Ways to Exercise

Not everyone truly enjoys exercising. If you cringe at the idea of cardio, or wrinkle your nose at walking, you can increase your physical activity without a planned exercise routine.

- Throw the ball for your dog, but try to get to the ball before he does.

- Shop 'til you drop. Take one spin around the mall before you actually enter a store.

- Learn to juggle.

- Wash the car yourself instead of paying someone else to do it.

- Go canoeing or paddleboating.

- Do volunteer work with kids. Think: sports and scouts

- ◆ Play Active Video Games: Get active games like Wii Sports, Wii Fit or the fitness or dance XBox 360 Kinect games—they're a fun way to burn calories when it's cold outside. Just remember to tone down the pace if too high impact.

- ◆ Try aerobic yard work. Cut your grass with a push mower and lessen your contribution to global warming! Rake leaves or pull weeds—these activities all use muscles!

- ◆ Plant a garden. A bonus of gardening is enjoying the (organic) fruits of your labor, which can be used in the future for baby food!

- ◆ Play ping-pong or Frisbee.

- ◆ Make your house-cleaning more aerobic. Do it faster and don't stop between chores. Make sure you use both sides of your body for chores so that your workout is balanced. Put on some great music—it will help motivate you. For more household exercise ideas, see www.nutritiontwins.com/nutrition-twins-good-morning-america-easy-household-exercises

- ◆ If the idea of working up a sweat while exercising is a turn-off, think about trying yoga.

For a comprehensive and motivating guide to exercise, which also dispels many of the myths of exercise during pregnancy, I recommend *Exercising Through Your Pregnancy* by James Clapp III, MD (Addicus Books, 2012)

Yoga: Perfect For Pregnancy and Postpartum

Christin Chan BA, MBA

Yoga can be very beneficial during and after pregnancy—especially when combined with a form of cardiovascular exercise, such as walking, in order to keep a woman in shape. It helps prepare a woman for the process of childbirth both mentally and physically.

Contributing to the reduction of worries through meditation practices, yoga encourages one to quiet the mind and heightens awareness of breath. This allows a woman to concentrate on being in the moment and letting everything else go. Of course, yoga also promotes flexibility and prepares the body for labor. Practicing yoga after delivery can help you get back in shape, reduces stress and it can be done at home while your baby is napping.

Here are some benefits to practicing yoga throughout pregnancy (and beyond):

- ◆ Generates blood circulation throughout the body which can help reduce swelling and water retention

- Builds strength in the body to carry weight during pregnancy and to carry the baby after birth

- Improves posture and eases back pain, carpel tunnel syndrome[36] and headaches

- May improve blood pressure[37]

- Promotes better sleep and mental alertness

- Reduces stress and anxiety by calming the body and mind through concentration of stillness[38]

- Because yoga can improve mental health, it could also be good for the "baby blues."

- Safely opens hips and strengthens the lower body for childbirth

- Group yoga classes are a great way to meet other mothers for moral support

To gain these benefits, here are some examples of postures that can be performed daily. If you are new to yoga, it's best to work with a yoga instructor at first. For more support, you can always use props such as yoga blocks, bolsters, straps, blankets, chairs, or even the wall.

Breathing

Learning to breathe deeply and relax will help with the demands of labor pain and childbirth. It is essential to concentrate on how to breathe fully and steadily, taking in air through the nose, filling the lungs with air and exhaling, pulling the stomach into the spine. Listen to the sounds of your breathing.

Seated or Floor Postures

These postures help ease back pain, strengthen the spine, open up the pelvis, and stretch the hamstrings:

- Cat/Cow Pose

- Bound Angle Pose

- Seated Wide-Legged Forward Bend

- Knee to Head Forward Bend

- Squat + Kegel Exercise - Doing this everyday will help to relax and open up the pelvis and strengthen upper legs. Kegel exercises can also be done while squatting. The easiest way to do this is to use a yoga bolster. This should be done while sitting on a yoga bolster with legs open like in a squat, using the elbows to push the knees open with palms together in front of your heart.

Standing postures

These strengthen leg muscles and help with reducing swelling and inflammation in the legs, knees, and ankles. These postures also help with backache and sciatica while strengthening joints and improving balance. Examples include:

♦ Extended Triangle Pose

♦ Side Angle Pose

♦ Warrior I and Warrior II

♦ Chair Pose

Balance postures

These maintain posture and elongate the spine. They include:

♦ Standing Tree Pose

♦ Warrior III

Relaxation

The most important part of yoga is to give yourself enough time to rest after your practice. Lay on your left side with knees bent. If you want to get more comfortable, place a bolster between your legs. Soften your breath. Allow your shoulders to sink down. Relax your entire body into the mat. Take this time to connect your breath to your baby.

What Not to Do

♦ Avoid inverted poses such as headstands or handstands, or any other postures where the head is below the heart. These types of poses can cause dizziness and risk to your baby if you fall.

♦ Avoid lying flat on your back after the first trimester to prevent a decrease in blood flow to the placenta.

♦ Avoid any deep twists or stretches in the abdominals.

♦ Avoid any deep forward or back bends to prevent tear or strain in muscles.

♦ If you have pubic symphysis diastasis, which is the pain in the pubic bone created by the separation of the ligaments around the pelvic joint, keep your legs closed in the postures.

- If you have placenta previa (also called low-lying placenta), where your placenta covers your cervix, avoid squatting. It's best to get your health care provider's OK before doing any exercise if you have this condition.

Christin is a Registered Yoga Teacher and Prenatal Fitness Educator.

Exercise After Pregnancy

Pregnancy is sometimes the beginning of weight problems for women. You may never get around to losing the last 10 pounds (4.5 kg) or perhaps you even gain weight due to the stress of a new baby. If you add another 5 to 10 extra pounds (2 to 5 kg) with another pregnancy, before you know it, you're 20 to 30 pounds (9 to 15 kg) overweight, which puts you at risk for chronic disease, as well as putting stress on your joints and heart.

Research has shown that people who exercise regularly lose more weight and have the best odds of keeping it off. Combining exercise with diet helps preserve muscle mass, which is important for weight loss! Other benefits of exercising include improved cardiovascular fitness, lowered heart rate, lowered blood pressure, decreased blood lipids, decreased blood sugar, toned muscles, less body fat, improved immunity, and more!

After your baby's birth, it may be a while before you feel motivated to exercise. That's okay—you have just gone through one of life's biggest events. You may need some time to get used to having a baby in the house and to set up a new routine. (I needed four months to adjust!) Remember those hormones that made your joints more elastic so that your pelvis could stretch for childbirth? Weeks will pass before those hormones drop to their normal levels. Most health care providers will approve an exercise program after the six-week check-up. Until then, walking is generally fine.

How to Get Your Exercise Groove Back

- Start at your own pace, no matter how slow it seems.

- Wear your baby. Dance, walk, stand…carrying around an 8-15 pound (3.5-7 kg) "weight" burns extra calories. It also makes your baby feel secure and cared for. You can also do sitting or standing exercises using your baby as the weight.

- Continue your pelvic tilts and Kegels as a good start that will help you get stronger and heal.

- Stretching is important, even if you don't feel like exercising.

- Find activities you enjoy and include other family members if possible.

- Join a fitness class for moms and babies. You won't feel as though you're the only one with a big tummy, you can meet other moms, and you won't need daycare.

- Schedule your time. While you're at home the first six weeks, the days seem to drift by. A schedule that includes some physical activity will give you a sense of purpose and structure.

- Consider investing in a personal trainer to help you get started.

- There is one post-pregnancy exercise every mom does a lot—lifting your baby—and holding him in position to feed. This can take a toll on back, arm and elbow muscles. Focus on stretching and strengthening those areas.

Use Technology To Help you Get Motivated

- Workouts to go: Would you like a personal trainer on your phone or iPad? FitnessBuilder.com has more than 750 video workouts, 5,600 exercise image and videos and audio coaching that can be downloaded to your phone, iPod or computer.

- Track your exercise. I can't go on a walk without turning on my Endomondo "app" (www.endomondo.com). It tells me how fast I walk, how many calories I burn, and my speed. The routes are mapped and it's fun to look back and see the different walks I've taken, especially when I'm traveling. Some "apps" can work with a heart monitor to easily track your heart rate.

- Thousands of exercise videos are now available, but how can you tell which are best? A company called Collage Video does the research for you. Every video they sell has been tested by a fitness instructor certified by the American Council on Exercise (ACE) and also by a "regular person". The videos are also rated for exercise level, choreography and toning emphasis. Online clips and customer ratings also help get a feel for each video. www.collagevideo.com

The most important aspect of exercising is simply doing it. Do whatever it takes to get started and surround yourself with support to continue.

Check out these on-line fitness resources:

- Exercise guidelines from the American College of Obstetricians and Gynecologists www.acog.org/~/media/for%20patients/faq119.ashx

- FitPregnancy Magazine www.fitpregnancy.com

- Prenatal Fitness: The Expert Dr. Michelle Mottola www.youtube.com/watch?v=SsEKcpnviVg

Questions You May Have

Q: Won't exercise make me more tired?

A: At first you may feel a little more tired after exercising while pregnant. This tiredness is a result of the extra weight you are carrying and the extra blood that must be pumped through your heart. (During the first trimester, hormonal changes can also cause fatigue.) However, since exercise increases endurance, you will gradually feel less tired as your body gets accustomed to exercise. Of course, if you're already exercising, you shouldn't feel as tired. If you do, you may not be eating enough foods or the right foods.

Q: How will I know if I'm eating enough while exercising during pregnancy?

A: The rule of thumb here is to eat when you're hungry and to watch your weight gain. If you're not gaining enough, you need to eat more. If you have a busy schedule and just can't seem to eat enough, you may need to slow down. (See page 200 for snack ideas.)

Q: I'm on bed-rest. How can I prevent my body from turning into flab?

A: Pregnancy often causes us to make changes in our lifestyle and habits—bed-rest takes this to the extreme. First the bad news—while on bed-rest, you'll lose muscle tone and take a few steps backwards in your fitness level. The Good News—if your health care provider gives the OK, doing some stretching and isometric exercises while on bed-rest can help you retain some of your muscle tone, reducing your risk of blood clots, improving circulation, and increasing your endurance during labor. Bed-rest Fitness, an exercise video that follows the ACOG Exercise during Pregnancy Guidelines is now available. It was developed by Darline Turner-Lee, Physician's Assistant and Certified Exercise Specialist, during her own pregnancy. Find it at www.nextstepfitness.com

Keep in mind that after you have your baby, your endurance for exercise will be very low. You'll need to start out slowly. I thought I would need practically forever to get back into shape after I was off bed-rest. However, in about a month, my endurance returned to almost normal. Your body will bounce back, and you can become fit again, so think of your situation as a temporary one.

Q: My back hurts all the time lately. What can I do?

A: Your complaint is a common one—up to ⅔ of women complain of low back pain. I can sympathize with you. During the last two months of my pregnancy, I couldn't sweep and mop the kitchen floor in the same afternoon because my back hurt so much. I finally wised up and delegated both jobs to my husband.

Your back undergoes a great deal of stress during pregnancy. Most traditional back-strengthening exercises are not recommended during pregnancy because you perform them lying on your back. However, research shows that pelvic tilts and water exercise reduce pain intensity and related sick leave from back pain. Acupuncture is also a very effective treatment for both back and pelvic pain.[39] Women who do exercise regularly may be less likely to experience low back and pelvic join pain in mid pregnancy and postpartum depression after pregnancy.[40]

STOCKING THE PREGNANT KITCHEN

What You'll Find:

- Your Kitchen: Time to Take Inventory

- A Peek in my Kitchen

- Using Food Labels to Your Advantage

- Eating on a Budget

- Stocking the Kitchen Toolbox

- Keeping the Vitamins in Your Veggies

- Boost Your Veggies: Twelve Ways

- Cooking Meats, Poultry and Fish

- Eating Cleaner And Greener

Frequently Asked Questions:

- How can reading the food label help me eat healthier?

- Are there food additives I should avoid?

- How long is it safe to keep leftovers?

- Which artificial sweeteners are safe during pregnancy?

- Which foods should I buy organic?

SCAN HERE FOR CHAPTER UPDATES

Well, I hope the previous 14 chapters have motivated you to eat well! If your diet is already good, you may not need much help. But if you're turning over a new leaf nutritionally, you may be thinking, "Where do I begin?" The best place to start improving your diet is of course, your own kitchen. First, you need to identify your shopping and eating habits so you can change them if needed.

Your Kitchen: Time to Take Inventory

1. What takes up most of the space in your freezer? Frozen vegetables? Ice cream? Frozen juice? Fish, chicken, or meat? Fish sticks? Frozen dinners? Frozen pies or cheesecakes? Pizza? French fries?
2. Does the door of your fridge hold soda and energy drinks?
3. Are your produce drawers bulging with fresh fruits and veggies (some of them organic), or do they contain only a few lonely, shriveled carrots or dead spinach?
4. Does your pantry hold lots of convenience foods? Canned vegetables and fruits? Potato chips? Candy?
5. Do you keep on hand a mix of grains, such as pasta, bulgur, quinoa, whole-wheat flour, wheat germ, oats, and barley, or just white flour, instant mashed potatoes, ramen noodles, and white rice?
6. Do you keep a variety of vegetables in the house, or do you regularly eat your standard two favorite vegetables and fruits?

A Peek in My Kitchen

People are always curious about how I eat at home. I think they envision my family eating perfectly all the time because I'm a registered dietician. They don't realize that we are just like any other family; we have our habits, our likes, and our dislikes. To show you how my family eats and shops, I'll let you take a peek in my kitchen.

In My Pantry

◆   Canned tomatoes, tomato sauce

◆   Jars of spaghetti sauce without meat

◆   Canned black beans, vegetarian refried beans, kidney beans, chickpeas

◆   Dried lentils, split peas, black beans, pinto beans

◆   Tuna pouches

◆   White, whole-wheat and buckwheat flours

◆   Skim evaporated milk

- Yeast, sugar, brown sugar, molasses, honey

- Pasta, white and brown rice, bulgur wheat, quinoa, barley, whole wheat couscous

- Sun-dried tomatoes

- Kashi Go Lean Crunch, Uncle Sam's Cereal, Raisin Bran, All Bran, old-fashioned oatmeal, grits, Multibran Chex, Bare Naked Granola, Cheerios, Nature's Path Organic Oatmeal

- Raisins, dried cranberries, dried blueberries, dates, figs

- Canola oil, olive oil, light soy sauce, walnut oil

- Nuts: Almonds, cashews, pistachios, pecans, sesame seeds, walnuts, peanuts

- Regular and decaf black tea, organic Chai tea, fair trade Costa Rican coffee

- Too many spices to mention

- Apple cider, white, balsamic, red wine, rice and tarragon vinegars

- Crackers: Triscuit, Wheat Thins Flat Breads and Milton's Whole Grain

- Cookies: Fig Newtons, LU Petit Beurre

- Toblerone, Milka or Ghirardelli chocolate (Our motto: Buy the best, but eat one piece at a time!)

- Tortilla Chips, Garden of Eatin' Blue Corn Tortilla Chips, pretzels, light popcorn

In My Freezer

- Nutri-Grain, Kashi or Van's waffles

- Trout, tilapia, salmon, shrimp, barramundi

- Boneless, skinless chicken thighs

- Top or bottom round, natural ground beef, sirloin and minute steaks

- Pork loin chops or pork loin roast

- Mashed bananas (to use in banana bread or pancakes)

- Chopped spinach or broccoli, mixed vegetables, peas, corn

- Frozen meatballs

- Boca or Gardenburger veggie burgers

- Frozen harvest from the garden: tomatillos, pasta sauce, green chiles

- Frozen soups, chilis, etc

- Homemade pesto

- Homemade sofrito (combination of onion, garlic, bell pepper and cilantro)

In My Refrigerator

- 1% DHA-fortified, organic milk

- Omega-3 or cage-free eggs

- Cheese: Brie, feta, part-skim mozzarella, reduced-fat or regular Cheddar, fresh Parmesan

- Greek yogurt

- Iced tea

- Miscellaneous meat, fish, or chicken, thawing

- Fat-free sour cream

- Lean ham

- Brummel & Brown Yogurt Spread

- Kerrygold Irish butter

- Natural-style peanut butter

- Mayonnaise, homemade vinaigrette dressing, homemade Ranch dressing (almost fat-free), barbecue sauce, teriyaki marinade, ketchup, hoisin sauce, grated ginger, chopped garlic in a jar, Dijon mustard, capers, horseradish, wheat germ, whole and ground flaxseed and wheat bran (in fridge to prevent rancidity)

In My Produce Drawers

Generally bulging with produce in season, produce from the garden with a few favorite fruits and veggies that I buy year round, like blueberries and lettuce.

Using Food Labels to Your Advantage

Chances are, you're more concerned about what you eat now than you were just a few months ago. In fact, your favorite new pastime may be studying food labels.

What Can You Learn?

Food labels contain a lot of helpful information, courtesy of the U.S. Food and Drug Administration (FDA) and Health Canada, which use the same labeling system. In the UK, Australia and New Zealand, similar information is provided with slightly different requirements. While labels in the US contain information based on a standard serving size, other countries require that nutrient info be listed based on a 100 g or 100 ml serving. You'll notice that some manufacturers are also putting their own "front of package" labeling that calls out things like calories, fat, protein, and sodium. This type of labeling has been used successfully in the US, Sweden, the Netherlands, and the UK.[1] This makes it easier to quickly scan, but sometimes you need to dig deeper on the Nutrition Facts Label to find the information you need.

Label Basics

Pesticide Use

A "certified organic" seal indicates the product has been grown using approved organic agricultural methods. Synthetic fertilizers, sewage sludge, irradiation, and genetic engineering may not be used in the US. A full discussion of organics is in the Eating Cleaner and Greener section on page 371.

Serving Size

While you *might* share your 20 oz. or half-liter soda with a friend, you're more likely to drink it all yourself. (If label information is based on a 100 g serving, ask yourself, is this the amount I'll really consume?) Pay attention to the serving size listed compared to how much you will actually eat or drink. Calculate accordingly.

Ingredient List

This is where you can find things you want to avoid—added sugars, preservatives, food colors and potential allergens. Ingredients are listed in order of weight, so ingredients that appear first in the list are found in larger amounts.

Daily Value

Calories, fat, carbohydrate and protein are listed as a percentage of a "standard" 2,000 calorie diet, which is most likely less than what you'll need while pregnant. . Vitamins A, C, calcium and iron are listed as a percentage of the Daily Value, which gives you a general idea of nutrient content. Though it doesn't necessarily reflect your exact needs while pregnant, it gives you a general idea of whether the nutrient in the food is significant or barely there. Important pregnancy nutrients such as choline, lutein, magnesium and DHA are listed only voluntarily by the manufacturer.

Nutrition Claims

There are many. Here are the most important ones and what they mean (Per standard serving)[2,3]:

- **Fat-free:** Less than ½ gram of fat and no added fat

- **Low-fat:** Contains three grams of fat or less

- **Light (or lite):** Has at least ⅓ fewer calories than or ½ the fat of a comparable product. Can also mean that a low-calorie, low-fat food has had its sodium reduced by 50 percent.

- **Excellent source of, High or Rich:** Contains 20 percent or more of the Daily Value for a particular nutrient

- **Healthy:** Must also be low-fat, low in saturated fat, contain less than 95 mg cholesterol and at least 10% of the Daily Value for vitamins A, C, calcium, iron, protein, or fiber

- **Good Source Of:** Contains 10 to 19 percent of the Daily Value of a nutrient

- **Lean:** No more than 10 g total fat, 4.5 g saturated fat and 95 mg cholesterol

- **Extra Lean:** No more than 5 g total fat, 2 g saturated fat and 95 mg cholesterol

- **Natural:** This is an approved claim for meats and eggs only. If you see it on other products, it can mean **anything!**

To find out which non-government claims are reliable, see www.nrdc.org/living/labels/food.asp

Claims for Meat, Poultry and Eggs

Besides nutrition and organic claims, there are also voluntary claims about livestock products and how the animals were treated. Some definitions from USDA:

- **Free-range:** The flock was provided shelter in a building, room, or area with unlimited access to food, fresh water, and continuous access to the outdoors during their production cycle. The outdoor area may or may not be fenced and/ or covered with netting-like material. This claim is regulated by the USDA.

- **Cage-free:** The flock was able to freely roam in a building or enclosed area with unlimited access to food and fresh water during their production cycle.

- **Natural:** Meat, poultry, and egg products labeled as "natural" must be minimally processed and contain no artificial ingredients. (Under this definition, most fresh poultry, meat and pork qualify as natural.) However, the natural label **only** applies to *processing* of meat and egg products, not to farm practices.

- ◆ **Grass-fed:** Animals receive a majority of their nutrients from grass throughout their life, while organic animals' pasture diet may be supplemented with grain. Also USDA regulated, *the grass-fed label does not limit the use of antibiotics, hormones, or pesticides.* Meat products may be also labeled as grass-fed organic.

- ◆ **Pasture-raised:** USDA has not developed a labeling policy for pasture-raised products, yet.

- ◆ **Humane:** Multiple labeling programs make claims that animals were treated humanely during the production cycle. However, these labeling programs are not regulated.

Fish is recommended during pregnancy. For a full discussion on which fish are healthiest, see page 127.

Fish Labeling

Look at these labeling terms and tips to make sure your fish is good for you and the planet.

Country of Origin Labeling

Indicates the country in which the product was grown or raised. Buying local and domestic makes a smaller energy footprint and can also be safer. In the US, imported farm-raised shellfish is often turned away by inspectors because they contain illegal chemical residues.

Organic

The United States lacks organic standards for fish, but you may see organic seals on fish that's certified by a third-party such as the UK Soil Association (www. soilassociation.org/certification) or Germany's Naturland. The USDA is working on new rules for organic aquaculture.

Best Aquaculture Practices

Indicates that certified shrimp farms and hatcheries and seafood processing plants protect biodiversity, food safety, and worker rights.

Dolphin-Safe

Ensures that certified tuna fisheries utilize specific methods that protect the marine ecosystem and do not harm dolphins.

Marine Stewardship Council

Certifies well-managed fisheries with healthy populations that are captured without damaging ocean ecosystems. MSC (Marine Stewardship Council) Certified product have the blue label. This certification does not evaluate mercury or PCB contamination. www.msc.org

Wild-Caught

Indicates fish were not farm-raised.

For more info about label reading:

- www.fda.gov/Food/ResourcesForYou/Consumers/NFLPM/ucm274593.htm

- www.nhs.uk/Livewell/Goodfood/Pages/food-labelling.aspx

- www.foodstandards.gov.au/consumerinformation/labellingoffood/interactivelabelpost3614.cfm

Take a Closer Look At These:

- *Your* serving size and its calories, sugar and fat

- **Fiber:** the more the better—29 grams a day is the goal.

- **Sodium:** Amount is listed by stated serving size. Watch out for foods containing over 400 mg per serving (The DRI for sodium during pregnancy is 1,500 mg; most people consume much more than that.)

- **Sugar:** As little added sugar as possible. Note that natural sugar from fruit and milk is also listed under "sugar" so this number may be misleading. See the many names for, and more info about sugar on page 70 and page 72

- **Saturated fat and trans fat:** as little as possible

- **Preservatives, artificial colors, artificial sweeteners, etc:** least is best. More about preservatives is on page 364

- Additional added nutrients and herbs—some of which you have never heard of—which may not be necessary or safe: you'll find these in protein bars/ drinks and medicinal foods

---

Check out this great book about label reading: *Read It Before You Eat It* by Bonnie Taub-Dix MS, RD

Sweeteners

Nutritive sweeteners have calories: the most common sweetener is sucrose or table sugar. (A complete list of sweeteners is on page 72.) All those different terms for sweeteners can make it difficult to decipher the label. For example, since ingredients are listed by weight, you'd expect to see something with a large percentage of sugar to have sugar listed as the first ingredient, right? Not necessarily. In the case where there are multiple sweeteners—such as brown rice syrup, evaporated cane juice and agave syrup—they'd be scattered in different places on the ingredient list. But, if you added them together in one category of "sweetener" it would move to the top of the ingredient list and be a more accurate representation of how much sweetener is in a product. Pay attention to them on the ingredient list. Sweeteners make your food taste good—but they also provide empty calories.

Non-nutritive sweeteners are calorie-free; sugar alcohols may have fewer calories but may also be calorie-free. They are also listed on the ingredient label. Check out a full discussion on page 368.

Sodium

You need more sodium during pregnancy due to the increase in your blood volume—twenty-five percent of your weight gain is fluid. Still, it's easy to get *too much sodium* in your diet, especially if you eat out frequently, or eat many processed foods. The upper limit of sodium recommended during pregnancy is 2,300 mg, found in about a teaspoon (5 ml) of salt. A typical fast food burger has 1,000 mg; so does a large dill pickle, a cup of consommé and a 4 ounce (115 g) bratwurst. It's easy to get *all* your sodium for the day in *one meal* when eating out!

Slowing down on Sodium:

♦ If you follow the Eating Expectantly Diet—mostly unprocessed foods—and you watch your sodium when eating out, you should have no worries about having too much sodium.

♦ If you eat out more than twice a week or often eat foods containing more than 1,000 mg sodium per serving, it's a good idea to take a close look at your total sodium intake and possibly cut back.

♦ Potassium counteracts the effects of sodium in your diet, so eat more potassium-rich foods when you've eaten extra salt. (It's a good idea even when you don't eat too much salt.) See page 218 for potassium content of foods.

♦ For more information on hypertension during pregnancy, see page 256.

Sodium increases blood pressure in people who are sensitive to it; it also causes your body to retain fluid. While some swelling is normal, especially after the 5th month, you may notice more swelling when you've eaten extra salt. Too much sodium may do more than just increase fluid retention. Animal studies show that a high salt diet during pregnancy may "program" offspring for high blood pressure, problems with kidney development and cardiovascular problems.[4,5] But very low sodium diets have been shown to cause similar problems in animals[6]—which is why you'll never see recommendations for women to follow a low-sodium diet during pregnancy. In fact, you won't see a whole lot of specific advice about which level of salt intake during pregnancy is best. So, like much of the dietary advice given here, for sodium, moderation is best! Check in with your health care provider on her opinion about sodium intake during pregnancy.

Most Common Sources of Sodium in the Diet

You might be surprised—the food that contributes the most sodium in a person's diet is bread!

- Breads and rolls
- Cold cuts and cured meats
- Pizza
- Poultry
- Soups

- Sandwiches
- Cheese
- Pasta dishes
- Meat dishes
- Snacks

Source: www.cdc.gov/vitalsigns/Sodium/index.html

Use By and Sell By Dates

Pay attention to the dates on the package to ensure the food is fresh and safe when you buy it. It is not required in the U.S., (except on infant formula) but many manufacturers list it voluntarily.[7] However, in Canada[8], the UK[9], and in Australia and New Zealand,[10] a "use by" or "best by" date is required.

While the US federal government does not require a dating system, package dating is required in more than 20 states. A "use by" date—determined by the manufacturer—is generally the last date recommended for the use of the product while at peak quality, and doesn't determine safety. But even if the product "expires" during home storage, it should be safe, wholesome and of good quality if handled properly.[11]

Canned food often has use-by dates. Acidic foods like tomatoes and pineapple will be at peak quality for 12-18 months, while canned meat fish and most other vegetables have a quality shelf life of 2-5 years, if the can is in good condition and has been kept in a cool, dry place.[12]

Eggs and Use By Dates

Eggs are often stamped with the date they are packaged; however, the Julian system of dating is used. The number is a three-digit code that represents the consecutive day of the year starting with January 1 as 001 and ending with December 31 as 365. A "use by" or "sell by" date is not required by the Federal government, but may be by state law. For best quality, use eggs within 4 to 5 weeks beyond the packing date.[13] The "sell by" date will usually expire during that length of time, but the eggs are perfectly safe to use.[14]

Is it Still Good?

Use this chart to learn how long you should store food in the refrigerator and freezer. Note that *freezer storage times are based on quality, not safety.* Frozen foods remain safe indefinitely.

Fish & Seafood	You Can Keep It Up To This Long	
	Refrigerator 40°F (4° C) or less	Freezer 0°F (-18° C)
Fresh fish	2 days	6 months
Cooked fish	4 days	6 month
Smoked fish	14 days	2 months
Canned seafood (after opening, out of can)	4 days	2 months
Fresh shrimp, scallops, crawfish, squid	2 days	6 months

Meats	You Can Keep It Up To This Long	
	Refrigerator 40°F (4° C) or less	Freezer 0°F (-18° C)
Raw roasts, steaks, chops	5 days	12 months
Raw livers, raw heart, raw kidneys and other variety meats	2 days	4 months
Raw ground meat, raw sausage of any type	2 days	4 months
Sliced bacon, uncooked	7 days	1 month
Lunch meat	5 days opened, 2 weeks unopened	2 months
Cooked meat dishes and leftovers	4 days	3 months

Poultry & Eggs	You Can Keep It Up To This Long	
	Refrigerator 40°F (4° C) or less	Freezer 0°F (-18° C)
Fresh poultry	2 days	12 months
Cooked poultry	4 days, unless covered in broth or gravy, then 1-2 days	6 months
Fresh eggs	5 weeks	Don't freeze
Raw yolks or whites	4 days	1 year
Liquid pasteurized eggs or egg substitutes-opened	3 days	Don't freeze
Liquid pasteurized eggs or egg substitutes-unopened	10 days	1 year

Other Foods	You Can Keep It Up To This Long	
	Refrigerator 40°F (4° C) or less	Freezer 0°F (-18° C)
Cooked pasta	5 days	2 weeks
Leftovers	4 days	3 months
Soups and stews	4 days	3 months
Store-cooked convenience meals	4 days	Don't freeze

 Sources: www.fda.gov, www.foodsafety.gov www.fda.gov/downloads/Food/ResourcesForYou/HealthEducators/ucm109315.pdf - This chart in Spanish: www.fda.gov/Food/ResourcesForYou/HealthEducators/ucm109318.htm

Storing for Safety and Quality

It's best to store food in food-safe plastic containers or BPA-free resealable bags. You can also use glass jars, but you run the risk of the jars breaking. Food expands as it freezes, so leave room at the top of the container—½ inch (1.25 cm) for small jars, 1.5 inches (3.75 cm) for large jars.

To preserve quality for freezing, remove meat, poultry and fish from Styrofoam trays and wrap tightly in freezer paper, resealable bags or vacuum seal bags. Removing all the air prevents freezer burn.

Label food with what it is and the date. See page 140 for a complete discussion about which plastics are safe to store food in.

Did you know?

The average person makes 200 food decisions every day!

Eating on a Budget

Raising a child is expensive! If you are pregnant with your first child, you may be discovering that just furnishing a nursery can cost a bundle! When looking at your food budget, the first thing to look at, is how much you spend on eating out. One friend who regularly stops for a coffee at her favorite café before work was surprised that when she added it up, she was spending $100 a month, at a minimum! Think about how many pounds of organic fruits and veggies *that would buy*! You might not think of coffee or a cold drink that you pick up at a convenience store as "eating out", but it sure does eat up your food budget! The tips below can help you eat a nutritious diet and limit your food costs.

Find recipes, menus, and a newsletter to help you eat healthy and cheap at www.nutritionbudgeteer.com/Pages/default.aspx. Written by Dr. Barb, a registered dietitian.

Investing in the Long Term

Making a few investments with a long-term goal of cutting your food budget can make a big difference:

Buy a Deep Freezer

Deep freezers aren't cheap, but they can allow you to buy food in bulk and stock up on sale items, as well as cook ahead and freeze. A grocer in my city often has buy-one-get-one-free sales with no limit on the number of items one can buy. If you could buy enough chicken for three months and get it for half-price, that would be quite a bargain. If you live near a cattle ranch, you can invest in a side of beef (or split it with a friend) and get a great deal on very lean cuts of meat. Even if you don't live near a ranch, you can buy certified organic, natural beef shipped to your door from www.alderspring.com, www.uswellnessmeats.com and many other online sources.

Cook Once: Eat Twice or Thrice

Make a double (or triple) pot of beans, chili or lentil soup and freeze half. This ready-made meal will be wonderful on a cold winter night. You can also freeze your leftovers instead of eating them every night for a week (or throwing them out when you get tired of them!) Consider freezing small portions in microwave-safe containers for homemade frozen dinners.

Buy Food in Bulk

This only works if you will actually use the food. If half of it spoils before you use it, bulk food is no bargain! Think of your friends when you want to buy large quantities. I've split large containers of food with friends—such as 3-pound (1.5 kg) containers of artichoke hearts or feta cheese.

Plant a Big Garden

Fresh produce can be expensive. Growing your own and canning or freezing what you can't eat right away can save you a bushel of money, especially during the winter. There's nothing more satisfying than growing and preserving your own. I'm lucky to have a husband with a green thumb. Even living in a dry southwest climate, we're able to enjoy organic zucchini, okra, basil, tomatoes, corn, chiles, cantaloupe and watermelon all summer. Swiss chard, kale, lettuce and tomatillos are fall favorites. See what gardening mom extraordinaire Connie Evers has to say on the subject:

Growing Food for Your Growing Baby by Connie Evers MS, RD

If you are attempting to "go organic" during your pregnancy, consider growing some of your own food in containers or raised garden beds. As you grow your baby, you can also grow nutrient-rich foods that are fresh, local, organic and affordable.

What you plant will depend on your space and also your growing zone. During the early spring, plant nutrient-rich "cool crops" such as kale, arugula, spinach, chard, pea pods, lettuce, carrots, beets and broccoli. Crops that grow better in hot weather include squash, tomatoes, tomatillos, chiles, eggplant, peppers, green beans and corn. Your local or regional Cooperative Extension office is a great free source for gardening information specific to your region. Master gardeners have been trained and can answer just about any of your questions. You can also find information about your specific geographical zone by visiting www.garden.org/regional/ and entering your zip code.

Even the smallest yard or apartment balcony offers a place to cultivate fresh herbs, vegetables, berries and even dwarf citrus trees. Smaller, yet taller, raised plots (4' X 4' X 30-32" high - 1.2 m X 1.2 m X 0.8 m high) are easier to manage and minimize the need to stoop or kneel. Container gardening is also a great option when space is limited.

An organic garden starts with organic soil and organic seeds or plant starts. Garden soil should be dark brown and feel loose in your hands. For the best success and safety, fill your containers or garden beds with organic, compost-rich soil. Always use an organic fertilizer and avoid any chemical-based pesticides. Garden centers and online catalogs offer a variety of natural solutions to ward off insects, birds and even hungry critters.

As your baby grows, your garden can also provide a source for organic homemade baby food. If you have been eating fresh produce during pregnancy and while breastfeeding, your baby has already been exposed to the taste of your garden veggies!

Connie Evers, MS, RD has been gardening since she was a child. She exposed her three children to garden-fresh veggies, herbs and berries from the time they were "buns in the oven!" She is the author of *How to Teach Nutrition to Kids*, **4th ed. www.nutritionforkids.com**

Check out these resources for container gardening:

◆   www.earthbox.com

◆   ag.arizona.edu/pubs/garden/mg/vegetable/container.html

◆   lifeonthebalcony.com/

Shop Smarter with Fooducate
Download Fooducate, a free app designed to help you "eat a bit better." Fooducate is a fantastic tool to rate what's in your pantry now, as well as help you find better choices at the grocery store. Just scan the food's barcode, and you see its grade plus an explanation. I rate this "app" A+! www.fooducate.com

Smart Shopping on a Budget

◆   Clip coupons and shop the sales.

◆   Shop alone. If you take children (or partner) with you, make sure they aren't hungry or tired as this can significantly increase impulse buys. Reducing distractions will help you concentrate on reading labels and comparing products and prices.

◆   Never shop hungry—everything looks good, and you're more likely to buy more "splurge" items and high calorie snacks. In fact, it's a good idea to grab an apple or banana to eat on the way to the store to make sure you don't get hungry while there.

- Make a menu based on what's on sale, and then make a list. Always follow your list—this saves money by avoiding impulse buys.

- Plan your menus with leftovers in mind. Think of different menus you can do with one dish. (Sort of like shopping for clothes—coordinates that go with each other.) For example, you could make beef fajitas the first night and fiesta salad with beans and beef strips a few days later, or you could freeze the leftover fajita fixings in individual containers for future lunches or quick dinners. Ditto with beans. Cook white beans; put some in chili, make a dip and freeze the rest. Most people end up throwing a lot of food away because they forget about it, get tired of it, or just don't like leftovers.

- Go to farmers' markets. In the summer, farmers' market prices are often cheaper than supermarket prices and most of the food is locally grown. You also support your local farmers. You can often buy big bunches of fresh herbs like basil at a cheap price—make it into pesto and freeze in small batches (Ice cube trays or baby food jars work great!)

- Shop at wholesale clubs like Sam's and Costco. They now carry a variety of less expensive organic foods.

- Buy your bread at a thrift store—or make your own. It's a great way to save money on a common staple. Making your own specialty breads is easy with a bread machine.

- If you buy staples such as beans, cereals, dried fruit and oats from bulk containers, you not only save money, but you also reduce packaging to help the environment. However, if you have allergies, keep in mind that bulk buying can be fraught with cross-contamination of allergens. Make sure to keep flour, rice and other dry goods in well-sealed containers to keep the bugs away.

- Get the best per-pound value. Fruit sold in 5-pound (2.5 kg) bags is often cheaper than fruit by the pound but packaged vegetables are not always cheaper. Mushrooms and tomatoes are good examples of this. Packaged ready-to-eat salads are more expensive than the individual ingredients. But sometimes the cost of convenience is worth it if it means you eat healthier.

What to Do with All Those Groceries?

So, if shopping and cooking is new to you, you may need help knowing what to do with all those groceries so you don't waste money on spoiled food! Here's a quick guide to help you get organized with storing your groceries:

- Fresh meats, chicken and seafood that you plan to eat immediately—up to 2 days—keep in the refrigerator.

- Fresh meats, chicken and seafood to eat later in the week—freeze. If bought in large quantities, divide first. (I like to add marinade at this point, so while they are freezing and defrosting, they'll be picking up flavors in the marinade.)

- Produce that you intend to cook but can't eat in a few days—chop and steam briefly to make it recipe-ready. Cool, then freeze.

- Food that you rarely need or need in small amounts (like tomato paste)—buy canned (BPA free) or in a jar and portion out in an ice cube tray. Freeze and store cubes for future use.

- If you can't use the whole bunch of fresh herbs you purchase, consider putting some in your bottle of olive oil or vinegar—it's a tasty way to add flavor and antioxidants to your cooking.

- Whole grains, nuts and seeds that you eat infrequently—wheat germ, bran, flaxseed, sesame seed, nuts—keep in the refrigerator.

Thanks to Julia Moszkowicz for her assistance with this section.

Stocking the Kitchen Toolbox

To make tasty, nutritious meals with minimum hassle, I consider the following tools essential for a cook who wants to eat well but doesn't have lots of time to waste in the kitchen:

- Blender and / or food processor. One of these is essential for making quick soups, bean dips, nut butters, low-fat cheese dips, and smoothies. A Magic Bullet works well for small quantities like smoothies. But invest in a heavy-duty blender or Vita Mix for bigger jobs.

- Citrus juice press: The perfect manual tool when you want to quickly squeeze all the juice you can without straining your hand in the process.

- Crockpot: Pour ingredients in. Turn on low. Return from work 8 hours later with dinner ready and smelling wonderful. What could be better than that?

- Cutting board: While it's still debated whether wood or plastic is best in terms of food safety, wood is the more natural and probably the safest choice. Research has shown that bacteria that get into the wood get carried into the interior of the wood where it's trapped and eventually dies off. Wood is also easier on your knives and won't accumulate many knife cuts because it can "heal" itself to a certain extent. According to the Food and Drug Administration's Food Code, a cutting board made from a hard wood with a closed grain like maple may be used in restaurants.[15] And if it's good enough for restaurants, it's good enough for home. You can sanitize wood cutting boards by heating in the microwave.

- Food thermometer: Using one is the most reliable method of determining whether food is cooked to the right temperature. If you like your meat on the pink side, you definitely need a thermometer to make sure you have cooked your food enough to kill bacteria.

- Garlic press: Garlic is a staple ingredient in most kitchens—and so is a press.

- Knives: If you don't have a few good quality ones, chopping and slicing will be a real pain, in more ways than one!

- Mandoline slicer: With that you can slice or dice an onion, or julienne zucchini in about 30 seconds!

- Microplane Zester/Grater: Whether it's grating lemon or fresh parmesan cheese, you'll find this tool is 100 times better than using the fine section of your cheese grater!

- Microwave. I didn't realize how much I used mine until I started creating the recipes for this book. Though most people use microwaves just for warming leftovers or heating water, using them for cooking can be a real timesaver. Microwave cooking can also preserve nutrients.

- Mini-chopper: Whether it's a manual or electric, a mini chopper is perfect for chopping onion, garlic, nuts etc. I'm a big Pampered Chef fan and they have both a hand chopper and a mini food processor (also manual) that makes chopping a breeze.

- Pots and pans: Of course, everyone needs some of these. Invest in a few good quality ones—for a full discussion see page 138.

- Salad spinner: I love salad, but I hate washing and drying lettuce leaves. We received a salad spinner as a wedding gift many years ago and after washing lettuce for hundreds (maybe thousands) of salads, it's still going strong. This tool will save money if you use it instead of buying bags of ready-made salads.

- "Stick" blender: also called an immersion blender (Emeril Lagasse calls these "boat motor blenders"!). This tool is great to make pureed sauces on the stove and small quantities of smoothies now, and the perfect tool for making homemade baby food later!

Keeping the Vitamins in Your Veggies

Which vegetables are better—frozen, canned, bottled or fresh? It's a toss-up—depending... Nothing beats freshly picked food straight from your own garden. However, research shows that frozen vegetables can actually have a similar nutrient content to fresh, and even some canned vegetables have higher antioxidant availability compared to fresh. How you cook your veggies also matter; the healthiest is steaming and pressure cooking, followed by baking/grilling. When foods are over-cooked or cooked in a lot of water they lack flavor, become mushy, and lose water-soluble vitamins like riboflavin, folate and vitamin C.

Nutrient Content Varies

Fresh vegetables may not be very fresh by the time you buy them, and they're even less fresh if they stay several days (or weeks) in your refrigerator. For example, fresh peas lose 50% of their vitamin C content in the first 24-48 hours after picking. Fresh spinach, when left in your refrigerator for 7 days, can lose 75% of its vitamin C content.[16]

Frozen vegetables such as green beans, sweet corn and peas contain similar levels of vitamin C, fiber, magnesium, and potassium as fresh vegetables.[17] The vitamin C level in quick frozen green beans, carrots and spinach are comparable to that of fresh vegetables.[18]

In some cases, carotenoids like lycopene are better absorbed from foods after they've been cooked or processed. For example, the bioavailability of lycopene from tomato sauce is higher than from fresh tomatoes.[19]

Canned vegetables may not seem as nutritious as fresh, but research shows that by the time the food gets to your table, the nutrient content of fresh, frozen and canned is similar.[20] If canned or bottled is the only way you eat vegetables that are lengthy to prepare—beans or pasta sauce, for example—then the payoff is worthwhile. Buy pantry foods in BPA-free cans, in glass jars or Tetra-paks when possible. However, canned foods have much more sodium than fresh or frozen.

Caring for Vegetables

♦   Store veggies in your refrigerator crisper in their bags.

♦   To keep lettuce and other greens fresh, remove rubber bands and ties, wrap in paper towels and then store in their bags. Wash right before eating to delay spoilage.

♦   If you like to chop up your vegetables ahead of time so that they're easier to eat later, store them in a zipper bag, letting the air out first. Wrapping them with paper towels save some nutrients that are light or air sensitive.

♦   Avoid soaking vegetables for long periods of time; soaking for 2 minutes is the best way to remove dirt from some foods, like spinach or strawberries. But if you leave vegetables soaking too long, they'll lose water-soluble vitamins.

Veggie Cooking Tips

◆ To cook vegetables in the microwave, add 1 or 2 tablespoons of water to veggies in a glass bowl and vented cover or with microwave-safe wrap, venting one corner. After the microwave cycle is finished, let the vegetables stand a few minutes while covered to continue cooking. This method is wonderful for cooking cubed potatoes; they are so moist, and they taste great without any added fat. (See the *Eating Expectantly Cookbook* for variations on this recipe.)

◆ If you want veggies to stop cooking so they stay crisp, immerse them in cool water.

◆ When stir-frying, put more dense vegetables in the pan first. For example, start with onion, and spices for flavor, then add carrots, celery, cabbage, and broccoli. At the end, add softer vegetables such as garlic and fresh herbs, peas, mushrooms, and greens.

◆ For steaming, a stainless steel, bamboo or silicone steaming basket is cheap and efficient. Or purchase a "universal steamer" pan, which fits over a traditional saucepan, and lets you cook pasta and steam veggies at the same time. (Don't you just love multi-tasking products?)

◆ When cooking in water or steaming, use just enough water to prevent scorching. Cut large vegetables in smaller pieces to shorten cooking time.

◆ Pressure-cooking has seen a comeback as a faster, nutrient-friendly way to cook. A wonderful resource for pressure-cooking (and vegetarian eating) is Jill Nussinow MS, RD, also known as The Veggie Queen. Her newest book *The New Fast Food: The Veggie Queen Pressure Cooks Whole Food Meals in Less than 30 Minutes* as well as a blog, recipes and cooking tips can be found at www. theveggiequeen.com.

Boost Your Veggies: Twelve Ways

So, 3 cups (750 ml) of vegetables a day sounds like a lot? These shopping and cooking tips will help you eat the green and orange stuff you and your baby need. (Many creative veggie recipes are found in the Eating Expectantly Cookbook.)

1. Veg-Up your sandwich. Add grated carrots, sliced cucumbers, mushrooms, avocado, corn, spinach leaves—anything to give your sandwich more crunch and vitamins.
2. Have a green smoothie—throw some spinach or kale leaves into your favorite berry or banana smoothie.
3. Start winter evenings with a cup of veggie soup—either broth or blended.

4. Start your meals with a raw veggie or cooked veggie salad of some kind. This will slow down your eating and add an extra veggie.

5. Keep raw carrots, celery, peppers and other snacking veggies at eye level in the fridge for easy grabbing.

6. Put spinach or lightly cooked sliced veggies instead of meat into your lasagna or stuffed pasta shells.

7. Don't forget foods with processed tomatoes—salsa and pasta sauce—they are an easy way to stack on the veggies.

8. Beans (black, pinto, chickpeas or white) make a great dip.

9. When you make a salad, make enough for a few days. Wrap in paper towel in a zipper bag so that you have the makings of a meal-sized salad the next day.

10. Buy veggies that are fun and easy to eat: baby carrots, julienne carrots, broccoli slaw, grape tomatoes.

11. Have a veggie for dessert—pumpkin, sweet potato or acorn squash.

12. Keep frozen peas on hand—they're easy to defrost and you can throw them in a salad, in pasta or stir-fry.

Cooking Meats, Poultry and Fish

"Throw another shrimp on the barbie!" brings a smile to many. And while there's nothing quite like a summer barbecue, grilling and cooking animal proteins at high temperatures produces heterocyclic amines (HCAs), compounds formed when amino acids react with creatine in muscle; and polycyclic aromatic hydrocarbons (PAHs), formed when fat from meat drips onto hot coals and produces smoke. Both HCAs and PAHs are linked with increased risk of cancer.

Decreasing HCAs and PHAs.

Don't toss out your grill yet—there are many things you can do to decrease the HCAs and PHAs in your food.[21]

♦   Not Too Hot: Low temperature cooking—below 325°F (165°C) such as stewing, boiling or poaching produces insignificant amounts of HCAs. Higher temperature cooking methods like broiling, pan-frying and grilling produce large amounts of HCAs.

♦   Not Too Long: Avoid cooking for long periods of time at a high temperature. Charring for example, also increases HCAs. Using food that is smaller—such as shish-kabobs or using boneless chicken—allows food to cook quicker. If you accidentally char your food, trim off the damaged section and discard.

♦   Keep it Moist: Marinating your food before grilling reduces HCAs. Using ingredients such as cider vinegar, lemon juice, olive oil and herbs like rosemary and turmeric decrease HCAs even more.[22,23]

- ◆ Cut the Fat: Choose the leanest cuts, remove skin and visible fat before cooking.

- ◆ Reduce Drips and Flare-Ups: Avoid mashing burgers with a spatula or piercing food with a fork while on the grill. This increases the juice that drips on the coals and causes flare-ups which produce PAHs. Use tongs instead of a fork to turn meat. Cooking food adjacent to, rather than directly over the heating element can also reduce flare-ups.

- ◆ Pre-Cook Before Grilling: Cook food that will take longer to grill, such as bone-in chicken or a large pork loin, to reduce grilling time. Put it on the grill immediately after microwaving.

- ◆ Say No to Well-Done: For your food to be "done", it doesn't have to be well-done! In one study, meats and fish cooked to an internal temperature considered well-done had 3.5 times more HCAs than those cooked to a lower temperature. Steaks, roasts and chops are safe to eat when cooked to medium, reaching an internal temperature of 145°F (65°C). Give those foods a 3-minute rest time before testing. Hamburgers should never be eaten unless they reach an internal temperature of 160°F (70°C), regardless of color.[24]

- ◆ Banish the Bacon: When compared to beef and chicken, fried pork had significantly more HCAs, and bacon had the highest.[25] Just one more reason to quell your craving for bacon and other fried foods.

Eating Cleaner And Greener

What is clean eating?

Eating foods as close to their natural state, minimally processed and with no additives.

Food Additives

Generally we think of food additives as things added to foods to improve a food's taste or appearance. In a broader sense, food additives also include substances that become part of a food product unintentionally during the processing, production, transportation or storage of that food. For example, the material a food is packaged in can migrate in small amounts to the food. So—anything that comes into contact with food can be considered an additive and therefore has to be safe.

Food additives are used to protect our food from spoilage, lengthen shelf life, enhance flavors, improve nutritional value, and add color or texture. For example, many foods are fortified with vitamins and minerals, and those fortifications are considered additives. Some fat-free products contain plant gums or seaweed derivatives that have been used safely for centuries. These are also considered additives. Some additives are healthier than others, as you'll see below.

Types of Food Additives and Uses

This list gives you just a few examples of the many additives used in food:

- Antimicrobials: Prevent food spoilage from bacteria, mold, or fungus. Calcium propionate, for example, is used to keep bread from molding.

- Antioxidants: Prevent oil-containing foods from going rancid; also delay browning. Vitamin C (ascorbic acid) and vitamin E (alpha-tocopherol) are commonly used antioxidants. After the discovery that vitamin C (ascorbic acid) inhibited production of nitrosamines in cured meats, it or its "chemical cousin" erythorbic acid, became a required additive.[26]

- Coloring agents (natural, nature-identical, and synthetic): Added to a product because consumers expect it to be a certain color. Most foods we eat have some added coloring—even Cheddar cheese!

- Curing agents: Prevent spoilage in meats. Sodium nitrate is a curing agent found in smoked meats. Celery powder and celery juice (also listed as "natural flavoring" on the label) is also used as a curing agent.

- Fat replacers or fat substitutes: Replace the properties of fat. They may be added to provide moisture or the taste or texture of fat. Fat replacers include natural plant substances, such as guar gum, xanthan gum, and carageenan, or they may be products developed specifically for replacing fat such as Olestra (a fat substitute found in some light and fat-free chips).

- Flavor or flavorant: Directly or indirectly add flavor to a product. For example, some flavorants affect the taste of a food through the sense of smell. Natural orange flavor may be used in a candy for taste, while limonene may be added to give the food an orange scent, which enhances flavor.

- Flavor enhancers: Enhance flavor without leaving flavors of their own. Monosodium glutamate (MSG) occurs naturally in food and is sometimes added to food to bring out natural flavors.

- Natural and artificial flavorings: Add flavor lost in processing or increases natural flavor.

- Preservatives: Help give food a longer shelf life by delaying spoilage.

- ◆ Texturizing Agents: used to modify the overall texture or 'mouthfeel' of food.

- ◆ Emulsifiers: Help evenly distribute tiny particles of liquid; keep oil and water mixed, as in creamy salad dressings.

- ◆ Miscellaneous: Other types of additives include leavening agents, propellants, pH control agents, humectants, dough conditioners, and anti-caking agents.

- ◆ Nutrients: Vitamins, minerals, and fiber are often added to replace nutrients lost in processing or to improve nutritional value. Inulin is a relatively new fiber added to many foods.

- ◆ Stabilizers or thickeners: Provide body or texture. Gums and other thickeners are used in fat-free salad dressings to give them the consistency of regular dressing. Phosphates and dough conditioners play a major role in modifying food texture.

- ◆ Sweeteners (including natural and artificial): Sweeten the taste of foods.

Are Food Additives Safe?

The vast majority of food additives are safe; some are uniformly beneficial while others are questionable. For example, sodium nitrite, which is found in cured meats, can be converted to nitrosamines, which cause cancer in animals and may be carcinogenic in humans too.

Other food additives may cause reactions in sensitive individuals. For example, up to 10 percent of the population is sensitive to sulfites, an anti-browning agent found in dried fruits, in some foods on salad bars and in some beer and wine. Monosodium glutamate (MSG) causes side effects in a small number of people.

Questionable Food Additives[27]

According to the Center for Science in the Public Interest[28], a science-based consumer advocacy group, some food additives would be better left on the shelf. However, with most issues regarding eating, you'll find conflicting opinion about these additives' safety. If in doubt, check in with your health care provider.

- ◆ Artificial Coloring: Blue 2, Green 3, Orange B, Red 3, Yellow 5, Yellow 6—for various reasons, including possibly causing cancer in animals.

- ◆ Butylated hydroxyanisole (BHA): suspected of being a human carcinogen. It's also added to cosmetics.

- ◆ Caramel coloring: This widely used food color is sometimes made with ammonia, which produces two chemicals considered to be cancer-causing by the World Health Organization (WHO). Cola type drinks contain relatively large amounts while things like soy sauce and bread have much smaller amounts.

- Cyclamate: Banned in the US, but available in most other countries including Canada, Australia and Mexico. The WHO and the Scientific Committee on Food (SCF) of the European Commission have also approved its use in many foods and drinks.

- Olestra: reduces the ability to absorb fat-soluble carotenoids; can cause diarrhea and loose stools. Found in some fat-free chips.

- Potassium Bromate: an additive in bread, which may cause cancer in humans. It has been banned in Canada, Europe, Brazil and China. In California, its use requires a cancer warning on the label.

- Propyl Gallate: There have been suggestions that this preservative may cause cancer in lab animals.

- Saccharin: Crosses the placenta during pregnancy. Advice regarding this sweetener has changed over the years and it's now regarded to be OK during pregnancy. However, there are plenty of less controversial sweeteners on the market.

- Sodium nitrite and sodium nitrate: consumption of these additives during pregnancy is associated with brain cancer in children as well as birth defects and risk of miscarriage.[29,30,31] Nitrates have been detected in breast milk; the amount increases with mom's intake.[32]

- Stevia: Recently approved in the US, and although used elsewhere for many years, not much research has been done on its effect during pregnancy or breastfeeding.

If you have questions about food additives, here is where to find answers:

- Helpful links about food additives in the US: www.nutrition.gov/whats-food/food-additives

- Health Canada: www.hc-sc.gc.ca/fn-an/securit/addit/index-eng.php

- Food Standards Australia New Zealand: www.foodstandards.gov.au/consumerinformation/additives/

- European Union: www.food.gov.uk/policy-advice/additivesbranch/enumberlist

- Chart of additives categorized by safety: www.cspinet.org/reports/chemcuisine.htm

- Complete alphabetic list of food additives and their uses: nutritiondata.self.com/topics/food-additives

What about "Naturally Cured?"

Labels that say "No added nitrate or nitrite" still may contain both substances due to the addition of natural curing agents—celery powder/ juice or other vegetable powders. Some vegetables are naturally high in nitrate, which has the same important preserving functions as added sodium nitrite or nitrate. Naturally cured products still contain nitrites, as found in a small Cook's Illustrated study.

Confusing? Yes! Just when you thought it was safest to buy "natural" and "nitrate-free" lunchmeat and bacon, you've now got to wonder. But thankfully, some completely nitrate and nitrite free bacon, lunchmeats and sausage are available from www.uswellnessmeats.com and Applegate Farms Organic and Natural Meats (found at natural food stores). These products are "uncured" which means they MUST be refrigerated at all times—nitrate preservatives present in cured meats prevent bacterial growth. I love the ingredient label on the Applegate Farms Natural Roast Beef: Beef, water, salt, pepper. You can't get cleaner than that! www.applegate.com.

How to Limit Food Additives

♦ Eat as many "whole foods" as possible, limiting mixes, processed and convenience foods—generally things found in a box or bag.

♦ Make sure to eat a wide variety of foods.

♦ If you do buy prepared or boxed foods, a quick measurement of the ingredient list can be a red flag for additives. If it's very long, take a closer look. A long list of ingredients may be the result of added vitamins and minerals; on the other hand, it can be from a lot of preservatives.

♦ Avoid cured meats and hot dogs containing nitrates or nitrites. There are many reasons to avoid cured meats, detailed elsewhere in this book. Although a rare slice of bacon is probably no cause for worry, a regular diet of cured meats requires more consideration.

♦ If you buy packaged snacks foods, look for those with no preservatives. My favorite savory snacks—baked corn tortilla chips and Triscuits—only contain three or four ingredients and no preservatives.

Artificial Sweeteners

Artificial or non-nutritive sweeteners are common additives. If you're avoiding sugary foods and drinks to help control blood sugar or weight gain, you may still want an occasional "something sweet." Should you eat products sweetened with artificial sweeteners? Saccharin (found in Sweet 'n Low), aspartame (found in NutraSweet), acesulfame K (found in Sweet One and Sunette), and sucralose (found in Splenda) have all been approved for use during pregnancy, and the American Diabetes Association OK's their use in moderation. (Although the Canadian Diabetes Association recommends avoiding saccharin and cyclamate.) Many health care providers would prefer that their patients avoid artificial sweeteners or consume them in moderation. A moderate intake of artificial sweeteners would be one or two servings a day. Consult with your health care provider for individualized recommendations.

Check out the chart below for more information about nonnutritive sweeteners (Not an all-inclusive list):

Brand Name/ European Union E-number	Countries Approved In*	Acceptable Daily Intake (ADI) for 150 lb (68 kg) person		Notes
		Number of 12 oz. (375 ml) drinks	Number of packets	
Acesulfame-K				
Sweet One Sunett E950	US, Australia, Canada	25	20	Often used in combination with other non-nutritive sweeteners.
Aspartame				
Nutrasweet Equal E951	US, Australia, EU, Canada	14	68	Loses sweetness when heated. People with PKU should limit intake.
Cyclamate				
Sucaryl Assugrin SugarTwin E952	Ireland, Australia, European Union In Canada & UK only as tabletop sweetener	4.5	Not determined	Once thought to be carcinogenic. Not recommended during pregnancy in Canada.[33]
Monk Fruit Extract (Luo Han Guo)				
Nectresse	US	Not determined	Not determined	Approved in 2012 in US, is a natural sweetener containing the sugar alcohol erythritol.

Brand Name/ European Union E-number	Countries Approved In*	Acceptable Daily Intake (ADI) for 150 lb (68 kg) person		Notes
		Number of 12 oz. (375 ml) drinks	Number of packets	
Neotame				
In Australia-New Zealand: NutraSweet E961	US, Canada, Australia, New Zealand, European Union	Not in carbonated beverages	No consumer product	Not in widespread use in the US. Chemically related to aspartame but safe for those with PKU.
Saccharin				
Sweet n' Low Sweet Twin Necta Sweet E954	US, Australia In Canada, only as tabletop sweetener	42	8.5	Crosses the placenta; slow fetal clearance. Not recommended in Canada during pregnancy. Best to avoid.[34]
Sucralose				
Splenda Sugar-Free Natura E955	US, Australia, Canada	15	30	No known safety issues during pregnancy or lactation.
Stevia (steviol glycosides, rebaudioside A, stevioside)				
Truvia PureVia Sweet Leaf E960	US, European Union, Australia, New Zealand	16	30	Research regarding use during pregnancy is limited. Best to avoid.[35]
Thaumatin				
Talin E957	Australia, New Zealand Approved as a flavoring but not a sweetener in the US	ADI not determined due to good safety profile	No consumer product	Naturally occurring plant protein. Used as a flavor enhancer due to extreme sweetness.

Eating Organic

There is a strong slant in this book towards eating cleaner—eating foods as close to their natural state as possible and staying away from unwanted chemicals. Buying organic foods definitely fits into the "eating clean" lifestyle. However, realistically speaking, it may not be practical (or budget-friendly) to buy all your foods organic. This section will help you navigate through the growing number of organic foods and help decide which ones should be in your shopping cart.

What's Organic?

In the US, USDA certified organic foods are grown and processed according to federal guidelines which address soil quality, animal raising practices, pest and weed control, and use of additives. Synthetic fertilizers, sewage sludge, irradiation, and genetic engineering may not be used.[36] Canada, the European Union, Australia, New Zealand and many other countries have similar certified organic programs. The policies outlined here apply to US organic certification.[37]

Produce: Can be called organic if it's certified to have grown on soil that had no prohibited substances applied for **three years** prior to harvest. Prohibited substances include most synthetic fertilizers and pesticides. When a grower has to use a synthetic substance to achieve a specific purpose, the substance must first be approved according to criteria that examine its effects on human health and the environment.

Meat: Regulations require that animals are raised in living conditions accommodating their natural behaviors (like the ability to graze on pasture), fed 100% organic feed and forage, and don't receive antibiotics or hormones.

Processed, multi-ingredient foods: USDA standards specify additional considerations. Regulations prohibit organically processed foods from containing artificial preservatives, colors, or flavors and require that their ingredients are organic, with some minor exceptions. Processed organic foods may contain some approved non-agricultural ingredients, like enzymes in yogurt, pectin in fruit jams, or baking soda in baked goods. Additional criteria for certification include:

- ◆ *100% organic:* The product must contain only organically produced ingredients

- ◆ *Organic:* The product must contain at least 95% organically produced ingredients. The other 5% are ingredients that are not available as organic or appear on an approved list.

- ◆ *Made with organic ingredients:* Processed foods may bear this label if they contain at least 70% organic ingredients—for example, soup made with organic peas, potatoes and carrots. "Made with organic" products will not bear the USDA organic seal, but, as with all other organic products, must still identify the USDA-accredited certifier.

Why Should You Eat Organic?

Most people choose organic for the health benefits—both to people and the planet. I discussed the problems with pesticides and other environmental chemicals on page 146. However, one statistic is worth repeating: organophosphate pesticide exposure during pregnancy can lower IQ in children.[38] A decrease in IQ by just 2 points can affect lifetime learning and earning potential. The risk from dietary exposure to pesticides is greatest during pregnancy and childhood, when the developing brain and nervous system is most vulnerable.[39]

However, the answer to the question "Is Organic Healthier?" is not straightforward. Looking at nutrient content, The Organic Center found that in matched pairs of organic vs. conventionally grown produce, organic was nutritionally superior in 61% of cases.[40] A study from the Newcastle University in the UK also showed an increase in nutrient content of conventional vs. organic produce.[41] But a just-published study from Stanford University, which analyzed more than 200 studies, concluded that *on average,* organic food offered no nutritional benefits over conventionally grown or raised. The study did confirm that choosing organic reduces exposure to pesticides and to antibiotic-resistant bacteria, which were found more often in conventionally raised pork and chicken.[42] Because research methodologies differ between studies and because nutrient content of produce varies greatly due to climate, soil and other variables, nutrient content is difficult to compare, which makes a "final answer" difficult to obtain.

What's GMO?

Organic foods are not allowed to be "GMO". GMO stands for Genetically Modified Organism—also called Genetically Engineered Organism or GEO. A GMO is one that has altered genetic material. Using recombinant DNA technology, genes from one organism are inserted into the DNA of another with a specific goal of improving the properties of the organism. Genetically modified foods are very controversial, especially in Europe and Japan. GMO labeling is required in the European Union, Australia, Japan, China and Russia, but not in the US.

Which Foods Should You Buy Organic?

The question I'm often asked is:"Which foods should I buy organic?" My answer is always:"It depends on what you eat!"

1. Take a look at the foods you eat—categorize them into groups depending on how often you eat them: several times a day, once daily, a few times a week, weekly, bi-weekly, monthly, or rarely.

2. Check out which foods in your locale have the highest pesticide residues. In the US, I recommend the Environmental Working Group's (EWG) Shopper's Guide to produce, which is an analysis of USDA data. While this list may not apply to produce from other countries, it gives you an idea of which types of produce generally have the highest levels of pesticides. The full list is found at www.ewg. org/foodnews/list/. From this list, EWG compiled a list of the "Dirty Dozen" and "Clean 15" Listed below.[43]

Environmental Working Group's Dirty Dozen: Produce with the Most Pesticide Residues *Consider Buying Organic if You Eat Regularly*		
1. Apples	5. Strawberries	9. Lettuce
2. Celery	6. Nectarine - non US	10. Cucumber
3. Sweet bell peppers	7. Grapes	11. Blueberries - US
4. Peaches	8. Spinach	12. Potatoes

Clean 15: Produce with the Least Pesticide Residues *Buying Organic is Not a Necessity*		
1. Onions	6. Sweet peas (frozen)	11. Cantaloupe – US
2. Sweet Corn	7. Asparagus	12. Sweet potatoes
3. Pineapples	8. Mangoes	13. Grapefruit
4. Avocado	9. Eggplant	14. Watermelon
5. Cabbage	10. Kiwi	15. Mushrooms

3. Next, check out how your most frequently eaten foods compare to their pesticide residue content. For the foods you eat often that have a lot of pesticides, try to buy those organic. Obviously, the produce with the lowest pesticide content will have the lowest priority for buying organic.

4. As a cheaper alternative to buying organic, for foods containing the highest levels of pesticides, grow your own! For example, apples, peaches and nectarines are some of the highest in pesticide residues—plant some trees! Spinach is one of the healthiest foods you can eat, but it's number 8 on the list. Luckily, it's also very easy to grow, along with kale, chard and other leafy greens.

5. Because pesticides and other chemicals tend to accumulate in the fat and skin of meat, poultry, fish and dairy products, choose lean and low-fat or skim

versions and trim off visible fat to reduce pesticides and other environmental chemicals. Buying organic meats, pork and poultry is also an option. Consider buying organic milk if you drink it daily.

For information on pesticide use around the world: Pesticide Action Network International www.pan-international.org/panint/?q=node/33

Eating Clean Helps You Go the Distance by By Diane Welland MS, RD

Eating clean is all about eating whole, natural, unprocessed foods. It's about eating "real" food that doesn't come out of a box, bag, package or can. This means focusing on fresh fruits, veggies, lean fresh meat, fish and poultry, legumes and whole grains. I also include cheese, yogurt, unsalted nut butters, whole grain breads, low sodium salsa, tomato sauce and fruit-sweetened jams and chutneys in my repertoire.

Eating clean is a good practice to stay healthy and feel good all your life, but particularly if you are pregnant and especially if you are an older mom, like I was. Since I was 42 years old when I was pregnant and had other children, I knew it would be important to keep my energy up and my weight down, as well as avoid salty foods that could lead to bloating.

If you can only do three things, try these—they worked for me:

1. Minimize the processed foods. Give up the frozen dinners, bagged frozen fish sticks or chicken tenders, which are also loaded with sodium: instead plan ahead. Double the amount of clean meals that you make and freeze half of it for later when you feel too tired to make supper—this works well for soups, stews, chili, pastas and chicken. I also usually made a few individual portions for when my husband was working late. Then my go-to meal for the kids and me was fruit, yogurt and nuts or granola. Perfect for a light dinner.

2. Switch to whole grains. Stock your pantry with whole grain breads and pastas, brown rice, quinoa, barley and oatmeal. These foods help you feel full, are an easy make-ahead side dish, and will keep you regular. Most grains will keep cooked for a week or more in the fridge. For a quick meal add them to sautéed veggies with beans, nuts, cheese or tofu.

3. Focus on eating some protein, carbohydrate and fat at every meal and snack— this can be a bit hard when you get those carb cravings. In addition to lean meat, fish and chicken, I often nibbled on cheese, yogurt and almond butter with apples. My favorite snack: Banana Peanut Butter Chocolate Roll Ups: Spread peanut butter on a whole wheat tortilla, top with ½ banana sliced in half lengthwise, sprinkle with a few shavings of dark chocolate, then roll it up.

Diane Welland is the author of *The Complete Idiot's Guide to Eating Clean* and *The Complete Idiot's Guide to Belly Fat Weight Loss*. For more tips and recipes on eating clean check out her blog: www.eatwelleatclean.com

EATING OUT AND EATING IN

What You'll Find:

- Kitchens are Gathering Cobwebs

- Pitfalls of Eating Out

- At Your Favorite Type of Restaurant

- Get a Healthier Meal, Just by Asking

- Choosing Nutritious Fast Foods

- Last-Minute Meals from What's in the Pantry

- Choosing Frozen Meal Options

Frequently Asked Questions:

- How can I eat healthier when eating out?

- How can I avoid food poisoning when eating out?

- What are some healthy options at Mexican food restaurants? Indian? Italian?

- Are there healthier fast food options?

- What are some foods I can keep on hand to make a super quick meal?

SCAN HERE FOR CHAPTER UPDATES

Kitchens are Gathering Cobwebs

Cooking has become something of a spectator sport for many. We might love watching Iron Chefs competing or Ellie Krieger whip up some luscious low-fat meals, but when it comes down to eating, many of us would rather make reservations than make dinner! That might be especially true when you're pregnant. We spend a lot on food prepared away from home—in the US, about half of every food dollar is spent eating out—and we eat away from home an average of four times a week. Is it possible to eat out on a regular basis (and eat nutritiously) without going over your target weight? The answer is yes, but you have to be careful and choose wisely.

The great part of eating out is, you're not the cook! No prep, standing over the stove or cleaning up. The bad thing? You're not the cook; you have no control and thus limited knowledge about how your food is actually being prepared. It helps to know what stands between you and a healthy meal when eating out. This section will give you the tools you need to have your "cake" and eat it too—a yummy restaurant meal that is also healthy for you and your baby.

Pitfalls of Eating Out

Eating out, whether it is quick-service or fine dining, has nutrition pitfalls in common. The good news is there are ways to sidestep around them.

Large Portions

People like value for their money, which is why restaurants keep dishing out large, value-size portions. Ironically, the most expensive meals—found in fine-dining restaurants—often have portions that are more appropriate than other restaurant meals.

Sidesteps

♦　Order appetizers instead of entrees. This is one of my favorite tools because I find the appetizer menu is often more creative and allows you to try several small dishes. One of my favorites is to order a tasty mixed green salad along with an appetizer-size of crab cakes. With some bread it's a perfectly balanced and tasty meal. The appetizer and side dish section of the menu is also where you might find some interesting vegetable dishes.

♦　Know that you don't have to order the "value" meal or the bigger portion that is only pennies more. It's tempting to get a good deal, but just remember that your baby is sharing all that extra fat and calories with you. At the drive-thru, order the sandwich and water, diet soda or tea, skip the fries, and get a side salad instead.

- Order a kid's meal—often the perfect sized portion at the drive-thru, and now you have the choice of a fruit (and milk) at some chains (Don't do this at a sit-down restaurant however, or you'll get chicken nuggets and fries!)

- Request that half your order be put in a to-go box before you are served. This helps you avoid the temptation of cleaning your plate, when you know you shouldn't. You also end up with lunch or dinner for tomorrow!

- Share the entrée with your dining partner. This is another strategy I often use—each of us orders a salad, soup or vegetable appetizer (not fried) and then we split an entrée. Most restaurants are used to this—others charge a plate-splitting fee—which is fine; you still save money, fat and calories in the long run.

Fruits and Vegetables are Few and Far Between

Sidesteps

- Start every meal with a salad or a vegetable (not creamy) soup.

- Choose steamed or grilled vegetables—often available as side orders.

- Look to the dessert menu for ideas; if you see cheesecake with fresh strawberries, you know they've got strawberries in the house. Ask for a dish of them for dessert.

- Order fruit at the drive thru. As the focus on child obesity continues to make headlines, fast-food chains are adding fruit to their menu, but you might have to hunt for it. I love McDonald Apple Dippers—without the caramel sauce—great for on the go.

- Eat a fruit before you leave home. Grab some grapes for the car on the way to lunch or dinner. You'll make sure to get a fruit in, and it will also take an edge off your hunger.

More Opportunities for Food Borne Illness

When you think of all the people at a restaurant who have their hands on your food before you eat it, there are many opportunities to pick up a bug or two.

Sidesteps

- Stay away from restaurants that have questionable food safety practices such as servers not washing hands after touching money, their hair or nose.

- If food doesn't feel cold enough or cooked well enough, return it.

- Ask a lot of questions to make sure there are no raw eggs, or other raw foods or unpasteurized cheese in what you plan to order.

- Avoid prepared deli salads; only order dishes with deli meats if they are heated to steaming. See page 130 for more tips.

Fat, Fat, Everywhere

One thing is for sure—everything at a restaurant will have more fat than if you had prepared it at home. Fat not only makes food tastes good, it also keeps food from drying out, important in commercial cooking. During pregnancy, fatty and fried foods can aggravate heartburn, and of course, add even more to your expanding width.

Sidesteps

- Ask a lot of questions—and if the servers don't know (they often don't), ask for the manager. Ask questions about the use of added fat and oils. The addition of oil at the last minute to fajitas for example, or butter on the top of a steak, fish or chowder can significantly increase hidden fat, or turn an otherwise healthy food such as grilled asparagus, into a higher-fat food.

- Skip fried foods; opt for grilled or "dry-fried" instead. Dry-fried is a healthier cooking technique which has little or no added fat.

- Order sauces, salad dressings and oils on the side.

- Seek out restaurants known to serve healthier options. Restaurants that are more health conscious are popping up everywhere.

- Look for "fatty" menu terms (fried, battered, crusted, smothered, creamed etc.) and either skip them or ask that they be modified. For example, although I love the taste of Alfredo sauce, the fat and calories aren't worth it. So I ask the waiter to put marinara sauce with a touch of the Alfredo—I call this concoction pink sauce. You get a touch of cream without nearly the fat of Alfredo. You can get the same flavor at home by mixing some fat-free sour cream into your marinara or puttanesca sauce. Vodka sauce is similar but it has more cream (and of course vodka, which you should avoid anyway!)

Whole Grains are the Exception

This is slowly changing too. For example, at PF Chang and Pei Wei, brown rice is an option; other Asian restaurants are following their lead.

Sidesteps

◆ Check out the side dishes.

◆ Ask for a whole grain bun, even if it's not usually the option for your sandwich or burger. Restaurants like Chili's and Red Robin offer this alternative but you have to ask for it. Many fast food outlets offer a grilled chicken sandwich with a whole grain (or at least partial whole grain) bun.

◆ Choose whole grains at sandwich shops when available, and they often are.

◆ Plan ahead *before* eating out and boost whole grains at other meals and snacks.

Unknown Calorie Counts

You probably know there are more calories in a fast-food burger than one you make at home—but how many more? Luckily it's getting easier to find out.

Sidesteps

◆ Check out the menu. McDonald's, some Starbucks and Dunkin' Donuts are now posting calorie counts on menu boards and at drive-thrus. In the US, calories will soon be posted on all menus, as required by an FDA labeling requirement.[1] This will hopefully drive consumers to choose more healthy options, which will motivate restaurants to expand their menus for health-conscious diners.

◆ Check out a restaurant's nutrient info on it's website.

◆ It's safe to assume that calorie counts will be more than you think—order less.

◆ Read books about dining out healthfully—a few are listed on page 393.

◆ There are many phone "apps" that have nutrient info for fast food.

The Urge to Splurge is Rampant

When I was growing up, eating out was a special occasion and a splurge. As restaurant eating has become an everyday way of life for many, the urge to splurge has stuck with it. This means more fat, saturated fat, trans fat, sodium and much fewer whole grains, fruits, vegetables and dairy products than we would have at home.

Sidestep

I urge you to change your attitude about eating out. Instead of splurging, take on the challenge of seeing how healthy you can eat, and then you'll have room for the occasional splurge!

Lack of Low-fat Dairy

In many restaurants, the only dairy in the house is high-fat cheese or whole milk.

Sidesteps

♦ While skim and low-fat milk is still pretty rare, 2% milk is becoming more available. Order it.

♦ Yogurt is also becoming more common. One of my favorites is the Fruit & Yogurt Parfait at McDonald's. Parfaits are also available at airports.

♦ Ice cream is a splurge, and not a great calcium source, unless it's low-fat! (On the other hand, ice cream has a lower Glycemic Index than low-fat ice cream.) That said, there are many options for low-fat and frozen yogurt—just watch the portion size as these options still contain lots of sugar.

♦ When cheese is an option, keep these fat contents in mind:

Cheese: Grams Fat per Ounce (30 g) (unless noted otherwise)	
American (1 slice 0.65 oz. 19 g)	4.5
American made with 2% milk: (1 slice 0.65 oz. 19 g)	2.5
Brie	8
Camembert	7
Cheddar	9
Cottage cheese, full-fat, ½ cup (125 ml)	4.5
Cottage cheese, low-fat	3
Cream cheese, 2 tablespoons	10
Cream cheese, low-fat, 2 tablespoons	5
Gjetost	8
Mozzarella, part skim milk	5
Mozzarella, whole milk	6
Monterey Jack or Muenster	8.5
Parmesan, grated, 5 tablespoons	7
Queso Asadero or Chihuahua	8
Provolone	7.5
Roquefort	9
Soft goat cheese	6
Swiss	8
Velveeta (Queso is sometimes made from this)	6

For eating advice about cheese see page 130.

Pre-Meal Appetizers

If restaurants served carrot sticks instead of chips before a meal, we'd all be thinner and healthier! Whether it's a basket of warm bread or chips and salsa, it's hard to resist temptation when it's right in front of you.

Sidesteps

♦ Say "no, gracias" to the chips when they bring them to the table—same for bread and other freebies, unless the offering is a veggie tray. Instead, order a cup of vegetable soup, a salad or other low-cal munchie. Or ask for a few whole grain crackers, not a whole basket.

♦ Instead, have a snack before eating out—a fruit, some raw veggies, or a cup of soup or hot decaf tea.

♦ Also say no thanks to the server who asks if you want to start with an appetizer, unless it's one of the above. Check out the calorie and fat contents of some popular restaurant appetizers that recently got the accolade as some of the Worst Foods in America by Men's Health Magazine[2]:

Outback Steakhouse Aussie Cheese Fries with Ranch Dressing	2,900 calories, 182 g fat, 240 g carbs
Chili's Awesome Blossom	2,710 calories, 203 g fat, 194 g carbs, 6,350 mg sodium
On the Border Stacked Nachos	2,740 calories, 166 g fat, 191 g carbs, 5,280 mg sodium

Saturated in Salt

While sodium needs increase during pregnancy, they are nowhere near the sodium contained in a typical fast-food meal. Having too much salt can affect blood pressure and swelling. Foods to watch out for—French fries, chips, salty condiments and extras like soy sauce, pickles or pickled veggies, ham, pepperoni, salad dressings, olives and sauces. Soups also tend to be loaded with salt. "Smoked" also mean salty.

Sidesteps

♦ Instead of using salt at the table, use a squeeze of lemon or lime which adds flavor as well as vitamin C to your meal. A squirt of lime in a vegetable soup really adds zip. Lemon on asparagus is also tasty.

♦ At Asian restaurants, ask that your food be prepared without soy sauce or MSG. Request low sodium soy sauce at the table.

Free Refills and Super-Size Drinks

Sure, you're getting great value for the money—just 50 cents more for double the size! But—what you save in cash goes to extra calories you don't need.

Sidesteps

◆ You'll save the most money if you stick with drinking water (a squeeze of lemon or lime adds so much!)

◆ If you're tempted by free refills (and who isn't), order something calorie-free— tea (ask for it to be watered down or dilute yourself at the self-serve to cut the caffeine) or sugar-free lemonade.

◆ If you've got to get the "real thing", order a small or kid's size—not "value" size—and order a glass of water with it.

◆ At restaurants where servers may automatically bring refills, tell them at the beginning that you don't want a second helping.

Dessert to Die For

If you're tempted by "Death by Chocolate" and other decadent favorites, keep in mind that a dessert could exceed your entire meal's calories!

Sidesteps

◆ Sharing is the best way to have your mousse and eat it too. Get one dessert for the table and pass it around. It's more fun that way and there's no guilt-to-go, either.

◆ Order a to-go box when you order dessert and immediately stash most of it there.

◆ Find a dessert that's fruit based (not the gloppy stuff that's squeezed between pie crusts!) I'm talking fresh berries with cream—light on the cream.

◆ Go with a single scoop of sorbet or ice cream—not the whole sundae.

At Your Favorite Type of Restaurant

Use these ideas to guide you the next time you eat out:

Breakfast

Tips

- Eggs are a great breakfast choice; poached will save you lots of fat—especially if you ask for no added butter or oil!

- Ask how many eggs are in that omelet—sometimes it's as many as four! If that's the case, ask for a smaller omelet or share.

- Choose beans—a common choice in the U.K. and Australia, and in Mexican restaurants in the U.S.

- Skip the skillet meals that have extra cheese and fat.

- Skip the juice; order a fresh fruit cup or half a grapefruit.

- Skip the biscuits.

- If you order pancakes or toast, ask that butter be served on the side, not on top.

- Choose whole grains when possible, but keep in mind that some bran and other muffins are loaded with fat.

- Scones—make them just an occasional splurge and go easy on the clotted cream!

Healthy Choices

- Vegetable omelet or frittata. Ask for low-fat cheese inside and salsa on the side to boost veggies. Shrimp & crab are good filling options.

- Huevos Rancheros—a good balance of protein, carb and veggie. Ask that the base tortillas be steamed, not fried. Ask for "easy on the cheese."

- Poached or scrambled eggs with whole grain toast or muffin.

- Breakfast sandwich with ham, egg and cheese.

- Oatmeal or muesli is a perfect choice. Pair it with a glass of milk for protein.

Deli

Tips

- Choose whole grain bread and ask for extra veggies. (Subway is great for that.)

- If you skip the cheese, you'll hardly miss it.

- Order a 6" (15 cm) or small instead of large sandwich. Or order just a half-sandwich. Get a salad or cup of veggie soup on the side. Subway has a great selection of low-fat soups.

- Skip the extra oil on the sandwich and choose low-fat sauces.

- Be cautious with tuna and chicken salads; they are sometimes loaded with fat.

- To skip the nitrates (and possibly the *listeria*) order a non-deli meat sandwich like an all veggie sandwich with cheese instead of deli meat, or a hot meat sandwich like steak or grilled chicken breast.

- Ask for avocado instead of mayo to boost monounsaturated fat.

Healthy Choices

- Chicken Breast Sandwich or Salad

- Steak Sandwich

- Veggie sandwich

- Tuna sandwich

- Minestrone or veggie soup as a side

Mexican

Tips

- Skip the chips; order beans OR rice, not both. Ask for side of veggies or salad instead.

- Beware of fried and cheesy entrees and appetizers (such as queso dip.)

- Choose corn tortillas instead of flour.

Healthy Choices

- Bean burritos

- Black beans

- Caldo de Pescado, Caldo de Res, or Caldo de Pollo (vegetable soups with either fish, beef or chicken)

- Tortilla soup (but skip the tortilla pieces and extra cheese)

- Grilled shrimp or fish tacos

- Fish, steak or shredded beef, and grilled chicken dishes are good choices

Italian

Tips

- Choose a salad or minestrone soup to start.

- Beware dishes stuffed with cheese or topped with creamy or buttery sauces.

- If pizza is an option, choose thin crust, vegetarian.

- Beware of meats and veggies which are breaded and fried first, like eggplant or chicken parmesan, veal saltimbocca, chicken or veal picatta.

Healthy Choices

- Shrimp or chicken pasta primavera

- Mussels—steamed or cooked in broth

- Angel hair pasta with clam sauce

- Vegetarian lasagna

- Any red-sauce based dish; ask that they go light on the cheese

Asian

While there are good choices at Asian restaurants, there are just as many bad ones.

Tips

♦ Miso soup is very healthy because the miso is made from fermented soybeans, which contain probiotics. But it can also be high in sodium.

♦ Avoid sashimi, which is always raw.

♦ Most broth soups are a good choice, but high in sodium.

♦ Choose meals with veggie/protein mixtures.

♦ Check out the dishes containing seafood and tofu.

♦ Beware of lo-mein—it can be super high in fat.

♦ Watch out for fried and crispy menu options—won tons, egg rolls, cashew chicken, crispy noodles, deep-fried, coconut-crusted.

♦ Sweet and sour offers the worst dietary choice—deep-fried chicken, shrimp or pork, topped with a sweet sauce packed with artificial colors!

♦ Choose Asian restaurants that are willing to change how they prepare the food. For example, at Pei Wei, you can have it made exactly to your liking!

Healthy Choices

♦ Lettuce wraps

♦ Shrimp, chicken or Beef and Broccoli or any other meat/veggie combo

♦ "Bowls" which are one dish meals with meats, noodles and veggies

♦ Rice Paper or Vietnamese Spring/salad Rolls—they aren't fried

♦ Sushi made with cooked seafood such as California Rolls

♦ Cabbage slaw

♦ Pad Thai

♦ Thai Beef Salad

Middle Eastern

Tips

♦ There are many healthy options to choose from. If you order hummus or Baba Ganoush, ask that it not be garnished with extra oil. Although it's healthy olive oil, you still don't want to have too much. Hummus and Baba Ganoush contain a super nutrient-rich ingredient—sesame seed paste (tahini.)

♦ Ask for raw veggies with hummus and other dips to avoid eating too much pita bread.

♦ Olives are healthy but very salty, so eat in moderation.

♦ While falafel is vegetarian, keep in mind that the chickpea-based balls are fried.

♦ For dishes with feta cheese, ask if the cheese is made from pasteurized milk.

Healthy Choices

♦ Lentil soup

♦ Fasolia (Greek baked beans)

♦ Tabouli salad

♦ Baba Ganoush

♦ Tomato and cucumber salad

♦ Eggplant-tomato salad

♦ Hummus

♦ Yogurt salad

♦ Kafta

♦ Chicken shawarma or shish taouk

♦ Kababs

♦ Vegetable tagine

Indian

Tips

♦ Curries may contain a lot of oil but are rich in antioxidant-rich spices like turmeric and cumin. Watch portion size and make sure other foods you order are low in fat.

♦ Order more grilled dishes like kebabs or tikka (these dishes are without curry and dry—less oil is used to make them.)

♦ Ask about ghee (clarified butter) or coconut oil, which may be used in some food prep or added at the end. Ask to skip it or for another oil to be used.

♦ If ordering a vegetable dish request that it be made with less oil.

♦ Skip the naan, which is made from refined white flour.

♦ Eat whole grain breads instead of rice. If eating rice, then practice portion control. Try to have more vegetables and less rice.

♦ Ask for salad with the dishes; they will bring you lettuce, onion, tomato and some cucumber.

♦ Lentils are a good dish to order and usually will be called "daal" on the menu.

Healthy Choices

♦ Tandoori dishes

♦ Chicken tikka

♦ Kebabs

♦ Gobhi Matar Tamatar (cauliflower, peas and tomatoes)

♦ Sabzi dish (vegetable dish)

♦ Bread choices which are usually whole grain: Chapatti, Roti—however avoid if soaked in fat.

♦ Pappadam bread—made with lentils

♦ Salad

♦ Lentils or daal

Thanks to Madiha Ahmad MS for her contribution to this section.

Continental/Fusion Cuisine

More upscale restaurants offer some healthy but also very rich choices. They are more likely to accommodate specific dietary requests and cater to not-on-the-menu food combinations. You also may find more whole grains like quinoa, millet, brown rice and vegetable side dishes. The fancier the place, the more likely the chef may be willing to whip up something special for you!

Menu Watch

These terms should be red flags to ask more questions:

♦ Au gratin

♦ Batter-fried / pan-fried

♦ Bisque or chowder—indicates soup made with heavy cream

♦ Buttered / creamed

♦ Casserole—sometimes made with a sauce or cheese

♦ Crispy / coated / breaded

♦ Scalloped / Escalloped—often in a cream sauce with buttery crumbs on top

♦ Hollandaise, mornay, remoulade, béarnaise—all creamy sauces

♦ Smothered

♦ Stroganoff

Instead look for these terms:

♦ En Papillote (generally steamed in parchment paper or other natural packaging like a lotus leaf)

♦ En-brochette—means "on a skewer" and usually includes vegetables

♦ Grilled

♦ Poached

♦ Roasted

♦ Steamed

♦ Stewed

♦ Stir-fried

Healthy Choices

◆ Gazpacho, or broth soup

◆ Steamed shellfish or scallops

◆ Tenderloin of beef or pork

◆ Blackened, grilled or poached, steamed fish, chicken, meat, etc.

◆ These types of sauces are usually healthy: Reductions and coulis (usually fruit or vegetable based)

◆ Tomato or fruit based sauces or salsas

Get a Healthier Meal, Just by Asking

Much to the embarrassment of the rest of my family, I **always** ask a lot of questions about how food is prepared and follow them with polite requests about how I would **like** it prepared. I think Meg Ryan said it best when she ordered pie in the movie "When Harry Met Sally."

My take on this—you should get what you want (and NOT what you don't want!) when you're paying for it! Just remember to tip nicely for the extra trouble!

Questions to Ask

First, find out how the food is prepared:

◆ Is that fried or grilled? Is it deep-fried or pan-fried?

◆ If fried can I get it grilled instead?

◆ Is there cream in that soup? Is it just a little or is it a lot?

◆ Is there sauce on the entrée? What's the sauce made of?

◆ Do you put any extra oil or butter on after it's cooked?

◆ Is there whipped cream on that?

◆ How much oil is it cooked with?

◆ Is the dish made with soy sauce or MSG?

◆ Is salt added to the food during cooking? Or at the end of preparation?

Eat Out Healthy by Dr. Jo Lichten, PhD, RD

Eating healthy during pregnancy is important, but that doesn't mean you can't eat out at a restaurant—even fast food restaurants. There are plenty of healthful options when dining out when you keep these tips in mind:

◆ Split a meal with a friend. Most restaurants entrees contain more than 1,000 calories—way more than most women need, even when they're eating for two.

◆ Request veggies and/or fruits. Most restaurants have fruits and vegetables available, even if they're not on the menu. These might include a fruit cup, sliced tomatoes, mini carrots, or a salad. Ask!

◆ Get dressings, butters, and sauces on the side. These extras can often double the calories of a meal. Get them on the side so you can practice "dip 'n stab"— dip your fork into the dressing or sauce, then into the food so you get great taste with every bite.

◆ Full nutritional information is often available at most restaurants' websites.

◆ Here are my "Go-To" Menu Items:

Applebee's:
◆ Weight Watchers or "Under 500 calorie" entrees
Boston Market:
◆ Roasted Turkey Breast or Skinless Chicken Breast
◆ Fresh Steamed Vegetables, Green Beans, and New Potatoes
Burger King:
◆ Veggie Burger, no mayo
◆ Whopper Jr., no mayo
Chick-Fil-A:
◆ Yogurt Parfait with granola
◆ Multigrain Oatmeal
◆ Chargrilled Chicken Sandwich
◆ Cool Wraps (skip the dressing)
Chili's:
◆ Guiltless Grills including sirloin, chicken sandwiches, wraps, and salads
Chipotle Mexican Grill:
◆ Naked Chicken Burrito on top of lettuce (with beans, guacamole and pico de gallo)
Denny's:
◆ Fit Fare menu items including eggs, chicken and fish dishes

McDonald's:
- ◆ Egg McMuffin
- ◆ Fruit 'n Yogurt Parfait with granola
- ◆ Oatmeal
- ◆ Premium Grilled Chicken Sandwich

Starbucks:
- ◆ Perfect Oatmeal
- ◆ Bistro Box including Chicken & Hummus or Chipotle Chicken Wraps

Subway:
- ◆ Double meat sub (turkey, ham or roast beef) on six inch (15 cm) 9 grain wheat bread. Ask for it to be heated. Skip the oil and mayo.

Taco Bell:
Fresco-style Bean Burrito or Taco (crunchy or soft)

Wendy's:
- ◆ Plain Baked Potato topped with small Chili (without cheese)
- ◆ Half portion Grilled Chicken Salad (get the dressing on the side and use sparingly)
- ◆ Ultimate Chicken Grill Sandwich

Joanne Lichten PhD, RD (a.k.a. "Dr. Jo"), America's On-The-Go Health Guru, is an accomplished author, speaker, freelance writer and media spokesperson who inspires busy people to stay healthy, sane, and productive. Her latest book, *Eat Out Healthy* (2012) is the complete handbook for health conscious individuals who enjoy eating out. Find it and other books at www.drjo.com

Choosing Nutritious Fast Foods

You can't make an informed decision about your fast-food choices simply by looking at the menu—you need to find the nutrition information. This is available on fast-food chains' websites, mobile phone "apps" and are sometimes posted at the restaurant. You can also find nutrition information for many fast food and other restaurants at www.calorieking.com and at www.nutritiondata.com

Check Out Your Favorite Fast Foods on the Web!
- ◆ www.arbys.com
- ◆ www.carlsjr.com
- ◆ www.mcdonalds.com
- ◆ www.tacobell.com
- ◆ www.burgerking.com
- ◆ www.dominos.com
- ◆ www.pizzahut.com
- ◆ www.tcby.com

Chipotle: Food Made with Integrity

At a conference a few years ago, I heard a Chipotle executive explain the restaurant's commitment to using more natural and sustainable foods. Each time they added new locations, they signed on another family farm to provide naturally-raised pork. They built sustainability while building their burrito empire. Impressive. Other examples of building a more natural food culture at Chipotle[3]:

♦ Whenever possible, they use meat from animals raised without the use of antibiotics or added hormones.

♦ They use organic and local produce when practical. In 2012, 40% of the beans used were organic.

♦ They use dairy from cows raised without the use of synthetic hormones.

♦ They support family farms that respect the land and the animals in their care.

Recommended books on the topic:

Eat Out Healthy, How to Eat Healthy When You're Not at Home and *How to Stay Healthy & Fit On the Road The Ultimate Health Guide for Road Warriors* by Dr. Joanne Lichten. Check out her newsletter and other books at www.drjo.com

"Clean" Fast Food? Not Really

This book suggests you eat "cleaner and greener." You may be wondering what fast food is doing here? The truth is, fast food doesn't really fit into the "cleaner and greener" model of eating. Reality check: sometimes fast food is better than no food, and, well, sometimes, mama's just gotta have her burger!

Typical fast food is very processed and usually has many preservatives and lots of sodium. However, there is a growing sustainability and health movement among restaurants. See sidebar about a leader in this area—Chipotle. Among the fast food chains, McDonald's has pledged to reduce sodium across their menu board, has already reduced sodium in all chicken items and plans to offer more seasonal fruits and vegetables. It's a great start and other chains should be following their lead.

Fast food has been offering some healthy options like grilled chicken sandwiches for a long while, but consumers don't always follow through with ordering them, leading to them being taken off the menu. Some healthy choices that are readily available: Fruit 'N Yogurt Parfait, Fruit and Walnuts Salad, Mango-Pineapple Smoothie at McDonald's, oatmeal at both Burger King and McDonald's and baked potatoes and Chili at Wendy's. A veggie burger is available at Burger King and at many fast food restaurants outside the US. Subway has been on the healthy bandwagon for a long time—offering low-fat mayo, low-fat deli meats, whole grain breads, baked chips, yogurt parfait, broth-based veggie soups and apple slices. The bottom line: there are plenty of unhealthy food choices when eating fast, but there are plenty of good ones, too (check a food's ingredient list for additives). And even if you do make a less-than-healthy choice, just don't do it too often!

Tips for Making Fast-Food Meals More Nutritious

- Remember that having a food high in vitamin C with your meal will increase the amount of iron your body absorbs. Drink orange juice; eat a salad with high-in-C veggies, like tomatoes, broccoli or cauliflower; choose fresh fruit or vegetables from the salad bar.

- When given the choice of cheese, ask for Swiss or part-skim mozzarella.

- Bring along fresh fruit or vegetables to go with your meal (or eat one before you get there) or order a side salad.

- If you are trying to keep your weight-gain down, choose lower-calorie fare such as grilled chicken/fish or bean burritos.

- Skip the additional toppings such as cheese or sour cream, but do choose guacamole or avocado instead of mayonnaise when available.

- Choose low-calorie or fat-free salad dressings.

- If you have trouble with heartburn, avoid French fries, burgers, fried pies, and other fried and greasy foods.

- Remember that sandwiches with deli meats should be eaten only if heated, and cold salads from delis should be avoided.

Last-Minute Meals from What's in the Pantry

We're most tempted to eat out when we feel there's nothing on hand to eat or no time to cook. How many times have you come home from work, looked in your refrigerator and exclaimed, "There's nothing to eat!" You may have forgotten to look in the pantry, which is sometimes overlooked but contains a smorgasbord of meal ideas. From a well-stocked pantry, freezer (and a few cheeses) you can make many main dishes!

Ingredients to Keep on Hand

- Pasta (dry and frozen cheese ravioli)

- Marinara sauce

- Pizza crust, pita bread or French bread

- Cooked shrimp

- Leftover or canned chicken

- Canned or jarred mushrooms, artichoke hearts, olives, asparagus

- Roasted red peppers

- Low sodium mushroom soup

- Evaporated milk

- Mozzarella, Parmesan, cream cheese, cottage cheese

- Salmon

- Bread crumbs

- Lemon juice

- Olive oil

- Vegetarian refried beans

- Bulgur wheat or whole grain couscous

- Corn

- Canned tomatoes

- Black or kidney beans

- Chickpeas

- Pineapple tidbits

- Fresh potatoes

- Tofu

- Frozen vegetables

Main Dishes that Can be Made

(Some of these can be found in the *Eating Expectantly Cookbook*)

- Angel hair with shrimp and marinara sauce

- Ravioli with creamy mushroom sauce

- Chicken and asparagus over whole grain couscous
- Chicken tetrazzini
- Breadcrumb topped shrimp over angel hair with lemon and capers
- Pizza with artichoke hearts, red peppers and olives
- Shrimp with roasted red pepper sauce
- Vegetarian lasagna (with tofu)
- Layered cheesy pasta bake
- Fettuccine Alfredo
- Tuna casserole
- Tuna salad
- Tuna "ceviche" salad
- Baked Tomato and bulgur wheat with chicken and beans
- Bulgur wheat salad with chick peas, olives and lemon
- Chicken salad
- Bean tostadas
- Chicken tostadas
- Mexican tofu tostadas
- Chicken salad with pineapple
- Baked potatoes with chicken topping
- Italian potato "nachos"
- Shrimp and potato chowder
- Black Bean and Corn Salad
- Vegetarian chili
- Black bean soup
- Black bean and chicken stew
- Hoppin' John

Choosing Frozen Meal Options

Convenience foods such as frozen dinners are becoming more and more popular. Some are better than others. Consider these questions when choosing frozen meals:

♦ Does the product provide a balanced meal (including protein, starch, and vegetable and/or fruit)? If not, add a fruit and/or vegetable and dairy serving.

♦ How much fat does the product contain? Look for no more than about 10 grams of fat per 300 calories.

♦ What is the sodium content? More than 500 milligrams per serving could be excessive.

♦ Is the product a good value? One often pays for convenience. When checking the price of a convenience food, make sure to consider the cost of ingredients that you add, such as chicken or tuna.

♦ Does the product contain a lot of additives and preservatives? One benefit of frozen foods is it doesn't *have* to have preservatives. Even so, some still do.

♦ Reading nutrition labels can help you pick the healthiest meals. By studying labels, you can pick meals with lower fat, lower sodium, fewer additives, or more vitamin C. Scanning the percentage of vitamins A and C at the bottom of a label can help you determine the amount and quality of fruits and vegetables in a meal.

> For a list of 20 top choices of healthy frozen dinners (with less than 600 mg of sodium) from Kathleen Zelman MPH, RD and WebMD: www.webmd.com/diet/features/top-12-healthy-frozen-dinners.

Watching Your Sodium

You can decrease your daily sodium intake by limiting canned or convenience foods to a few times a week; also try to eat plenty of potassium-rich foods to balance out the sodium. If you had hypertension or kidney disease before you became pregnant, (or if it appeared during your pregnancy) your health care provider may ask you to moderate your salt intake. It will be important for you to read food labels for sodium content. (See page 259 for more information about sodium recommendations during pregnancy.)

Look for frozen meals that contain no more than 500 milligrams of sodium. That's much less than regular frozen dinners, which can contain as many as 1,200 milligrams of sodium per serving. Canned soups and stews are also notorious for being high in sodium. Two exceptions are Healthy Choice and Campbell's Select

Soups. Amy's Organics has a line of "Lighter in Sodium" products that include soups, sauces and frozen entrees that have 340 mg of sodium—or less. An easy way to spot an item that is lower in sodium—look for one labeled "healthy"—it must contain 480 mg or less of sodium or "reduced sodium" which must have at least 25% less sodium than a reference food. To make a low sodium claim, a food has to contain 140 mg per typical serving—but this level of sodium is difficult to meet in frozen dinners and canned foods. For more labeling information info, see page 346.

Going Meatless?

If you prefer meatless meals, Cascadian Farms and Amy's brands are both meatless and organic.

Meal Starters

These offer yet another choice for a quick, nutritious meal; they can be prepared in the microwave or on the stove top. Some include meat or chicken, such as Tyson Fajita Kit and Bertolli Meal Starter. Others, like Green Giant Create-A-Meal and Birds Eye Meal Starter, don't, so you can choose whether to add chicken, shrimp, or beef or soy crumbles. One benefit of meal starters is that if you cook them as little as possible, the vegetables will retain more vitamins. Many of these meals are especially nutritious because they include a lot of vegetables.

Budget Frozen Food

Pot Pies, Frozen Pizza, Fried Chicken, Chicken Nuggets, Fish Sticks are cheaper than other frozen dinners, but they get 50 percent or more of their calories from fat. However, many "light" versions of these foods are now available. These are better (but more expensive) choices. If you choose these, just don't make a regular habit of it. And watch out for indigestion due to their high fat content.

Burritos and Pocket Sandwiches

These foods are often less expensive than other convenience foods, but they are missing the vegetables. I recently spotted some frozen organic bean burritos at my local Costco—a great find! As with other convenience foods, check the label for fat and sodium, and choose light versions when available. Make sure to add some fruit and vegetables and milk to make a balanced meal.

End Note

I hope you've enjoyed reading *Eating Expectantly*. If you have, please, let others know via amazon.com. You can send your comments to EatingExpectantly@gmail.com.

REFERENCES

Chapter 1
Contemplating Pregnancy

1.   CDC/AATSDR Preconception Care Work Group and the Select Panel on Preconception Care. Recommendations to improve preconception health and health care—United States. MMWR 2006: Apr; 55(RR06);1-23. [Cited 14-Dec-12]. Available from: http://www.cdc.gov/mmwr/preview/mmwrhtml/rr5506a1.htm

2.   Murphy V, Namazy J, Powell H, Schatz M, Chambers C, Attia J, et al. A meta-analysis of adverse perinatal outcomes in women with asthma. BJOG 2011;118:1314-1323. [Cited 16-Oct-11]. Available from: http://www.ncbi.nlm.nih.gov/pubmed/21749633

3.   Centers for Disease Control & Prevention [Preconception Care Questions and Health Care.] May 2012. [Cited 14-Dec-12]. Available from: http://www.cdc.gov/preconception/planning.html

4.   Centers for Disease Control & Prevention [Preconception Care Questions and Health Care.] May 2012. [Cited 14-Dec-12]. Available from: http://www.cdc.gov/preconception/planning.html

5.   Ismail-Beigi F, Catalano PM, Hanson RW. Metabolic programming: fetal origins of obesity and metabolic syndrome in the adult. Am J Physiol Endocrinol Metab. 2006 Sep;291(3):E439-40.

6.   Barker DJP. Mothers, babies and health in later life. Edinburgh: Churchill Livingstone 1998.

7.   Vignini A, Raffaelli F, Cester A, Iannilli A, Cherubini V, Mazzanti L, Nanetti L. Environmental and genetical aspects of the link between pregnancy, birth size, and type 2 diabetes. Curr Diabetes Rev. 2012 May;8(3):155-61.

SCAN HERE FOR   REFERENCE UPDATES

8.　　Calkins K, Devaskar SU. Fetal origins of adult disease. Curr Probl Pediatr Adolesc Health Care. 2011 Jul;41(6):158-76.

9.　　Dyer JS, Rosenfeld CR. Metabolic imprinting by prenatal, perinatal, and postnatal overnutrition: a review. Semin Reprod Med. 2011 May;29(3):266-76.

10.　　Boney CM, Verma A, Tucker R, Vohr BR. Metabolic syndrome in childhood: association with birth weight, maternal obesity, and gestational diabetes mellitus. Pediatrics. 2005 Mar;115(3):e290-6.

11.　　Ovesen P, Rasmussen S, Kesmodel U. Effect of pre-pregnancy maternal overweight and obesity on pregnancy outcome. Obstet Gynecol. 2011 Aug;118(2 Pt 1):305-12.

12.　　Boney CM, Verma A, Tucker R, Vohr BR. Metabolic syndrome in childhood: association with birth weight, maternal obesity, and gestational diabetes mellitus. Pediatrics. 2005 Mar;115(3):e290-6.

13.　　Mandal D, Manda S, Rakshi A, Dey RP, Biswas SC, Banerjee A. Maternal obesity and pregnancy outcome: a prospective analysis. J Assoc Physicians India. 2011 Aug;59:486-9.

14.　　Ovesen P, Rasmussen S, Kesmodel U. Effect of pre-pregnancy maternal overweight and obesity on pregnancy outcome. Obstet Gynecol. 2011 Aug;118(2 Pt 1):305-12.

15.　　Hobbs CA, Cleves MA, Karim MA, Zhao W, MacLeod SL. Maternal folate-related gene environment interactions and congenital heart defects. Obstet Gynecol. 2010 Aug;116(2 Pt 1):316-22.

16.　　Oken E, Taveras EM, Kleinman KP, Rich-Edwards JW, Gillman MW. Gestational weight gain and child adiposity at age 3 years. Am J Obstet Gynecol. 2007 Apr;196(4):322.e1-8.

17.　　Gale CR, Javaid MK, Robinson SM, Law CM, Godfrey KM, Cooper C. Maternal size in pregnancy and body composition in children. J Clin Endocrinol Metab. 2007 Oct;92(10):3904-11.

18.　　Vickers MH. Developmental programming of the metabolic syndrome - critical windows for intervention. World J Diabetes. 2011 September 15;2(9): 137–148.

19.　　U.S. Department of Health and Human Services. 2008 Physical Activity Guidelines for Americans. Washington (DC): U.S. Department of Health and Human Services; 2008. Office of Disease Prevention and Health Promotion Publication No. U0036. Available from: http://www.health.gov/paguidelines

20.　　Ramadhani MK, Grobbee DE, Bots ML, Castro Cabezas M, Vos LE, Oren A, et al. Lower birth weight predicts metabolic syndrome in young adults: the Atherosclerosis Risk in Young Adults (ARYA)-study. Atherosclerosis. 2006 Jan;184(1):21-7.

21.　　Bihl GR. Intrauterine growth and disease in later life. Highlights from the 9th Asian congress of nephrology. February 2003. Available from: http://www.medscape.com/viewarticle/453242

22.   Barker DJ. Fetal origins of coronary heart disease. BMJ. 1995 July;311:171–174. http://www.bmj.com/content/311/6998/171?ijkey=2997c5e1ebf782339057289d2fbc426b040b0ae5&keytype2=tf_ipsecsha

23.   Briana DD, Malamitsi-Puchner A. Intrauterine growth restriction and adult disease: the role of adipocytokines. Eur J Endocrinol. 2009 Mar;160(3):337-47.

24.   Grotto D, Zied E. The Standard American Diet and its relationship to the health status of Americans. Nutr Clin Pract. 2010 Dec;25(6):603-12.

25.   Office on women's health. US Department of Health and Human Services. Women on track with health screenings; healthy eating and exercise lacking. May 2007. [Cited 4-Oct-07]. Available from: http://www.womenshealth.gov/news/pr/2007.NWHW.htm

26.   What We Eat in America, NHANES 2007-2008, Day 1 dietary intake data, weighted; MyPyramid Food Intake Patterns. [Cited 6-Nov-11]. Available from: http://www.mypyramid.gov/downloads/MyPyramid_Food_Intake_Patterns.pdf

27.   Leung BM, Kaplan BJ. Perinatal depression: prevalence, risks, and the nutrition link—a review of the literature. J Am Diet Assoc. 2009 Sep;109(9):1566-75.

28.   Knudsen VK, Orozova-Bekkevold IM, Mikkelsen TB, Wolff S, Olsen SF. Major dietary patterns in pregnancy and fetal growth. Eur J Clin Nutr. 2008 Apr;62(4):463-70.

29.   Shaw GM, Carmichael SL, Yang W, Selvin S, Schaffer DM. Periconceptional dietary intake of choline and betaine and neural tube defects in offspring. Am J Epidemiol. 2004 Jul 15;160(2):102-9.

30.   Crider KS, Bailey LB, Berry RJ. Folic acid food fortification-its history, effect, concerns, and future directions. Nutrients. 2011 Mar;3(3):370-84.

31.   Tinker SC, Cogswell ME, Devine O, Berry RJ. Folic acid intake among U.S. women aged 15-44 years, National Health and Nutrition Examination Survey, 2003-2006. Am J Prev Med. 2010 May;38(5):534-42.

32.   Shiraishi M, Haruna M, Matsuzaki M, Ota E, Murayama R, Murashima S. Association between the serum folate levels and tea consumption during pregnancy. Biosci Trends. 2010 Oct;4(5):225-30.

33.   Allan K, Devereux G. Diet and asthma: nutrition implications from prevention to treatment. J Am Diet Assoc. 2011 Feb;111(2):258-68.

34.   Alwan NA, Greenwood, DC, Simpson, NA, McArdle HJ, Godfrey KM, Cade JE. Dietary iron during early pregnancy and birth outcomes in a cohort of British women. Hum Reprod. 2011 April;26(4): 911–9.

35.   Casanueva E, Viteri FE. Iron and oxidative stress in pregnancy. J Nutr. 2003 May;133(5 Suppl 2):1700S-1708S.

36.   Leung BM, Kaplan BJ. Perinatal depression: prevalence, risks, and the nutrition link—a review of the literature. J Am Diet Assoc. 2009 Sep;109(9):1566-75.

37.   Depression and Pregnancy. Office of Teratology Information Specialists. January 2011. [Cited 5-Nov-11]. Available from: http://www.otispregnancy.org/otis-fact-sheets-s13037#4

38.   Diabetes and Pregnancy. Office of Teratology Information Specialists. April 2011. [Cited 5-Nov-11]. Available from: http://www.otispregnancy.org/otis-fact-sheets-s13037#4

39.   Ziegler O, Sirveaux MA, Brunaud L, Reibel N, Quilliot D. Medical follow up after bariatric surgery: nutritional and drug issues. General recommendations for the prevention and treatment of nutritional deficiencies. Diabetes Metab. 2009 Dec;35(6 Pt 2):544-57.

40.   Okun ML, Schetter CD, Glynn LM. Poor sleep quality is associated with preterm birth. Sleep. 2011 Nov 1;34(11):1493-8.

41.   Organization of Teratology Specialists. Alcohol and Pregnancy. September 2010. [Cited 12-Nov-11]. Available from: http://www.otispregnancy.org/otis-fact-sheets-s13037#6

42.   von Kries R, Bolte G, Baghi L, Toschke AM; GME Study Group. Parental smoking and childhood obesity—is maternal smoking in pregnancy the critical exposure? Int J Epidemiol. 2008 Feb;37(1):210-6.

43.   Salmasi G, Grady R, Jones J, McDonald SD; Knowledge Synthesis Group. Environmental tobacco smoke exposure and perinatal outcomes: a systematic review and meta-analyses. Acta Obstet Gynecol Scand. 2010;89(4):423-41.

44.   March of Dimes. Smoking During Pregnancy. April 2010. [Cited 13-Nov-11]. Available from: http://www.marchofdimes.com/pregnancy/alcohol_smoking.html

45.   Cohen LS, Altshuler LL, Harlow BL, Nonacs R, Newport DJ, Viguera AC, et al. Relapse of major depression during pregnancy in women who maintain or discontinue antidepressant treatment. JAMA. 2006 Feb 1;295(5):499-507. Erratum in: JAMA. 2006 Jul 12;296(2):170.

46.   European Society of Human Reproduction and Embryology (ESHRE) (2011, July 5). Gum disease can increase the time it takes to become pregnant. ScienceDaily. [Cited 30-Jun-12]. Available from: http://www.sciencedaily.com/releases/2011/07/110705071548.htm

47.   Boggess KA, Edelstein BL. Oral health in women during preconception and pregnancy: implications for birth outcomes and infant oral health. Matern Child Health J. 2006 Sep;10(5 Suppl):S169-74.

48.   Chavarro JE, Rich-Edwards JW, Rosner BA, Willett WC. Use of multivitamins, intake of B vitamins, and risk of ovulatory infertility. Fertil Steril. 2008 Mar;89(3):668-76.

49.   Jung A, Strauss P, Lindner HJ, Schuppe HC. Influence of heating car seats on scrotal temperature. Fertil Steril. 2008 Aug;90(2):335-9. Epub 2007 Oct 24.

50.   Ivell R. Lifestyle impact and the biology of the human scrotum. Reprod Biol Endocrinol. 2007 Apr 20;5: 15.

51.   Moretti ME, Bar-Oz B, Fried S, Koren G. Maternal hyperthermia and the risk for neural tube defects in offspring: systematic review and meta-analysis. Epidemiology. 2005 Mar;16(2):216-9.

52.   Suarez L, Felkner M, Hendricks K. The effect of fever, febrile illnesses, and heat exposures on the risk of neural tube defects in a Texas-Mexico border population. Birth Defects Res A Clin Mol Teratol. 2004 Oct;70(10):815-9.

53.   Nestler JE, Jakubowicz DJ, Reamer P, Gunn RD, Allan G. Ovulatory and metabolic effects of D-chiro-inositol in the polycystic ovary syndrome. N Engl J Med. 1999 Apr 29;340(17):1314-20.

54.   Iuorno MJ, Jakubowicz DJ, Baillargeon JP, Dillon P, Gunn RD, Allan G, et al. Effects of d-chiro-inositol in lean women with the polycystic ovary syndrome. Endocr Pract. 2002 Nov-Dec;8(6):417-23.

55.   Anderson J. Nutrition and oral contraceptives. December 2010. [Cited 22-Nov-11]. Available from: http://www.ext.colostate.edu/pubs/foodnut/09323.html

56.   Mahmud M, Mazza D. Preconception care of women with diabetes: a review of current guideline recommendations. BMC Women's Health. 2010 Jan 31;10:5. [Cited 20-Nov-11]. Available from: http://www.biomedcentral.com/1472-6874/10/5

Chapter 2
Fueling Your Fertility

1.   Society for Reproductive Medicine. Weight [Cited 13-Nov-11] Available from: http://www.reproductivefacts.org/topics/detail.aspx?id=1763

2.   Beyene J, Han Z, Liao G, Mulla S, McDonald SD; Knowledge Synthesis Group. Maternal underweight and the risk of preterm birth and low birth weight: a systematic review and meta-analyses. Int J Epidemiol. 2011 Feb;40(1):65-101.

3.   Nohr EA, Vaeth M, Rasmussen S, Ramlau-Hansen CH, Olsen J. Waiting time to pregnancy according to maternal birthweight and prepregnancy BMI. Hum Reprod. 2009 Jan;24(1):226-32.

4.   Position of the American Dietetic Association and American Society for Nutrition. Obesity, reproduction and pregnancy outcomes. J Am Diet Assoc. 2009;109:918-927.

5.   Position of the American Dietetic Association and American Society for Nutrition. Obesity, reproduction and pregnancy outcomes. J Am Diet Assoc. 2009;109:918-927.

6.   Clark AM, Ledger W, Galletly C, Tomlinson L, Blaney F, Wang X, et al. Weight loss results in significant improvement in pregnancy and ovulation rates in anovulatory obese women. Hum Reprod. 1995 Oct;10(10):2705-12.

7.   Ramlau-Hansen CH, Thulstrup AM, Nohr EA, Bonde JP, Sørensen TI, Olsen J. Subfecundity in overweight and obese couples. Hum Reprod. 2007 Jun;22(6):1634-7.

8.　　　Chavarro JE, Toth TL, Wright DL, Meeker JD, Hauser R. Body mass index in relation to semen quality, sperm DNA integrity, and serum reproductive hormone levels among men attending an infertility clinic. Fertil Steril. 2010 May 1;93 (7):2222-31.

9.　　　Kay VJ, Barratt CLR. Male obesity: impact on fertility. British Journal of Diabetes & Vascular Disease 2009 Sept/Oct;9(5): 237-241.

10.　　　Grassi A. The Dietitian's Guide to Polycistic Ovary Syndrome. Luca Publishing. Haverford PA. 2007.

11.　　　Brand-Miller J, Colagiui, S, Foster-Powell K, and Wolever, TM. The New Glucose Revolution, 3rd edition, Marlowe & Company. New York. 2007. p. 121.

12.　　　Agrassi A. Obstructive sleep apnea and PCOS.[Cited 14-Dec-12]. Available from: http://www.pcosnutrition.com/links/blogs/obstructive-sleep-apnea-and-pcos.html

13.　　　Farrell K, Antoni M. Insulin resistance, obesity, inflammation and depression in polycystic ovary syndrome: biobehavioral mechanisms and interventions. Fertil Steril. 2010 October;94(5): 1565–1574.

14.　　　Chavarro JE, Rich-Edwards JW, Rosner BA, Willett WC. Caffeinated and alcoholic beverage intake in relation to ovulatory disorder infertility. Epidemiology. 2009 May;20(3):374-81.

15.　　　Hackney AC. Effects of endurance exercise on the reproductive system of men: the "exercise-hypogonadal male condition". J Endocrinol Invest. 2008 Oct;31(10):932-8.

16.　　　Melo MA, Soares SR. Cigarette smoking and reproductive function. Curr Opin Obstet Gynecol. 2008 Jun;20(3):281-91.

17.　　　American Society for Reproductive Medicine. Smoking and Infertility. 11/2003 [Cited 25-Nov-11]. Available from: http://www.asrm.org/FactSheetsandBooklets/

18.　　　Marchetti F, Rowan-Carroll A, Williams A, Polyzos A, Berndt-Weis M, Yauk C. Side stream tobacco smoke is a male germ cell mutagen. Proceedings of the National Academy of Sciences. Available from: http://www.pnas.org/cgi/doi/10.1073/pnas.1106896108

19.　　　Elizabeth H. Ruder, Terryl J. Hartman, Jeffrey Blumberg, Marlene B. Goldman. Hum Reprod Update. 2008 Jul-Aug;14(4):345-57.

20.　　　Fasano A, Berti I, Gerarduzzi T, Not T, Colletti RB, Drago S, et al. Prevalence of celiac disease in at-risk and not-at-risk groups in the United States: a large multicenter study. Arch Intern Med. 2003 Feb 10;163(3):286-92.

21.　　　Green PHR, Stavropoulos SN, Panagi SG, Goldstein SL, Mcmahon DJ, Absan H, et al.Characteristics of adult celiac disease in the USA: results of a national survey. Am J Gastroenterol. 2001 Jan;96(1):126-31.

22.　　　"Celiac Disease." National Digestive Diseases Information Claring House. [Cited 3-Dec-11] Available from: http://digestive.niddk.nih.gov/ddiseases/pubs/celiac/#what

23.   Ladenson PW, Singer PA, Ain KB, Bagchi N, Bigos ST, Levy EG, et al. American Thyroid Association guidelines for detection of thyroid dysfunction. Arch Intern Med. 2000 Jun 12;160(11):1573-5.

24.   Jana SK, K NB, Chattopadhyay R, Chakravarty B, Chaudhury K.Upper control limit of reactive oxygen species in follicular fluid beyond which viable embryo formation is not favorable. Reprod Toxicol. 2010 Jul;29(4):447-51.

25.   Agarwal A, Gupta S and Sharma RK. Role of oxidative stress in female reproduction. Reproductive biology and endocrinology. 2005 July14;(3):28.

26.   Galan P, Viteri FE, Bertrais S, Czernichow S, Faure H, Arnaud J, et al. Serum concentrations of beta-carotene, vitamin C and E, zinc, and selenium are influenced by age, diet smoking status, alcohol consumption and corpulence in a general French adult population. Eur J Clin Nutr 2005 Oct;59(10): 1181-1190.

27.   Ebisch IM, Thomas CM, Peters WH, Braat DD, Steegers-Theunissen RP. The importance of folate, zinc and antioxidants in the pathogenesis and prevention of sub fertility. Human Reproductive Update 2007 Mar-April;13(2):163-174. Review.

28.   Gharagozloo P, Aitken RJ. The role of sperm oxidative stress in male infertility and the significance of oral antioxidant therapy. Hum Reprod. 2011 Jul;26(7):1628-40.

29.   Schmid TE, Eskenazi B, Marchetti F, Young S, Weldon RH, Baumgartner A, Anderson D, Wyrobek AJ. Fertil Steril. Micronutrients intake is associated with improved sperm DNA quality in older men. 2012 Nov;98(5):1130-1137.e1. doi: 10.1016/j.fertnstert.2012.07.1126. Epub 2012 Aug 27.

30.   Carlsen MH et al. The total antioxidant content of more than 3100 foods, beverages, spices, herbs and supplements used worldwide. Nutrition Journal 2010 Jan 9:3. doi:10.1186/1475-2891-9-3.

31.   Pellegrini N. Total antioxidant capacity of plant foods, beverages and oils consumed in Italy assessed by three different in vitro assays. J Nutr. 2003 Sep 133(9): 2812-2819.

32.   Kubota C, McCune LM, Stendell-Hollis NR, Thomson CA. Cherries and health: a review. Crit Rev Food Sci Nutr. 2011 Jan;51(1):1-12.

33.   Balabanič D, Rupnik M, Klemenčič AK. Negative impact of endocrine-disrupting compounds on human reproductive health. Reprod Fertil Dev. 2011;23(3):403-16.

34.   Said TM, Ranga G, Agarwal A. Relationship between semen quality and tobacco chewing in men undergoing infertility evaluation. Fertil Steril 2005 Sep;84(3):649-53.

35.   Deepinder F, Makker K, Agarwal A. Cell phones and male infertility: dissecting the relationship. Reprod Biomed Online. 2007 Sep;15(3):266-70.

36.   De Iuliis GN, Newey RJ, King BV, Aitken RJ. Mobile phone radiation induces reactive oxygen species production and DNA damage in human spermatozoa in vitro. PLoS One. 2009 Jul 31;4(7):e6446.

37.   World Health Organization. Electromagnetic fields and public health: fact sheet #193. June 2011. [Cited 30-Jun-12] Available from: http://www.who.int/mediacentre/factsheets/fs193/en/

38.   Du Plessis SS, Cabler S, McAlister DA, Sabanegh E, Agarwal A. The effect of obesity on sperm disorders and male infertility. Nat Rev Urol. 2010 Mar;7(3):153-61.

39.   nway MD, Leathers C, Skinner MK. Endocrine disruptor vinclozolin induced epigenetic transgenerational adult-onset disease. Endocrinology 2006 Dec;147(12): 5515-5523.

40.   Pauli EM, Legro RS, Demers LM, Kunselman AR, Dodson WC, Lee PA. Diminished paternity and gonadal function with increasing obesity in men. Fertil Steril. 2008 Aug;90(2):346-51.

41.   Eskenazi B, Kidd SA, Marks AR, Sloter E, Block G, Wyrobek AJ. Antioxidant intake is associated with semen quality in healthy men. Hum Reprod. 2005 Apr;20(4):1006-12.

42.   Chavarro JE, Rich-Edwards JW, Rosner BA, Willett WC. Dietary fatty acid intakes and the risk of ovulatory infertility. Am J Clin Nutr. 2007 Jan;85(1):231-7.

43.   Attaman JA, Toth TL, Furtado J, Campos H, Hauser R, Chavarro JE. Dietary fat and semen quality among men attending a fertility clinic. Hum Reprod. 2012 May;27(5):1466-74.

44.   Tavilani H, Doosti M, Nourmohammadi I, Mahjub H, Vaisiraygani A, Salimi S, et al. Lipid composition of spermatoazoa in normozoospermic and athenozoospermic males. Prostaglandins, Leukotrienes and Essential Fatty Acids. 2007 July;77(1): 45-50.

45.   Chavarro JE, Furtado J, Toth TL, Ford J, Keller M, Campos H, et al. Trans-fatty acid levels in sperm are associated with sperm concentration among men from an infertility clinic. Fertil Steril. 2011 Apr;95(5):1794-7.

46.   Chavarro JE, Rich-Edwards JW, Rosner BA, Willett WC. A prospective study of dietary carbohydrate quantity and quality in relation to risk of ovulatory infertility. Eur J Clin Nutr. 2009 Jan;63(1):78-86.

47.   Katcher HI, Legro RS, Kunselman AR, Gillies PJ, Demers LM, Bagshaw DM, et al. The effects of a whole grain enriched hypocaloric diet on cardiovascular disease risks in men and women with metabolic syndrome. Am J Clin Nutr. 2008;87(1)79-90.

48.   Crozier SJ, Preston AG, Hurst JW, Payne MJ, Mann J, Hainly L, et al. Cacao seeds are a "Super Fruit": A comparative analysis of various fruit powders and products. Chem Cent J. 2011 Feb 7;5:5.

49.   American Chemical Society (2009, November 11). New evidence that dark chocolate helps ease emotional stress. Science Daily, [Cited 4-Feb-12.]Available from: http://www.sciencedaily.com/releases/2009/11/091111123612.htm

50.   Robbins WA, Xun L, Fitzgerald LZ, Esguerra S, Henning SM, Carpenter CL. Walnuts improve semen quality in men consuming a Western-style diet: randomized control dietary intervention trial. Biol Reprod. 2012 Oct 25;87(4):101. doi: 10.1095/biolreprod.112.101634.

Chapter 3
Knowledgeable Pregnancy

1.   Siega-Riz AM, Herrmann TS, Savitz DA, Thorp JM. Frequency of eating during pregnancy and its effect on preterm delivery. Am. J. Epidemiol. 2001 Apr 1;53(7): 647-652

2.   Institute of Food Technologists. (2012, June 29). Skipping breakfast can lead to unhealthy habits all day long. Science Daily. [Cited 1-Jul-12]. Available from http://www.sciencedaily.com/releases/2012/06/120629143045.htm

3.   Javaid MK, Crozier SR, Harvey NC, Gale CR, Dennison EM, Boucher BJ, et al. Maternal vitamin D status during pregnancy and childhood bone mass at age 9 years: a longitudinal study. Lancet. 2006 Jan 7;367(9504):36-43.

4.   Hofmeyer GJ, Duley L, Atallah A. Dietary calcium supplementation for prevention of hypertension related problems: a systematic review and commentary. BJOG. 2007 Aug;114(8): 933-43.

5.   Imdad A, Jabeen A, Bhutta ZA. Role of calcium supplementation during pregnancy in reducing risk of developing gestational hypertensive disorders: a meta-analysis of studies from developing countries. BMC Public Health. 2011 Apr 13;11 Suppl 3:S18. Review.

6.   Bodnar LM, Catov JM, Simhan HN, Holick MF, Powers RW, Roberts JM. Maternal vitamin D deficiency increases the risk of preeclampsia. J Clin Endocrinol Metab. 2007;92(9):3517–3522.

7.   Sørensen IM, Joner G, Jenum PA, Eskild A, Torjesen PA, Stene LC. Maternal serum levels of 25-hydroxy-vitamin D during pregnancy and risk of type 1 diabetes in the offspring. Diabetes. 2012 Jan;61(1):175-8.

8.   Whitehouse AJ, Holt BJ, Serralha M, Holt PG, Kusel MM, Hart PH. Maternal Serum Vitamin D Levels During Pregnancy and Offspring Neurocognitive Development. Pediatrics. 2012 Mar;129(3):485-93.

9.   Belderbos ME, Houben ML, Wilbrink B, Lentjes E, Bloemen EM, Kimpen JL, et al. Cord blood vitamin D deficiency is associated with respiratory syncytial virus bronchiolitis. Pediatrics. 2011 Jun;127(6):e1513-20.

10.   Bodnar LM, Simhan HN, Powers RW, Frank MP, Cooperstein E, Roberts JM. High prevalence of vitamin D insufficiency in black and white pregnant women residing in the northern United States and their neonates. J Nutr. 2007 Feb;137(2):447-52.

11.   Harvey NC, Javaid K, Bishop N, Kennedy S, Papageorghiou AT, Fraser R, Gandhi SV, Schoenmakers I, Prentice A, Cooper C. MAVIDOS Maternal Vitamin D Osteoporosis Study: study protocol for a randomized controlled trial. Trials. 2012 Feb 7;13(1):13.

12.   Holick MF, Binkley NC, Bischoff-Ferrari HA, Gordon CM, Hanley DA, Heaney RP, Murad MH, Weaver CM; Endocrine Society. Evaluation, treatment, and prevention of vitamin D deficiency: an Endocrine Society clinical practice guideline. J Clin Endocrinol Metab. July 2011;96(7):1911–1930.

13.   Food and Nutrition Board, Institute of Medicine. Dietary Reference Intakes: Calcium and Vitamin D. Washington DC: The National Academies Press; 2011.

14.   Vitamin D and calcium; updated Dietary Reference Intakes. Health Canada. December 2010. [Cited 25-Feb-12]. Available from: http://www.hc-sc.gc.ca/fn-an/ nutrition/vitamin/vita-d-eng.php.

15.   Vitamin D supplementation: Recommendations for Canadian mothers and infants First Nations, Inuit and Métis Health Committee, Canadian Paediatric Society (CPS) Paediatr Child Health. 2007;12(7):583-9. Reaffirmed March 2012. [Cited 17-Nov-12] Available from: http://www.cps.ca/english/statements/ii/fnim07- 01.htm#RECOMMENDATIONS

16.   Vidailhet M, Mallet E, Bocquet A, Bresson JL, Briend A, Chouraqui JP, et al. Comité de nutrition de la Société française de pédiatrie. Vitamin D: Still a topical matter in children and adolescents. A position paper by the Committee on Nutrition of the French Society of Paediatrics. Arch Pediatr. 2012 Mar;19(3):316-28.

17.   Li W, Green TJ, Innis SM, Barr SI, Whiting SJ, Shand A, et al. Suboptimal vitamin D levels in pregnant women despite supplement use. Can J Public Health. 2011 Jul-Aug;102(4):308-12.

18.   Vitamin D Council. UVB exposure: sunlight and indoor tanning. September 2011. [Cited 17-Nov-12] Available from: http://www.vitamindcouncil. org/about-vitamin-d/how-to-get-your-vitamin-d/uvb-exposure-sunlight-and- indoor-tanning/

19.   Edvardsen K, Brustad M, Engelsen O, Aksnes L The solar UV radiation level needed for cutaneous production of vitamin D3 in the face. A study conducted among subjects living at a high latitude (68 degrees N). Photochemical and Photobiological Sciences. 2007 Jan;6(1):57-62.

20.   British Paediatric Respiratory Society British Society of Paediatric Gastroenterology, Hepatology and Nutrition. A survey of healthcare professionals' awareness of vitamin D supplementation in pregnancy, infancy and childhood- midwives, gps and health visitors have their say. Arch Dis Child. 2011;96:A16-A18 doi:10.1136/adc.2011.212563.32

21.   Scholl TO. Iron status during pregnancy: setting the stage for mother and infant. American Journal of Clinical Nutrition. 2005 May;81(5):1218S-1222S.

22. Jonnalagadda SS, Harnack L, Liu RH, McKeown N, Seal C, Liu S, et al. Putting the whole grain puzzle together: health benefits associated with whole grains--summary of American Society for Nutrition 2010 Satellite Symposium. J Nutr. 2011 May;141(5):1011S-22S.

23. Qiu C, Coughlin KB, Frederick IO, Sorensen TK, Williams MA. Dietary fiber intake in early pregnancy and risk of subsequent preeclampsia. Am J Hypertens. 2008 Aug;21(8):903-9.

24. Livesey G, Taylor R, Hulshof T, Howlett J. Glycemic response and health--a systematic review and meta-analysis: relations between dietary glycemic properties and health outcomes. Am J Clin Nutr. 2008 Jan;87(1):258S-268S.

25. Burani, J. Gushers and Tricklers: Practical Use of the Glycemic Index. Presentation at the American Diabetes Association Southern Regional Conference. Marco Island, Florida. May 2006.

26. Moshfegh AJ, Friday AJ, Goldman JP, Chug Ahuja JK. Presence of Inulin and Oligofructose in the Diets of Americans. J. Nutr. 1999 Jul;129(7 Suppl):1407S-11S. [Cited 13-Aug-12]. Available from: http://jn.nutrition.org/content/129/7/1407S.full

27. Sajilata MG, Rekha SS, Kulkarni PR. Resistant Starch—A Review. Comprehensive Reviews in Food Science and Food Safety. 2006;(5)1:1-17. Available from: http://onlinelibrary.wiley.com/doi/10.1111/j.1541-4337.2006.tb00076.x/pdf

28. Team Nord. Safety evaluation of fructans. Copenhagen: Nordic Council of Ministers. 2000.

29. USDA. Sugar and sweeteners yearbook table. Table 51 and 52. Updated 5/24/11. [Cited 22-Jan-12]. Available from: http://www.ers.usda.gov/Briefing/Sugar/Data.htm

30. Jackson BP, Taylor VF, Karagas MR, Punshon T, Cottingham KL 2012. Arsenic, organic foods, and brown rice syrup. Environ Health Perspect. 2012 May;120(5):623-6. [Cited 23-Feb-12]. Available from: http://www.ncbi.nlm.nih.gov/pmc/articles/PMC3346791/

31. Johnson RK, Appel LJ, Brands M, Howard BV, Lefevre M, Lustig RH, Sacks F, Steffen LM, Wylie-Rosett J; American Heart Association Nutrition Committee of the Council on Nutrition, Physical Activity, and Metabolism and the Council on Epidemiology and Prevention. Dietary sugars intake and cardiovascular health: a scientific statement from the American Heart Association. Circulation. 2009 Sep 15;120(11):1011-20. [Cited 17-Nov-12]. Available from: http://circ.ahajournals.org/content/120/11/1011.long

32. Koletzko B, Cetin I, Brenna JT; Perinatal Lipid Intake Working Group; Dietary fat intakes for pregnant and lactating women. Br J Nutr. 2007 Nov;98(5):873-7.

33. Micha R, Mozaffarian D. Saturated fat and cardiometabolic risk factors, coronary heart disease, stroke, and diabetes: a fresh look at the evidence. Lipids. 2010 Oct;45(10):893-905.

34.   Assunção ML, Ferreira HS, dos Santos AF, Cabral CR Jr, Florêncio TM. Effects of dietary coconut oil on the biochemical and anthropometric profiles of women presenting abdominal obesity. Lipids. 2009 Jul; 44(7):593-601.

35.   St-Onge MP, Bosarge A. Weight-loss diet that includes consumption of medium-chain triacylglycerol oil leads to a greater rate of weight and fat mass loss than does olive oil. Am J Clin Nutr. 2008 Mar;87(3):621-6.

36.   American Heart Association. Know your fats. Updated 2-8-12. [Cited 28-Feb-12]. Available from: http://www.heart.org/HEARTORG/Conditions/ Cholesterol/PreventionTreatmentofHighCholesterol/Know-Your-Fats_ UCM_305628_Article.jsp

37.   Haahtela T, Valovirta E, Kauppi P, Tommila E, Saarinen K, von Hertzen L, Mäkelä MJ. The Finnish Allergy Programme 2008-2018 - scientific rationale and practical implementation. Asia Pac Allergy. 2012 October; 2(4): 275–279

38.   Eur Respir J. 2010 Jun;35(6):1228-34. Kramer MS. Cochrane Database Syst Rev. 2000; CD000133. Maternal antigen avoidance during pregnancy for preventing atopic disease in infants of women at high risk.

39.   Salvatore S, Keymolen K, Hauser B, Vandenplas Y. Intervention during pregnancy and allergic disease in the offspring. Pediatr Allergy Immunol. 2005; 16:558-66.

40.   Greer FR, Sicherer SH, Burks AW; American Academy of Pediatrics Committee on Nutrition; American Academy of Pediatrics Section on Allergy and Immunology. Effects of early nutritional interventions on the development of atopic disease in infants and children: the role of maternal dietary restriction, breastfeeding, timing of introduction of complementary foods, and hydrolyzed formulas. Pediatrics. 2008 Jan;121(1):183-91. doi: 10.1542/peds.2007-3022.

41.   American Academy of Allergy, Asthma and Immunology. Prevention of Allergies and Asthma in Children: Tips to Remember. [Cited 27-Jan-13]. Available from: http://www.aaaai.org/conditions-and-treatments/library/at-a-glance/ prevention-of-allergies-and-asthma-in-children.aspx

42.   Prescott SL,Tang M ASCIA Position Statement: Summary of Allergy Prevention in Children, as published in the Medical Journal of Australia 2005; 182 (9): 464-467. March 2010. [Cited 27-Jan-13]. Available from: http://www.allergy. org.au/health-professionals/papers/allergy-prevention-in-children

43.   Høst A, Halken S, Muraro A, Dreborg S, Niggemann B, Aalberse R, Arshad SH, von Berg A, Carlsen KH, Duschén K, Eigenmann PA, Hill D, Jones C, Mellon M, Oldeus G, Oranje A, Pascual C, Prescott S, Sampson H, Svartengren M, Wahn U, Warner JA, Warner JO, Vandenplas Y, Wickman M, Zeiger RS. Dietary prevention of allergic diseases in infants and small children. Pediatr Allergy Immunol. 2008 Feb;19(1):1-4.

44. Maslova E, Granström C, Hansen S, Petersen SB, Strøm M, Willett WC, Olsen SF. Peanut and tree nut consumption during pregnancy and allergic disease in children-should mothers decrease their intake? Longitudinal evidence from the Danish National Birth Cohort.

45. Willers SM, Wijga AH, Brunekreef B, Kerkhof M, Gerritsen J, Hoekstra MO, de Jongste JC, Smit HA. Eur Respir J. Maternal food consumption during pregnancy and the longitudinal development of childhood asthma. Am J Respir Crit Care Med. 2008 Jul 15;178(2):124-31.

46. Dotterud CK, Storrø O, Johnsen R, Oien T. Probiotics in pregnant women to prevent allergic disease: a randomized, double-blind trial. Br J Dermatol. 2010 Sep;163(3):616-23.

47. Wickens K, Black PN, Stanley TV, Mitchell E, Fitzharris P, Tannock GW, Purdie G, Crane J; Probiotic Study Group. J Allergy Clin Immunol. A differential effect of 2 probiotics in the prevention of eczema and atopy: a double-blind, randomized, placebo-controlled trial. 2008 Oct;122(4):788-94.

48. Torres-Borrego J, Moreno-Solís G, Molina-Terán AB. Diet for the prevention of asthma and allergies in early childhood: much ado about something? Allergol Immunopathol (Madr). 2012 Jul-Aug;40(4):244-52.

49. Erkkola M, Nwaru BI, Kaila M, Kronberg-Kippilä C, Ilonen J, Simell O, Veijola R, Knip M, Virtanen SM. Risk of asthma and allergic outcomes in the offspring in relation to maternal food consumption during pregnancy: a Finnish birth cohort study. Pediatr Allergy Immunol. 2012 Mar;23(2):186-94.

50. Torres-Borrego J, Moreno-Solís G, Molina-Terán AB. Diet for the prevention of asthma and allergies in early childhood: much ado about something? Allergol Immunopathol (Madr). 2012 Jul-Aug;40(4):244-52.

51. Lumia M, Luukkainen P, Tapanainen H, Kaila M, Erkkola M, Uusitalo L, Niinistö S, Kenward MG, Ilonen J, Simell O, Knip M, Veijola R, Virtanen SM. Dietary fatty acid composition during pregnancy and the risk of asthma in the offspring.Pediatr Allergy Immunol. 2011 Dec;22(8):827-35.

52. Castro-Rodriguez JA, Garcia-Marcos L, Sanchez-Solis M, Pérez-Fernández V, Martinez-Torres A, Mallol J. Pediatr Pulmonol. 2010 Apr;45(4):395-402. Olive oil during pregnancy is associated with reduced wheezing during the first year of life of the offspring.

Chapter 4
Eating Expectantly Diet

1. Goy YI, Bollano E, Eiarson TR, Koren G. Prenatal multivitamin supplementation and rates of congenital anomalies: a meta analysis.. Journal of obstetrics and gynaecology Canada. 2006 Aug; 28(8):680-9.

2.   Shah PS, Ohlsson A. Effects of prenatal multimicronutrient supplementation on pregnancy outcomes: a meta-analysis. CMAJ. Jun 9 2009; 180(12):E99-108.

3.   Public Health Committee of the American Thyroid Association, Becker DV, Braverman LE, Delange F, Dunn JT, Franklyn JA, Hollowell JG, Lamm SH, et al. Iodine supplementation for pregnancy and lactation-United States and Canada: recommendations of the American Thyroid Association. Thyroid. 2006 Oct; 16(10):949-51.

4.   Teran E, Hernandez I, Nieto B, Tavara R, Ocampo JE, Calle A. Coenzyme Q10 supplementation during pregnancy reduces the risk of pre-eclampsia. Int J Gynaecol Obstet. 2009 Apr; 105(1):43-5.

5.   Natural Medicines Comprehensive Database. Coenzyme Q-10. Updated 2-28-12. [Cited 29-Feb-12]. Available from: http://naturaldatabase. therapeuticresearch.com/nd/Search.aspx?pt=100&id=938&ds=&name=CoQ10+%2 8COENZYME+Q-10%29&searchid=33081344&cs=&s=ND

6.   Cavalli P, Tonni G, Grosso E, Poggiani C. Effects of inositol supplementation in a cohort of mothers at risk of producing an NTD pregnancy. Birth Defects Res A Clin Mol Teratol. 2011 Nov;91(11):962-5. doi: 10.1002/bdra.22853.

7.   Wilson MP, Hugge C, Bielinska M, Nicholas P, Majerus PW, Wilson DB. Neural tube defects in mice with reduced levels of inositol 1,3,4-trisphosphate 5/6-kinase. Proc Natl Acad Sci U S A. 2009 Jun 16;106(24):9831-5.

8.   Natural Medicines Comprehensive Database. Inositol. Updated 2-28-12. [Cited 29-Feb-12]. Available from: http://naturaldatabase.therapeuticresearch.com/ nd/Search.aspx?cs=&s=ND&pt=100&id=299&ds=&name=INOSITOL&search id=33081344

9.   Center for Disease Control and Prevention. Recommendations to prevent and control iron deficiency in the United States. MMWR. April 3, 1998. 47(RR-3):1-36.

10.   Cockell KA, Miller DC, Lowell H. Application of the Dietary Reference Intakes in developing a recommendation for pregnancy iron supplements in Canada. Am J Clin Nutr. 2009 Oct; 90(4):1023-8.

11.   Office of Dietary Supplements, National Institutes of Health. Dietary Supplement Fact Sheet: Iron. Reviewed 8-24-07. [Cited 28-Feb-12]. Available from: http://ods.od.nih.gov/factsheets/iron/#en36

12.   Ettinger AS, Hu H, Hernandez-Avila M. Dietary calcium supplementation to lower blood lead levels in pregnancy and lactation. J Nutr Biochem. 2007 Mar; 18(3):172-8.

13.   Koletzko B, Cetin I, Brenna JT; Perinatal Lipid Intake Working Group; Child Health Foundation; Diabetic Pregnancy Study Group; European Association of Perinatal Medicine; European Association of Perinatal Medicine; European Society for Clinical Nutrition and Metabolism; European Society for Paediatric Gastroenterology, Hepatology and Nutrition, Committee on Nutrition; International Federation of Placenta Associations; International Society for the Study of Fatty Acids and Lipids. Dietary fat intakes for pregnant and lactating women. Br J Nutr. 2007 Nov; 98(5):873-7.

14.   American Pregnancy Association. Omega 3 fish oil and pregnancy. Updated 12/2011 [Cited 29-Feb-12] Available from: http://www.americanpregnancy.org/pregnancyhealth/omega3fishoil.html

15.   Medicinenet.com Probiotics symptoms, causes, treatment. 8/1/2008.[Cited 29-Feb-12] Available from: http://www.medicinenet.com/probiotics/page5.htm

16.   Doege K, Grajecki D, Zyriax BC, Detinkina E, Zu Eulenburg C, Buhling KJ. Impact of maternal supplementation with probiotics during pregnancy on atopic eczema in childhood--a meta-analysis. Br J Nutr. 2012 Jan; 107(1):1-6.

17.   Othman M, Neilson JP, Alfirevic Z. Probiotics for preventing preterm labour. Cochrane Database Syst Rev. 2007 Jan; 24(1):CD005941.

18.   Brantsaeter AL, Myhre R, Haugen M, Myking S, Sengpiel V, Magnus P, et al. Intake of probiotic food and risk of preeclampsia in primiparous women: the Norwegian Mother and Child Cohort Study. Am J Epidemiol. 2011 Oct 1; 174(7):807-15.

Chapter 5
Weight Gain: What You Need To Know

1.   Stotland NE. Body mass index, provider advice and gestational target weight gain. 2005 Mar;105(3) 633-638.

2.   Crane JM, White J, Murphy P, Burrage L, Hutchens D. The effect of gestational weight gain by body mass index on maternal and neonatal outcomes. J Obstet Gynaecol Can. 2009 Jan;31(1):28-35.

3.   Webb JB, Siega-Riz AM, Dole N. Psychosocial Determinants of Adequacy of Gestational Weight Gain. Behavior and Psychology Obesity. 2009:17(2) 300–309. doi:10.1038/oby.2008.490

4.   Hurley KM, Caulfield LE, Saco LA, Costigan KA, DiPietro JA. Psychosocial influences in dietary patterns during pregnancy. J Am Diet Assoc 2005;105:963–966.

Chapter 6
Keeping Your Baby's Environment Safe

1.　　Tobacco Use and Pregnancy, Centers for Disease Control and Prevention. 3/23/12. [Cited 5-Jul-12]. Available from: http://www.cdc.gov/reproductivehealth/tobaccousepregnancy/

2.　　Day, MD, Day NL. Developmental consequences of prenatal tobacco exposure. Curr Opin Neurol. 2009 April;22(2): 121–125.[Cited 5-Jul-12]. Available from: http://www.ncbi.nlm.nih.gov/pmc/articles/PMC2745235/

3.　　American Pregnancy Association. November 2006. [Cited 18-Aug-12]. Available from: http://www.americanpregnancy.org/pregnancycomplications/placentalabruption.html

4.　　Neuman A, Hohmann C, Orsini N, Pershagen G, Eller E, Fomsgaard Kjaer H, et al. Maternal Smoking in Pregnancy and Asthma in Preschool Children: a Pooled Analysis of 8 Birth Cohorts. Am J Respir Crit Care Med. 2012 Nov 15;186(10):1037-43

5.　　Rückinger S, Rzehak P, Chen CM, Sausenthaler S, Koletzko S, Bauer CP, et al. GINI-plus Study Group. Prenatal and postnatal tobacco exposure and behavioral problems in 10-year-old children: results from the GINI-plus prospective birth cohort study. Environ Health Perspect. 2010 Jan;118(1):150-4.

6.　　Ekblad M, Gissler M, Lehtonen L, Korkeila J. Prenatal smoking exposure and the risk of psychiatric morbidity into young adulthood. Arch Gen Psychiatry. 2010 Aug;67(8):841-9.

7.　　Goldschmidt L, Cornelius MD, Day NL. Prenatal cigarette smoke exposure and early initiation of multiple substance use. Nicotine Tob Res. 2012 Jun;14(6):694-702.

8.　　Key AP, Ferguson M, Molfese DL, Peach K, Lehman C, Molfese VJ. Smoking during pregnancy affects speech-processing ability in newborn infants. Environ Health Perspect. 2007 Apr;115(4):623-9.

9.　　Yilmaz G, Caylan ND, Karacan CD. Effects of Active and Passive Smoking on Ear Infections. Curr Infect Dis Rep. 2012 Feb;14(2):166-174

10.　　Mitchell EA, Beasley R, Keil U, Montefort S, Odhiambo J; and the ISAAC Phase Three Study Group. The association between tobacco and the risk of asthma, rhinoconjunctivitis and eczema in children and adolescents: analyses from Phase Three of the ISAAC programme. Thorax 2012 Jun 12. [Cited 6-Jul-12]. Available from: http://www.ncbi.nlm.nih.gov/pubmed/22693180

11.　　Cogswell ME, Weisberg P, Spong C. Cigarette Smoking, Alcohol Use and Adverse Pregnancy Outcomes: Implications for Micronutrient Supplementation. J Nutr. 2003 May;133(5 Suppl 2):1722S-1731S. Review. [Cited 6-Jul-12]. Available from: http://jn.nutrition.org/content/133/5/1722S.full

12.   March of Dimes. Alcohol during pregnancy. March 2012. [Cited 6-Jul-12]. Available from: http://www.marchofdimes.com/pregnancy/alcohol_indepth.html

13.   Danish studies suggest low and moderate drinking in early pregnancy has no adverse effects on children aged five. BJOG. [Cited 20-Jun-12]. Available from: http://www.bjog.org/details/news/2085661/Danish_studies_suggest_low_and_moderate_drinking_in_early_pregnancy_has_no_adver.html

14.   Chen JH. Maternal Alcohol Use during Pregnancy, Birth Weight and Early Behavioral Outcomes. Alcohol Alcohol. 2012 Nov;47(6):649-56. doi: 10.1093/alcalc/ags089. Epub 2012 Aug 14.

15.   Carter RC, Jacobson JL, Molteno CD, Jiang H, Meintjes EM, Jaconson SW, et al. Effects of Heavy Prenatal Alcohol Exposure and Iron Deficiency Anemia on Child Growth and Body Composition through Age 9 Years. Alcohol Clin Exp Res. 2012 Nov;36(11):1973-82. doi: 10.1111/j.1530-0277.2012.01810.x

16.   Centers for Disease Control and Prevention. Alcohol use in pregnancy. October 2010. [Cited 1-Dec-12]. Available from: http://www.cdc.gov/ncbddd/fasd/alcohol-use.html

17.   International Council on Alcohol Policies. International guidelines on drinking during pregnancy. December 2009. [Cited 1-Dec-12]. Available from: http://www.icap.org/Table/InternationalGuidelines

18.   CARE Study Group. Maternal caffeine intake during pregnancy and risk of fetal growth restriction: a large prospective observational study. BMJ. 2008 Nov 3;337:a2332. doi: 10.1136/bmj.a2332. Erratum in: BMJ. 2010;340. doi: 10.1136/bmj.c2331.

19.   CARE Study Group. Maternal caffeine intake during pregnancy and risk of fetal growth restriction: a large prospective observational study. BMJ. 2008 Nov 3;337:a2332. doi: 10.1136/bmj.a2332. Erratum in: BMJ. 2010;340. doi: 10.1136/bmj.c2331.

20.   Weng X, Odouli R, Li DK. Maternal caffeine consumption during pregnancy and the risk of miscarriage: a prospective cohort study. Am J Obstet Gynecol. 2008 Mar;198(3):279.e1-8.

21.   Robinson LE, Spafford C, Graham TE, Smith GN. Acute caffeine ingestion and glucose tolerance in women with or without gestational diabetes mellitus. J Obstet Gynaecol Can. 2009 Apr; 31(4):304-12. [Cited 7-Jul-12.] Available from: http://www.ncbi.nlm.nih.gov/pubmed/19497149

22.   Committee Opinion No. 462: Moderate Caffeine Consumption During Pregnancy Obstetrics & Gynecology. 2010 August;116(2, Part 1):467-468.

23.   The March of Dimes, Caffeine in pregnancy. [Cited 8-Jul-12]. Available from: http://www.marchofdimes.com/pregnancy/nutrition_caffeine.html

24.   Pregnancy and food safety. New South Wales Food Authority. March 2012. [Cited 1-Dec-12]. Available from: http://www.foodauthority.nsw.gov.au/consumers/life-events-and-food/pregnancy/

25.   National Health Service. Should I limit caffeine during pregnancy. July 2011. [Cited 7-Jul-12]. Available from: http://www.nhs.uk/chq/pages/limit-caffeine-duringpregnancy.aspx?categoryid=54&subcategoryid=130

26.   Natural Medicines Comprehensive Database. [Cited 8-Jul-12]. Available from: http://www.naturaldatabase.com

27.   Natural Medicines Comprehensive Database. [Cited 8-Jul-12]. Available from: http://www.naturaldatabase.com

28.   United States Environmental Protection Agency. Persistent Organic Pollutants: A Global Issue, A Global Response. 12/09. [Cited 12-Jul-12]. Available from: http://www.epa.gov/oia/toxics/pop.html

29.   United States Environmental Protection Agency. Persistent Organic Pollutants: A Global Issue, A Global Response. December 2009. [Cited 12-Jul-12]. Available from: http://www.epa.gov/oia/toxics/pop.html

30.   Lee DH, Lee IK, Song K, Steffes M, Toscano W, Baker BA, et al. (2006). A strong dose-response relation between serum concentrations of persistent organic pollutants and diabetes - Results from the National Health and Examination Survey 1999-2002. Diabetes Care. 29(7), 1638-1644. [Cited 30-Aug-12]. Available from: http://care.diabetesjournals.org/content/29/7/1638.long

31.   Environmental Protection Agency. Persistent Organic Pollutants: A Global Issue, A Global Response December 2009 [Cited 26-Aug-12]. Available from: http://www.epa.gov/oia/toxics/pop.html

32.   Balabanič D, Rupnik M, Klemenčič AK. Negative impact of endocrine-disrupting compounds on human reproductive health. Reprod Fertil Dev. 2011;23(3):403-16.

33.   Giordano F, Abballe A, De Felip E, di Domenico A, Ferro F, Grammatico P, et al. Maternal exposures to endocrine disrupting chemicals and hypospadias in offspring. Birth Defects Res A Clin Mol Teratol. 2010 Apr;88(4):241-50.

34.   Dindyal S. The sperm count has been decreasing steadily for many years in Western industrialised countries: Is there an endocrine basis for this decrease?. The Internet Journal of Urology. 2004;2(1). [Cited 1-Dec-12]. Available from: http://www.ispub.com/journal/the-internet-journal-of-urology/volume-2-number-1/the-sperm-count-has-been-decreasing-steadily-for-many-years-in-western-industrialised-countries-is-there-an-endocrine-basis-for-this-decrease.html

35.   Bonacasa B, Siow RC, Mann GE. Impact of dietary soy isoflavones in pregnancy on fetal programming of endothelial function in offspring. Microcirculation. 2011 May; 18(4):270-85. doi: 10.1111/j.1549-8719.2011.00088.x. [Cited 2-Sep-12]. Available from: http://www.ncbi.nlm.nih.gov/pubmed/21418378

36.   United States Environmental Protection Agency. BPA alternatives in thermal paper partnership. 8/20/12. [Cited 31-Aug-12]. Available from: http://www.epa.gov/dfe/pubs/projects/bpa/index.htm

37.   U.S. Environmental Protection Agency. Bisphenol A Action Plan; 29 March 2010 [Cited 18-Aug-12]. Available from: http://www.epa.gov/oppt/existingchemicals/pubs/actionplans/bpa_action_plan.pdf

38.   United States Food and Drug Administration. Bisphenol A (BPA): Use in Food Contact Application. March 2012. [Cited 18-Aug-12]. Available from: http://www.fda.gov/newsevents/publichealthfocus/ucm064437.htm

39.   World Health Organization. Dioxins and their effects on health. Fact sheet No 225. May 2010. [Cited 27-Aug-12]. Available from: http://www.who.int/mediacentre/factsheets/fs225/en/

40.   Environmental Protection Agency. An inventory of sources and environmental releases of dioxin-like compounds in the United States for the years 1987, 1995, and 2000. 2006. [Cited 28-Aug-12]. Available from: http://cfpub.epa.gov/ncea/cfm/recordisplay.cfm?deid=159286

41.   World Health Organization European Centre for Environment and Health. International Programme on Chemical Safety. Assessment of the health risk of dioxins: reevaluation of the Tolerable Daily Intake. May 1998. [Cited 2-Dec-12]. Available from: http://www.who.int/ipcs/publications/en/exe-sum-final.pdf

42.   World Health Organization. Dioxins and their effects on health. Fact sheet no 225. May 2010. [Cited 27-Aug-12]. Available from: http://www.who.int/mediacentre/factsheets/fs225/en/

43.   The Breast Cancer Fund. BPA in Thanksgiving Canned Food. November 2011. [Cited 31-Aug-12]. Available from: http://www.breastcancerfund.org/big-picture-solutions/make-our-products-safe/cans-not-cancer/bpa-thanksgiving-food.html

44.   Agency for toxic substances and disease registry. (ATSDR) ToxFAQs™ for Polychlorinated Biphenyls (PCBs). Updated March 2011. [Cited 14-Jul-12]. Available from: http://www.atsdr.cdc.gov/toxfaqs/tf.asp?id=140&tid=26#bookmark09

45.   United States Environmental Protection Agency. Persistent Organic Pollutants: A Global Issue, A Global Response. December 2009. [Cited 28-Aug-12]. Available from: http://www.epa.gov/oia/toxics/pop.html

46.   UN Environmental Protection Agency. Health effects of PCBs. Updated 4-12. [Cited 14-Jul-12]. Available from: http://www.epa.gov/osw/hazard/tsd/pcbs/pubs/effects.htm

47.   McAuliffe ME, Williams PL, Korrick SA, Altshul LM, Perry MJ. Environmental exposure to polychlorinated biphenyls and p,p'-DDE and sperm sex-chromosome disomy. Environ Health Perspect. 2012 Apr; 120(4):535-40.

48.   Agency for toxic substances and disease registry. (ATSDR) Public health implications of exposure to polychlorinated biphenyls (PCBs). August 2008. [Cited 28-Aug-12]. Available from: http://www.atsdr.cdc.gov/dt/pcb007.html

49.   Susan G Komen for the Cure. Breast Cancer Research Studies. Table 27: Blood organochlorine levels and breast cancer risk. August 2012. [Cited 31-Aug-12]. Available from: http://ww5.komen.org/BreastCancer/Table27Bloodorganochlorinelevelsandbreastcancerrisk.html

50.   Mnif, W, Hassine AIH, Bouaziz A, Bartegi A, Thomas A, Roig B. Effect of Endocrine Disruptor Pesticides: A Review. Int J Environ Res Public Health. 2011 June; 8(6): 2265–2303. [Cited 28-Aug-12]. Available from: http://www.ncbi.nlm.nih.gov/pmc/articles/PMC3138025/

51.   CDC (Centers for Disease Control and Prevention).. Third National Exposure Report. 2005 [Cited 19-Feb-08]. Available from: http://www.cdc.gov/exposurereport/report.htm

52.   Duty SM, Singh NP, Silva MJ, Barr DB, Brock JW, Ryan L, et al. The relationship between environmental exposures to phthalates and DNA damage in human sperm using the neutral comet assay. Environmental Health Perspectives. 2003 Jul;111(9):1164-9.

53.   Duty SM, Silva MJ, Barr DB, Brock JW, Ryan L, Chen Z, et al. Phthalate Exposure and Human Semen Parameters. Epidemiology. 2003 May;14(3):269-77.

54.   Swan SH, Main KM, Liu F, Stewart SL, Kruse RL, Calafat AM, et al. Study for Future Families Research Team. Decrease in anogenital distance among male infants with prenatal phthalate exposure. Environ Health Perspect. 2005 Aug;113(8):1056-61.

55.   James-Todd T, Stahlhut R, Meeker JD, Powell S-G, Hauser R, Huang T, et al. Urinary Phthalate Metabolite Concentrations and Diabetes among Women in the National Health and Nutrition Examination Survey (NHANES) 2001-2008. Environ Health Perspect. 2012 September;120(9): 1307–1313. Available from: http://www.ncbi.nlm.nih.gov/pmc/articles/PMC3440117/

56.   United States Environmental Protection Agency. Inorganic arsenic. TEACH chemical summary. August 2007. [Cited 14-Jul-12]. Available from: http://www.epa.gov/teach/

57.   Arsenic in your juice: How much is too much? Consumer Reports Magazine. January 2012. [Cited 5-Jul-12]. Available from: http://www.consumerreports.org/cro/consumer-reports-magazine-january-2012/arsenic-in-your-juice/index.htm#groundwater

58.   Arsenic in your juice: How much is too much? Consumer Reports Magazine. January 2012.[Cited 5-Jul-12]. Available from: http://www.consumerreports.org/cro/consumer-reports-magazine-january-2012/arsenic-in-your-juice/index.htm#groundwater

59.   Food Standards Australia New Zealand. Arsenic. August 2012. [Cited 31-Aug-12]. Available from: http://www.foodstandards.gov.au/consumerinformation/arsenic.cfm

60.   United States Environmental Protection Agency. Inorganic arsenic. TEACH chemical summary. Revised 8/07. [Cited 14-Jul-12]. Available from: http://www.epa.gov/teach/

61.   Hamadani JD, Tofail F, Nermell B, Gardner R, Shiraji S, Bottai M, Arifeen SE, Huda SN, Vahter M. Critical windows of exposure for arsenic-associated impairment of cognitive function in pre-school girls and boys: a population-based cohort study. Int J Epidemiol. 2011 Dec;40(6):1593-604.

62.   Gilbert-Diamond D, Cottingham KL, Gruber JF, Punshon T, Sayarath V, Gandolfi AJ, et al. Rice consumption contributes to arsenic exposure in US women. Proc Natl Acad Sci USA. 2011 Dec 20; 108(51):20656-60.

63.   Jackson BP, Taylor VF, Karagas MR, Punshon T, Cottingham KL. Arsenic, organic foods, and brown rice syrup. Environ Health Perspect 2012 May;120(5):623-6.

64.   Meharg AA, Lombi E, Williams PN, Scheckel KG, Feldmann J, Raab A, et al. Speciation and localization of arsenic in white and brown rice grains. Environ Sci Technol. 2008 Feb 15;42(4):1051-7.

65.   Consumer Reports Magazine. Arsenic in your food. November 2012. [Cited 2-Dec-12]. Available from: http://www.consumerreports.org/cro/magazine/2012/11/arsenic-in-your-food/index.htm

66.   Consumer Reports Magazine. Arsenic in your food. November 2012. [Cited 2-Dec-12]. Available from: http://www.consumerreports.org/cro/magazine/2012/11/arsenic-in-your-food/index.htm

67.   US Environmental Protection Agency. Cadmium compounds. Updated July 2007 [Cited 14-Jul-12]. Available from: http://www.epa.gov/ttn/atw/hlthef/cadmium.html

68.   US Environmental Protection Agency. Waste minimization: Cadmium. Updated April 2012.[Cited 14-Jul-12]. Available from: http://www.epa.gov/wastes/hazard/wastemin/priority.htm

69.   Buck Louis GM, Sundaram R, Schisterman EF, Sweeney AM, Lynch CD, Gore-Langton RE, et al. Heavy metals and couple fecundity, the LIFE Study. Chemosphere. 2012 Jun;87(11):1201-7.

70.   Thompson J, Bannigan J Cadmium: toxic effects on the reproductive system and the embryo. Reprod Toxicol. 2008 Apr;25(3):304-15.

71.   Queiroz EK, Waissmann W. Occupational exposure and effects on the male reproductive system. Cad Saude Publica. 2006 Mar;22(3):485-93. Review.

72.   Agency for Toxic Substances and Disease Registry. ToxFAQs for Cadmium. Updated March 2011. [Cited 15-Jul-12]. Available from: http://www.atsdr.cdc.gov/toxfaqs/tf.asp?id=47&tid=15

73.   Bonithon-Kopp C, Huel G, Moreau T, Wendling R. Prenatal exposure to lead and cadmium and psychomotor development of the child at 6 years. Neurobehav Toxicol Teratol. 1986 May-Jun;8(3):307-10.

74.   Ciesielski T, Weuve J, Bellinger DC, Schwartz J, Lanphear B, Wright RO. Cadmium exposure and neurodevelopmental outcomes in U.S. children. Environ Health Perspect. 2012 May;120(5):758-63. Available from: http://dx.doi.org/10.1289/ehp.1104152

75.   Dartmouth Toxic Metals. Superfund Research Program. November 2010. [Cited 31-Aug-12]. Available from http://www.dartmouth.edu/~toxmetal/toxic-metals/more-metals/cadmium-faq.html

76.   Bendell LL, Chan K, St. Clair T, Walling H. Proceedings of the workshop; Cadmium in Shellfish from the Pacific Northwest: Status and Health Concerns. Simon Fraser University. May 2010.

77.   FDA Office of Regulatory Affairs. ORA Laboratory Manual. Volume IV Orientation and Training. Section 6 Elemental Analysis. Revised January 2012. [Cited 31-Aug-12]. Available from: http://www.fda.gov/downloads/ScienceResearch/UCM092243.pdf

78.   FDA Office of Regulatory Affairs. ORA Laboratory Manual. Volume IV Orientation and Training. Section 6 Elemental Analysis. Revised January 2012. [Cited 31-Aug-12]. Available from: http://www.fda.gov/downloads/ScienceResearch/.../UCM092243.pdf

79.   Agency for Toxic Substances and Disease Registry. ToxFAQs for Lead. Updated March 2011. [Cited 5-Jul-12]. Available from: http://www.atsdr.cdc.gov/toxfaqs/tf.asp?id=93&tid=22

80.   Buck Louis GM, Sundaram R, Schisterman EF, Sweeney AM, Lynch CD, Gore-Langton RE, et al. Heavy metals and couple fecundity, the LIFE Study. Chemosphere. 2012 Jun;87(11):1201-7.

81.   Center for Disease Control and Prevention. Are You Pregnant? Prevent lead poisoning. Start now. Updated 11/29/10. [Cited 9-Jul-12]. Available from: http://www.cdc.gov/nceh/lead/tips/pregnant.htm

82.   March of Dimes. Staying safe: mercury. August 2009. [Cited 12-Jul-12]. Available from: http://www.marchofdimes.com/pregnancy/stayingsafe_mercury.html

83.   Hujoel PP, Lydon-Rochelle M, Bollen AM, Woods JS, Geurtsen W, del Aguila MA. Mercury exposure from dental filling placement during pregnancy and low birth weight risk. Am J Epidemiol. 2005 Apr 15; 161(8):734-40.

84.   Watson GE, Lynch M, Myers GJ, Shamlaye CF, Thurston SW, Zareba G, et al. Prenatal exposure to dental amalgam: evidence from the Seychelles Child Development Study main cohort. J Am Dent Assoc. 2011 Nov;142(11):1283-94.

85.   US Environmental Protection Agency. Mercury: Health Effects. February 2012. [Cited 31-Aug-12]. Available from: http://www.epa.gov/hg/effects.htm

86.   Deshayne B. Fell, Ann E. Sprague, Ning Liu, Abdool S. Yasseen, Shi-Wu Wen, et al. H1N1 Influenza Vaccination During Pregnancy and Fetal and Neonatal Outcomes. Am J Public Health. 2012 Jun;102 (6): e33-40.

87.   Centers for disease control and prevention. Listeria prevention. [Cited 23-Jul-12]. Available from: http://www.cdc.gov/listeria/prevention.html

88.   Australia and New Zealand. Pregnancy and healthy eating. October 2011. [Cited 2-Sep-12]. Available from: http://www.foodstandards.gov.au/consumerinformation/pregnancyandhealthyeating/

89.   National Health Service. Can I eat smoked fish and cold meats during pregnancy? April 2011. [Cited 2-Sep-12]. Available from: http://www.nhs.uk/chq/Pages/eating-smoked-fish-and-cold-meats-during-pregnancy.aspx

90.   La Listeriose. Institut Pasteur. February 2009 [Cited 13-Dec-12]. Available from: http://www.pasteur.fr/ip/easysite/pasteur/fr/presse/fiches-sur-les-maladies-infectieuses/listeriose

91.   March of Dimes. Pregnancy Complications: Listeriosis. Februuary 2012. [Cited 3-Dec-12]. Available from: http://www.marchofdimes.com/pregnancy/complications_toxoplasmosis.html

92.   Center for Food Safety and Applied Nutrition. US Food and Drug Administration. Bad Bug Book, 2nd ed. April 2012. [Cited 1-Sep-12]. http://www.fda.gov/food/foodsafety/foodborneillness/foodborneillnessfoodbornepathogensnaturaltoxins/badbugbook/default.htm

93.   Lafferty K. Can the common brain parasite toxoplasma gondii, influence human culture? Proc Biol Sci. 2006 November 7;273(1602): 2749–2755. [Cited 24-Jul-12]. Available from: http://www.ncbi.nlm.nih.gov/pmc/articles/PMC1635495/

94.   Consumer Reports. Greener choices for a better planet. Water filters: green buying guide. February 2012. [Cited 10-Jul-12]. Available from http://www.greenerchoices.org/products.cfm?product=waterfilter

95.   Centers of Disease Control and Prevention. An ounce of prevention keeps the germs away: Seven steps to a safer healthier home. [Cited 29-Jul-12]. Available from: http://www.cdc.gov/ounceofprevention

96.   Kilonzo Nthenge A, Chen FC, Godwin SL. Efficacy of home washing methods in controlling surface microbial contamination on fresh produce. J Food Prot. 2006 Feb;69(2):330-4.

97.   Lukasik J, Bradley ML, Scott TM, Dea M, Koo A, Hsu WY, et al. Reduction of poliovirus 1, bacteriophages, Salmonella montevideo, and Escherichia coli O157:H7 on strawberries by physical and disinfectant washes. J Food Prot. 2003 Feb;66(2):188-93.

98.   Health Canada. Safe internal temperatures. August 2010. [Cited 28-Jul-12]. Available from: http://www.hc-sc.gc.ca/fn-an/securit/kitchen-cuisine/cook-temp-cuisson-eng.php

99.   Health Canada. It's your health: The Safe Use of Cookware. 2006. [Cited 28-Jul-12]. Available from: http://www.hc-sc.gc.ca/hl-vs/iyh-vsv/prod/cook-cuisinier-eng.php

100.   Consumer Union. Kitchen cookware buying guide. Updated July 2012. [Cited 29-Jul-12]. Available from: http://www.consumerreports.org/cro/kitchen-cookware.htm

101.   Consumer Union. Kitchen cookware buying guide. Updated July 2012. Available from: http://www.consumerreports.org/cro/home-garden/kitchen/kitchen-cookware/kitchen-cookware-recommendations/cookware.htm

102.   Hamilton J. Plastic's new frontier: no scary chemicals. March 4, 2011. [Cited 1-Sep-12]. Available from: http://www.npr.org/2011/03/04/134240436/plastics-new-frontier-no-estrogenic-activity

103.   United States Department of Agriculture. Food Safety and Inspection Service. Cooking safely in the microwave. May 2011. [Cited 1-Sep-12]. Available from: http://www.fsis.usda.gov/FACTSheets/Cooking_Safely_in_the_Microwave/index.asp#3

104.   US Food and Drug Administration. FDA Continues to study BPA. March 2012. [Cited 28-Jul-12]. Available from: http://www.fda.gov/ForConsumers/ConsumerUpdates/ucm297954.htm

105.   Hjortebjerg D, Andersen AM, Garne E, Raaschou-Nielsen O, Sørensen M. Non-occupational exposure to paint fumes during pregnancy and risk of congenital anomalies: a cohort study. Environ Health. 2012 Aug 14;11(1):54.

106.   Centers for Disease Control and Prevention. National Center for Environmental Health. Ettinger AS, Wengrovitz AG, editors. Guidelines for the Identification and Management of Lead Exposure in Pregnant and Lactating Women. Nov 2010.

107.   Anway MD, Leathers C, Skinner MK. Endocrine disruptor vinclozolin induced epigenetic transgenerational adult-onset disease. Endocrinology. 2006 Dec;147(12):5515-23.

108.   Rutala WA, Barbee SL, Aguiar NC, Sobsey MD, Weber DJ. Antimicrobial activity of home disinfectants and natural products against potential human pathogens. Infect Control Hosp Epidemiol. 2000 Jan;21(1):33-8.

109.   Center for disease control and prevention. Healthcare Infection Control Practices Advisory Committee. Guideline for disinfection and sterilization in healthcare facilities, 2008. Updated 2009. [Cited 5-Aug-12]. Available from: http://www.cdc.gov/hicpac/Disinfection_Sterilization/7_0formaldehyde.html

110.   Fragrance. The campaign for safe cosmetics. 2011. [Cited 4-Aug-12]. Available from: http://safecosmetics.org/article.php?id=222

111.   Director General for Health and Consumers. European Commission. SCCS Final opinion on fragrance allergens in cosmetic products now available. July 2012. [Cited 4-Aug-12]. Available from: http://ec.europa.eu/dgs/health_consumer/dyna/enews/enews.cfm?al_id=1283

112.   DEHP information center. [Cited 4-Aug-12]. Available from: http://www.dehp-facts.com/restrictions

113.   EWG (Environmental Working Group). Cosmetics with banned and unsafe ingredients. Table 1 – Banned in other countries. 2007. [Cited 5-Aug-12]. http://www.ewg.org/node/22624

114.   Nanotechnology. The campaign for safe cosmetics. 2011. [Cited 4-Aug-12]. Available from: http://safecosmetics.org/article.php?id=222

115.   California department of toxic substances control. Unsupportable claims in nail care products. April 2012. [Cited 4-Aug-12]. Available from: http://dtsc.ca.gov/PollutionPrevention/SaferNailProducts.cfm

116.   Brazilian Blowout Material Data Safety Sheet: BB-001. Revised 2/1/12. [Cited 7-Jul-12]. Available from: http://www.brazilianblowout.com/_literature_72696/Material_Safety_Data_Sheet.pdf

Chapter 7
First Trimester

1.   Mayo Clinic. Pregnancy Week by Week.Fetal Development: The First Trimester. July 23, 2011. [Cited 22-Jan-12]. Available from: http://www.mayoclinic.com/health/prenatal-care/PR00112

2.   Mayo Clinic. Pregnancy Week by Week.Fetal Development: The First Trimester. July 23, 2011. [Cited 22-Jan-12]. Available from: http://www.mayoclinic.com/health/prenatal-care/PR00112

3.   Food and Nutrition Board, Institute of Medicine. Dietary Reference Intakes. Recommended Intakes for Individuals, Macronutrients. Dietary Reference Intakes for Energy, Carbohydrate, Fiber, Fat, Fatty Acids, Protein and Amino Acids. p 653. Washington DC; National Academies Press: 2002. Available from: http://www.nap.edu/openbook.php?record_id=10490&page=653

4.   Zhang C, Qiu C, Hu F, David RM, van Dam RM. Bralley A, Williams MA. Maternal plasma 25-hydroxyvitamin D concentrations and the risk for gestational diabetes mellitus. PLoS One. 2008;3(11):e3753. [Cited 1-Feb-2012]. Available from: http://www.ncbi.nlm.nih.gov/pmc/articles/PMC2582131/?tool=pubmed

5.   Zhang C, Williams MA, Sorensen TK, King IB, Kestin MM, Thompson ML, Leisenring WM, Dashow EE, Luthy DA. Maternal plasma ascorbic acid (vitamin C) and risk of gestational diabetes mellitus. Epidemiology. 2004 Sep;15(5):597-604.

6.   Zhang C, Williams MA, King IB, Dashow EE, Sorensen TK, Frederick IO, Thompson ML, Luthy DA. Vitamin C and the risk of preeclampsia--results from dietary questionnaire and plasma assay. Epidemiology. 2002 Jul;13(4):409-16.

7.   Barclay L, Nghiem HT. ACOG Guidelines for Treating Nausea and Vomiting in Pregnant Women Reviewed. Medscape Education Clinical Briefs. November 2010. [Cited 12-26-11]. Available from: http://www.medscape.org/viewarticle/730520

8.	Jueckstock JK, Kaestner R, Mylonas I. Managing hyperemesis gravidarum: a multimodal challenge. BMC Med. 2010 Jul 15;8:46. [Cited 26-Dec-11]. Available from: http://www.biomedcentral.com/1741-7015/8/46

9.	Pepper GV, Craig Roberts S. Rates of nausea and vomiting in pregnancy and dietary characteristics across populations. Proc Biol Sci. 2006 Oct 22;273(1601):2675-9. [Cited 16-Dec-11]. Available from: http://www.ncbi.nlm.nih.gov/pmc/articles/PMC1635459/?log$=activity

10.	The American College of Obstetricians and Gynecologists. ACOG Practice Bulletin No. 52. American College of Obstetricians and Gynecologists. Obstet Gynecol 2004;103:803-15. March 2004.

11.	The American College of Obstetricians and Gynecologists. ACOG Practice Bulletin No. 52. American College of Obstetricians and Gynecologists. Obstet Gynecol 2004;103:803-15. March 2004.

12.	Smith C, Crowther C, Beilby J. Pregnancy outcome following women's participation in a randomized controlled trial of acupuncture to treat nausea and vomiting in early pregnancy. Complement Ther Med. 2002 Jun;10(2):78-83.

13.	Smith C, Crowther C, Willson K, Hotham N, McMillian V. A randomized controlled trial of ginger to treat nausea and vomiting in pregnancy. Obstet Gynecol. 2004 Apr;103(4):639-45.

14.	Jednak MA, Shadigian EM, Kim MS, Woods ML, Hooper FG, Owyang C, Hasler WL. Protein meals reduce nausea and gastric slow wave dysrhythmic activity in first trimester pregnancy. Am J Physiol. 1999 Oct;277(4 Pt 1):G855-61.

15.	Food cravings and what they mean. [Cited 4-Feb-12]. Available from: http://www.babycenter.com/0_food-cravings-and-what-they-mean_1313971.bc

16.	Huck O, Tenenbaum H, Davideau JL. Relationship between Periodontal Diseases and Preterm Birth: Recent Epidemiological and Biological Data. J Pregnancy. 2011: 164654. Epub 2011 Oct 30. [Cited 27-Dec-11. Available from: http://www.ncbi.nlm.nih.gov/pmc/articles/PMC3205685/?tool=pubmed

17.	Dasanayake AP, Gennaro S, Hendricks-Muñoz KD, Chhun N. Maternal periodontal disease, pregnancy, and neonatal outcomes. MCN Am J Matern Child Nurs. 2008 Jan-Feb;33(1):45-9.

18.	Ruma M, Boggess K, Moss K, Jared H, Murtha A, Beck J, Offenbacher S. Maternal periodontal disease, systemic inflammation, and risk for preeclampsia. Am J Obstet Gynecol. 2008 Apr;198(4):389.e1-5. Epub 2008 Mar 4.

19.	Offenbacher S, Lin D, Strauss R, McKaig R, Irving J, Barros SP, Moss K, Barrow DA, Hefti A, Beck JD. Effects of periodontal therapy during pregnancy on periodontal status, biologic parameters, and pregnancy outcomes: a pilot study. J Periodontol. 2006 Dec;77(12):2011-24.

20.	Personal communication. Dr. Don Callan. 2-28-08

21.	Personal communication. Dr. Gary Bourgeois 2-28-08

22.	The American Academy of Periodontology. [Cited 8-Dec-12]. Available from: http://www.perio.org/consumer/risk-factors

23.   American Academy of Pediatric Dentistry (AAPD). Guideline on perinatal oral health care Chicago (IL). 2011. [Cited 27-Dec-11]. Available from: http://www.aapd.org/media/policies.asp

24.   American Academy of Pediatric Dentistry (AAPD). Guideline on perinatal oral health care. Chicago (IL): 2011. [Cited 27-Dec-11]. Available from: http://www.aapd.org/media/policies.asp

25.   Al-Zahrani MS. Increased intake of dairy products is related to lower periodontitis prevalence. J Periodontol. 2006 Feb;77(2):289-94.

26.   Merchant AT. Pitiphat W, Franz M, Joshipura KJ. Whole grain and fiber intakes and periodontitis risk in men. American Journal of Clinical Nutrition. 2006 Jun;83(6):1395-1400.

27.   Slawik S, Staufenbiel I, Schilke R, Nicksch S, Weinspach K, Stiesch M, Eberhard J. Probiotics affect the clinical inflammatory parameters of experimental gingivitis in humans. Eur J Clin Nutr. 2011 Jul;65(7):857-63. doi:10.1038/ejcn.2011.45.

28.   Shimazaki Y, Shirota T, Uchida K, Yonemoto K, Kiyohara Y, Iida M, Saito T, Yamashita Y. Intake of dairy products and periodontal disease: the Hisayama Study. J Periodontol. 2008 Jan;79(1):131-7.

Chapter 8
Second Trimester

1.   Mayo Clinic. Pregnancy Week by Week. Fetal Development: The First Trimester. July 2011. [Cited 9-Dec-12]. Available at http://www.mayoclinic.com/health/fetal-development/PR00113/NSECTIONGROUP=2

2.   What your baby looks like this week. www.babycenter.com. [Cited 9-Dec-12]. Available from: http://www.babycenter.com/fetal-development-week-by-week

3.   What your baby looks like this week. www.babycenter.com. [Cited 9-Dec-12]. Available from: http://www.babycenter.com/fetal-development-week-by-week

4.   Mayo Clinic. Pregnancy Week by Week. Fetal Development: The First Trimester. July 2011. [Cited 22-Jan-12]. Available from: http://www.mayoclinic.com/health/fetal-development/PR00113/NSECTIONGROUP=2

5.   Food and Nutrition Board, Institute of Medicine. Weight gain during pregnancy: reexamining the guidelines. p 2. Washington, DC. The National Academies Press; 2009). [Cited 20-Jan-12]. Available from: http://www.nap.edu/openbook.php?record_id=12584&page=2

6.   Nicklas, T.A., Qu, H., Hughes, S.O., Wagner, S.E., Foushee, H.R., Shewchuk, R.M. 2009. Prevalence of self-reported lactose intolerance in multiethnic sample of adults. Nutrition Today. 44(5): 222-227.

7.   Eunice Kennedy Shriver National Institute of Child Health and Human Development and NIH Office of Medical Applications of Research. NIH Consensus Development Conference. Lactose Intolerance and Health. February 22-24, 2010. [Cited 9-Dec-12]. Available from: http://consensus.nih.gov/2010/lactosestatement.htm

8.   Dehkordi N, Rao DR, Warren AP, Chawan CB. Lactose malabsorption as influenced by chocolate milk, skim milk, sucrose, whole milk, and lactic cultures. J Am Diet Assoc. 1995 Apr;95(4):484-6.

9.   Lee CM, Hardy CM. Cocoa feeding and human lactose intolerance. Am J Clin Nutr. 1989 May;49(5):840-4.

10.   Recker RR, Bammi A, Barger-Lux MJ, Heaney RP. Calcium absorbability from milk products, an imitation milk, and calcium carbonate. Am J Clin Nutr. 1988 Jan;47(1):93-5.

11.   Institute of Medicine. Food and Nutrition Board. Dietary Reference Intakes for Vitamin A, Vitamin K, Arsenic, Boron, Chromium, Copper, Iodine, Iron, Manganese, Molybdenum, Nickel, Silicon, Vanadium and Zinc. Washington, DC: National Academy Press; 2001.

12.   Kannan S. Factors in vegetarian diets influencing iron and zinc bioavailability. Vegetarian Nutrition: a dietetic practice group of the American Dietetic Association. 2012. [Cited 3-Jan-12]. Available from: http://vndpg.org/articles/Iron-and-Zinc-Bioavailability-in-Vegetarian-Nutrition.php

13.   Office of Dietary Supplements: National Institutes of Health. Dietary supplement fact sheet: Iron. August 2007. [Cited 3-Jan-12]. Available from: http://ods.od.nih.gov/factsheets/iron

14.   Kobayashi M, Nagatani Y, Magishi N, Tokuriki N, Nakata Y, Tsukiyama R, Imai H, Suzuki M, Saito M, Tsuji K. Promotive effect of Shoyu polysaccharides from soy sauce on iron absorption in animals and humans. Int J Mol Med. 2006 Dec;18(6):1159-63.

15.   Mangels R. The Everything Vegan Pregnancy Book. P 43. Adams Media: Avon Massachusetts; 2011.

16.   Macfarlane BJ, van der Riet WB, Bothwell TH, Baynes RD, Siegenberg D, Schmidt U, Tal A, Taylor JR, Mayet F. Effect of traditional oriental soy products on iron absorption. Am J Clin Nutr. 1990 May;51(5):873-80.

17.   Bihl G. Iron deficiency and gastric bypass surgery. Medscape Today News. January 2003. [Cited 3-Jan-12] Available from: http://www.medscape.com/viewarticle/448249

18.   Meltz, Wendy. "Fantastic Fruit." Nutrition Action Health Letter. May 1998.

19.   National Digestive Diseases Information Clearinghouse (NDDIC). A service of the National Institute of Diabetes and Digestive and Kidney Diseases (NIDDK), National Institutes of Health (NIH) Constipation. July 2007. [Cited 5-Jan-12]. Available from: http://digestive.niddk.nih.gov/ddiseases/pubs/constipation/index.aspx

20.   King S, Laplante DP. The effects of prenatal maternal stress on children's cognitive development: Project Ice Storm. Stress. 2005 Mar;8(1):35-45.

21.   Talge NM, Neal C, Glover V; Early Stress, Translational Research and Prevention Science Network: Fetal and Neonatal Experience on Child and Adolescent Mental Health. Antenatal maternal stress and long-term effects on child neurodevelopment: how and why? J Child Psychol Psychiatry. 2007 Mar-Apr;48(3-4):245-61.

22.   Beijers R, Jansen J, Riksen-Walraven M, de Weerth C. Maternal prenatal anxiety and stress predict infant illnesses and health complaints. Pediatrics. 2010 Aug;126(2):e401-9.

23.   Davis EP, Sandman CA. The timing of prenatal exposure to maternal cortisol and psychosocial stress is associated with human infant cognitive development. Child Dev. 2010 Jan-Feb;81(1):131-48.

24.   Van den Bergh BR, Marcoen A. High antenatal maternal anxiety is related to ADHD symptoms, externalizing problems, and anxiety in 8- and 9-year-olds. Child Dev. 2004 Jul-Aug;75(4):1085-97.

25.   Ghosh JK, Wilhelm MH, Dunkel-Schetter C, Lombardi CA, Ritz BR. Paternal support and preterm birth, and the moderation of effects of chronic stress: a study in Los Angeles county mothers. Arch Womens Ment Health. 2010 Aug;13(4):327-38.

Chapter 9
Third Trimester

1.   Mayo Clinic. Pregnancy Week by Week. Fetal Development: The Third Trimester. July 23, 2011. [Cited 27-Jan-12]. Available from: http://www.mayoclinic.com/health/fetal-development/PR00114

2.   WebMD. Your Pregnancy Week by Week. Week 26-30. [Cited 27-Jan-12]. Available from: http://www.webmd.com/baby/guide/your-pregnancy-week-by-week-weeks-26-30

3.   WebMD. Your Pregnancy Week by Week. Week 31-34. [Cited 27-Jan-12]. Available from: http://www.webmd.com/baby/guide/your-pregnancy-week-by-week-weeks-31-34

4.   WebMD. Your Pregnancy Week by Week. Week 31-34. [Cited 27-Jan-12]. Available from: http://www.webmd.com/baby/guide/your-pregnancy-week-by-week-weeks-35-40

5.   National Heart, Lung and Blood Institute. What is the DASH eating plan? November 11, 2010. [Cited 14-Jan-12]. Available from: http://www.nhlbi.nih.gov/health/health-topics/topics/dash/

6.   Saftlas AF, Triche EW, Beydoun H, Bracken MB. Does chocolate intake during pregnancy reduce the risks of preeclampsia and gestational hypertension? Ann Epidemiol. 2010 Aug;20(8):584-91.

7.   Triche EW, Grosso LM, Belanger K, Darefsky AS, Benowitz NL, Bracken MB. Chocolate consumption in pregnancy and reduced likelihood of preeclampsia. Epidemiology. 2008 May;19(3):459-64.

8.   Kim H, Hwang JY, Ha EH, Park H, Ha M, Lee SJ, Hong YC, Chang N. Association of maternal folate nutrition and serum C-reactive protein concentrations with gestational age at delivery. Eur J Clin Nutr. 2011 Mar;65(3):350-6. Epub 2010 Dec 22. Erratum in: Eur J Clin Nutr. 2011 Jul;65(7):878.

9.   Shiraishi M, Haruna M, Matsuzaki M, Ota E, Murayama R, Watanabe E, Sasaki S, Yeo S, Murashima S. Association Between Oxidized LDL and Folate During Pregnancy. Biol Res Nurs. 2011 Dec 15. [Epub ahead of print]

10.   Jain S, Sharma P, Kulshreshtha S, Mohan G, Singh S. The role of calcium, magnesium, and zinc in pre-eclampsia. Biol Trace Elem Res. 2010 Feb;133(2):162-70.

11.   Shin JS, Choi MY, Longtine MS, Nelson DM. Vitamin D effects on pregnancy and the placenta. Placenta. 2010 Dec;31(12):1027-34.

12.   Brantsaeter AL, Myhre R, Haugen M, Myking S, Sengpiel V, Magnus P, Jacobsson B, Meltzer HM. Intake of probiotic food and risk of preeclampsia in primiparous women: the Norwegian Mother and Child Cohort Study. Am J Epidemiol. 2011 Oct 1;174(7):807-15.

13.   Hofmeyr GJ, Lawrie TA, Atallah AN, Duley L. Calcium supplementation during pregnancy for preventing hypertensive disorders and related problems. Cochrane Database Syst Rev. 2010 Aug 4;(8):CD001059.

14.   Miller, G.D., J.K. Jarvis, and L.D. McBean. Handbook of Dairy Foods and Nutrition. 3rd ed. Boca Raton, FL: CRC Press; 2007. p. 99-139.

15.   Zhang C, Liu S, Solomon CG, Hu FB. Dietary fiber intake, dietary glycemic load, and the risk for gestational diabetes mellitus. Diabetes Care. 2006 Oct;29(10):2223-30.

16.   Wang Y, Storlien LH, Jenkins AB, Tapsell LC, Jin Y, Pan JF, Shao YF, Calvert GD, Moses RG, Shi HL, Zhu XX. Dietary variables and glucose tolerance in pregnancy. Diabetes Care. 2000 Apr;23(4):460-4.

17.   Ley SH, Hanley AJ, Retnakaran R, Sermer M, Zinman B, O'Connor DL. Effect of macronutrient intake during the second trimester on glucose metabolism later in pregnancy. Am J Clin Nutr. 2011 Nov;94(5):1232-40.

18.   Zhang C, Qiu C, Hu FB, David RM, van Dam RM, Bralley A, Williams MA. Maternal plasma 25-hydroxyvitamin D concentrations and the risk for gestational diabetes mellitus. PLoS One. 2008;3(11):e3753.

19.   Zhang C, Williams MA, Sorensen TK, King IB, Kestin MM, Thompson ML, Leisenring WM, Dashow EE, Luthy DA. Maternal plasma ascorbic acid (vitamin C) and risk of gestational diabetes mellitus. Epidemiology. 2004 Sep;15(5):597-604.

20.   Medline Plus. Preeclampsia. September 12, 2011. [Cited 14-Jan-12]. Available from: http://www.nlm.nih.gov/medlineplus/ency/article/000898.htm

21.   Thompson KT and Logomarsino J. The effects of calcium and magnesium supplementation in preeclamptic women: is there a relationship between preeclampsia and peripartum cardiomyopathy? Women's Health Report. A quarterly publication of Women's Health Dietetic Practice Group. Spring 2010.

22.   Magnesium. Linus Pauling Institute. Oregon State University. August 2008. [Cited 28-Jan-12]. Available from: http://lpi.oregonstate.edu/infocenter/minerals/magnesium/

23.   Hajjar IM, Grim CE, George V, Kotchen TA. Impact of diet on blood pressure and age-related changes in blood pressure in the US population: analysis of NHANES III. Arch Intern Med. 2001 Feb 26;161(4):589-93.

24.   New SA, Robins SP, Campbell MK, Martin JC, Garton MJ, Bolton-Smith C, Grubb DA, Lee SJ, Reid DM. Dietary influences on bone mass and bone metabolism: further evidence of a positive link between fruit and vegetable consumption and bone health? Am J Clin Nutr. 2000 Jan;71(1):142-51.

25.   Pubmed Health. Muscle Cramps. July 23, 2010. [Cited 2-Mar-12]. Available from: http://www.ncbi.nlm.nih.gov/pubmedhealth/PMH0003677/

26.   World Health Organization. United Nations Children's Fund & International Council for the Control of Iodine Deficiency Disorders. Assessment of iodine deficiency disorders and monitoring their elimination. 2nd ed. Geneva, Switzerland: WHO; 2007.

27.   Jiang X, Yan J, West AA, Perry CA, Malysheva OV, Devapatla S, Pressman E, Vermeylen F, Caudill MA. Maternal choline intake alters the epigenetic state of fetal cortisol-regulating genes in humans. FASEB J. 2012 Aug;26(8):3563-74. doi:10.1096/fj.12-207894.

28.   Lien EL, Hammond BR. Nutritional influences on visual development and function. Prog Retin Eye Res. 2011 May;30(3):188-203. doi: 10.1016/j.preteyeres.2011.01.001.

29.   Mangels, AR, Holden, JM, Beecher, GR, Forman, MR, Lanza, E. Carotenoid content of fruits and vegetables: an evaluation of analytic data. J Am Diet Assoc. 1993. 93:284-296.

30.   Handelman, G. J., Nightingale, Z. D., Lichtenstein, A. H., Schaefer, E. J. & Blumberg, J. B. (1999) Lutein and zeaxanthin concentrations in plasma after dietary supplementation with egg yolk. Am. J. Clin. Nutr. 70:247-251.

31.   Craig WJ, Mangels AR; American Dietetic Association. Position of the American Dietetic Association: vegetarian diets. J Am Diet Assoc. 2009 Jul;109(7):1266-82.

32.   Bonzini M, Coggon D, Palmer KT. Risk of prematurity, low birthweight and pre-eclampsia in relation to working hours and physical activities: a systematic review. Occup Environ Med. 2007 Apr;64(4):228-43.

33. Moazzez R, Bartlett D, Anggiansah A. The effect of chewing sugar-free gum on gastro-esophageal reflux. J Dent Res. 2005 Nov;84(11):1062-5.

34. Medline Plus. Aloe. 4/7/2011 [Cited 28-Jan-12]. Available from: http://www.nlm.nih.gov/medlineplus/druginfo/natural/607.html

35. Medline Plus. Aloe. 4/7/2011 [Cited 28-Jan-12]. Available from: http://www.nlm.nih.gov/medlineplus/druginfo/natural/881.html

36. Natural Medicines Comprehensive Database. Papaya. [Cited 28-Jan-12]. Available from: http://naturaldatabase.therapeuticresearch.com/nd/Search.aspx?cs=&s=ND&pt=100&id=488&ds=safety

Chapter 10
Vegetarian Eating

1. American Dietetic Association. Position Paper of the American Dietetic Association: Vegetarian Diets. J Am Diet Assoc. 2009. (109):1266-1282. [Cited 18-Aug-12]. Available from: http://www.eatright.org/about/content.aspx?id=8357

2. American Dietetic Association. Position Paper of the American Dietetic Association: Vegetarian Diets. J Am Diet Assoc. 2009. (109): 1266-1282. [Cited 18-Aug-12]. Available from: http://www.eatright.org/about/content.aspx?id=8357

3. Key TJ, Davey GK, Appleby PN. Health benefits of a vegetarian diet. Proc Nutr Soc. 1999 May;58(2):271-5

4. Ornish D, Scherwitz LW, Billings JH, Brown SE, Gould KL, Merritt TA, Sparler S, Armstrong WT, Ports TA, Kirkeeide RL, Hogeboom C, Brand RJ. Intensive lifestyle changes for reversal of coronary heart disease. JAMA. 1998 Dec 16;280(23):2001-7.

5. Lindbloom EJ. Long-term benefits of a vegetarian diet. Am Fam Physician. 2009 Apr 1;79(7):541-2.

6. American Dietetic Association. Position Paper of the American Dietetic Association: Vegetarian Diets. J Am Diet Assoc. 2009. (109): 1266-1282. [Cited 18-Aug-12]. Available from: http://www.eatright.org/about/content.aspx?id=8357

7. Farmer B, Larson BT, Fulgoni VL 3rd, Rainville AJ, Liepa GU. A vegetarian dietary pattern as a nutrient-dense approach to weight management: an analysis of the national health and nutrition examination survey 1999-2004. J Am Diet Assoc. 2011 Jun;111(6):819-27.

8. Messina V, Melina V, Mangels AR. A new food guide for North American vegetarians. Can J Diet Pract Res. 2003 Summer;64(2):82-6.

9. Food and Nutrition Board , Institute of Medicine. Dietary Reference Intakes for Vitamin A, Vitamin K, Arsenic, Boron, Chromium, Copper, Iodine, Iron, Manganese, Molybdenum, Nickel, Silicon, Vanadium, and Zinc. Washington DC: National Academies Press; 2001.

10.   Pramyothin P, Holick MF. Curr Opin Gastroenterol. 2012 Mar;28(2):139-50. Vitamin D supplementation: guidelines and evidence for subclinical deficiency.

11.   Glerup H, Mikkelsen K, Poulsen L, Hass E, Overbeck S, Thomsen J, Charles P, Eriksen EF. Commonly recommended daily intake of vitamin D is not sufficient if sunlight exposure is limited. J Intern Med. 2000 Feb;247(2):260-8.

12.   Armas LA, Hollis BW, Heaney RP. Vitamin D2 is much less effective than vitamin D3 in humans. J Clin Endocrinol Metab. 2004 Nov;89(11):5387-91.

13.   Higdon J, Drake VD. Iodine. Linus Pauling Institute. March 2010. [Cited 22-Dec-12]. Available from: http://lpi.oregonstate.edu/infocenter/minerals/iodine/

14.   American Dietetic Association. Position Paper of the American Dietetic Association: Vegetarian Diets. J Am Diet Assoc. 2009. (109):1266-1282. [Cited 18-Aug-12]. Available from: http://www.eatright.org/about/content.aspx?id=8357

15.   Barnard ND, Cohen J, Jenkins DJ, Turner-McGrievy G, Gloede L, Jaster B, Seidl K, Green AA, Talpers S. A low-fat vegan diet improves glycemic control and cardiovascular risk factors in a randomized clinical trial in individuals with type 2 diabetes. Diabetes Care. 2006 Aug;29(8):1777-83.

Chapter 11
High-Risk Pregnancy

1.   American Diabetes Association. Diabetes Basics. January 2011. [Cited 13-Aug-12]. Available from: http://www.diabetes.org/diabetes-basics/diabetes-statistics/

2.   American Diabetes Association. What is gestational diabetes? [Cited 13-Aug-12]. Available from: http://www.diabetes.org/diabetes-basics/gestational/what-is-gestational-diabetes.html

3.   American Diabetes Association. Standards of medical care in diabetes--2012. Diabetes Care. 2012 Jan;35 Suppl 1:S11-63. [Cited 14-Sep-12]. Available from: http://care.diabetesjournals.org/content/35/Supplement_1/S11.full#sec-11

4.   American Diabetes Association. Standards of medical care in diabetes--2012. Diabetes Care. 2012 Jan;35 Suppl 1:S11-63. [Cited 14-Sep-12]. Available from: http://care.diabetesjournals.org/content/35/Supplement_1/S11.full#sec-11

5.   Kim SY, England JL, Sharma JA, Njoroge T. Gestational diabetes mellitus and risk of childhood overweight and obesity in offspring: a systematic review. Exp Diabetes Res. 2011;2011:541308.

6.   US Department of Health and Human Services. National Diabetes Information Clearing House. What I need to know about Gestational Diabetes. December 2011. [Cited 8-13-12]. Available from: http://diabetes.niddk.nih.gov/dm/pubs/gestational/#6

7.   Ferrara A. Increasing prevalence of gestational diabetes mellitus: a public health perspective. Diabetes Care. 2007 Jul;30 Suppl 2:S141-6.

8.   Academy of Nutrition and Dietetics. Evidence Analysis Library. Gestational Diabetes. 2008. [Cited 24-Sep-12]. Available from: http://www.adaevidencelibrary.com

9.   Academy of Nutrition and Dietetics. Evidence Analysis Library. Gestational Diabetes. 2008. [Cited 24-Sep-12]. Available from: http://www.adaevidencelibrary.com

10.   Tucker KL, Morita K, Qiao N, Hannan MT, Cupples LA, Kiel DP. Colas, but not other carbonated beverages, are associated with low bone mineral density in older women: The Framingham Osteoporosis Study. Am J Clin Nutr. 2006 Oct;84(4):936-42.

11.   Gutiérrez OM, Wolf M, Taylor EN. Fibroblast growth factor 23, cardiovascular disease risk factors, and phosphorus intake in the health professionals follow-up study. Clin J Am Soc Nephrol. 2011 Dec;6(12):2871-8. [Cited 22-Dec-2012]. Available from: http://cjasn.asnjournals.org/content/6/12/2871.short

12.   Tucker KL, Morita K, Qiao N, Hannan MT, Cupples LA, Kiel DP. Colas, but not other carbonated beverages, are associated with low bone mineral density in older women: The Framingham Osteoporosis Study. Am J Clin Nutr. 2006 Oct;84(4):936-42.

13.   American Diabetes Association. Prenatal Care. [Cited 14-Sep-12]. Available from: http://www.diabetes.org/living-with-diabetes/complications/pregnant-women/prenatal-care.html

14.   Cranmer H. Neonatal hypoglycemia. Medscape Reference. Updated September 2011. [Cited 14-Sep-12] Available from: http://emedicine.medscape.com/article/802334-overview

15.   American Diabetes Association. Standards of medical care in diabetes--2012. Diabetes Care. 2012 Jan;35 Suppl 1:S11-63. [Cited 14-Sep-12]. Available from: http://care.diabetesjournals.org/content/35/Supplement_1/S11.full#sec-11

16.   American Diabetes Association. How to treat gestational diabetes. [Cited 14-Sep-12]. Available from: http://www.diabetes.org/diabetes-basics/gestational/how-to-treat-gestational.html

17.   March of Dimes. Pregnancy Complications: High blood pressure during pregnancy. March 2012. [Cited 15-Aug-12]. Available from: http://www.marchofdimes.com/pregnancy/complications_highbloodpressure.html

18.   Report of the National High Blood Pressure Education Program Working Group on High Blood Pressure in Pregnancy. Am J Obstet Gynecol. 2000 Jul;183(1):S1-S22.

19.   WebMD. Preeclampsia and eclampsia. August 2012. [Cited 15-Aug-12]. Available from: http://www.webmd.com/baby/guide/preeclampsia-eclampsia

20. Dennedy MC, Avalos G, O'Reilly MW, O'Sullivan EP, Gaffney G, Dunne F. ATLANTIC-DIP: raised maternal body mass index (BMI) adversely affects maternal and fetal outcomes in glucose-tolerant women according to International Association of Diabetes and Pregnancy Study Groups (IADPSG) criteria. J Clin Endocrinol Metab. 2012 Apr;97(4):E608-12.

21. Hypertension in pregnancy. The management of hypertensive disorders during pregnancy. National Collaborating Centre for Women's and Children's Health. London (UK): National Institute for Health and Clinical Excellence (NICE); 2010 Aug. 46 p. (Clinical guideline; no. 107). [Cited 14-Sep-12]. Available from: http://www.guideline.gov/content.aspx?id=24122

22. March of Dimes. Pregnancy Complications: High blood pressure during pregnancy. March 2012. [Cited 15-Aug-12]. Available from: http://www.marchofdimes.com/pregnancy/complications_highbloodpressure.html

23. Carson MP. Hypertension and pregnancy. Medscape Reference. February 2012. [Cited 15-Aug-12]. Available from: http://emedicine.medscape.com/article/261435-overview#aw2aab6b7

24. National Heart, Lung and Blood Institute. US Department of Health and Human Services. Your guide to lowering your blood pressure with DASH. NIH Publication No. 06-4082. Revised April 2006. [Cited 22-Dec-12]. Available from http://www.nhlbi.nih.gov/health/public/heart/hbp/dash/new_dash.pdf

25. Roussell MA, Hill AM, Gaugler TL, West SG, Heuvel JP, Alaupovic P, Gillies PJ,Kris-Etherton PM. Beef in an Optimal Lean Diet study: effects on lipids, lipoproteins, and apolipoproteins. Am J Clin Nutr. 2012 Jan;95(1):9-16.

26. Torres SJ, Nowson CA. A moderate-sodium DASH-type diet improves mood in postmenopausal women. Nutrition. 2012 Sep;28(9):896-900.

27. Health Canada. Sodium and Nutrition. June 2012. [Cited 14-Sep-12]. Available from: http://www.hc-sc.gc.ca/fn-an/nutrition/sodium/index-eng.php

28. Food and Nutrition Board, Institute of Medicine, National Academies. Dietary Reference Intakes for Water, Potassium, Sodium, Chloride, and Sulfate. Washington DC: National Academies Press; 2005.

29. Australian government: National Health and Medical Research Council. Nutrient Reference Values. Sodium. [Cited 14-Sep-12]. Available from: http://www.nrv.gov.au/nutrients/sodium.htm

30. Centers for Disease Control and Prevention. Americans consume too much sodium. February 2011. [Cited 17-Aug-12]. Available from: http://www.cdc.gov/features/dssodium/

31. Hofmeyr GJ, Atallah AN, Duley L. Calcium supplementation during pregnancy for preventing hypertensive disorders and related problems. Cochrane Database Syst Rev. 2006 Jul 19;(3):CD001059.

32.   Conde-Agudelo A, Romero R, Kusanovic JP, Hassan SS. Supplementation with vitamins C and E during pregnancy for the prevention of preeclampsia and other adverse maternal and perinatal outcomes: a systematic review and meta-analysis. Am J Obstet Gynecol. 2011 Jun;204(6):503.e1-12.

33.   Scholl TO, Chen X, Goldberg GS, Khusial PR, Stein TP. Maternal diet, C-reactive protein, and the outcome of pregnancy. J Am Coll Nutr. 2011 Aug;30(4):233-40.

34.   Furness DL, Dekker GA, Roberts CT. DNA damage and health in pregnancy. J Reprod Immunol. 2011 May;89(2):153-62.

35.   Bodnar LM, Catov JM, Klebanoff MA, Ness RB, Roberts JM. Prepregnancy body mass index and the occurrence of severe hypertensive disorders of pregnancy. Epidemiology. 2007 Mar;18(2):234-9.

36.   Kennedy DA, Woodland C, Koren G. Lead exposure, gestational hypertension and pre-eclampsia: a systematic review of cause and effect. J Obstet Gynaecol. 2012 Aug;32(6):512-7.

37.   Martin JA, Hamilton BE, Sutton PD, Ventura SJ, Menacker F, Kirmeyer S, Munson ML; Centers for Disease Control and Prevention National Center for Health Statistics National Vital Statistics System. Births: final data for 2005. Natl Vital Stat Rep. 2007 Dec 5;56(6):1-103.

38.   Luke B, Eberlein T. When you're expecting twins, triples or quads: proven guidelines for a healthy multiple pregnancy. Harper Collins: New York; 2011.

39.   Food and Nutrition Board, National Library of Medicine. Kathleen M. Rasmussen and Ann L. Yaktine, Editors; Committee to Reexamine IOM Pregnancy Weight Guidelines; Institute of Medicine; National Research Council. Weight Gain During Pregnancy: Reexamining the Guidelines. Washington DC: National Academies Press; 2009.

40.   Flidel-Rimon O, Rhea DJ, Keith LG, Shinwell ES, Blickstein I. Early adequate maternal weight gain is associated with fewer small for gestational age triplets. J Perinat Med. 2005;33(5):379-82.

41.   Luke B, Eberlein T. When you're expecting twins, triples or quads: proven guidelines for a healthy multiple pregnancy. Harper Collins: New York; 2011.

42.   Lantz ME, Chez RA, Rodriguez A, Porter KB. Maternal weight gain patterns and birth weight outcome in twin gestation. Obstet Gynecol. 1996 Apr;87(4):551-6.

43.   Vitamin and Mineral Supplements: Your Nutrition Insurance Policy. [Cited 14-Sep-12]. Available from: http://www.drbarbaraluke.com/vitamin.aspx

44.   Livingston G and Cohn D. The New Demography of American Motherhood. Pew Research Center August 19, 2010. [Cited 16-Aug-12]. Available from: http://pewresearch.org/pubs/1586/changing-demographic-characteristics-american-mothers

45.   Lisonkova S, Janssen PA, Sheps SB, Lee SK, Dahlgren L. The effect of maternal age on adverse birth outcomes: does parity matter? J Obstet Gynaecol Can. 2010 Jun;32(6):541-8.

46.   Wang Y, Tanbo T, Abyholm T, Henriksen T. The impact of advanced maternal age and parity on obstetric and perinatal outcomes in singleton gestations. Arch Gynecol Obstet. 2011 Jul;284(1):31-7.

47.   Lao TT, Ho LF, Chan BC, Leung WC. Maternal age and prevalence of gestational diabetes mellitus. Diabetes Care. 2006 Apr;29(4):948-9

48.   Blankenship J. Pregnancy after surgical weight loss: nutrition care and recommendations. Weight Management Matters. 2005; 3(1)6-8.

49.   Allied Health Sciences Section Ad Hoc Nutrition Committee, Aills L., Blankenship J, Buffington C, Furtado M, Parrott J. ASMBS Allied Health Nutritional Guidelines for the Surgical Weight Loss Patient. Surg Obes Relat Dis. 2008 Sep-Oct;4(5 Suppl):S73-108. [Cited 22-Dec-12]. Available from: http://asmbs.org/2012/06/asmbs-integrated-health-nutritional-guidelines-for-the-surgical-weight-loss-patient/

50.   Allied Health Sciences Section Ad Hoc Nutrition Committee, Aills L, Blankenship J, Buffington C, Furtado M, Parrott J. ASMBS Allied Health Nutritional Guidelines for the Surgical Weight Loss Patient. Surg Obes Relat Dis. 2008 Sep-Oct;4(5 Suppl):S73-108. [Cited 22-Dec-12]. Available from: http://asmbs.org/2012/06/asmbs-integrated-health-nutritional-guidelines-for-the-surgical-weight-loss-patient/

51.   Xanthakos SA. Nutritional deficiencies in obesity and after bariatric surgery. Pediatr Clin North Am. 2009 Oct;56(5):1105-21.

52.   Xanthakos SA. Nutritional deficiencies in obesity and after bariatric surgery. Pediatr Clin North Am. 2009 Oct;56(5):1105-21.

Chapter 12
Considering Breastfeeding

1.   American Academy of Pediatrics. Section on Breastfeeding. Policy Statement: Breastfeeding and the use of human milk. Pediatrics. 2012 Mar;129 (3):e827–e841.

2.   World Health Organization. Health Topics: Breastfeeding. [Cited 16-Sep-12) Available from: http://www.who.int/topics/breastfeeding/en/

3.   Chirico G, Marzollo R, Cortinovis S, Fonte C, Gasparoni A. Antiinfective properties of human milk. J Nutr. 2008 Sep;138(9):1801S-1806S. [Cited 30-Dec-12]. Available from: http://jn.nutrition.org/content/138/9/1801S.long

4.   Schweigert FJ, Bathe K, Chen F, Büscher U, Dudenhausen JW. Effect of the stage of lactation in humans on carotenoid levels in milk, blood plasma and plasma lipoprotein fractions. Eur J Nutr. 2004 Feb;43(1):39-44. Epub 2004 Jan 6.

5.   American Academy of Pediatrics. Section on Breastfeeding. Policy Statement: Breastfeeding and the use of human milk. Pediatrics. 2012 Mar;129 (3):e827–e84.1.

6.   American Academy of Pediatrics. Section on Breastfeeding. Policy Statement: Breastfeeding and the use of human milk. Pediatrics. 2012 Mar;129 (3):e827–e84.1.

7.   Dennis CL, McQueen K. The relationship between infant-feeding outcomes and postpartum depression: a qualitative systematic review. Pediatrics. 2009 Apr;123(4):e736-51.

8.   James DC, Lessen R; American Dietetic Association. Position of the American Dietetic Association: promoting and supporting breastfeeding. J Am Diet Assoc. 2009 Nov;109(11):1926-42.

9.   Amorim AR, Linne YM, Lourenco PM. Diet or exercise, or both, for weight reduction in women after childbirth. Cochrane Database Syst Rev. 2007 Jul 18;(3):CD005627.

10.   Dietary Reference Intakes for Water, Potassium, Sodium, Chloride, and Sulfate The National Academies Press. Washington DC; 2005.

11.   Institute of Medicine. Nutrition During Lactation. The National Academies Press. Washington DC. 1991. [Cited 16-Sep-12]. Available from: http://www.nap.edu/openbook.php?record_id=1577&page=101

12.   American Academy of Pediatrics. Policy Statement: Breastfeeding and the use of human milk. Pediatrics. 2012 Mar;122 (5):1142-1152.

13.   Wagner CL, Greer FR and the American Academy of Pediatrics Section on Breastfeeding and Committee on Nutrition. Prevention of Rickets and Vitamin D Deficiency in Infants, Children, and Adolescents. Pediatrics. 2008 Nov;129 (3):e827–e841.

14.   Bjørnerem A, Ahmed LA, Jørgensen L, Størmer J, Joakimsen RM. Breastfeeding protects against hip fracture in postmenopausal women: the Tromsø study. J Bone Miner Res. 2011 Dec;26(12):2843-50. doi: 10.1002/jbmr.496.

15.   Caudill MA. Pre- and postnatal health: evidence of increased choline needs. J Am Diet Assoc. 2010 Aug;110(8):1198-206.

16.   Eichenfield LF, Hanifin JM, Beck LA, Lemanske RF Jr, Sampson HA, Weiss ST, Leung DY. Atopic dermatitis and asthma: parallels in the evolution of treatment. Pediatrics. 2003 Mar;111(3):608-16.

17.   Sicherer SH, Munoz-Furlong A, Sampson HA. Prevalence of peanut and tree nut allergy in the United States determined by means of a random digit dial telephone survey: a 5-year follow-up study. J Allergy Clin Immunol. 2003 Dec;112(6):1203-7.

18.   Greer FR, Sicherer SH, Burks AW; American Academy of Pediatrics Committee on Nutrition; American Academy of Pediatrics Section on Allergy and Immunology. Effects of early nutritional interventions on the development of atopic disease in infants and children: the role of maternal dietary restriction, breastfeeding, timing of introduction of complementary foods, and hydrolyzed formulas. Pediatrics. 2008 Jan;121(1):183-91.

19.   Greer FR, Sicherer SH, Burks AW; American Academy of Pediatrics Committee onNutrition, American Academy of Pediatrics Section on Allergy and Immunology. Effects of early nutritional interventions on the development of atopic disease in infants and children: the role of maternal dietary restriction, breastfeeding, timing of introduction of complementary foods, and hydrolyzed formulas. Pediatrics. 2008 Jan;121(1):183-91.

20.   Australasian Society of Clinical Immunology and Allergy. Allergy Prevention in Children. January 2010. [Cited 16-Sep-12]. Available from: http://www.allergy.org.au/patients/allergy-prevention/allergy-prevention-in-children

21.   Australasian Society of Clinical Immunology and Allergy. Allergy Prevention in Children. January 2010. [Cited 16-Sep-12]. Available from: http://www.allergy.org.au/patients/allergy-prevention/allergy-prevention-in-children

22.   National Institutes of Health. Dietary Supplement Fact Sheet: Vitamin B12. June 24, 2011. [Cited 6-Aug-12]. Available from: http://ods.od.nih.gov/factsheets/VitaminB12-HealthProfessional/

23.   American Academy of Pediatrics. Section on Breastfeeding. Policy Statement: Breastfeeding and the use of human milk. Pediatrics. 2012 Mar;129 (3):e827–e841.

24.   Rubin LP, Chan GM, Barrett-Reis BM, Fulton AB, Hansen RM, Ashmeade TL, Oliver JS, Mackey AD, Dimmit RA, Hartmann EE, Adamkin DH. Effect of carotenoids supplementation on plasma carotenoids, inflammation and visual development in preterm infants. J Perinatol. 2012 Jun;32(6):418-24. doi: 10.1038/jp.2011.87.

25.   American Academy of Pediatrics. Section on Breastfeeding. Policy Statement: Breastfeeding and the use of human milk. Pediatrics. 2012 Mar;129 (3):e827–e841.

26.   American Academy of Pediatrics Committee on Drugs. Transfer of drugs and other chemicals into human milk. Pediatrics. 2001 Sep;108(3):776-89.

27.   Oddy WH. Infant feeding and obesity risk in the child. Breastfeed Rev. 2012 Jul;20(2):7-12.

28.   Horta BL, Bahl R, Martines JC, Victora CG. Systematic reviews and meta-analysis. Geneva: World Health Organization; 2007. Evidence on the long-term effects of breastfeeding.

29.   Duration of breastfeeding and risk of overweight: a meta-analysis. Harder T, Bergmann R, Kallischnigg G, Plagemann A Am J Epidemiol. 2005 Sep 1; 162(5):397-403.

Chapter 13
First Weeks With baby

1.   US National Library of Medicine. Postpartum depression. A.D.A.M. Medical encyclopedia. September 2010. [Cited 10-Aug-12]. Available from: http://www. ncbi.nlm.nih.gov/pubmedhealth/PMH0004481/

2.   US National Library of Medicine. Fact Sheet: depression after childbirth—what can help. February 2010. [Cited 10-Aug-12]. Available from: http://www.ncbi. nlm.nih.gov/pubmedhealth/PMH0005000/

3.   Cassidy-Bushrow AE, Peters RM, Johnson DA, Li J, Rao DS. Vitamin D Nutritional Status and Antenatal Depressive Symptoms in African American Women. J Womens Health (Larchmt). 2012 Nov;21(11):1189-95.

4.   Mokhber N, Namjoo M, Tara F, Boskabadi H, Rayman MP, Ghayour-Mobarhan M,Sahebkar A, Majdi MR, Tavallaie S, Azimi-Nezhad M, Shakeri MT, Nematy M, Oladi M,Mohammadi M, Ferns G. Effect of supplementation with selenium on postpartum depression: a randomized double-blind placebo-controlled trial. J Matern Fetal Neonatal Med. 2011 Jan;24(1):104-8.

5.   Etebary S, Nikseresht S, Sadeghipour HR, Zarrindast MR. Postpartum depression and role of serum trace elements. Iran J Psychiatry. 2010 Spring;5(2):40-6.

6.   Gunderson EP, Abrams B. Epidemiology of gestational weight gain and body weight changes after pregnancy. Epidemiol Rev. 1999;21(2):261-75.

7.   Østbye T, Krause KM, Lovelady CA, Morey MC, Bastian LA, Peterson BL, Swamy GK,Brouwer RJ, McBride CM. Active Mothers Postpartum: a randomized controlled weight-loss intervention trial. Am J Prev Med. 2009 Sep;37(3):173-80 [Cited 11-Aug-12]. Available from: http://www.ncbi.nlm.nih.gov/pmc/articles/ PMC2774935/?tool=pubmed

8.   Hetherington MM, Boyland E. Short-term effects of chewing gum on snack intake and appetite. Appetite. 2007 May;48(3):397-401.

9.   Paula J. Geiselman, Corby Martin, Sandra Coulon, Donna Ryan, and Megan Apperson. Effects of chewing gum on specific macronutrient and total caloric intake in an afternoon snack. FASEB J. 2009 23:101.3.

10.   FRC Research corporation. The impact of chewing gum on consumer stress levels. June 2006.

11.   NWCR Facts. The National Weight Control Registry. [Cited 31-Dec-12]. Available from: http://www.nwcr.ws/Research/default.htm

12.   NWCR Facts. The National Weight Control Registry. [Cited 31-Dec-12]. Available from: http://www.nwcr.ws/Research/default.htm

13.   NWCR Facts. The National Weight Control Registry. [Cited 31-Dec-12]. Available from: http://www.nwcr.ws/Research/default.htm

14. Kiernan M, Moore SD, Schoffman DE, Lee K, King AC, Taylor CB, Kiernan NE, Perri MG. Social support for healthy behaviors: scale psychometrics and prediction of weight loss among women in a behavioral program. Obesity (Silver Spring). 2012 Apr;20(4):756-64. doi: 10.1038/oby.2011.293.

15. Vander Wal JS, Marth JM, Khosla P, Jen KL, Dhurandhar NV. Short-term effect of eggs on satiety in overweight and obese subjects. J Am Coll Nutr. 2005 Dec;24(6):510-5.

16. National Institutes of Health, National Heart, Lung and Blood Institute, North American Association for the Study of Obesity. The Practical Guide; Identification, evaluation and treatment of overweight and obesity in adults. 2000.

17. Gunderson EP, Rifas-Shiman SL, Oken E, Rich-Edwards JW, Kleinman KP, Taveras EM, Gillman MW. Association of fewer hours of sleep at 6 months postpartum with substantial weight retention at 1 year postpartum. Am J Epidemiol. 2008 Jan 15;167(2):178-87.

18. Maturi MS, Afshary P, Abedi P. Effect of physical activity intervention based on a pedometer on physical activity level and anthropometric measures after childbirth: a randomized controlled trial. BMC Pregnancy Childbirth. 2011; 11: 103. [Cited 11-Aug-12]. Available from: http://www.ncbi.nlm.nih.gov/pmc/articles/PMC3292461/?tool=pubmed

19. Turner-McGrievy GM, Barnard ND, Scialli AR. A two-year randomized weight loss trial comparing a vegan diet to a more moderate low-fat diet. Obesity. (Silver Spring). 2007 Sep;15(9):2276-81.

20. Berkow SE, Barnard N. Vegetarian diets and weight status. Nutr Rev. 2006 Apr;64(4):175-88.

21. Conde-Agudelo A, Rosas-Bermúdez A, Kafury-Goeta AC. Birth spacing and risk of adverse perinatal outcomes: a meta-analysis. JAMA. 2006 Apr 19;295(15):1809-23.

22. Linné Y, Dye L, Barkeling B, Rössner S. Weight development over time in parous women--the SPAWN study--15 years follow-up. Int J Obes Relat Metab Disord. 2003 Dec;27(12):1516-22.

Chapter 14
Fitting Fitness In

1. American College of Obstetricians and Gynecologists (2002, reaffirmed 2007). Exercise during pregnancy and the postpartum period. ACOG Committee Opinion No. 267. Obstetrics and Gynecology, 99(1): 171–173.

2. Sports Medicine Australia. Exercise in pregnancy fact sheet. [Cited 24-Feb-12]. Available from: http://sma.org.au/resources/policies/active-women/

3. Royal College of Obstetricians and Gynaecologists. Statement No. 4. Exercise in pregnancy. January 2006.

4. Mottola M. Exercise and pregnancy: Canadian guidelines for health care professionals. Government of Alberta. 2011 June. [Cited 1-Jan-13] Available from: http://www.centre4activeliving.ca/publications/wellspring/2011/aug-pregnancy.html

5. Canadian society for exercise physiology. Physical activity readiness medical examination for pregnancy (PARmed-X for pregnancy). 2002. [Cited 1-Jan-13]. Available from: http://www.csep.ca/cmfiles/publications/parq/parmed-xpreg.pdf

6. Owe KM, Nystad W, Bø K. Correlates of regular exercise during pregnancy: the Norwegian Mother and Child Cohort Study. Scand J Med Sci Sports. 2009 Oct;19(5):637-45.

7. Ruchat SM, Davenport MH, Giroux I, Hillier M, Batada A, Sopper MM, Hammond JM, Mottola MF. Nutrition and exercise reduce excessive weight gain in normal-weight pregnant women. Med Sci Sports Exerc. 2012 Aug;44(8):1419-26.

8. Teychenne M, Ball K, Salmon J. Physical activity and likelihood of depression in adults: a review. Prev Med. 2008 May;46(5):397-411.

9. Carek PJ, Laibstain SE, Carek SM. Exercise for the treatment of depression and anxiety. Int J Psychiatry Med. 2011;41(1):15-28.

10. Gjestland K, Bø K, Owe KM, Eberhard-Gran M. Do pregnant women follow exercise guidelines? Prevalence data among 3482 women, and prediction of low-back pain, pelvic girdle pain and depression. Br J Sports Med. 2012 Aug.

11. Gjestland K, Bø K, Owe KM, Eberhard-Gran M. Do pregnant women follow exercise guidelines? Prevalence data among 3482 women, and prediction of low-back pain, pelvic girdle pain and depression. Br J Sports Med. 2012 Aug.

12. Curtis K, Weinrib A Katz J. Systematic review of yoga for pregnant women: current status and future directions. Evid Based Complement Alternat Med. 2012 Aug; 2012: 715942. doi: 10.1155/2012/715942

13. Babbar S, Parks-Savage AC, Chauhan SP. Yoga during pregnancy: a review. Am J Perinatol. 2012 Jun;29(6):459-64.

14. Price BB, Amini SB, Kappeler K. Exercise in pregnancy: effect on fitness and obstetric outcomes-a randomized trial. Med Sci Sports Exerc. 2012 Dec;44(12):2263-9. doi: 10.1249/MSS.0b013e318267ad67.

15. The American College of Obstetricians and Gynecologists. Exercise during pregnancy. Frequently asked questions. FAQ 0119. August 2011. [Cited 1-Jan-13]. Available from: http://www.acog.org/~/media/For%20Patients/faq119.ashx

16. Nieman DC, Henson DA, Austin MD, Brown VA. Immune response to a 30-minute walk. Med Sci Sports Exerc. 2005 Jan;37(1):57-62.

17. Palomba S. et al. Structured exercise training programme versus hypocaloric hyperproteic diet in obese polycystic ovary syndrome patients with anovulaotry infertility; a 24 week pilot study. Hum Reprod. 2008 Mar;23(3):642-50

18. Jackson G. The importance of risk factor reduction in erectile dysfunction. Current Urology Reoirt 2007; 8(6):463-6.

19.   Melzer K, Schutz Y, Boulvain M, Kayser B. Physical activity and pregnancy. cardiovascular adaptations, recommendations and pregnancy outcomes. Sports Med. 2010 Jun 1;40(6):493-507. doi: 10.2165/11532290-000000000-00000.

20.   National Health Service (UK). Exercise in pregnancy. [Cited 1-Jan-13]. Available from: http://www.nhs.uk/conditions/pregnancy-and-baby/pages/pregnancy-exercise.aspx#close

21.   American pregnancy association. Kegels. [Cited 1-Jan-13]. Available from: http://www.americanpregnancy.org/labornbirth/kegelexercises.htm

22.   Davies GA, Wolfe LA, Mottola MF, MacKinnon C, Arsenault MY, Bartellas E, Cargill Y, Gleason T, Iglesias S, Klein M, Martel MJ, Roggensack A, Wilson K, Gardiner P, Graham T, Haennel R, Hughson R, MacDougall D, McDermott J, Ross R,Tiidus P, Trudeau F; SOGC Clinical Practice Obstetrics Committee, Canadian Society for Exercise Physiology Board of Directors. Exercise in pregnancy and the postpartum period. J Obstet Gynaecol Can. 2003 Jun;25(6):516-29. [Cited 18-Feb-12]. Available from: http://www.sogc.org/guidelines/public/129E-JCPG-June2003.pdf

23.   Tobias DK, Zhang C, van Dam RM, Bowers K, Hu FB. Physical activity before and during pregnancy and risk of gestational diabetes mellitus: a meta-analysis. Diabetes Care. 2011 Jan;34(1):223-9.

24.   American College of Obstetricians and Gynecologists (2002, reaffirmed 2007). Exercise during pregnancy and the postpartum period. ACOG Committee Opinion No. 267. Obstetrics and Gynecology, 99(1): 171–173.

25.   Davies GA, Wolfe LA, Mottola MF, MacKinnon C, Arsenault MY, Bartellas E, Cargill Y, Gleason T, Iglesias S, Klein M, Martel MJ, Roggensack A, Wilson K, Gardiner P, Graham T, Haennel R, Hughson R, MacDougall D, McDermott J, Ross R,Tiidus P, Trudeau F; SOGC Clinical Practice Obstetrics Committee, Canadian Society for Exercise Physiology Board of Directors. Exercise in pregnancy and the postpartum period. J Obstet Gynaecol Can. 2003 Jun;25(6):516-29. [Cited 18-Feb-12]. Available from: http://www.sogc.org/guidelines/public/129E-JCPG-June2003.pdf

26.   American College of Obstricians and Gynecologists. Exercise during pregnancy and the postpartum period. ACOG Committee Opinion No. 267. Reaffirmed 2009. Obstet Gynecol 2002;99:171-173.

27.   Davies GA, Wolfe LA, Mottola MF, MacKinnon C, Arsenault MY, Bartellas E, Cargill Y, Gleason T, Iglesias S, Klein M, Martel MJ, Roggensack A, Wilson K, Gardiner P, Graham T, Haennel R, Hughson R, MacDougall D, McDermott J, Ross R,Tiidus P, Trudeau F; SOGC Clinical Practice Obstetrics Committee, Canadian Society for Exercise Physiology Board of Directors. Exercise in pregnancy and the postpartum period. J Obstet Gynaecol Can. 2003 Jun;25(6):516-29. [Cited 18-Feb-12]. Available from: http://www.sogc.org/guidelines/public/129E-JCPG-June2003.pdf

28. The American College of Obstetricians and Gynecologists. Exercise during pregnancy. Frequently asked questions. FAQ 0119. August 2011. [Cited 1-Jan-13]. Available from: http://www.acog.org/~/media/For%20Patients/faq119.ashx

29. Davies GA, Wolfe LA, Mottola MF, MacKinnon C, Arsenault MY, Bartellas E, Cargill Y, Gleason T, Iglesias S, Klein M, Martel MJ, Roggensack A, Wilson K, Gardiner P, Graham T, Haennel R, Hughson R, MacDougall D, McDermott J, Ross R,Tiidus P, Trudeau F; SOGC Clinical Practice Obstetrics Committee, Canadian Society for Exercise Physiology Board of Directors. Exercise in pregnancy and the postpartum period. J Obstet Gynaecol Can. 2003 Jun;25(6):516-29. [Cited 18-Feb-12]. Available from: http://www.sogc.org/guidelines/public/129E-JCPG-June2003.pdf

30. The American College of Obstetricians and Gynecologists. Exercise during pregnancy. Frequently asked questions. FAQ 0119. August 2011. [Cited 1-Jan-13]. Available from: http://www.acog.org/~/media/For%20Patients/faq119.ashx

31. Davies GA, Wolfe LA, Mottola MF, MacKinnon C, Arsenault MY, Bartellas E, Cargill Y, Gleason T, Iglesias S, Klein M, Martel MJ, Roggensack A, Wilson K, Gardiner P, Graham T, Haennel R, Hughson R, MacDougall D, McDermott J, Ross R,Tiidus P, Trudeau F; SOGC Clinical Practice Obstetrics Committee, Canadian Society for Exercise Physiology Board of Directors. Exercise in pregnancy and the postpartum period. J Obstet Gynaecol Can. 2003 Jun;25(6):516-29. [Cited 18-Feb-12]. Available from: http://www.sogc.org/guidelines/public/129E-JCPG-June2003.pdf

32. Davies GA, Wolfe LA, Mottola MF, MacKinnon C, Arsenault MY, Bartellas E, Cargill Y, Gleason T, Iglesias S, Klein M, Martel MJ, Roggensack A, Wilson K, Gardiner P, Graham T, Haennel R, Hughson R, MacDougall D, McDermott J, Ross R,Tiidus P, Trudeau F; SOGC Clinical Practice Obstetrics Committee, Canadian Society for Exercise Physiology Board of Directors. Exercise in pregnancy and the postpartum period. J Obstet Gynaecol Can. 2003 Jun;25(6):516-29. [Cited 18-Feb-12]. Available from: http://www.sogc.org/guidelines/public/129E-JCPG-June2003.pdf

33. Mottola MF. Exercise and pregnancy: Canadian guidelines for health care professionals. Wellspring. Volume 22(4) June 2011. [Cited 1-Jan-13] Available from: http://www.centre4activeliving.ca/publications/wellspring/2011/aug-pregnancy.html

34. Mottola MF. Exercise prescription for overweight and obese women: pregnancy and postpartum. Obstet Gynecol Clin North Am. 2009 Jun;36(2):301-16, viii.

35. Mottola MF, Giroux I, Gratton R, Hammond JA, Hanley A, Harris S, McManus R,Davenport MH, Sopper MM. Nutrition and exercise prevent excess weight gain in overweight pregnant women. Med Sci Sports Exerc. 2010 Feb;42(2):265-72.

36. Garfinkel MS, Singhal A, Katz WA, Allan DA, Reshetar R, Schumacher HR Jr. Yoga-based intervention for carpal tunnel syndrome: a randomized trial. JAMA. 1998 Nov 11;280(18):1601-3.

37.   Okonta NR. Does yoga therapy reduce blood pressure in patients with hypertension: an integrative review. Holist Nurs Pract. 2012 May-Jun;26(3):137-41.

38.   Smith JA, Greer T, Sheets T, Watson S. Is there more to yoga than exercise? Altern Ther Health Med. 2011 May-Jun;17(3):22-9.

39.   Pennick VE and Young G. Interventions for preventing and treating pelvic and back pain in pregnancy. Cochrane Database of Systematic Reviews. 1998. Issue 3. Updated 2007.

40.   Gjestland K, Bø K, Owe KM, Eberhard-Gran M. Do pregnant women follow exercise guidelines? Prevalence data among 3482 women, and prediction of low-back pain, pelvic girdle pain and depression. Br J Sports Med. 2012 Aug 17.

Chapter 15
Stocking The Pregnant Kitchen

1.   US Department of Health and Human Services. Policy Research for Front of Package Nutrition Labeling: Environmental Scan and Literature Review. February 2011. [Cited 2-Sep-12]. Available from: http://aspe.hhs.gov/sp/reports/2011/FOPNutritionLabelingLitRev/index.shtml#3.4.3

2.   U.S. Food and Drug Administration. 10. Appendix B: Additional Requirements for Nutrient Content Claims. May 2011. [Cited 2-Sep-12]. Available from: http://www.fda.gov/Food/GuidanceComplianceRegulatoryInformation/GuidanceDocuments/FoodLabelingNutrition/FoodLabelingGuide/ucm064916.htm

3.   U.S. Food and Drug Administration. 9. Appendix A: Definitions of Nutrient Content Claims. July 2011. [Cited 2-Sep-12]. Available from: http://www.fda.gov/Food/GuidanceComplianceRegulatoryInformation/GuidanceDocuments/FoodLabelingNutrition/FoodLabelingGuide/ucm064911.htm

4.   Piecha G, Koleganova N, Ritz E, Müller A, Fedorova OV, Bagrov AY, Lutz D, Schirmacher P, Gross-Weissmann ML. High salt intake causes adverse fetal programming—vascular effects beyond blood pressure. Nephrol Dial Transplant. 2012 Sep;27(9):3464-76. doi: 10.1093/ndt/gfs027.

5.   Coimbra TM, Francescato HD, Balbi AP, Marin EC, Costa RS. Renal Development and Blood Pressure in Offspring from Dams Submitted to High-Sodium Intake during Pregnancy and Lactation. Int J Nephrol. 2012;2012:919128.

6.   Koleganova N, Piecha G, Ritz E, Becker LE, Müller A, Weckbach M, Nyengaard JR, Schirmacher P, Gross-Weissmann ML. Both high and low maternal salt intake in pregnancy alter kidney development in the offspring. Am J Physiol Renal Physiol. 2011 Aug;301(2):F344-54.

7.   US FDA. Did you know that a store can sell food past the expiration date? Updated April 2012. [Cited 12-Aug-12]. Available from: http://www.fda.gov/AboutFDA/Transparency/Basics/ucm210073.htm

8.   Health Canada. Nutrition labeling. September 2010. [Cited 12-Aug-12]. Available from: http://www.hc-sc.gc.ca/fn-an/label-etiquet/nutrition/index-eng.php

9.   Food standards agency. Understanding food labeling rules. [Cited 12-Aug-12]. Available from: http://www.food.gov.uk/scotland/regsscotland/ull/

10.   Food standards Australia New Zealand. Use by and best before dates. July 2012. [Cited 12-Aug-12]. Available from: http://www.foodstandards.gov.au/consumerinformation/labellingoffood/usebyandbestbeforeda5593.cfm

11.   US FDA. Did you know that a store can sell food past the expiration date? Updated April 2012. [Cited 12-Aug-12]. Available from: http://www.fda.gov/AboutFDA/Transparency/Basics/ucm210073.htm

12.   USDA Food Safety and Inspection Service: Fact Sheets: Food product dating. September 2011. [Cited 2-Sep-12]. Available from: http://www.fsis.usda.gov/Factsheets/Food_Product_dating/#2

13.   Egg facts and fun. Julian dates. [Cited 6-Sep-12]. Available from: http://www.incredibleegg.org/egg-facts/eggcyclopedia/j/julian-dates

14.   USDA Food Safety and Inspection Service: Fact Sheets: Food product dating. September 2011. [Cited 2-Sep-12]. Available from: http://www.fsis.usda.gov/Factsheets/Food_Product_dating/#2

15.   US Food and Drug Administration. FDA Food Code 2009: Chapter 4 - Equipment, Utensils and Linens. 2009. [Cited 23-Sep-12]. Available from: http://www.fda.gov/food/foodsafety/retailfoodprotection/foodcode/foodcode2009/ucm188064.htm

16.   Bruhn CM, Rickman JC, Barrett DM PhD, Review Nutritional comparison of fresh, frozen and canned fruits and vegetables. Part 1. Vitamins C and B and phenolic compounds. J Sci Food Agric 87:930–944 (2007).

17.   Makhlouf J et al. Some nutritional characteristics of beans, sweet corn and peas (raw, canned, and frozen) produced in the province of Quebec. Food Research International. 1995; 28:253-259.

18.   Favell DJ. A comparison of the vitamin C content of fresh and frozen vegetables. Food Chemistry. 1998;62:59-64.

19.   Shi J., LeMaguer M. Lycopene in tomatoes: chemical and physical properties affected by food processing. 2000; 40(1):1-42.

20.   Bruhn CM, Rickman JC, Barrett DM PhD, Review Nutritional comparison of fresh, frozen and canned fruits and vegetables. Part 1. Vitamins C and B and phenolic compounds. J Sci Food Agric 87:930–944 (2007).

21.   Food Safety Network, University of Guelph. What are safe grilling practices? 2003. [Cited 7-Sep-12]. Available from: http://www.foodsafety.ksu.edu/articles/533/grilling_factsheet.pdf

22.   Puangsombat K, Jirapakkul W, Smith JS. Inhibitory activity of Asian spices on heterocyclic amines formation in cooked beef patties. J Food Sci. 2011 Oct;76(8):T174-80. doi: 10.1111/j.1750-3841.2011.02338.x.

23. Consumer Reports: Greener choices, products for a better planet. Get out and grill. healthy cooking tips. July 2010 [Cited 7 Sep-12]. Available from: http://www.greenerchoices.org/products.cfm?product=0710grilltips

24. Puangsombat K, Gadgil P, Houser TA, Hunt MC, Smith JS. Occurrence of heterocyclic amines in cooked meat products. Meat Sci. 2012 Mar;90(3):739-46.

25. Puangsombat K, Gadgil P, Houser TA, Hunt MC, Smith JS. Occurrence of heterocyclic amines in cooked meat products. Meat Sci. 2012 Mar;90(3):739-46.

26. Scanlan R. Nitrosamines and cancer. November 2010. [Cited 8-Sep-12]. Available from: http://lpi.oregonstate.edu/f-w00/nitrosamine.html

27. Food Additives. Center for Science in the Public Interest. [Cited 12-Aug-12]. Available from: http://www.cspinet.org/reports/chemcuisine.htm

28. Food Additives. Center for Science in the Public Interest. [Cited 12-Aug-12]. Available from: http://www.cspinet.org/reports/chemcuisine.htm

29. Pogoda JM, Preston-Martin S. Maternal cured meat consumption during pregnancy and risk of paediatric brain tumour in offspring: potentially harmful levels of intake. Public Health Nutr. 2001 Apr;4(2):183-9.

30. Huncharek M, Kupelnick B. A meta-analysis of maternal cured meat consumption during pregnancy and the risk of childhood brain tumors. Neuroepidemiology. 2004 Jan-Apr;23(1-2):78-84.

31. Pogoda JM, Preston-Martin S, Howe G, Lubin F, Mueller BA, Holly EA, Filippini G, Peris-Bonet R, McCredie MR, Cordier S, Choi W. An international case-control study of maternal diet during pregnancy and childhood brain tumor risk: a histology-specific analysis by food group. Ann Epidemiol. 2009 Mar;19(3):148-60. doi: 10.1016/j.annepidem.2008.12.011.

32. US Environmental Protection Agency. Nitrates and Nitrites, Toxicity and Exposure Assessment for Children. May 2007. [Cited 3-Jan-13]. Available from: http://www.epa.gov/teach/chem_summ/Nitrates_summary.pdf

33. Gougeon R. Spidel M, Lee K, Field CJ. Canadian Diabetes Association National Nutrition Committee Technical Review: Non-nutritive Intense Sweeteners in Diabetes Management. Can J Diab. 2004 (28) 4:385-389.

34. Gougeon R. Spidel M, Lee K, Field CJ. Canadian Diabetes Association National Nutrition Committee Technical Review: Non-nutritive Intense Sweeteners in Diabetes Management. Can J Diab. 2004 (28) 4:385-389.

35. Food Additives. Center for Science in the Public Interest. [Cited 12-Aug-12]. Available from: http://www.cspinet.org/reports/chemcuisine.htm

36. United States Department of Agriculture. Agriculture Marketing Department. National organic program. June 2012. [Cited 12-Aug-12]. Available from: http://www.ams.usda.gov/AMSv1.0/nop

37.   United States Department of Agriculture. Agriculture Marketing Department. National organic program. June 2012. [Cited 12-Aug-12]. Available from: http://www.ams.usda.gov/AMSv1.0/ams.fetchTemplateData.do?template=Template C&navID=NationalOrganicProgram&leftNav=NationalOrganicProgram&page=NOPConsumers&description=Consumers&acct=nopgeninfo

38.   Bouchard MF, Chevrier J, Harley KG, Kogut K, Vedar M, Calderon N, Trujillo C, Johnson C, Bradman A, Barr DB, Eskenazi B. Prenatal exposure to organophosphate pesticides and IQ in 7-year-old children. Environ Health Perspect. 2011 Aug;119(8):1189-95. doi: 10.1289/ehp.1003185.

39.   Eskenazi B, Rosas LG, Marks AR, Bradman A, Harley K, Holland N, Johnson C, Fenster L, Barr DB. Pesticide toxicity and the developing brain. Basic Clin Pharmacol Toxicol. 2008 Feb;102(2):228-36. The Organic Center. Today's Science Insight. April 2011. [Cited 9-8-12]. Available from: http://www.organiccenter.org/dailylog.php?action=detail&dailylogId=65&categoryId=2

40.   Benbrook C, Zhao X, Yanez J, Davies N, Andrews P. New Evidence Confirms the Nutritional Superiority of Plant-Based Organic Foods. State of Science Review. The Organic Center. March 2008. [Cited 8-Sep-12]. Available from: http://www.organic-center.org/science.nutri.php?action=view&report_id=126

41.   Brandt K, L eifert C, Sanderson R, Seal CJ. Agroecosystem Management and Nutritional Quality of Plant Foods: The Case of Organic Fruits and Vegetables. Critical Reviews in Plant Sciences 2011; (30)1-2.

42.   Smith-Spangler C, Brandeau ML, Hunter GE, Bavinger JC, Pearson M, Eschbach PJ,Sundaram V, Liu H, Schirmer P, Stave C, Olkin I, Bravata DM. Are organic foods safer or healthier than conventional alternatives?: a systematic review. Ann Intern Med. 2012 Sep 4;157(5):348-66.

43.   Environmental Working Group. 2012 Shopper's Guide to Pesticides in Produce. June 2012. [Cited 8-Sep-12]. Available from: http://www.ewg.org/foodnews/list/

Chapter 16
Eating Out

1.   US Food and Drug Administration. Overview of FDA Proposed Labeling Requirements for Restaurants, Similar Retail Food Establishments and Vending Machines. November 2012. [Cited 3-Jan-13]. Available from: http://www.fda.gov/Food/LabelingNutrition/ucm248732.htm

2.   Goulding, M. The 20 worst foods in American. Men's Health Magazine. 2008. [Cited 17-Aug-12]. Available from: http://www.menshealth.com/20worst/worstfood.html

3.   What is Food with Integrity? [Cited 8-18-12]. Available from http://www.chipotle.com/en-US/fwi/fwi.aspx

INDEX

Academy of Nutrition and Dietetics, 80, 228, 229, 259

Acesulfame K, 164, 368-369

Acupuncture, 43, 170, 342

Additives
- chemical, 124
- food, 252, 364-368, 371

Aerobic exercise, 292, 313

Ahmad, Madiha, 388

Alcohol, 26
- avoiding, 114
- breastfeeding and, 300
- fertility and, 27, 46
- pregnancy and, 114

Activity, physical, 254, 324-325
- tips for, 334-336

Additives, food, 364-368

Agave, 70, 72

Allergies
- preventing in pregnancy, 83-84
- preventing in breastfeeding, 278, 295, 296

Almonds, 33, 93, 166, 215

Anemia, 61, 187, 189, 232

Antioxidants
- content of food, 33, 49-50
- fertility and, 33, 46, 48-49, 52
- pre-eclampsia and, 260
- pregnancy and, 164, 166

American Academy of Pediatrics, 84, 292, 293, 296, 299, 300

American Association of Allergy, Asthma and Immunology, 84

American Association of Diabetes Educators, 247

American Cancer Society, 113

American College of Obstetricians and Gynecologists, 116, 168, 170, 332, 340

American Council on Exercise, 340

American Dental Association, 177

American Diabetes Association, 34, 247, 248, 255, 369

American Heart Association, 78, 80, 81, 228

American Institute for Cancer Research, 228

American Society for Metabolic and Bariatric Surgery, 274

American Society of Reproductive Medicine, 45

American Thyroid Association, 47

Apps (phone applications), 108, 127, 253,

Arachidonic acid, 79

Artificial
- coloring, 151, 365, 366
- flavors, 365
- sweeteners, 368-370

Arsenic, 71, 124, 125

Aspartame, 368-370

Australia, 68, 114, 116, 124, 131, 146, 151, 240, 259, 369

Aversions, food, 173

Avocado, 193, 219, 230, 384
- recommended fat, 92
- superfood and, 33, 93

Bad habits, 112-119

Bacteria, dental health and, 27, 28, 177

Bacteria, destroying, 148

Bacteria, foodborne 129-140
- Campylobacter, 129
- Clostridium botulinum, 129
- E coli, 129, 148
- Listeria, 30, 129-131,
- organic and, 372
- Salmonella, 129, 148
- Staph, 129, 148

Bacterial infection, 102
Bacteria, probiotic, 67, 101
Bad bugs, 129, 132, 134, 135
Backache, 338
Baby blues, 306, 337
Beef
- BOLD diet and, 258
- choline and, 220
- cooking and, 137, 140
- iron and, 24
- multiple pregnancy and, 265
- natural, 355
- superfood and, 33, 93
Beer
- breastfeeding and, 300
- ginger, 170
- sulfites in, 366
Bedrest, 246, 267
- eating while on, 269
- exercise and, 335, 341
- resources for, 271
- survival tips, 270
Before Baby Diet, 28
Blood supply, 104, 332
Blood pressure, 256-258
- age and, 272
- diet and, 54, 78, 192, 214, 220, 229, 352, 381
- fat and 78
- PCOS and, 40
- pre-eclampsia and, 16
- preventing 207-208, 261, 273, 299, 325, 339
- trying to conceive and, 16,17, 20
Blood sugar
- controlling, 25, 34, 53, 62, 171, 178, 248,
    249-253, 255
- diet and, 63, 64, 71, 73, 115, 162, 192, 199, 244
- exercise and, 254, 329
- glycemic index and, 63
- high, 63, 212, 247
- low, 40, 171, 173
- prenatal programming and, 20
Blueberries, 33,93, 196, 345
BMI (Body Mass Index), 22
- categories, 105
- fertility and, 35,
- gaining according to, 105, 157, 183
- health risks and, 261,
Bone development, 59, 99
BPA (bisphenol A), 121-122, 128, 140, 141, 144
Brain development, 23, 78, 79, 114, 126, 203,
    220-222, 251, 255

Breastfeeding
- and allergies, 294-297
- barriers for, 279-284
- benefits of, 256, 278-279
- eating for, 289-294
- caffeine and, 300
- premature infants and, 298-299
- for special groups, 297
- weight loss during, 318-320
- work and, 286-287
Brown rice syrup, 71
Buckwheat, 31,33,75
Budget
- eating on, 355-358

Caesarean section, 20, 105, 346
Caffeine 115-117
- breastfeeding and, 300
- chocolate milk and, 187,
- infertility and, 44
- recommendations, 28, 44
Calcium
- blood pressure and, 208-210, 258-259, 273
- breastfeeding and, 293
- functions, 59
- food/beverage sources, 215
- and lactose intolerance, 186
- and lead, 126
- requirements, 214
- sneaking into diet, 216
- supplements, 98-100, 189
- vegetarian diet and, 230, 233
Calories
- how to add, 110
- needed during pregnancy, 87, 157, 181, 210
- needed during breastfeeding, 289
- splurge, 87, 93
- translating fat to, 81
- weight loss and, 307, 313-316-
Canada, 23, 80, 98, 114, 137, 151, 228, 259, 324,
    327, 367, 370
Carbohydrates, 101, 62-75
- diabetes and, 71, 226, 250, 251
- recommendations, 87, 251
- sugar and, 70-72
CDC (US Centers for Disease Control and
    Prevention), 16, 129, 249,
Chan, Christin, 336
Cheese 91, 110, 130, 131, 178, 352
- calcium content and, 215, 216
- cottage, 76, 91,110, 171, 216

- fat content in, 380
Chemicals, environmental, 119-129, 146-149, 373
- beauty care and, 149-152
- breastfeeding and, 301
- in tap water, 132-134
- plastics and, 141-143
- smoking and, 26, 45
- workplace and, 30,
Cherries, 49, 50
Chewing gum, 307
Chocolate
- antioxidants and, 53
- caffeine in, 117
- preeclampsia and, 208
Celiac disease, 46-47
- diet for, 75-77
Center for Science in the Public Interest (CSPI), 117, 164, 196, 366,
Choline, 23, 33, 57, 96, 163, 220, 293, 294
Cleaning
- kitchen, 135,
- produce, 135
- products, 123, 147, 148, 149
Clif Kit's organic bars, 70, 75
Coffee, 44, 115, 116
Cold cuts, 130, 352
Coloring, artificial, 365, 366
Constipation
- fiber and, 62, 191-193
- tips for preventing, 201-203
Consumer Reports Magazine, 124, 132
Complications, pregnancy, 20, 104, 109, 246-247
Cooking
- food safety and, 363,
- microwave, 140
- vitamins and, 362
Cookware
- safer 138, 139
Cosmetics, safe, 150-152
Corn syrup, high fructose, 70, 72
Cravings
- causes of, 173
- channeling, 174-176
Culturelle (probiotic), 102
Curing agents, 365, 368
Cytomegalovirus (CMV), 30

Dad
- diet tips for, 50-52
- fertility and, 28, 50

Daily BFFFs, 95
Dairy products, 91, 178
- what counts as a serving, 32
Delivery
- eating after, 304
- what to expect after, 314
Dental care, 27, 176-178
Depression, 25, 306
- nutrition and 25, 108, 306
DHA (docohexaenoic acid), 79, 101, 127, 292
Diabetes, (also see gestational diabetes), 248
- risk factors for, 247
- testing for, 208, 248, 255
Diets
- BOLD, 258-260
- DASH, 258-260
- Eating Expectantly 86-87
- evaluating, 312
- Mediterranean, 84
- multiples and, 264-266
- twelve steps to a healthy, 57
Drugs
- breastfeeding and, 297
- dangers of during pregnancy, 26-27, 114
Duker Freuman, Tamara, 76
Dunaway Teh, Ann, 319

Eating Expectantly Diets, 86-93
- 1st Trimester, 159
- 2nd Trimester, 182
- 3rd Trimester, 211
- Before Baby, 31
- Best for Breastfeeding, 289
- Lose that Baby Fat, 316
Eczema, 84, 102, 295, 296
Eating
- clean, 364-374
- to prevent allergies, 83, 84, 295, 296
- vegetarian, 228-241
Eating disorders, 47-48, 308
Eating out
- at your favorite restaurant, 383-390
- fast food and, 391-392
- food safety and, 377-378
- pitfalls of, 376-382
- sodium and, 351
- vegetarian, 241-243
Eggs
- choline content of, 220
- cooking, 138
- health benefits, 57, 108, 163

- labeling of, 353
Endocrine disrupting chemicals, 120
- avoiding, 128
- BPA (bisphenol A), 121, 122
- dioxins, 121
- PCBs (polycholorinated biphenyls), 122
- pesticides, 123
- phthalates, 123
Energy, tips for increasing, 222
Energy drinks, 116
Environmental Protection Agency (EPA), 120,
    129, 132, 147
Environmental Working Group (EWG), 151, 373
Emotions, 106, 246,
Equal (aspartame), 360, 370
Essential fats. See fats
Estrogen, 38, 39, 42, 120, 141, 168
Exercise
- benefits of, 43, 61, 107, 202, 204, 254, 324-326
- guidelines for
-- pregnancy, 324, 332-333
-- postpartum, 307
- ideas, 333-335
- kegels, 327
- pelvic tilt, 326
- tips, 328-330
- yoga, 336-339
European Commision, 79, 367
European Union, 121, 126, 151, 152, 369, 371,
    372
Evers, Connie, 356

Fast food,
- healthier choices, 392
Fat 78-83
- body, 34, 38, 39, 120
- fertility, 34, 38, 39, 44, 53
- how much, 82
- monounsaturated, 79
- needs during breastfeeding, 292
- needs during pregnancy, 81
- omega-3 fats, 79
- polyunsaturated, 79
- recommended, 80
- saturated, 53, 79, 80-81, 84, 292
- trans, 80-81
- watching your,
Fertility
- dad's diet and, 50-52
- factors you can control, 43-50
- nutrition and, 23-25

- seven tips to fuel your, 52-54
- weight and, 21-22, 38-39
Fetal development
- in 1st trimester, 156
- in 2nd trimester, 180
- in 3rd trimester, 206
Fatigue, 172, 222, 341
Fiber
- diabetes and, 192, 251
- focus on, 62
- food sources, 193-195
Fish and seafood
- consumption advisories, 127, 130, 134
- cooking and internal temperatures, 137
- DHA content of, 101
- environmental contaminants and, 101, 127
- labeling, 349-350
- recommended, 127
- storing, 353
Fitness. See exercise
Fluids
- breastfeeding and, 292
- morning sickness and, 169
- pregnancy and, 62, 95
First trimester
- calorie needs for, 157
- developmental highlights in, 156-157
- diet challenges during, 168-173
- power nutrients for, 164
- weight gain for, 157
Flaxseed, 93, 101, 194, 220
Folate (folic acid)
- before pregnancy, 23, 24, 28, 49, 96
- food sources of, 24
- importance of, 208
- recommendations for, 24
Food additives, 364-370
Food allergies, eating to prevent
- during pregnancy, 83
- while breastfeeding, 295-296
Food aversions, 173, 174
Foodborne illness
- common sources of, 132, 135
- during breastfeeding, 301
- during pregnancy, 30-31, 129
Food cravings, 173, 174
Food labeling
- basics, 347
- nutrition claims and, 348-350
- use-by and sell-by dates, 352-353
Food planning, menus, 158, 184, 213

Food safety
- eating out and, 377-378
- grocery handling for, 137, 358
- international advice, 131
- tips for, 134-145
Food storage
- safe time for, 144, 353
- safe containers for, 140-143
- tips for, 144
Food Standards Australia New Zealand, 367
France, 60, 131
Freezing foods, 344, 355
Frozen meals, choosing, 397
Fructose, 71
Fruit
- getting more on your plate, 196-198
- healthiest, 196
- super, 93-94
- what counts as a serving, 90
Fruit juice, 195, 196

Gaining weight. See weight gain
Gas
- breastfeeding and, 294, 295
- causes, 67, 75, 186, 193, 201
Gastric bypass, 190, 273, 274
Genetic counseling, 17
Gestational diabetes, 248-252
- after pregnancy, 255
- diet for, 251-252
- effects on baby, 20, 248, 249
- managing, 250-251, 253, 255
- PCOS and, 42
- preventing, 20, 61, 71, 78, 105, 165, 167, 208,
    209
Ginger, morning sickness and, 170
Good Belly, 102, 202
Glucose. See blood sugar
Glucose tolerance test, 208
Gluten free
- eating, 75-76
- products, 69, 77
- resources, 76
Gluten-free pregnancy, 76-77
Gluten intolerance/sensitivity, 47
- breastfeeding and, 278
Glycemic index, 63, 64-66
Glycemic load, 64-66
GMO (genetically modified organism),
Gnu bars, 70, 110, 193

Grains
- gluten-free, 75
- what's a serving of, 88
- whole, 54, 61, 87, 178, 192, 378
Grassi, Angela, 41, 42
Green cleaning products, certified, 147
Green vitamins, 96
Greener living
- around the house, 146-148
- beauty care and, 149-153
- cleaning tips, 147-148
- disinfectants, 148
- eating and, 58, 364-374, 393
- fragrance and, 149-150
- in a nutshell, 153
Grotto, Dave, 51, 289
Gum disease, 27, 176, 177

Hand washing, 134
Health Canada, 137, 151, 347, 367
Healthy diet
- twelve steps to a, 57
Heartburn, 58, 78, 213, 223-225, 273, 378
Heart disease, 20, 40, 78, 121
Heavy metals
- Arsenic, 26, 71, 124
- Cadmium, 124, 125, 126
- Lead, 26, 28, 30, 99, 125, 126, 132, 144, 146,
    150, 190, 260, 293
- Mercury, 126, 127,
Hemorrhoids, 192, 225
Herbal
- caution with, 29, 98
- supplements, 97, 116, 117
- teas, 117-119
High blood pressure, 256-258
- diet for preventing, 207, 210, 258, 352
- lead and, 260
- pregnancy and
Hi-Maize resistant starch, 68, 192
High risk pregnancy
- bedrest and, 267
- emotions during, 246
- gastric bypass, after 273
- gestational diabetes, 248
- high blood pressure, 256
- multiple pregnancy, 261
- older moms 35, 271
- preexisting diabetes, 248
- resources for, 247
Honest Company, The, 149

Hormones, 208, 223, 278, 294, 339, 349
Hospital and breastfeeding, 281-283
Hunger
- signs in baby, 283
Hydrogenated fats, 80
Hyperemesis gravidarum, 168, 261
Hypertension. *See high blood pressure*

Ideal body weight, 34, 39, 48, 52, 229, 261
Immune system, 67, 119, 121, 146, 278
Infertility, 38-40, 43-49
Inositol, 31, 96
Insulin, 42, 52, 53, 208, 255
Iodine, 220, 233, 235, 294
Iron
- breastfeeding and, 293, 298
- calcium taken with, 99
- deficiency, 61, 87, 189, 190, 274
- enhancers, 57, 188-189, 233
- food sources of, 88, 190-191
- inhibitors, 189-190
- low birthweight and, 24
- multiple births and, 261
- need for, 187
- supplements, 96, 98-99
- vegetarian eating and, 188, 232

Kashi bars, 70, 74, 110
Kegel exercise, 172, 326, 337
Ketones, 162, 274
Kind bars, 69
Kitchen
- a peak in my, 344
- cleaning, 134-135
- toolbox, 359

Lacto-ovo vegetarian menu, 238
Lactose intolerance, 186-187
Lakatos Shames, Tammy, 330
Larabar, 69, 193, 200
Lead, (also *see heavy metals*)
- avoiding, 100, 126, 144
- calcium and, 99
- harmful effects of, 126
Legumes, 93, 121, 194, 218, 251, 260
Leftovers
- reheating, 137
- storing, 141, 354
Lentils, 91, 93, 163, 388
Lichten, Jo, 391, 393
Life's DHA, 101, 234,

Linoleic acid, 79, 236
Listeria monocytogenes 131, 384
Liver, 220
Losing weight
- breastfeeding and, 291
- exercise for,
- expectations for, 313-314
- fertility and, 38, 39
- post pregnancy, 316
- sleep and, 310
- tips for, 309-310
Luna bars, 69, 75, 110, 170
Lutein, 216, 220, 294
Lycopene, 52, 237, 361

Magnesium, 208, 217-218
Manganese, 164, 293
March of Dimes, 17, 29, 114, 116, 203
Margarine, 81, 110
Meal planning
- vegetarian, 230
Meat
- cooking, 363-364
- food safety and, 130, 131, 136, 137, 353,
- nutrition in, 57, 163, 188, 259, 265, 294
- nutrition claims for, 349-350
Medications, 27, 99, 114, 189, 248, 297
Menus
- sample, 82-83, 185, 212, 237-238, 304
- planning, 358
Mercury, 126, 127
Metabolic syndrome, 20, 51, 53, 299, 325
Mexico, 126, 127, 367
Microwave cooking, 140
Milk
- benefits of, 59,
- chocolate, 187
- lactose intolerance and, 186
- nutrition and, 59, 214, 220, 233
- protein in, 162, 163, 164
- tips for using, 216
- superfood and, 33
- unpasteurized, 130
Miscarriage, 45-48, 75, 126
- caffeine and, 115
- listeria and, 130
Monounsaturated fat, 78, 384
Morning sickness, 168-171
Moszkowicz, Julia, 359
Multiple pregnancy, 261-267
MyPlate, 58, 73, 86, 87, 196, 318

National Health Service (UK), 80, 116
National Sanitation Foundation (NSF), 132
Natural Medicines Database, 96, 118
Nausea
- tips to relieve, 58, 78, 169-171
- prenatal vitamins and, 96
Nectresse sweetener, 72, 369
Nervous system, 78, 115, 121, 122, 126, 206, 220, 264, 372
Neural tube, 23, 24, 28, 29, 96, 157, 221
New Zealand, 124, 234, 240, 370
Niacin, 222, 240
Nitrates 28, 134, 367, 368, 384
NSW Health (Australia), 116
Nursing. See breastfeeding
Nutrasweet (aspartame), 368-370
Nutrients
- calcium, 59, 99, 214
- carbohydrate, 62
- choline, 23, 33, 57, 96, 163, 220, 293, 294
- copper, 33, 34, 49, 61, 126, 128, 138
- fat, 53, 78, 81
- folate/folic acid, 96, 208
-- birth defects and, 23
-- food sources, 24
- iodine, 220, 233, 235, 294
- iron, 61, 87, 88, 189, 190, 274
- magnesium, 208, 217-218
- potassium, 218-219, 259
- protein, 90-91, 160-164
- vitamin A, 28, 29, 220
- vitamin B6, 170, 221
- vitamin B12, 190, 232, 240
- vitamin C, 49, 52, 167
- vitamin D, 59-61
- vitamin E, 49, 166
- zinc, 49, 126, 165
Nutrition
- for dads, 50-52
- prenatal programming and, 19-20
Nutrition facts label, 347
Nuts
- allergies and, 84
- nutrients and, 230, 259, 296
- superfoods and, 33, 93

Oatmeal, 33, 63, 68,
Obesity, preventing, 79, 104, 249, 278, 310
Oils
- canola, 79, 80, 82, 236
- olive, 80, 82, 84, 93, 236, 363

- what counts as a serving, 92
Omega-3 fatty acids
- alpha linolenic acid, 79, 84, 101, 235
- DHA, 79, 101, 127, 292
- food sources of, 101
- multiples and, 264-265
- supplements, 101, 230, 264, 292
- vegetarian eating and, 230
Omega-6 fatty acids, 79, 236
Organic
- benefits of, 123, 372
- definition, 347, 349, 371-372
- Dirty Dozen, 373
- food labeling and, 347, 371
- gardening, 356
- meat and poultry, 347, 355
- recommendations for, 373-374
Osteoporosis, 59, 186, 293, 325
OTIS (Office of Teratology Information Specialists), 26
Ovulation, 38, 39, 42, 46, 53, 325
Overweight
- risks of, 20, 247
- trying to conceive while, 21-22, 38, 39
- weight gain for, 105, 183, 210

Palmer, Sharon, 236
Pasta, low carb, (Dreamfields) 68
PCBs (polychlorinated biphenyls), 122-123, 127, 301
PCOS (polycystic ovary syndrome), 31, 40-43, 51
Peanuts
- allergies and, 84, 295, 296
Pecans, 33, 49, 54, 194, 265
- superfood, 93
Pelvic tilt, 326
Persistent organic pollutants (POPs), 120, 128, 129
Painting, 30, 146, 152
Pest control, 146
Pesticides, 120, 123, 146, 372-374
- fertility and, 50, 52
Phosphorus, 253
Phthalates, 140, 142-143, 149, 152
Physical activity guidelines, 21
Pica, 173, 190
PKU, 369-370
Placenta, 104, 115, 164
Plastic
- cooking and, 139, 140

- moving away from, 141
- recycling codes and uses, 142-143
Polyunsaturated fats, 78
Pork, 91, 137, 165, 364, 372, 393
Portion sizes, 87, 95
Postpartum
- eating for, 317
- exercise for, 339-340
- weight loss during, 291, 306-307, 318-320
- what to expect, 313
Postpartum depression, 293, 306
Potassium, 218-219, 259
Potatoes, 63, 66, 93, 373
Poultry, 144, 162, 188, 258, 354
Prebiotics, 67, 68
Preeclampsia
- fiber and, 62, 191
- nutrition and, 102, 207-208, 259-261
- risk factors, 16, 27, 203, 257
- symptoms, 107, 256,
Pre-existing diabetes, 25, 248
Preparing for next pregnancy, 321
Pre-pregnancy
- diet for, 23-24, 32-33
- visit, 16-17
Premature infants
- breastfeeding, 278, 298-299
- preventing, 61, 62, 104, 112, 177
Prenatal programming, 19-22
Prenatal supplements. See supplements
Prenatal visits
- dental care and, 27-28
- importance of, 34
Preservatives, 253, 368, 394
Preterm labor, 102, 265
Probiotics
- benefits of, 84, 95, 98, 101-102, 296
- sources of, 102
Produce wash, 136
Progesterone, 201
Protein
- breastfeeding needs for,
- complementary, 228
- egg, 163
- food sources of, 161, 162
- needs for, 160-161
- quality of, 162-163
- vegetarian sources of, 231
- what counts as an ounce, 90-91
Protein supplements, 163, 274

Psychological factors, 109
- depression, 25, 40, 246, 253
- stress, 29, 41, 48, 203-204, 255, 307
- weight gain and, 108, 109, 203
Pumpkin seeds, 33, 93, 176, 191

Quinoa, 75, 88, 94, 125,
Quiz
- how's your diet, 183, 226
- pre-pregnancy, 18
- will you gain too much weight, 106

Registered Dietitian (RD), 41, 76, 244
Refrigerator
- keeping clean, 136
- storing food in, 137, 144, 353-354
- safe temperature for, 144
Resistant starch, 53, 62, 68
Rest, 172, 206
Restaurants. See eating out
- Rice milk, 125, 214

Saccharin (Sweet'N Low), 367, 368, 369, 370
Salmon, 60, 93, 101, 127, 215, 265
Salmonella, 129, 148
Salt. See sodium
Santerre, Charles, 127
Saturated fat, 53, 79, 80-81, 84, 292
Seafood, smoked, 130
Second trimester, 179-201
Selenium, 33, 49, 166
Shopping, 239, 357-358
Simon, Judy, 254
Smoking, 45, 112, 113
Snack bars chart, 69
Snack ideas, 198, 199-200
Soda (soft drinks)
- caffeine content of, 116
- fertility and, 44, 53
- PCOS and, 41
- sugar content of, 73
Sodium
- dining out and, 381, 393
- food sources of, 351-352
- frozen meals and, 397-398
- labeling for, 348, 350
- requirements, 259, 260
Soy foods, 121, 163, 189, 295
Soyjoy bars, 69
Spinach, 33, 93, 294
Splenda (Sucralose), 368, 370

Spicy foods, 171, 181, 223
- breastfeeding and, 294
Sprouts, 145, 233
Stevia, 367, 370
Strawberries, 50, 65, 373
- superfood, 33
Strength training, 315, 330, 337
Stress, 29, 41, 48, 203-204, 255, 307
Sucralose (Splenda), 368, 370
Sugar, 70-73
- food content of, 73-75
- recommendations, 73
- slashing your, 212
Sugar alcohols. See sweeteners
Sunscreen, safe, 153
Super condiments, 94
Superfoods, Before Baby, 33
Superfoods, Eating Expectantly, 93-94
Supplements
- calcium, 99
- DHA, 101
- fertility, 49
- fish oil, 101
- herbal, 117, 164
- individual,
- iron, 98-99
- multiple pregnancy, 264
- prenatal, 96-97
- probiotic, 98, 102
- vegetarian, 234
- vitamin D, 96, 98, 214
Sushi, 145, 386
Swelling, 259, 332, 352
Sweet'N Low (saccharin), 367, 368, 369, 370
Sweeteners, 70-73
- artificial, 368
Swimming, 107, 129, 133, 250

Taste of Nature Bars, 70, 200
Tea, 24, 232
- herbal, 118-119
- caffeine and, 116
Teeth and gum changes, 176
Tempeh, 91, 93, 189, 231
Temperatures
- danger zone, 137, 140
- fertility and, 29, 39
- for cooking and storing, 137
Textured vegetable protein (TVP), 240
Thiamin, 25, 33, 222

Thyroid function
- fertility and, 47
Third trimester
- calorie needs for, 210
- developmental highlights in, 206
- diet challenges during, 222
- power nutrients for, 214
- weight gain for, 210
Tofu, 93, 216, 217
Toxoplasma parasite, 131,
Trans-fat, 80-81
Travel, 201, 288
Tree nuts, 84
Truvia sweetener (stevia), 370
Triplets. See multiple pregnancy
Tuna, 101, 127
Twins. See multiple pregnancy

UK (United Kingdom), 114, 116, 131, 228, 324
Underweight
- fertility and, 38, 39
- planning for pregnancy and, 21-22
- risks of, 104
- weight gain and, 105
USDA (United States Department of
    Agriculture), 80, 86, 348, 371, 373
USP (U.S. Pharmacopeial), 100
Uterus, 258, 279, 326

Van Dommelen, Marissa, 285
Vegetables
- caring for, 361
- cooking tips, 362
- getting more on your plate, 196
- food safety and, 135-136
- focus on, 195
- sea, 233
- starchy, 66, 87, 88
- super, 93
- what counts as a serving, 89
Vegetarian eating
- A to Z guide to, 239
- benefits of, 228
- breastfeeding and, 298
- eating out and, 241-242
- nutrient of concern, 231-236
- menus, 237-238
- weight loss and, 321
Vitamin A, 28, 29, 274
Vitamin B6, 170, 221
Vitamin B12, 190, 232, 240,

Vitamin C
- fertility and, 49, 52
- food sources of, 167
Vitamin D 59-61,
- high risk pregnancy and, 208
- breastfeeding and, 293
- PCOS and, 41
- recommendations for, 60, 98, 165, 293
- food sources, 217
- sunshine and, 60, 234
- vegetarian eating and, 234
Vitamin E, 49, 166
Vitamin K, 59, 240
Vitamin supplements. See supplements
Vitamins
- prenatal, 94, 98, 203
    See names of individual vitamins
Vision
- development of, 79, 131
- lutein and, 216, 220, 294
Vomiting. See morning sickness

Walnuts, 33, 49, 54, 79, 101, 236
Ward, Elizabeth, 318
Water
- filters, 132
- lead in, 132, 133
- importance of, 62
Weighing, tips for, 106
Weight
- where it goes, 104
- will you gain too much quiz, 106
Weight gain
- 1st trimester, 157
- 2nd trimester, 181
- 3rd trimester, 210
- avoiding too much, 107-108
- excessive and fast, 107
- monitoring, 106
- multiple pregnancy and, 263
- not enough, 109
- recommended, 105
Weight loss
- breastfeeding and, 291
- fertility and, 39, 273
- PCOS and, 41
- plans, evaluating, 312
- postpartum, 313-320
Welland, Diane, 374
Wheat germ, 33, 88, 165, 194

WHO (World Health Organization), 129, 220, 280, 367,
Whole grains, 61, 178, 192, 378
Work
- breastfeeding and going back to, 285-287
- environmental contaminants at, 30
- pregnancy and, 45, 222
Work-life balance, 288

Yakult, 67, 95, 102, 178
Yoga
- benefits, 336-337
- recommended poses, 337
Yogurt, 33, 91, 93, 95

Zinc, 49, 126, 165
- fertility and, 49
- food sources, 165
- vegetarian eating and, 235
Zing bars, 69, 110
Zisman, Carrie, 318

RECOMMENDED RESOURCES

Baby Care:
Mommy Calls: Dr. Tanya Answers Parents' Top 101 Questions About Babies and Toddlers by Tanya Remer Altmann MD, FAAP (American Academy of Pediatrics, 2008)
Caring for Your Baby and Young Child, 5th Edition: Birth to Age 5 (Shelov, Caring for your Baby and Young Child, Birth to Age 5, by The American Academy of Pediatrics, Tanya Remer Altmann MD, editor. (American Academy of Pediatrics, 2009)
Baby 411: Clear Answers & Smart Advice For Your Baby's First Year, 5th edition by Denise Fields and Ari Brown MD (Windsor Peak Press, 2011)

Breastfeeding:
The Nursing Mother's Companion, 6th Edition by Kathleen Huggins RN (Harvard Common Press, 2010)
Breastfeeding Made Simple: Seven Natural Laws for Nursing Mothers by Nancy Mohrbacher IBCLC FILCA and Kathleen Kendall-Tackett PhD IBCLC (New Harbinger Publications, 2010)
Oh, Yes You Can Breastfeed Twins! by April Rudat RD, (April Rudat Registered Dietitian LLC, 2007)

Clean Eating:
The Complete Idiot's Guide to Clean Eating by Diane Welland, MS, RD (Alpha, 2009)
Clean Eating for Busy Families: Get Meals on the Table in Minutes with Simple and Satisfying Whole-Foods Recipes You and Your Kids Will Love by Michelle Dudash MS, RD (Fair Winds, 2012)
The Big Green Cookbook: Hundreds of Planet-Pleasing Recipes and Tips for a Luscious, Low-Carbon Lifestyle by Jackie Newgent RD (Houghton Mifflin Harcourt, 2009)

Diabetes:
Healthy You, Healthy Baby: A Mother's Guide to Gestational Diabetes by the Doctor's Dietitian Susan B. Dopart MS, RD, CDE (SGJ Publishing, 2012)
Diabetes Meal Planning Made Easy by Hope Warshaw MMSc, RD, CDE (American Diabetes Association, 2010)

Eating Out:
Eat Out Healthy by Dr. Jo Lichten (Nutrifit Publishing, 2012)
How to Stay Healthy & Fit On the Road: The Ultimate Health Guide for Road Warriors by Dr. Jo Lichten (Nutrifit Publishing, 2006)

Feeding Infants:
Baby Bites: Everything You Need to Know about Feeding Infants and Toddlers in One Handy Book by Bridget Swinney MS, RD (Meadowbrook Press, 2007)
Feeding Baby Green: The Earth Friendly Program for Healthy, Safe Nutrition During Pregnancy, Childhood, and Beyond by Alan Greene MD (Jossey-Bass, 2009)
The Best Homemade Baby Food on the Planet: Know What Goes Into Every Bite with More Than 200 of the Most Deliciously Nutritious Homemade Baby Food ... More Than 60 Purees Your Baby Will Love by Karin Knight RN and Tina Ruggiero MS, RD (Fair Winds Press, 2010)

Fitness:
Exercising Through Your Pregnancy, 2nd Edition by James Clapp III, MD (Addicus Books, 2012)
Nancy Clark's Sports Nutrition Guidebook by Nancy Clark RD (Human Kinetics, 2008)

Gluten-Free Eating:
Gluten-Free, Hassle Free: A Simple, Sane, Dietitian-Approved Program for Eating Your Way Back To Health by Marlisa

Brown RD, CDE, (Demos Health, 2009)
Gluten-Free Diet: A Comprehensive Resource Guide- Expanded and Revised Edition by Shelley Case RD, Iona Glabus and Brian Danchuk (Case Nutrition Consulting, 2010)
American Dietetic Association Easy Gluten-Free: Expert Nutrition Advice with More Than 100 Recipes by Marlisa Brown, MS, RD and Tricia Thompson MS, RD (Houghton Mifflin Harcourt, 2010)

Healthy Eating:
Joy Bauer's Food Cures: Eat Right to Get Healthier, Look Younger, and Add Years to Your Life by Joy Bauer and Carol Svec (Rodale, 2011)
Small Changes, Big Results, Revised and Updated: A Wellness Plan with 65 Recipes for a Healthy, Balanced Life Full of Flavor by Ellie Krieger MS, RD (Clarkson Potter, 2013)
The Best Things You Can Eat: For Everything from Aches to Zzzz, the Definitive Guide to the Nutrition-Packed Foods that Energize, Heal, and Help You Look Great by David Grotto, RD, LDN (De Capo, 2013)
Quick & Healthy Recipes and Ideas: For people who say they don't have time to cook healthy meals, 3rd Edition by Brenda Ponichtera RD (Small Steps Press, 2008)
The Food Lover's Healthy Habits Cookbook: Great Food & Expert Advice That Will Change Your Life by Janet Helm and The Cooking Light Editors (Oxmoor House, 2012)
MyPlate for Moms, How to Feed Yourself & Your Family Better by Elizabeth Ward MS, RD (Loughlin Press, 2011)
Nutrition at Your Fingertips by Elisa Zied MS, RD (Alpha, 2009)
Eat More of What You Love: Over 200 Brand-New Recipes Low in Sugar, Fat, and Calories by Marlene Koch (Running Press, 2012)
Read It Before You Eat It: How to Decode Food Labels and Make the Healthiest Choice Every Time by Bonnie Taub Dix MA, RD (Plume, 2010)
Gut Insight: Probiotics and Prebiotics for Digestive Health and Well-being by Jo Ann Hattner PH, RD with Susan Anderes MLIS (Hattner Nutrition, 2009)
101 Foods That Could Save Your Life by David Grotto RD (Bantam, 2010)

Multiples:
When You're Expecting Twins, Triplets or Quads; Proven Guidelines for a Healthy Multiple Pregnancies by Dr. Barbara Luke and Tamara Eberlein (Harper Resource, 3rd Edition, 2011)
Mothering Multiples: Breastfeeding and Caring for Twins or More! by Karen Kerkhoff Gromada, (LLL International, 2007)
It's Twins: Parent-to-Parent Advice from Infancy Through Adolescence. Susan Heim (Hampton Roads, 2007)

Pregnancy:
Expecting 411: Clear Answers & Smart Advice for Your Pregnancy by Michele Hakakha MD and Ari Brown MD (Windsor Peak Press, 2012)
Mayo Clinic Guide to a Healthy Pregnancy by Mayo Clinic (Good Books, 2011)

Trying to Conceive:
Before Your Pregnancy: A 90-Day Guide for Couples on How to Prepare for a Healthy Conception (2nd Ed.) by Amy Ogle, MS, RD and Lisa Mazzullo MD (Ballantine Books, 2011)
Tell Me What to Eat If I Am Trying to Conceive by Kimberly Tessmer RD, LD (New Page Books, 2009)

Vegetarian:
The Everything Vegan Pregnancy Book: All You Need to Know for a Healthy Pregnancy that Fits Your Lifestyle by Reed Mangels (2011, Adams Media)
The Plant-Powered Diet: The Lifelong Eating Plan for Achieving Optimal Health, Beginning Today by Sharon Palmer RD (The Experiment, 2012)
The New Fast Food: The Veggie Queen Pressure Cooks Whole Food Meals in Less than 30 Minutes by Jill Nussinow MS, RD (The Veggie Queen, 2011)

Weight Loss:
The Secret to Skinny: How Salt Makes You Fat, and the 4-Week Plan to Drop a Size and Get Healthier with Simple Low-Sodium Swaps by Lyssie Lakatos RD, CFT and Tammy Lakatos Shames RD, CFT (HCI, 2009)
Fire Up Your Metabolism: 9 Proven Principles for Burning Fat and Losing Weight Forever by Lyssie Lakatos RD, CFT and Tammy Lakatos Shames RD, CFT (Touchstone, 2004)
The Complete Idiot's Guide to Belly Fat Weight Loss by Claire M. Wheeler MD & Diane Welland MS, RD (Penguin, 2012)
The Dash Diet Weight Loss Solution: 2 Weeks to Drop Pounds, Boost Metabolism, and Get Healthy by Marla Heller MS, RD (Grand Central, 2012)
Train Your Brain to Get Thin: Prime Your Gray Cells for Weight Loss, Wellness, and Exercise by Melinda Boyd MPH, RD and Michele Noonan PhD (Adams Media, 2012)
The Flexitarian Diet: The Mostly Vegetarian Way to Lose Weight, Be Healthier, Prevent Disease, and Add Years to Your Life by Dawn Jackson Blatner RD (McGraw-Hill, 2010)